Asia Bible Commentary Series

JOHN

Westcott famously said that "only in India, when Christian thought had developed there, would St. John be fully understood" (thus C. F. Andrews). What he hoped can now be better imagined when one reads Johnson Thomaskutty's fascinating commentary on the Gospel of John. Knowing Christian and Asian traditions inside out, Thomaskutty draws a sustained comparison between John and the East and puts them into dialogue.

George van Kooten, PhD
Lady Margaret's Professor of Divinity,
University of Cambridge, UK

Written in and for an Asian context, Johnson Thomaskutty's commentary not only provides a clear analysis of the text of John's Gospel but also indicates points of contact and comparison with Asian religious and cultural traditions, and with contemporary Asian societies, which will be illuminating for many readers.

David G. Horrell, PhD
Professor of New Testament Studies,
University of Exeter, UK

Once again one of the most prolific and distinguished Asian biblical scholars, Dr. Thomaskutty, presents an insightful and dynamic interpretation of the Gospel of John within the diverse religious and cultural context of Asia. The combination of his in-depth biblical exegesis, rich knowledge of Asian traditions, and skillful context-text-context hermeneutics open fresh new insights and enrich our understanding of the Fourth Gospel. It is essential reading for anyone seeking to encounter the transformative power of God.

Xiaoli Yang, PhD
Honorary Research Associate and Adjunct Lecturer,
University of Divinity, Australia

This commentary by Johnson Thomaskutty is a profound exploration of the Gospel of John, providing readers with deep insights and cultural sensitivity. This commentary, blending rigorous scholarship with diverse Asian perspectives, unveils the profound realities of John's Gospel within the dynamic context of Asia. Thomaskutty's work not only offers fresh perspectives but also spiritual sustenance for those seeking a deeper understanding of the word.

This commentary bridges traditional wisdom with contemporary relevance, inviting readers to engage with the Gospel of John in a manner that resonates profoundly with Asian realities.

Biju Chacko, DTh
Principal and Professor of New Testament,
New Theological College, India

How can we, Indians in particular and Asians in general, read and understand the Bible in our cultural context without losing the core value of biblical text? This work of Dr. Johnson Thomaskutty is an answer to the question, representing a historical transition from the Greco-Roman and Jewish world of the Fourth Gospel (traditional Western interpretation) to the Jewish-Asian world of the Fourth Gospel. This book stands as an example for any Asian who wants to read the Bible in their own socio-religious-political contexts.

Thawng Ceu Hnin, PhD
Professor of New Testament,
Evangelical Theological Seminary, India

Asia Bible Commentary Series

JOHN

Johnson Thomaskutty

General Editor
Andrew B. Spurgeon

Old Testament Consulting Editors
Joseph Shao, Havilah Dharamraj, Koowon Kim

New Testament Consulting Editors
Steve Chang, Finny Philip, Samson Uytanlet

© 2025 Johnson Thomaskutty

Published 2025 by Langham Global Library
An imprint of Langham Publishing
www.langhampublishing.org

Langham Publishing and its imprints are a ministry of Langham Partnership

Langham Partnership
PO Box 296, Carlisle, Cumbria, CA3 9WZ, UK
www.langham.org

Published in partnership with Asia Theological Association

ATA
QCC PO Box 1454–1154, Manila, Philippines
www.ataasia.com

ISBNs:
978-1-78641-234-8 Print
978-1-78641-238-6 ePub
978-1-78641-239-3 PDF

Johnson Thomaskutty has asserted his right under the Copyright, Designs and Patents Act, 1988 to be identified as the Author of this work.

All rights reserved. No part of this publication may be reproduced, stored in a retrieval system or transmitted, in any form or by any means, electronic, mechanical, photocopying, recording or otherwise, without the prior written permission of the publisher or the Copyright Licensing Agency.

Requests to reuse content from Langham Publishing are processed through PLSclear. Please visit www.plsclear.com to complete your request.

Unless otherwise stated, Scripture quotations are from the New International Version, copyright © 2011. Used by permission. All rights reserved.

British Library Cataloguing-in-Publication Data
A catalogue record for this book is available from the British Library

ISBN: 978-1-78641-234-8

Cover & Book Design: projectluz.com

Langham Partnership actively supports theological dialogue and an author's right to publish but does not necessarily endorse the views and opinions set forth here or in works referenced within this publication, nor can we guarantee technical and grammatical correctness. Langham Partnership does not accept any responsibility or liability to persons or property as a consequence of the reading, use or interpretation of its published content.

To Leelamma Thomaskutty, "my dear mother,"
who was my first Bible teacher

To all Asian readers of the Bible
for their unique faith and identity

CONTENTS

Commentary

Series Preface xi
Author's Preface xiii
List of Abbreviations xv
Introduction 1
Commentary on John 17
Selected Bibliography 275

Topics

Johannine Metaphors 21
Johannine Women 30
The Seven Signs 34
Jews and Samaritans 59
Intercultural Communication 63
The "I Am" Sayings 90
Johannine Cultural Dynamics 253

SERIES PREFACE

What's unique about the Asia Bible Commentary Series? It is a commentary series written especially for Asian Christians, which incorporates and addresses Asian concerns, cultures, and practices. As Asian scholars – either by nationality, passion, or calling – the authors identify with the biblical text, understand it culturally, and apply its principles in Asian contexts to strengthen the churches in Asia. Missiologists tell us that Christianity has shifted from being a Western majority religion to a South, Southeastern, and Eastern majority religion and that the church is growing at an unprecedented rate in these regions. This series meets the need for evangelical commentaries written specifically for an Asian audience.

This is not to say that Asian churches and Asian Christians do not want to partner with Western Christians and churches or that they spurn Western influences. A house divided cannot stand. The books in this series complement the existing Western commentaries by taking into consideration the cultural nuances familiar to the Eastern world so that the Eastern readership is not inundated with Western clichés and illustrations that they are unable to relate to and which may not be applicable to them.

The mission of this series is "to produce resources that are biblical, pastoral, contextual, missional, and prophetic for pastors, Christian leaders, cross-cultural workers, and students in Asia." While using approved exegetical principles, the writers strive to be culturally relevant, offer practical applications, and provide clear explanations of the texts so that readers can grow in understanding and maturity in Christ and Christian leaders can guide their congregations into maturity. May we be found faithful in this endeavor and may God be glorified!

Andrew B. Spurgeon
General Editor

AUTHOR'S PREFACE

I owe my thanks to the many people who contributed to this commentary project. I thank Dr. Andrew Spurgeon, the general editor of Asia Bible Commentary Series, for his constant support, helpful suggestions, and critical evaluations on multifarious occasions.

I offer public thanks to the anonymous reviewers and readers of the manuscript for their clear and helpful criticisms. Thanks are also due to Langham Publishing for accepting this project for publication in the ABC Series.

I am grateful to the librarians at Union Biblical Seminary, Pune, and the United Theological College, Bengaluru, for their assistance in material collection.

I thank Prof. Dr. George van Kooten (Lady Margaret's Professor of Divinity, University of Cambridge, UK), Prof. Dr. David G. Horrell (Professor of New Testament Studies, University of Exeter, UK), Prof. Dr. Xiaoli Yang (University of Divinity, Australia), Dr. Biju Chacko (Principal and Professor of New Testament, New Theological College, India), and Dr. Thawng Ceu Hnin (Evangelical Theological Seminary, Hosur, India) for their endorsements of this commentary.

I am deeply indebted to my students, my colleagues, and the administration of the United Theological College, Bengaluru, for their intellectual and moral support. I also thank my family members for their sacrifice and continuous support. This commentary is dedicated to all Asian readers of the Bible for their unique faith and identity.

Johnson Thomaskutty
United Theological College, Bengaluru, India
July 2025

LIST OF ABBREVIATIONS

BOOKS OF THE BIBLE

Old Testament

Gen, Exod, Lev, Num, Deut, Josh, Judg, Ruth, 1–2 Sam, 1–2 Kgs, 1–2 Chr, Ezra, Neh, Esth, Job, Ps/Pss, Prov, Eccl, Song, Isa, Jer, Lam, Ezek, Dan, Hos, Joel, Amos, Obad, Jonah, Mic, Nah, Hab, Zeph, Hag, Zech, Mal

New Testament

Matt, Mark, Luke, John, Acts, Rom, 1–2 Cor, Gal, Eph, Phil, Col, 1–2 Thess, 1–2 Tim, Titus, Phlm, Heb, Jas, 1–2 Pet, 1–2–3 John, Jude, Rev

BIBLE TEXTS AND VERSIONS

Divisions of the canon

NT	New Testament
OT	Old Testament

Ancient texts and versions

LXX	Septuagint
MT	Masoretic Text

Modern versions

KJV	King James Version
NET	New English Translation
NIV	New International Version
NKJV	New King James Version
NRSV	New Revised Standard Version
RSV	Revised Standard Version

Journals, reference works, and series

BECNT	The Baker Exegetical Commentary on the New Testament
BINS	Biblical Interpretation Series of Brill

John

DJG	*Dictionary of Jesus and the Gospels*
JBL	*Journal of Biblical Literature*
JTS	*Journal of Tribal Studies*
NCBC	*New Cambridge Biblical Commentary*
NICNT	*New International Commentary on the New Testament*
SBL	Society for Biblical Literature
VWGTh	*Veröffentlichungen der Wissenschaftlichen Gesellschaft für Theologie*
WBC	Word Biblical Commentary
WUNT	*Wissenschaftliche Untersuchungen zum Neuen Testament*

INTRODUCTION

This commentary presents the Gospel of John within the wider Asian context, shaped by multireligious, multiethnic, multicultural, and pluralistic realities. Just as the Jesus movement emerged from the contextual realities of Jesus's time and first-century Judaism, understanding the Gospel of John through an Asian lens may provide a unique perspective.

The Gospel of John is one of the most significant writings of the New Testament (NT), appealing to Asian spirituality and ideals in multifaceted ways. It is a unique literary masterpiece that reflects the feelings and aspirations of many Asians. The Gospel's dynamic genre,[1] setting,[2] ideological constructs,[3] character development,[4] plot structures, and point of view reflect and reveal the Gospel's power to speak meaningfully into the situations of Asian communities.

This commentary adopts a *context-text-context* integration approach to establish the contemporary relevance of the Fourth Gospel. Readers of the commentary can see how the socioreligious and politico-cultural aspects align within the framework of the Johannine narrative to provide a new way forward. A cross-pollination of Johannine spirituality with contemporary socioreligious and politico-cultural aspects enables us to better understand its inclusive nature. This commentary foregrounds the Gospel's liberating, transformative, and accommodative aspects, reflecting its relevance to a broad spectrum of contemporary life.

The commentary begins with a succinct discussion of authorship, audience, date and place of composition, structure, and outline. It then attempts to situate the Gospel within the Asian context to derive an interpretative dynamism that takes account of diverse religious, cultural, and other contextual aspects.

---

1. David Hellholm, "The Problem of Apocalyptic Genre and the Apocalypse of John," *Semeia 36: Early Christian Apocalypticism, Genre and Social Setting* (Decatur: SBL/Scholars Press, 1986), 13.
2. James L. Resseguie, *Narrative Criticism of the New Testament: An Introduction* (Grand Rapids: Baker Academic, 2005), 87.
3. It deals with the development of the semantic, syntactic, and pragmatic integration of the text.
4. Cornelis Bennema, *Encountering Jesus: Character Studies in the Gospel of John* (Bangalore: Primalogue, 2009), 1–21.

John

AUTHORSHIP

The Johannine author, with his many mystical and ideological ideas, will resonate with many Asians. The Asian mindset of seeing the realities and reflecting is prominent in the Gospel, with the author declaring that "we have seen his glory" (1:14). The appearance of Thomas at significant narrative intervals (11:16; 14:5; 20:24–28; 21:1) and the *inclusio* created between John's thesis statement – "the Word was God" (1:1) – and its resolution through Thomas's utterance – "My Lord and my God!" (20:28) – may establish a link between John's Gospel and the Thomas community in India.[5]

The eyewitness in this Gospel is an unnamed disciple (19:26–35; 20:2) – sometimes referred to as the "Beloved Disciple" – who was also reclining close to Jesus during the Last Supper (13:23). Although recent scholarship proposes various candidates – Lazarus,[6] Thomas,[7] Mary Magdalene,[8] and John the son of Zebedee[9] – there are no convincing grounds to reject the traditional view that identifies the "Beloved Disciple" as John, son of Zebedee.[10] The Gospel reveals the author's familiarity with Jewish customs, beliefs, and festivals (2:6; 4:27; 5:10; 7:21–23, 37; 9:2, 14), Jewish history (4:9; 11:49; 18:13), and Palestinian geography (1:28; 2:1; 3:23; 4:46; 6:1; 12:1; 18:1; 21:1), supporting the view that the author was a Jew.[11] Another significant development in Johannine authorship is the community hypothesis,[12] where rather than attrib-

---

5. Johnson Thomaskutty, *Saint Thomas the Apostle: New Testament, Apocrypha, and Historical Traditions*, T & T Clark Jewish and Christian Texts Series 25 (London: Bloomsbury T & T Clark, 2018), 84–85; 148–150; 201–202.
6. Tobias Skinner, *The Gospel according to Lazarus* (UK: Watersgreen House, 2022).
7. James H. Charlesworth, *The Beloved Disciple: Whose Witness Validates the Gospel of John?* (Philadelphia: Trinity Press International, 1995).
8. Esther A. De Boer, *The Gospel of Mary: Listening to the Beloved Disciple* (London: T & T Clark International, 2004).
9. Richard Bauckham, *The Testimony of the Beloved Disciple: Narrative, History, and Theology in the Gospel of John* (Grand Rapids: Baker Academic, 2007).
10. Donald Guthrie, *New Testament Introduction* (Leicester: Apollos, 1990), 260. Also Craig L. Blomberg, *The Historical Reliability of John's Gospel: Issues and Commentary* (Leicester: Apollos, 2001), 23; Martin Hengel, *The Johannine Question* (London: SCM Press, 1989); Richard Bauckham, *Jesus and the Eyewitnesses: The Gospels as Eyewitness Testimony* (Grand Rapids: Eerdmans, 2006), 358–411.
11. Blomberg, *The Historical Reliability of John's Gospel*, 27.
12. J. Louis Martyn, *History and Theology in the Fourth Gospel* (Nashville: Abingdon, 1983); Reymond E. Brown, *Community of the Beloved Disciple* (New York: Paulist, 1979); R. Alan Culpepper, *The Johannine School: An Evaluation of the Johannine School Hypothesis based on the Investigation of the Nature of Ancient Schools* (Durham: Duke University, 1982); Oscar Cullmann, *The Johannine Circle* (London: SCM Press, 1976).

Introduction

uting authorship to a single individual, scholars link the Johannine traditions to a community, with John, the son of Zebedee, remaining at the focal point.

Similarly, church fathers like Irenaeus, Tertullian, Clement of Alexandria, Origen, and others support the view that this Gospel was written by John, son of Zebedee.[13] Irenaeus states, "John, the disciple of the Lord, who leaned on his breast, also published the Gospel while living at Ephesus in Asia" (*Adv. Haer.* 3.1.1).[14] Clement of Alexandria considers it a "spiritual Gospel" (Eusebius, *HE.* 6.14.7).[15] While Eusebius mentions John's association with Polycarp (*HE.* 5.4–8), Polycrates connects him with the city of Ephesus (Eusebius, *HE.* 4.14.1–8).[16] Papias valued the Gospel of John more highly than other Gospels he knew and regarded it as an authentic source.[17] The Gospel of John is often considered a "Gospel with an Indian spirit" – Indians in particular, and Asians in general, recognize the Gospel's universal significance "here" and "now."[18]

AUDIENCE

John's Gospel was written primarily for those who came to faith in Jesus under the leadership of the Beloved Disciple. This believing community faced opposition from the synagogue, and some were even excommunicated because of their faith (see 9:22; 12:42; 16:2). Jey J. Kanagaraj states, "In a context of such hostility, John offers hope of a heavenly life that is available even now for those who believe in Jesus."[19] John's purpose statement (20:30–31) invites people to put their faith in Jesus (*missionsschrift*) and aims to deepen the faith of the believing community (*gemeindeschrift*).[20] In that sense, the Gospel serves both a missional and a pastoral purpose.[21]

Louis Martyn suggests that John can be read as a two-level drama.[22] Adopting Martyn's suggestion, Blomberg comments, "This approach has

---

13. Guthrie, *New Testament Introduction*, 269–71. Other names suggested for authorship are: John of Jerusalem and John the Elder. Also Francis J. Moloney, *The Gospel of John* (Collegeville: The Liturgical Press,1998), 6–9.
14. Bauckham, *Jesus and the Eyewitnesses*, 452–58.
15. Marianne M. Thompson, "John, Gospel of," *DJG*, eds. Joel B. Green, Scot McKnight, and I. Howard Marshall (Downers Grove: InterVarsity Press, 1992), 369.
16. Bauckham, *Jesus and the Eyewitnesses*, 438–52.
17. Bauckham, 423.
18. Johnson Thomaskutty, *The Gospel of John: A Universalistic Reading*, Biblical Hermeneutics Rediscovered 25 (New Delhi: Christian World Imprints, 2020).
19. Jey J. Kanagaraj, *The Gospel of John: A Commentary* (Secunderabad: OM Books, 2005), 23.
20. A. Barus, "John 2:12–25: A Narrative Reading," *New Currents through John: A Global Perspective*, eds. F. Lozada, and T. Thatcher (Leiden/Boston: Brill, 2006), 140.
21. Johnson Thomaskutty, *The Gospel of John: A Universalistic Reading*, 92.
22. J. Louis Martyn, *History and Theology in the Fourth Gospel*.

assumed that the characters and issues highlighted in John refer (at least much of the time) not to the historical Jesus and his contemporaries but to the Christians in the Johannine community and their opponents (or other, more interested outsiders)."[23] While Jesus's ministry was focused on Jerusalem, John's community was based in Ephesus and consisted mostly of Gentiles. The narrator reinterprets and retells the story of Jesus to meet these new demands.[24] The language and literary style of John draw the attention of the reader toward "everywhere and ever" realities.[25]

DATE AND PLACE

Dating the Fourth Gospel is a herculean task. The scholarly consensus suggests a date between 85 and 110 CE,[26] and early second-century manuscripts such as the *Rylands Papyrus 457* (P52; 125–175 CE) and the *Egerton Papyrus 2* (end of the second century CE) support this view.[27] Despite arguments concerning John's dependency upon the Synoptics, there is no convincing evidence to prove this position. Paul N. Anderson argues that the Johannine traditions already existed alongside the synoptic traditions and that John would have undergone several editorial processes. According to Anderson, the Gospel would have developed as an autonomous tradition in the Palestinian context and later been finalized in Asia Minor.[28] However, J. A. T. Robinson suggests a date in the 60s CE.[29] Based on these scholarly perspectives, I suggest the following: The Johannine traditions developed from the early stages alongside other Gospel traditions; the Gospel underwent several editorial processes; and the canonical Gospel in its current form probably emerged between 90 and 110 CE. All these factors also indicate that the final draft of the Gospel was associated with the Ephesian context. So, the context of the writing is particular although its message remains universal.

---

23. Blomberg, *Historical Reliability of John's Gospel*, 61–62. Also Martyn, *History and Theology in the Fourth Gospel*.
24. Thomaskutty, *The Gospel of John: A Universalistic Reading*, 155–56.
25. Thomaskutty, 3–14.
26. Guthrie, *New Testament Introduction*, 297; Kanagaraj, *The Gospel of John*, 23. Blomberg suggests a date either to the late 80s or to the 90s. Blomberg, *Historical Reliability of John's Gospel*, 44; compare George R. Beasley-Murray, *John*, WBC 36 (Nashville: Thomas Nelson Publishers, 1999), lxxv–lxxviii.
27. Guthrie, *New Testament Introduction*, 297; compare Thompson, "John, Gospel of," 370.
28. Anderson, *From Crisis to Christ*, 138.
29. John A. T. Robinson, *The Priority of John* (London: SCM, 1985) and Thompson, "John, Gospel of," 370–71.

Introduction

STRUCTURE AND OUTLINE

The Gospel writers had their own criteria for determining what they included, and "whatever does not fit into the structures determined by those criteria is simply omitted."[30] Thus, John's Gospel has a unique structure that does not correspond with the Synoptic Gospels. Classical Johannine scholarship divides the Gospel into four parts: two smaller sections – the *Prologue* (1:1–18) and the *Epilogue* (21:1–25) – and two larger sections – the *Book of Signs* (1:19–12:50) and the *Book of Glory* (13:1–20:31).[31] After the *Prologue* (1:1–18), the evangelist narrates the life and ministry of Jesus with reference to seven signs and seven discourses (1:19–12:50).[32] John 13:1–20:31 centers around "the hour," the lifting up, and the glorification of the Son of Man. The climax of this second major section is the Gospel's purpose statement (20:30–31), and the narrator concludes with an *Epilogue* (21:1–25).[33]

Based on this, the Gospel can be outlined into four major sections: Prologue (1:1–18), Book of Signs (1:19–12:50), Book of Glory (13:1–20:31), and Epilogue (21:1–25). Further, the events in these sections can be divided into:

1:1–18 The Incarnation of the Word
1:19–2:12 The Beginning of Jesus's Ministry
    1:19–28 Day One
    1:29–34 Day Two
    1:35–42 Day Three
    1:43–51 Day Four
    1:43–51 Day Five (Implied)
    2:1–11 Day Six
    2:12 Day Seven
2:13–25 Cleansing the Temple at Jerusalem

---

30. Blomberg, *Historical Reliability of John's Gospel*, 54.
31. Raymond E. Brown, *The Gospel according to John*, vols. 1–2 (Garden City: Doubleday, 1966, 1970); Moloney, *Gospel of John*, 23–24; Rudolf Bultmann, *The Gospel of John: A Commentary* (Philadelphia: Westminster, 1970); C. H. Dodd, *The Interpretation of the Fourth Gospel* (Cambridge: University Press, 1960); C. K. Barrett, *The Gospel according to St. John: An Introduction with Commentary and Notes on the Greek Text* (London: SPCK, 1978); Johnson Thomaskutty, *Dialogue in the Book of Signs: A Polyvalent Analysis of John 1:19–12:50*, BINS 136 (Leiden/Boston: Brill, 2015).
32. Blomberg, *Historical Reliability of John's Gospel*, 55. Also Leon Morris, *The Gospel according to John*, NICNT, rev. ed. (Grand Rapids: Eerdmans, 1995).
33. Thompson, "John, Gospel of," *DJG*, eds. Joel B. Green, Scot McKnight, and I. Howard Marshall (Downers Grove: InterVarsity Press, 1992), 373–74.

John

3:1–21 Jesus and a Religiously Elite Person
3:22–36 Final Declaration of John the Baptist
4:1–42 Jesus and a Downtrodden Woman
    4:1–26 Jesus and the Samaritan Woman
    4:27–38 Jesus and the Disciples
    4:39–42 Jesus among the Samaritans
4:43–54 Jesus and a Royal Official
5:1–47 Jesus and the Invalid by the Pool
    5:1–18 Dialogue between Jesus and the Invalid
    5:19–30 The Authority of Jesus
    5:31–47 Witnesses Concerning Jesus
6:1–71 Jesus Is the Bread of Life
    6:1–15 Jesus Feeds a Multitude
    6:16–21 Jesus Walks on the Water
    6:22–59 Jesus's Bread of Life Discourse
    6:60–71 Responses from the Disciples
7:1–52 The First Tabernacles Discourse
    7:1–9 Jesus and His Unbelieving Brothers
    7:10–36 Jesus at the Feast of Tabernacles
    7:37–39 Prophecy Concerning Streams of Living Water
    7:40–52 Divided Opinions about Jesus
7:53–8:11 Jesus and the Adulterous Woman
    1. The Text of John
    2. An Interpretation of the Text
8:12–59 The Second Tabernacles Discourse
    8:12–20 Jesus Is the Light of the World
    8:21–30 Jesus's Foretelling of His Death
    8:31–38 True Discipleship and Freedom in Christ
    8:39–59 "Before Abraham was Born, I AM"
9:1–41 A Man Born Blind Receives Sight
    9:1–7 Jesus and the Man Born Blind
    9:8–12 The Man and His Neighbors
    9:13–17 The Man and the Pharisees
    9:18–23 The Pharisees and the Parents
    9:24–34 The Man's Expulsion from the Synagogue
    9:35–38 Jesus's Encounter with the Healed Man
    9:39–41 A Concluding Theological Message
10:1–21 Gate for the Sheep and the Good Shepherd

Introduction

    10:1–10 Jesus Is the Gate for the Sheep
    10:11–21 Jesus Is the Good Shepherd
10:22–42 Jesus during the Festival of Dedication
11:1–57 Jesus Raises Lazarus from the Dead
    11:1–6 A Concern of Mary and Martha
    11:7–16 Jesus and the Disciples
    11:17–27 Jesus and Martha
    11:28–37 Jesus and Mary
    11:38–44 Jesus Raises Lazarus
    11:45–57 Antagonism Against Jesus
12:1–50 End of Jesus's Public Ministry
    12:1–11 Mary Anoints Jesus
    12:12–19 Jesus Enters the City of Jerusalem
    12:20–22 The Greeks Come to Meet Jesus
    12:23–36 Jesus Predicts His Crucifixion
    12:37–41 Unbelief of the People
    12:42–50 Postlude to the Book of Signs
13:1–38 Foot Washing and the Foretelling of Jesus's Death
    13:1–20 Jesus Washes the Disciples' Feet
    13:21–35 Jesus Foretells His Betrayal
    13:36–38 Jesus Predicts Peter's Denial
14:1–31 Jesus Is the Way, the Truth, and the Life
    14:1–14 Jesus as the Way to the Father
    14:15–26 The Promise of the Holy Spirit
    14:27–31 Jesus's Offer of Enduring Peace
15:1–27 Jesus Is the True Vine and a Friend
    15:1–14 The Vine and the Branches
    15:15–17 Jesus as a Friend
    15:18–25 The World's Attitude Towards Believers in Christ
    15:26–27 Second Statement About the *Paraklētos*
16:1–33 Jesus's Warnings, Promises, and Prophecies
    16:1–6 Jesus's Warning of Persecution
    16:7–15 Third Introduction to the *Paraklētos*
    16:16–33 Jesus's Teaching on His Death and Resurrection
17:1–26 Jesus's High Priestly Prayer
    17:1–5 Jesus's Prayer for Himself
    17:6–19 Jesus's Prayer for the Disciples
    17:20–23 Jesus's Prayer for Future Believers Worldwide

17:24–26 Jesus's Prayer for the Twelve
18:1–19:42 The Passion of Jesus
   18:1–14 Jesus's Betrayal and Arrest
   18:15–27 Peter's Three Denials
   18:28–40 Jesus Before Pilate
   19:1–15 Pilate's Final Attempt to Release Jesus
   19:16–30 The Crucifixion of Jesus
   19:31–42 The Burial of Jesus
20:1–31 The Resurrection of Jesus
   20:1–10 Resurrection and the First Witnesses
   20:11–18 Jesus's Appearance to Mary Magdalene
   20:19–29 Two Appearances of Jesus to the Disciples
   20:30–31 The Gospel's Purpose Statement
21:1–25 The Epilogue of the Gospel
   21:1–14 Jesus's Appearance to Seven Disciples
   21:15–19 Dialogue Between Jesus and Peter
   21:20–25 Jesus and the Beloved Disciple

THE GOSPEL OF JOHN IN THE ASIAN CONTEXT

The Gospel of John offers a persuasive theological framework that resonates with Asian communities.[34] By engaging deeply with this Gospel, readers can derive contextually oriented and universally applicable messages.

1:1–18 The Prologue

John's *Prologue* (1:1–18) can be read as a rhythmic and responsive piece of rhetoric.[35] It displays all the features of a quasi-poem – a combination of prose and poetry – and sustains this style throughout. The orator maintains a rhythmic responsive style in presenting the text to the audience, similar to the dialogic and musical structure found in some twentieth-century stage performances.

The Johannine narrator introduces the first part of the Gospel through a *tri-level* – interactive, intra-textual, and intertextual – dialogue.[36] At the

---

34. Brown, *Gospel according to John*.
35. If we consider the prologue as a responsive reading between A and B, the following format shall explain the structure of the pericope – A: "In the beginning was the Word" and B: "And the Word was with God, and the Word was God. He was in the beginning with God." This format can be delved out throughout the pericope. Thomaskutty, *Gospel of John*, 41–42.
36. Also https://credomag.com/2013/02/intertextuality-and-intratextuality/. Compare M. W. G. Stibbe, *John*, Readings: A New Biblical Commentary (Sheffield: Sheffield Academic Press, 1993), 22.

Introduction

interactive level of the text, the narrator addresses the reader from an eternal point of view. At the *intra-textual level*, the *Prologue* is considered a wisdom hymn, woven into the opening of the Gospel to make the overall message comprehensible to the reader. Some key themes of the Gospel are first introduced in these verses: life (1:4), light (1:4), witness (1:7), true (in the sense of "genuine" or "ultimate," 1:9), the world (1:10), glory (1:14), and truth (1:14).[37] Throughout the Gospel, the *Logos* is depicted as a divine emissary in conflict with the world (1:9–10; 3:16–17, 19). The narrator also establishes an *intertextual* relationship between the story of Jesus and the story of Moses. The opening line echoes Genesis 1:1, and the *Prologue* identifies its protagonist as the *Logos* – the Word of God – thus placing the drama within a cosmic setting against the backdrop of the Old Testament (OT).[38] Comparisons between Jesus and Moses, and between Jesus's death and the exodus, recur throughout John.[39]

The Gospel begins with a familiar rhythm: "In the beginning was the *Word*, and the *Word* was with God, and the *Word* was God" (1:1, emphasis added). The book of Genesis also begins in a similar style: "In the beginning God created the heavens and the earth" (Gen 1:1). The affirmation of the incarnation – "The Word became flesh and made his dwelling among us" (1:14) – is a key theme of the Fourth Gospel.

Some Indian Christian theologians attempt to bridge the gap between Johannine and Indian traditions to foster interreligious dialogue. For instance, Keshub Chandra Sen understands *Brahman* as *Sat*, *Cit*, and *Ananda* (that is, "being," "intelligence," and "bliss"). For Sen, in the words of Boyd, "The *Logos*, then, who in eternity lay as it were asleep in God, is the Word of Creation, *Cit* (intelligence, wisdom), ever at work in the development of the created world, and in the fullness of time being born as man in Jesus of Nazareth."[40] Similarly, Brahmabandhav Upādhyāya (1861–1907) equates the Hindu concept of *Saccidānanda Brahman* with the Christian Trinity.[41] In *The Hymn of the Incarnation*, his Sanskrit hymn, Upādhyāya depicts Christ as both the "God-Man" and the *Logos*. Boyd puts it like this: "Christ is the Image of God (*Brahman*) and in him the eternal Word (Intelligence, *Cit*), the fullness of the Godhead, dwells. In the refrain, victory (*jai*) or glory is ascribed to him who

---

37. Thomaskutty, *Gospel of John*, 45–46.
38. Thomaskutty, 46.
39. Stibbe, *John*, 23.
40. R. M. Boyd, *An Introduction to Indian Christian Theology* (Delhi: ISPCK, 1969), 28.
41. Boyd, *Introduction to Indian Christian Theology*, 63–74.

9

is the true *Nara-Hari* ('Man-God')."[42] These dialogical interactions between the Johannine *Logos* and Indian traditions introduce new nuances for an Asian interpretation of the Fourth Gospel.

1:19–12:50 The Book of Signs

After the *Prologue*, the narrator introduces the first major part of the Gospel, often called the *Book of Signs* (1:19–12:50).[43] Raymond E. Brown divides this section into four subunits: the initial days of Jesus's revelation to his disciples through various titles (John 1:19–51); the first and second miracles at Cana (John 2–4); a third miracle and OT feasts and their replacements (John 5–10); and a fourth miracle – the raising of Lazarus – and its aftermath (John 11–12).[44]

In the first subsection (1:19–51), Jesus's name is revealed through various witnesses: "Lamb of God" (1:29, 35), "Messiah" (1:41), "the one" about whom Moses and the prophets wrote (1:45), "Son of God" (1:49), and "king of Israel" (1:49). Some of the key revelatory aspects of Jesus and his universal significance are made evident in this section.[45]

The second subsection (John 2–4) describes Jesus's circular mission journey that begins in Cana (2:1–11), proceeds through Jerusalem (2:13–22) and Samaria (4:1–42), and ends in Cana (4:43–54). The events recorded in these sections highlight Jesus's role as a giver of joy (2:1–11), a great teacher (3:1–21; 4:1–42), and provider of life (4:43–54).[46]

The third subsection (John 5–10) focuses on how Jesus fulfills various OT festivals through his ministry. Asians observe festivals such as Diwali, Onam, Pongal, Holi, and Ramadan. In this context, the Johannine narrative offers a rhetoric that is both friendly and contextually relevant. For instance, just as the festival of Booths or Tabernacles (7:2, 37) is associated with themes of light and water for ritual cleansing, in Hindu spirituality, Diwali is a festival of light that also involves water for purification.[47] Drawing these parallels can be helpful in sharing the gospel with a Hindu.

---

42. Boyd, 78.
43. Van Belle describes in detail the origin and development of the "Sēmeia [Sign] Hypothesis." Brown, *Gospel according to John*, xxviii–xxix.
44. Raymond E. Brown, *An Introduction to the New Testament* (Bangalore: Theological Publications in India, 2009), 338–51.
45. Thomaskutty, *Dialogue in the Book of Signs*, 92.
46. Kanagaraj, *Gospel of John*, 97–163.
47. "Diwali," *Britannica*, https://www.britannica.com/topic/Diwali-Hindu-festival; R. B. P. Singh, "Water Symbolism and Sacred Landscape in Hinduism: A Study of Benares (Vārāṇasi)," *Erdkunde* (Band 48/3, 1994), 210–27.

Introduction

The fourth subsection (John 11–12) is crucial as the death and resurrection of Lazarus prepare readers for Jesus's death and resurrection in the second major part of the Gospel.[48] Jesus's friendship with Lazarus and his family resonates with Asian readers, who place great value on friendship and can readily identify with Jesus as he mourns at the tomb of his friend Lazarus.

Asian readers will see several contextual and ideological resonances between the *Book of Signs* (1:19–12:50) and various aspects of Asian religious literature. Just as the *Rāmāyana* has been a perennial source of spiritual, cultural, and artistic inspiration for thousands of years, the Johannine narratives continue to inspire many with their spiritual insights,[49] cultural identification with the Johannine community, and artistic inspiration.[50] As Vālmîki, the great sage, presents Rāma, the ancient idol of the heroic ages, as the embodiment of truth and morality, the ideal son and husband, and, above all, the ideal king,[51] the Beloved Disciple presents Jesus, his protagonist, as the embodiment of truth (1:17; 14:6) and great morality, the ideal Son of God (1:34, 49), the bridegroom of the Johannine community (3:29), and the ideal king of Israel (1:49). The Johannine narrator skillfully weaves together drama, bhakti (devotion to a deity), and themes of pain and suffering in his portrayal of Jesus.

The seven signs in the *Book of Signs* (2:1–11; 4:46–54; 5:1–18; 6:1–15; 6:16–21; 9:1–41; 11:1–54) are narrated within the framework of the grand sign – the incarnation of the Word (1:1–18). Jesus's performance of these signs to reveal his identity resonates with Asian realities, and the signs are presented in a universalistic fashion in the Fourth Gospel.

13:1–20:31 The Book of Glory

The *Book of Signs* is followed by the second major part of the Gospel, traditionally called the *Book of Glory* (13:1–20:31). Brown subdivides this section into three parts: the Last Supper and Jesus's Farewell Discourse (John 13–17); Jesus's Passion and Death (John 18–19); and Four Post-Resurrection Appearances and a Declaration of Faith in the Risen Jesus (20:1–29), followed by the Gospel's Purpose Statement (20:30–31).[52]

---

48. Thomaskutty, *Dialogue in the Book of Signs*, 368–404.
49. Clement of Alexandria considers it as a *Spiritual Gospel*. Hypotyposes, cited in Eusebius, *HE* 6.14.7.
50. Refer to http://jyotiartashram.blogspot.com/.
51. Kamala Subramaniam, *Ramayana* (Mumbai: Bharatiya Vidya Bhavan, 2019), v.
52. Brown, *Introduction to the NT*, 351–60.

John

While the *Book of Signs* ends with Mary's anointing of Jesus's feet (12:1–8), the *Book of Glory* begins with Jesus washing the feet of the disciples (13:1–20). While the *Book of Signs* ends with the death and the raising of Lazarus (11:1–54), the *Book of Glory* focuses our attention on the death and the resurrection of Jesus (John 18–20). While the *Book of Signs* ends with Jesus weeping at the tomb of Lazarus (11:35), the *Book of Glory* ends with Mary Magdalene weeping at the tomb of Jesus (20:10–18).[53] Thus, there is a strong connection between the two major parts of the Gospel.

The Farewell Discourse (John 13–17) begins with Jesus's foot washing (13:1–20) and end with his high priestly prayer (17:1–26). In this prayer, Jesus prays for himself (17:1–5), his disciples (17:6–19), and future believers (17:20–26). In the Asian context, prayers are usually offered for personal edification, for relatives and friends, and for the world at large. Many scholars connect this prayer with Jesus's declaration, "I am the way and the truth and the life" (14:6). The prayers of Jesus in John make God's presence known universally.

The Passion Narrative (John 18–19) describes Jesus's betrayal and arrest (18:1–11), the trial before Annas and Caiaphas (18:12–14), Peter's three denials (18:15–27), the trial before Pilate (18:28–19:15), the crucifixion and death (19:16–37), and the burial (19:38–42). The irony of the cross is revealed through Jesus's final utterances: although rejected by his own people (1:10–11), Jesus protected his own (17:11–12) and, even at the moment of death, cared for his mother by entrusting her to the Beloved Disciple (19:26–27); the giver of living water was thirsty (19:28; compare 4:10–14), and the provider of the new wine – who was also the true vine – was given sour wine (19:28–29; compare 2:1–11; 15:1–5); and despite worldly persecution, he accomplished the task entrusted to him by the Father (19:30).[54]

John 20:1–29 describes the resurrection of Jesus and subsequent events. The section begins with an introduction, describing how Mary Magdalene came to the tomb, found it empty, and reported the news to Simon Peter and the Beloved Disciple (20:1–2). There are four scenes set in Jerusalem: a) Simon Peter and the Beloved Disciple run to the tomb and confirm the absence of Jesus's body (20:3–10); b) Mary Magdalene returns to the tomb, where two angels are now present (20:11–18); c) on the evening of Easter Sunday, the

---

53. These striking literary interconnections between the *Book of Signs* and the *Book of Glory* is rhetorical in the process of interpreting the Gospel as a whole.
54. J. B. Green, "Death of Jesus," *DJG*, eds. Joel B. Green, Scott McKnight, and I. Howard Marshall (Downers Grove: InterVarsity Press, 1992), 161–63.

disciples are behind locked doors for the fear of the Jews (20:19–25); and d) a week later, the disciples are gathered in the same place, this time with Thomas also present (20:26–29).[55] In the extended narrative framework of John's Gospel, Jesus's resurrection marks the culmination of his glorification.

The Gospel's purpose statement (20:30–31) clearly reveals the author's goal: that readers would come to faith or deepen their faith in Jesus as the Messiah, the Son of God, and, through this faith, receive eternal life in his name.[56]

In the *Book of Glory*, themes of pain and glory develop simultaneously. Jesus, the protagonist, and those who believe in him and follow him experience pain. But Jesus's suffering brings glory; the shameful cross becomes God's way of salvation. The glory of God and Jesus is further revealed through the resurrection, which is the climax of the story. John's narrative is a threnody – a poetic lament – that encompasses melody, comedy, and tragedy. In this way, Asian realities and literary features are integral to John's dialogue.

21:1–25 The Epilogue

The *Epilogue* of John is set in Galilee and can be divided into three sections: a) the appearance of Jesus and the miraculous catch of fish (21:1–14); b) the conversations between the risen Jesus and Peter (21:15–23); and c) the Gospel's conclusion (21:24–25).[57] Just as the Gospel begins with a double introduction (1:1–18; 1:19–51), it ends with a double conclusion (20:30–31; 21:1–25, especially verses 24–25).

In the first section (21:1–14), the gathering of seven disciples seems symbolic since this group represents the future community – the church.[58] While most of the disciples do not recognize Jesus, the Beloved Disciple exclaims, "It is the Lord!" (21:7). Achtemeier, Green, and Thompson say that "even after his resurrection, Jesus is not easily recognized, and the disciples must learn to recognize Jesus all over again."[59]

The second section (21:15–23) focuses on two central characters: Peter and the Beloved Disciple. Peter, who denied Jesus three times before a charcoal

---

55. Brown, *Introduction to the NT*, 359–60.
56. Brown, 360.
57. Brown, 360–61.
58. R. Schnackenburg, *The Gospel according to St. John*, vol. 3 (London: Burns & Oates, 1982), 78–79.
59. Paul J. Achtemeier, Joel B., Green, and Marianne M. Thompson, *Introducing the New Testament: Its Literature and Theology* (Grand Rapids: Eerdmans, 2001).

fire (18:15–27), is now reinstated in love and prepared for future mission (21:15–17). While the Beloved Disciple is the first to recognize the Lord (21:7), it is Peter who receives the command "Follow me" (21:19, 22) – this is the same command Jesus gave Philip (1:43), thus forming a larger *inclusion* within this Gospel.

Following the conclusion already given (20:30–31), another concluding statement is added in verses 24–25. The Beloved Disciple is identified "as the witness who stands behind the Gospel narrative and certifies the truth of his testimony."[60] In that sense, the entire story is narrated through the perspective of the Beloved Disciple.

The Gospel of John demonstrates several conceptual and ideological parallels beyond the South Asian context. A comparison may be drawn between Jesus's disciples and the disciples of Confucius, who followed their teacher closely, shared in his hardships, and were encouraged by their master to stand firm in times of trial.[61] Confucius also warned them to avoid greed and laziness and instilled in them moral and ethical principles for living a renewed life within their society.[62] Both Jesus and Confucius were teachers who taught great lessons. Just as the oral teachings of Confucius spread through his disciples to future generations, the Johannine community reinterpreted, developed, and expounded Jesus's teaching in response to changing needs. Just as the Beloved Disciple reinterpreted his master's teachings for his community, the teachings of Confucius were later compiled as *Analects*.[63]

The ancient *Guru-Shishya* (teacher-student) tradition of India dates back to the Upanishadic period.[64] Just as Jesus was a *walking teacher* (someone who taught while walking) and the disciples followed him, Asian religious teachers like Dronacharya, Buddha, Mahavira, and the Sikh Gurus imparted knowledge to their disciples while they walked together. The *Guru-Shishya* relationship is also emphasized in the Sikh religion. The Punjabi word *sikh* (meaning "learner") is related to the Sanskrit *shishya* (meaning "disciple"). Both Johannine and Asian religious traditions regard following the master an essential aspect of one's spirituality.

---

60. Brown, *Introduction to the NT*, 361.
61. For more details about here: https://plato.stanford.edu/entries/confucius/.
62. https://classroom.synonym.com/roles-of-the-disciples-in-confucianism-12086182.html.
63. https://classroom.synonym.com/roles-of-the-disciples-in-confucianism-12086182.html.
64. Surindar Singh Kohli, *The Sikh and Sikhism* (New Delhi: Atlantic Publishers, 1993), 18.

Introduction

CONCLUSION

The Gospel of John demonstrates several conceptual and ideological similarities with Asian contextual realities. The four parts of the Gospel (the *Prologue*, the *Book of Signs*, the *Book of Glory*, and the *Epilogue*), the ideology of discipleship, the semantics of signs, the "I am" statements, the characters and characterization, the mystical and religious aspects, and the dualistic framework of the Gospel fit well within the ideological framework of the Asian context. Truly, John is relevant for Asian readers.

JOHN 1:1–18

THE INCARNATION OF THE WORD

The *Prologue* (1:1–18) has features of poetry and a chiastic structure:
Jesus's *being* as the preincarnate Word (1:1–5)
  John's witness about the *becoming* nature of the
    Word (1:6–9)
Jesus's *becoming* flesh and living among humanity (1:10–14)
  John's witness concerning the preexistent nature of the
    Word (1:15)
The relevance of the revelation through the Word (1:16–18)

The passage functions as rhythmic prose, with Jesus and John the Baptist appearing in an alternative A-B-A-B-A sequence and has all the features of a quasi-poem – a combination of prose and poem. It reflects themes prevalent in many Asian religions: "life" (*jîva*), "light" (*jyoti* or *deepam*), "truth" (*satya*), "witness" (*sākshi*), "world" (*lōkum*), and "logos" (*vachan*).[1] An Asian reader can identify the poetic style of the *Prologue* with that found in other sacred texts such as the OT, the *Ramayana*, the *Mahabharata*, the *Dhammapada*, and the Qu'ran.

The first section (1:1–5) discusses the *being* nature of the preincarnate Word. *Logos* refers to the principle of reason or order immanent in the universe.[2] It directs the reader's attention to the beginning of all beginnings (1:1a). The undetermined chronology of the universe directs the reader's attention to the existence of the Word in the beginning. The Gospel begins by pointing to the existence of the Word *before time* (1:1a). John 1:1b explains the Word's presence "with God" (Gk: *pros*). In verse 1c, the narrator explains the Word's oneness with God through the clause "the Word was God."[3] In verse 1, the

---
1. All the terminologies in bracket are Sanskrit or Indian equivalents to the Johannine terms.
2. For Bruce, it is "the principle which imposes form on the material world and constitutes the rational soul in man." F. F. Bruce, *The Gospel of John: Introduction, Exposition, and Notes* (Grand Rapids: Eerdmans, 1983), 29.
3. Bruce states, "Since *logos* has the article preceding it, it is marked out as the subject. The fact that *theos* is the first word after the conjunction *kai* ('and') shows that the main emphasis of the clause lies on it. Had *theos* as well as *logos* been preceded by the article the meaning would have been that the Word shared the nature and being of God." Bruce, *Gospel of John*, 31.

three clauses are connected by the parataxis *kai* (and) and have the following narratorial emphasis: the autonomous existence of the Word in the beginning (1:1a), the relational nature of the Word with God (1:1b), and the oneness of the Word with God as inseparable but independent identities. This delineation of the Word gives the reader insight into the functional dynamism of the Word, who is connected to God as the source of absolute power (compare Col 1:15–20; Heb 1:2).

The essence of verse 1 is recapitulated in a simple idiom in verse 2. In verse 3, the expression "all things . . . without him nothing" clearly indicates the emergence of the universe through the Word.[4] The preposition *dia* (through) and the personal pronoun *autou* (him) together communicate the involvement of the preincarnate Word in creation (compare Col 1:15–20; Heb 1:2). The Word was the source of life, and that life was the light of all people (1:4). These expressions – "all things," "without him nothing," and "light of all mankind" show the Word's absolute authority over and ownership of all things. Themes such as Word, life, and light are presented as synonymous titles to refer to the same person. Jesus is the Word and the life-giving source who enlightens the universe.

The Word as the life-giving light (*jyoti* or *deepam*) introduces a sharp contrast with the spheres of darkness (*tamas*). The victory of the life-giving light over darkness is foretold with proleptic imagery – "the darkness has not overcome it" (1:5). The poetic style and literary artistry of John reach their zenith in verses 1–5, where Jesus, in the flesh, serves as the intermediary between the realms "from below" and "from above," transcending the limitations of time and space.

The narrator then turns to the character of John the Baptist. While Jesus is introduced from a "once before time perspective," John is introduced from a "once upon a time perspective." The narrator uses his storytelling skills in an idiomatic way: "There was a man sent from God whose name was John" (1:6). The oral and folkloric style of the Fourth Gospel has a persuasive appeal for Asian readers.[5] John appears as a forerunner, in contrast to the disciples who are called to be followers. John is the "witness" who testifies concerning the light. In an Indian setting, a witness (*sākshi*) appears in a courtroom setting

---

4. The term *panta* ("all") is used in its neuter form. It can mean "all [things]," animate and inanimate.
5. Edwin Jebaraj and Johnson Thomaskutty, "The Gospel of Mark," *An Asian Introduction to the New Testament* (Minneapolis: Fortress Press, 2022), 99.

to authenticate someone else's truthfulness. John's mission included guiding the world toward the light and helping people believe in the Word. John's testimony adds another layer to the dualistic framework of belief and unbelief. Just as Indian movies categorize characters as *nāyakan* (protagonist), villain (antagonist), friends of the *nāyakan*, and friends of the villain, the Johannine story identifies those who believe as friends of the *nāyakan* (Jesus) and those who do not believe as his enemies. The narrator affirms that John himself was not the light but a witness (*sākshi*) to the light. Verses 4–9 focus on Jesus's role as the true light that enlightens the world and John's role as his witness.

The narrator returns to the Word in verse 10, which states one of the grand ironies of the Gospel: Jesus's familiarity with the world, as its creator, is contrasted with the world's unfamiliarity with its creator (1:10b). Even though Jesus endured rejection by many, a large number of people received him and believed in his name (1:11). Those who believed in Jesus were given the power to become children of God (1:12). Receiving or accepting Jesus is the starting point of belief.

John's use of filial language – Father, Son, children – emphasizes that acceptance and belief in Jesus are requirements for becoming children of God. In Asia, where family ties are of great significance, this filial language of the Gospel resonates deeply. Children of God are not born of blood, nor of the will of the flesh, nor of the will of man.[6] Their spiritual birth as children of God begins with accepting and believing in the Word.

In verse 14, the narrator emphasizes the incarnation of the preincarnate Word. The Word becoming signifies means that the Word fully identifies with the world from below.[7] The Greek word *eskēnōsen*, derived from *skēnoō*, can mean to pitch a tent or tabernacle. Jesus's movement from heaven to earth is best described in terms of the Indonesian concept of a *perantau* (migrant).[8] This incarnate Word reflects the glory of the Father and exhibits the Father's grace and truth in full measure. Jesus's position as the Father's "one and only" (1:14, 18),[9] embodying the qualities of glory, grace, and truth, demonstrates

---

6. The Greek expression *egennēthēsan* refers to the physical or biological birth of a person.
7. The Greek word *sarx* can mean "flesh," "human nature," or "human frame."
8. Ekaputra Tupamahu, "The Gospel of Luke," *An Asian Introduction to the New Testament*, ed. Johnson Thomaskutty (Minneapolis: Fortress Press, 2022), 109–12.
9. The adjectival form can mean "only-begotten" or "only-born" (Luke 7:12; 8:42; 9:38; Heb 11:17) and *only-begotten* in respect of peculiar generation (John 1:14, 18; 3:16, 18; 1 John 4:9).

their oneness in substance (*homoousios*).[10] As Popley says, anyone can become a child of God, but Jesus alone is the Father's "one and only" (*ēkaputtiraṉ*).[11]

In verse 15, the narrator returns to John the Baptist, who faithfully testified to the Word's superiority. The Word's existence precedes and transcends John's testimony.

The last three verses of the *Prologue* (1:16–18) concerns the world at large. In verse 14, the narrator describes Jesus as glorious – as the Father's only Son, "full of grace and truth." In verse 16, he presents Jesus as the source of grace upon grace. As Jesus received grace from the fullness of the Father, those who believe in Jesus will receive grace from the Father's fullness. Here, grace upon grace – "grace in place of grace already given" (1:16) – can mean that the grace of Jesus builds upon the grace of the Father. There is a progression from the period of law (Moses) to the period of grace (Jesus). While Moses and the law were inadequate to save people permanently, Jesus's grace and truth sufficiently and permanently save people. Jesus saw the full glory of God and received grace and truth in full measure, which he then imparted to his people. Since Jesus was close to the Father's heart, he was able to access the full measure of heavenly glory, grace, and truth and impart it to the world. Jesus's benevolence to humanity is one of the hallmarks of John's story.

The *Prologue* introduces some key themes of the Gospel and presents the narrator's agenda in its simplest form. The passage highlights the *being* and *becoming* of the Word and the witness of John the Baptist. While Jesus was revealed as divine in his preincarnate stage (see 1:1c, 18), he became fully human in the incarnation. Word, life, light, glory, grace, and truth amplify the person and work of Jesus with rhetorical punch. The repeated use of "all" (1:3, 4, 7, 12, 16) and "full" or "fullness" (1:14, 16) demonstrate Jesus's total involvement in creation and his full equality with God.

In the Gospel of John, the incarnation and the motif of the Son of Man ascending and descending are central.[12] Although it is difficult to equate Hindu and Christian streams of thought, Asian readers may recognize parallels in God's descent to the world below, God's activity of saving humans in their

---

10. The Nicene (325 CE) creed affirms that God the Son and God the Father are of the same substance (*homoousios*).
11. H. A. Popley, *Paricutta Yōvāṉ eḻutiṉa cuvicēṣam, mūlamum uraiyum (The Gospel of John: Text and Commentary) ceṉṉai kirictava kalvi apivirutti caṅkam* (Chennai: SPCK, 1913), 24, 157. Also G. T. Basker, *Interpreting Biblical Texts: John and his Tamil Readers* (New Delhi: ISPCK, 2016), 23.
12. The debate on Boyd, *Introduction to Indian Christian Theology*, 80–82.

times of need, and the divine presence manifested in human form. In the Asian context, when people are gripped by fear or caught in dangerous situations, God's presence as life has profound significance. Suffering humanity may find comfort in the *Logos-Life-Light* – a paradigmatic message of hope for Asians.

JOHANNINE METAPHORS

Metaphors in the NT enable readers to connect the earthly with the heavenly, conveying meanings that are above and beyond their literal and conceptual semantics. The Fourth Gospel has a network of metaphors that demonstrate its soteriological framework to readers. While the Synoptic writers use the word *parabolē* (parable) for artistic portrayals, John uses the word *paroimia* (figure of speech) in a few instances (10:6; 16:25, 29) and explains in detail how Jesus is a figure of salvation through his acts of protection, guidance, shepherding, and laying down his life. While the Synoptic writers use "kingdom of God" or "kingdom of heaven" as an overarching metaphor for salvation, John uses "life" or "eternal life."

John's emphasis is reflected not only in his terminology but also in his conceptual framework. The Synoptic writers present God as a king of a kingdom – and hence his followers are dynamically aligned within that system as *subjects* of the king. But the Fourth Gospel depicts God as the Father of a family – and hence his followers are dynamically aligned within that system as *children* of the Father. This metaphorical difference points to John's emphasis on intimacy, familiarity, and responsibility within this Father-child relationship.[1]

Other metaphors such as life, light, witness, darkness, glory, children, dwelling, Father, and Son are found in the *Prologue* of John (1:1–18). The metaphor of following frames the Gospel (1:43; 21:19, 22), forming an *inclusio* – a parenthesis-like structure – that aligns with its soteriological framework. The metaphor of dove for the Holy Spirit (1:32) symbolizes the descent of God's presence into the world below. Jesus's metaphorical language is evident in his utterance at the temple: "Destroy this temple, and I will raise it again in three days" (2:19), which was a reference to his crucifixion and resurrection. His metaphorical speech emphasizing salvation is also apparent in his statements about his "hour" (2:4; 4:21, 23; 5:25, 28; 7:6, 8, 30; 8:20; 12:23) and about the Son of Man being "lifted up" (3:14; 12:32). Metaphors such as being "born from above" (3:3), being "born of water and the Spirit" (3:5), water and drinking (4:10–14; 7:37–38), work (5:17; 6:29), and judgment and testimony (5:19–47) elaborate further on soteriological themes within John's framework.[2]

In addition, the "I am" sayings of Jesus are profoundly metaphorical: bread (6:35, 41, 48), light (8:12; 9:5), gate (10:7, 9), shepherd (10:11), resurrection and life (11:25), way, truth, and life (14:6), and vine (15:1). To develop these key metaphors, the narrator uses a network of related imagery that highlights their salvific significance. For instance, the metaphor of bread in John 6 is amplified and expanded using related metaphors such as eating, filling the stomach (6:26, 51, 53), hunger and thirst (6:35), and food and drink (6:55).[3] The same is true for the shepherd (John 10) and vine (John 15) metaphors. One advantage for Asian readers is that many expressions and metaphors in John's Gospel reflect the flora and fauna of their own contexts. This enables them to be more creative in interpreting and expressing the sacred writings in light of their own realities.

---

1. Johnson Thomaskutty, "Metaphors of Salvation in the New Testament and Their Implications in Asia," *Exploring the New Testament in Asia: Evangelical Perspectives*, eds. Samson L. Uytanlet and Bennet Lawrence (Carlisle: Langham Global Library, 2024), 55–78.
2. David W. Wead, *The Literary Devices in John's Gospel*, The Johannine Monograph Series, revised and expanded edition (Eugene: Wipf & Stock, 2018).
3. Susan Hylen, *Allusion and Meaning in John 6*, BZNW 1377 (Berlin: Walter de Gruyter, 2005).

JOHN 1:19–2:12

THE BEGINNING OF JESUS'S MINISTRY

After the *Prologue* (1:1–18), the narrator focuses on Jesus's ministry. John 1:19–2:12 forms a single unit with seven subsections. Just as the Genesis creation story is narrated within a seven-day framework (Gen 1:3–2:3), John structures this episode around a seven-day motif: Day One (1:19–28); Day Two (1:29–34); Day Three (1:35–42); Day Four (1:43–51); Day Five (implied); Day Six (2:1–11); and Day Seven (2:12).

1:19–28 DAY ONE

John the Baptist appears again in the narrative as the one who bears "testimony" (1:19). When the Jewish leaders sent priests and Levites from Jerusalem to inquire about John's identity,[1] he denied that he was the Messiah.[2] The Jews questioned him further: "Then who are you? Are you Elijah? . . . Are you the Prophet?" (1:21). John responded with three negations in the following order: "I am not the Messiah" (1:20), "I am not" (1:21), and "No" (1:21). Beasley-Murray comments, "The question, 'Are you Elijah?' arises from Malachi 4:5 (compare Mal 3:1), promising the sending of Elijah before the Day of the Lord that Israel might avert its wrath (compare Sir 48:10)."[3] John's "I am not" statements (1:20–21) prepare the way for Jesus's "I am" statements in subsequent episodes (6:48; 8:12; 9:5; 10:7, 11; 11:25; 14:6; 15:1).

John the Baptist was identified with Elijah partly because of the similarity in their garments. The expectation of a coming prophet was rooted in Deuteronomy 18:15, 18. When questioned by the Jewish authorities, John the Baptist clearly affirmed his identity and mission.

The dialogue between John the Baptist and the Jewish leaders serves as a narrative rhetoric to reveal the Messiah to the world. While John was "sent from God" (*apestalmenos* in verse 6), the priests and Levites were "sent" by the Jewish leaders in Jerusalem (*apesteilan* in verse 19, *pempsasin* in verse 22, and *apestalmenoi* in verse 24).

---

1. The Jews are further identified as the Pharisees in verse 24.
2. Beasley-Murray, *John*, WBC 36 (Nashville: Thomas Nelson Publishers, 1999), 23.
3. Beasley-Murray, *John*, 23.

John

While the first three questions concern the identity of John the Baptist, the final two questions concern his activity: "Who are you? Give us an answer to take back to those who sent us. What do you say about yourself?" (1:22). John responded by identifying himself as the one whom Isaiah had prophesied about: "I am the voice of one calling in the wilderness, 'Make straight the way for the Lord'" (1:23; compare Isa 40:3). Here, the narrator uses a promise and fulfillment formula.

In verse 25, John the Baptist affirms three things: first, his baptism was only with water; second, Jesus was already among the people, although unrecognized; and third, John was unworthy even to untie the thongs of Jesus's sandal. In the Greco-Roman context, untying the master's sandal was a duty reserved for a slave. Here, John the Baptist regards himself as beneath even the status of a slave. In Brahmanical India, Dalits were not allowed to wear sandals and were expected to untie and clean the sandals of upper-caste people. In the honor-shame context of Asian cultures, touching someone else's sandal is considered shameful. Sandals are usually left outside homes and religious places because they are believed to carry the dirt of the world. Similarly, John considered himself inferior to Jesus, unworthy even to untie his sandals.

The geographical setting of the event – "Bethany on the other side of the Jordan" (1:28)[4] – alludes to Joshua's parting of the Jordan River for Israel's redemption (Josh 3:1–17) and suggests that Jesus was crossing the Jordan to form the new Israel.

1:29–34 DAY TWO

Asians are well attuned to various levels of religious discourse. Since nearly all major religions in Asia involve religious discourses in both private and public places, Asians can easily relate to John the Baptist's engagement in such practices. In John 1:29–34, John's speech in this section involves his declaration about the Lamb of God (1:29–31) and his eyewitness testimony about the Son of God (1:32–34).[5] The phrase "the next day" (1:29) marks the transition from the previous section (1:19–28). Having identified the one who stands among the people (1:26), John now reveals him to the public (1:29a). His declaration in verses 29–31 introduces the Lamb of God to the world, emphasizing the

---

4. This "Bethany" is different from the "Bethany" outside of Jerusalem.
5. Thomaskutty, *Dialogue in the Book of Signs*, 59.

following aspects:[6] Jesus is presented as the Lamb of God who takes away the sin of the world, signifying his salvific mission (1:29b);[7] the Baptizer reaffirms Jesus's superiority over himself, signifying Jesus's universal role (1:30a; compare 1:27); he emphasizes Jesus's preexistence by using the expression "he was before me" (1:30b; compare 1:1–5, 6–9, 10–14); the confession, "I myself did not know him" reveals John's own earthly status and his initial lack of understanding (1:31a); and John's baptism with water was so that Jesus might be revealed to Israel, pointing to John's unique role as the forerunner (1:31b). The title "Lamb of God" foreshadows the passion of Jesus. Although John the Baptizer's origins were earthly (1:31a), his special appointment as one sent from God makes him unique in this world (1:6).

The second section of this passage (1:29–34) focuses on John's eyewitness testimony: he saw the Spirit's descent upon Jesus like a dove, signifying divine endowment for ministry (1:32).[8] John served as a divine instrument (1:33a), beginning his ministry with water baptism – a role that marked him as a unique figure (1:33b). God's voice confirmed this mission by revealing to John that the one on whom the Spirit descended would baptize with the Holy Spirit (1:33c). The Baptizer's witness (1:32) and the divine oracle (1:33c) confirm to us that the Holy Spirit descended on Jesus. The Baptizer testified to Jesus's identity as the Lamb of God (1:29) and the Son of God (1:34).[9] Like a sannyasi (an Asian devotee), John the Baptizer practiced austerity, followed an ascetic lifestyle, discovered and revealed spiritual truths, and experienced a mystical union with God.[10]

Jesus was not a lamb offered by people *to* God but a lamb *from* God. Thus, the title "Lamb of God" transcends the traditional understanding of the Passover Lamb, reinterpreting an old symbol in a new way.[11] The passage

---

6. The term "Lamb of God" in the NT appears only in the Johannine writings (1:29, 36; and 27 times in Revelation).
7. Scholars associate the Lamb of God with: first, the Suffering Servant of Isaiah 53; second, the Triumphant Lamb of Revelation (Rev 7:17; 17:14); third, the Jewish understanding of a lamb who would lead the flock of God's people; and fourth, the Passover Lamb. Moloney, *Gospel of John*, 59.
8. Blomberg writes, "It is interesting that all four Gospels use simile for the Spirit coming 'like' or 'as' a dove (Matt 3:16; Mark 1:10; Luke 3:22; John 1:32), which may suggest a more subjective, spiritual experience rather than an actual vision of a bird that could be pinpointed to a precise moment." Blomberg, *Historical Reliability of John's Gospel*, 78.
9. Some manuscripts say, "the chosen one of God" while others say, "the Son of God." Moloney, *Gospel of John*, 59; also Beasley-Murray, *John*, 25–26.
10. Compare Basker, *Interpreting Biblical Texts*, 97–98.
11. Moloney, *Gospel of John*, 59.

emphasizes the connection between the Baptizer's *seeing* of events and his *testifying* about them to the world (1:34).

The work of the Lamb of God as one who "takes away the sin of the world" reveals his universal salvific role (1:29b) as the sacrificial lamb who saves people from their sinful nature.

The Holy Spirit remained upon Jesus, who is the Messiah, "the Lamb of God" (1:29), the one who surpasses the Baptizer (1:30), and "God's Chosen One" (1:34).[12] John the Baptizer was not merely the first witness to Jesus but a practitioner of Christian spirituality in a pluralistic context, a Christian mystic who proclaimed a universal message of salvation.

1:35–42 DAY THREE

The narrator introduces the events of the third day (1:35–42). At the beginning of the passage, John is depicted, according to the Greek text, as one who "again stood up," "having looked at," and "says" – verbs that position him for dramatic action. The two disciples with whom he was standing are introduced in verse 40. While one is identified as Andrew, the brother of Simon Peter, the other disciple remains anonymous.[13] The Baptizer introduced Jesus to the disciples as someone whom they did not know (1:26) but also someone from their own tradition (Judaism), foretold by their own scriptures. A clear distinction is made between John, as the forerunner sent from God (1:6, 33), and his two disciples who spoke with Jesus and received his invitation (1:37).

Jesus began his public speech with a question: "What do you want?" (1:38a). The disciples addressed him as "Rabbi," an Aramaic word meaning "Teacher," which the narrator translates for his Greek-speaking readers. The disciples' question – "Where are you staying?" – led to Jesus's invitation to "Come . . . and you will see" (1:39a). Jesus invited the two disciples to come and experience his spirituality and oneness with God. They followed him, saw where he was staying, and remained with him that day – and the narrator notes that it was about four o'clock in the afternoon.[14] Just as the Holy Spirit remained (*meno*) with Jesus (1:32, 33b), the disciples now remain (*meno*) with him (1:39). Andrew and the other disciple experienced the oneness of a mystical relationship with Jesus.

---

12. Thomaskutty, *Dialogue in the Book of Signs*, 60.
13. Beasley-Murray states Philip as the anonymous disciple since they pair up in 12:22. Beasley-Murray, *John*, 26–27.
14. Beasley-Murray suggests, "The hour mentioned suggests time for conversation, perhaps even that the disciples stayed overnight with Jesus." Beasley-Murray, *John*, 26.

Hospitality, an important Asian virtue, lies at the heart of this passage. Jesus invited these strangers to stay with him. Similarly, toward the end of the Gospel, Jesus prepared breakfast and extended his hospitality to the disciples (21:10–14). In this sense, the entire Gospel of John unfolds within an *inclusio* marked by Jesus's hospitality to the disciples (1:14, 39; 21:10–14).

Andrew found his brother Simon Peter and testified, "We have found the Messiah" (1:41). The narrator translates the Aramaic term "Messiah" into "Christ" for the benefit of his Greek-speaking audience. Asian devotees often guide others to their religious gurus; similarly, Andrew led Simon Peter to Jesus (v. 42a). The narrator records Simon's positive response to Andrew and their journey together to meet Jesus.

Andrew's actions exemplify the true marks of discipleship and evangelization: hearing about Jesus (1:37), following him (1:37), remaining with him (1:39), finding his brother (1:41a), testifying that Jesus is the Messiah (1:41b), and leading Simon to Jesus (1:42). Jesus tells Simon, "You are Simon son of John. You will be called Cephas" (1:42b).[15] Once again, the Aramaic word, "Cephas," is translated as "Peter" for the Greek-speaking audience (1:41b). This passage gradually shifts the focus away from the Baptizer and gently brings Jesus to the forefront.

1:43–51 DAY FOUR

The transition to the events of the fourth day (1:43–51) are marked by the phrase "the next day." Jesus decided to go to Galilee for the first time (1:43a) and invited Philip to follow him (1:43b). There is a clear progression in the theme of following Jesus from the previous day's events (1:37, 40) to the present day (1:43). Philip, from Bethsaida – the city of Andrew and Peter – found Nathanael and told him that he had found Jesus of Nazareth, the son of Joseph, describing him as "the one Moses wrote about in the Law, and about whom the prophets also wrote" (1:45). The first-person plural "we have found" might be a reference to the witness of Andrew, the anonymous disciple, Peter, and Philip. The reference to Torah and Prophets indicates that Jesus's coming reflects the fulfillment of the Scriptures. However, his coming from Nazareth and connection to Joseph went beyond traditional Jewish expectations of the Messiah. In their testimony, both Andrew and Philip used the first-person plural rather than the singular (1:41, 45). This indicates the communitarian – rather than the individualistic – emphasis of the Jesus movement and the

---

15. Beasley-Murray, *John*, 27; Blomberg, *Historical Reliability of John's Gospel*, 82.

Johannine community. This communal aspect resonates with Asian communities and serves as a significant connecting link for hermeneutical development in the Asian context.

Nathanael's response to Philip – "Nazareth! Can anything good come from there?" (1:46) – could be read as a well-known proverb or as a sarcastic statement conveying skepticism about the Messiah coming from an insignificant place like Nazareth.[16] Philip's reply, "Come and see," differs from Jesus's response to Andrew and his companion (1:39). Jesus credited Nathanael with all the virtues of a true Israelite (1:47), in contrast to the deceitfulness of Jacob, the first Israelite (Gen 25:19–34; 27:1–41). In response to Nathanael's question, Jesus responded, "I saw you while you were still under the fig tree before Philip called you" (1:48b). Like Jewish men of his time, Nathanael probably sat under the shade of a fig tree to study the Scriptures. Nathanael's utterance in verse 49 acknowledges Jesus as Rabbi – just as the first two disciples did (1:38b) – as Son of God – just as John the Baptist did (1:34) – and also as king of Israel, a unique understanding about Jesus thus far.[17] While acknowledging Nathanael's declaration, Jesus promised even greater revelations (1:50). A shift would take place in Nathanael's spiritual experience – from belief on the basis of *hearing* what Jesus said (1:50a) to belief on the basis of *seeing* greater things (1:50b). Jesus's promise to him in verse 51 is apocalyptic in nature: a vision about heaven being opened and the angels of God ascending and descending upon the Son of Man.[18] This marks the first occasion on which Jesus used a self-designation – "Son of Man" (1:51b) – to refer to himself.[19]

The narrator emphasizes the concept of the new Israel in an innovative way: Whereas Jacob was deceitful, Nathanael is described as being without deceit; and whereas Jacob had a vision of a ladder from heaven, Nathanael would see the ascending and descending of the Son of Man.[20] While Jesus affirmed Nathanael as a "true Israelite" (1:47), Nathanael acknowledged Jesus as "king of Israel" (1:49). The new Israel motif is central in this passage, with Jesus expecting Nathanael-like disciples under his kingship. Nathanael's posture

---

16. Blomberg says, "The fact that Philip is paired with Bartholomew in all three synoptic lists of the Twelve (Mark 3:18; Matt 10:3; Luke 6:14), coupled with the observation that Bartholomew (*bar Tholomais*) is a patronymic (meaning "son of Talmai"), nor a proper name, makes the frequent equation of Bartholomew with Nathanael defensible." Blomberg, *Historical Reliability of John's Gospel*, 82.
17. Blomberg, *Historical Reliability of John's Gospel*, 83; Moloney, *Gospel of John*, 61.
18. Blomberg, *Historical Reliability of John's Gospel*, 84; Moloney, *Gospel of John*, 62.
19. For more details, refer to Blomberg, *Historical Reliability of John's Gospel*, 84.
20. Beasley-Murray, *John*, 27–28.

under the fig tree (1:48b), his faith based on both hearing and seeing (1:45, 49; compare 1:51), and Philip's introduction of the Messiah as the one foretold in the Scriptures (1:45) point to a radical form of discipleship under Jesus's reign.

1:43–51 DAY FIVE

A fifth day is implicit between the fourth day (1:43–51) and the day of the wedding at Cana in Galilee (2:1–11). The reader can infer that there is a day between the first day of Jesus's journey to Galilee (1:43) and the "third day" (2:1). This implies that an entire day was spent traveling. The fifth day can be understood within the overall framework of the seven-day structure of John 1:19–2:12 and based on Jesus's three-day journey from the Transjordan area to Galilee.[21] Asian readers, who are accustomed to long hikes and treks through the countryside and mountains and religious pilgrimages to the hill country, can readily identify with Jesus's long journeys – and it is reasonable to assume that Jesus continued teaching his disciples during these journeys.

2:1–11 DAY SIX

The event in 2:1–11 develops across four levels: the setting of the story (2:1–2); the *request* of Mary, the mother of Jesus (2:3); Jesus's mild *rebuke* of Mary (2:4); and Jesus's *response* and subsequent signs (2:5–11).[22] In the Johannine narrative, Jesus reached Galilee on the sixth day – the narrator refers to this as the "third day" because it was the third day of a three-day journey.

The story centers around a wedding celebration. Jesus's mother was also present, and the word "invited" reveals that Jesus and his disciples were attending as invited guests. Asian readers can easily relate to this story as in their culture, too, weddings are important social events where communities gather. When the wine ran out, Jesus's mother informed him, "They have no more wine" (2:3). In many Asian cultures, wedding celebrations are attended not only by invited guests but also by uninvited individuals, especially poor people. The presence of unexpected guests can lead to a shortage of refreshments. Jesus's response to his mother may be understood as a mild rebuke, emphasizing that he does not act according to human timetables or familial obligations but in accordance with divine timing and heavenly ties.[23] Jesus's

---

21. Beasley-Murray, *John*, 31.
22. Moloney, *Gospel of John*, 70–71.
23. "Woman" is an ordinary mode of addressing females under every circumstance. Beasley-Murray, *John*, 34.

use of the word "woman" to address his mother can be read as a term of respect. Kanagaraj says, "The use of the Greek word is similar in many ways to *amma* ["mother"] in South Indian languages."[24] Jesus used the same word on the cross when he showed his care and affection for Mary by entrusting her to the Beloved Disciple (19:26–27).

> ## JOHANNINE WOMEN
>
> The women in John's Gospel show great devotion to Jesus and affirm their faith with profound depth and clarity. Jesus's mother, for example, appears in the context of both celebration – a wedding (2:1–5) – and sorrow – the cross (19:25–27). At the wedding in Cana, Mary demonstrated her faith by presenting a need to Jesus: "They have no wine" (2:3). She also accepted that he would only act in accordance with his "hour" (2:4) and instructed the servants to obey him: "Do whatever he tells you" (2:5). At the cross, she sacrificially released her firstborn and accepted the care of the Beloved Disciple (19:26–27).
>
> In John's Gospel, one of Jesus's most extensive theological discussions was with the Samaritan woman at the well (4:7–26). This stands in sharp contrast to his brief discussion with Nicodemus, a member of the Jewish ruling council, which concluded with a rebuke: "You are Israel's teacher . . . and do you not understand these things?" (3:10). The Samaritan woman knew about her forefathers and was familiar with scriptural prophecies, and she used this knowledge to challenge Jesus: "Are you greater than our father Jacob, who gave us the well and drank from it himself, as did also his sons and his livestock?" (4:12); "Our ancestors worshiped on this mountain, but you Jews claim that the place where we must worship is in Jerusalem" (4:20); and "I know that Messiah . . . is coming. When he comes, he will explain everything to us" (4:25). She did not hide her true situation from Jesus but confessed honestly, "I have no husband," and Jesus commended her honesty: "You are right when you say you have no husband" (4:17). She repeatedly addressed Jesus as *kyrios* (4:11, 15, 19), which the NIV

---

24. Kanagaraj, *Gospel of John*, 99.

translates as "Sir" but also means "Lord." She asked for the living water even though she had not fully grasped its significance: "Sir, give me this water so that I won't get thirsty and have to keep coming here to draw water" (4:15). Like an evangelist or missionary, she invited the people of her village, saying, "Come, see a man who told me everything I did. Could this be the Messiah?" (4:29). As a result of the Samaritan woman's faith and invitation, many from that town believed in Jesus (4:39).

Martha and Mary, along with their brother Lazarus, were deeply loved by Jesus (11:5). Mary and Martha demonstrated their love and faith by turning to Jesus for help and trusting that he could help. Knowing that Jesus – who was in a place several miles away – could prevent their brother's death, they sent a message to him: "Lord, the one you love is sick" (11:3). Despite trusting Jesus, both sisters expressed their disappointment – and perhaps even held him responsible – when they said, "If you had been here, my brother would not have died" (11:21, 32). However, this accusation or reproach was immediately followed by words of assurance and hope: "But I know that even now God will give you whatever you ask" (11:22). It is evident that Martha's theology was sound. When Jesus told her that Lazarus would rise again, she responded, "I know he will rise again in the resurrection at the last day" (11:24). After Jesus declared, "I am the resurrection and the life" (11:25), Martha confessed, "Yes, Lord . . . I believe that you are the Messiah, the Son of God, who is to come into the world" (11:27). Just as Nicodemus, a respected teacher and member of the Jewish ruling council, had acknowledged that Jesus had come from God (3:2), Martha openly acknowledged that Jesus had come from the Father. She referred to Jesus as "Teacher," "Messiah," "Son of God," and "Lord." Her sister Mary fell at Jesus's feet in a posture of worship (11:32). When Jesus asked where they had buried Lazarus, they said, "Come and see" (11:34), echoing Jesus's earlier invitation to his disciples (1:39). As a result of their faith, they witnessed the glory of God when Jesus raised their brother from the dead (11:40). Their faith also led others to believe in Jesus (11:45). Later, Mary demonstrated her gratitude and love by pouring about a pint of pure nard – an expensive perfume worth nearly a year's wages – on Jesus's feet and wiping them with her hair (11:2; 12:1–3, 5). Jesus told the disciples that Mary's act symbolically prepared him for burial (12:7) – a ritual washing he did not receive because he died on the eve of the day of Preparation. These sisters showed greater faith in Jesus than many of Jesus's male disciples.

Whereas the male disciples – except for the Beloved Disciple – were absent, four women stood faithfully at the foot of the cross:

Jesus's mother, Mary; her sister; Mary the wife of Clopas; and Mary Magdalene (19:25). On the morning of the first day of the week, Mary Magdalene arose early, while it was still dark, and went fearlessly to the tomb because of her great devotion to her master and Lord (20:1). She wanted to see Jesus but was shocked to find the stone moved away and the Lord's body missing. Greatly distressed, she reported this to Simon Peter and the Beloved Disciple, perhaps seeking their help (20:2). Peter and the other disciple confirmed that Jesus's body was gone. Yet they failed to understand Jesus's earlier words about rising from the dead (20:9). Instead of searching for his body, they returned to where they were staying (20:10). Mary, however, did not give up but remained outside the tomb crying (20:11). She explained to the two angels inside the tomb that "they have taken my Lord away . . . and I don't know where they have put him" (20:12–13). Turning around, she saw Jesus standing there but did not recognize him (20:14) – perhaps due to the dim light or her lack of understanding about the resurrection. When Jesus asked who she was looking for, Mary repeated her earlier complaint. She was determined to find Jesus's body and place it back in the tomb: "Tell me where you have put him, and I will get him" (20:15). It was only when Jesus called her by name that she recognized him and cried out, "Rabboni!" and clung to him (20:16–17a). Jesus then engaged in a brief theological discussion with her about his ascension to the Father (20:17b). Immediately after this, Mary went to the disciples and announced, "I have seen the Lord!" (20:18). In this way, she became the first witness to Jesus's resurrection.

Together, these examples reveal that the women in John's Gospel exercised their faith in both public and private spheres of life. John's retelling of these women's presence at key moments in Jesus's life illustrates the community's openness to affirming the status and role of women.[1]

Like these Johannine women, the women of Asia can be effective agents of liberation. Just as Mary, the mother of Jesus, played significant roles both at a wedding feast and at the cross, Asian women can assume important leadership roles in times of both joy and sorrow, guiding people to Christ. Like the Samaritan woman at the well, they can learn theology, question and challenge teachers to ensure that their teachings align with Scripture, and lead people in their own communities to Christ. Like Martha and Mary, Asian women can express deep faith in Christ, demonstrate devotion to God, and become channels of blessing to those around them. Like Mary of Bethany, they can model what it means to give the Lord their very best, including their most treasured

> possessions. Finally, like Mary Magdalene, Asian women can wait for the Lord, seek him persistently until they encounter him, and boldly tell others, "I have seen the Lord!"
>
> ---
>
> 1. Johnson Thomaskutty, "Johannine Women as Paradigms in the Indian Context," *Acta Theologica Supplementum* 27 (Bloemfontein: University of the Free State, 2019): 79–100.

The reference to "hour" points forward to the climax of the story.[25] There is a clear connection between the term "hour" in verse 4 and the term "glory" in verse 11. Jesus's hour is ultimately the Father's hour, revealing the moment of divine intervention in the ministry of Jesus.

Subsequent events are narrated in verses 5–11. Mary's instruction to the servants demonstrates her confidence that Jesus could do something to resolve the crisis. Beasley-Murray comments, "The Jewish requirements for which the jars were used included ritual cleansing of the hands through pouring water on them and washing of vessels (compare Mark 7:3–4)."[26] In the reference to "six stone water jars" (2:6), the number six – as a number of imperfection – has symbolic significance, pointing to the inadequacy of the purification system of Judaism (2:6).[27] Jesus's command to "fill the jars with water" (2:7a) and the transformation of the water into wine symbolically demonstrates the fullness of Christ's grace in contrast to the limitations of the old covenant (John 1:16–17).[28] Although caught between his earthly mother's request and his heavenly Father's hour, Jesus channeled the divine purpose to meet the earthly need – a helpful model of service for us all.

The statement made by the master of the banquet highlights the irony of this miracle. Jesus reversed the usual custom of serving the good wine first, followed by the inferior wine once the guests were drunk. Jesus transformed the situation of a lack of wine into a joyous occasion filled with superior and abundant wine. The words of the master of the banquet make it clear that the wine Jesus provided was superior in quality compared to even the choicest

---

25. Also references for "hour" (*hora*) in 7:6, 30; 8:20; 13:1; 17:1.
26. Beasley-Murray, *John*, 35.
27. Moloney, *Gospel of John*, 72.
28. Beasley-Murray, *John*, 35.

wine (2:10). In Greek mythology, Dionysus was the god of wine, religious ecstasy, and fertility. Jesus's role as a provider of the best wine (2:1–11) and as the true vine (15:1–5) would have resonated with the early Christians, who were familiar with the Dionysian myth.[29] Jesus turns situations of scarcity into abundance and enables people to overcome shameful situations with honor. Through the provision of superior wine, Jesus turned an occasion of shame into one of honor.

For the Jews, wine symbolized gladness. Through this sign, Jesus brought to the foreground the fullness of joy[30] that is associated with the arrival of God's kingdom.[31] The narrator concludes this story by saying that this was the first of Jesus's signs (1:11a). The expression "Cana in Galilee" (2:1, 11) forms an *inclusio* that brackets this story. Here begins a series of signs in the Gospel of John.[32] Through this sign, Jesus revealed his glory, and his disciples believed in him.[33]

> ### **THE SEVEN SIGNS**
>
> John's purpose statement (20:30–31) emphasizes three points: first, Jesus did many other signs in the presence of his disciples that are not recorded in the Fourth Gospel; second, those signs that were recorded were intended to persuade people to believe that Jesus is the Christ; and third, by believing that Jesus is the Son of God, people may have life in his name. The Gospel of John as a whole is structured around Jesus's signs, which were recorded to inspire faith among people, with faith in Jesus being the expected outcome of these signs. Paul N. Anderson says, "Distinctive in John are the ways that the signs of Jesus

---

29. Jae Hyung Cho, *This Is My flesh: John's Eucharist and the Dionysus Cult* (Eugene: Pickwick Publications, 2022), 1–21.
30. Johnson Thomaskutty, "New Joy of Salvation (John 2:1–12)," *Barnabas Today* (1 December 2020).
31. Blomberg, *Historical Reliability of John's Gospel*, 86.
32. The concept of sign is familiar in the OT; it is used to demonstrate the truth of God's word through his prophet (for example, Exod 3:12; 1 Sam 10:1–9) and so authenticate the prophet himself (for example, Exod 4:1–9). Beasley-Murray, *John*, 33.
33. Beasley-Murray, *John*, 35.

lead into expansions upon the spiritual meaning of Jesus's works, and in that sense, dialogues with and discourses by Jesus often follow the signs."[1] John's Gospel emphasizes seven of Jesus's signs.

Jesus's first sign was turning water into wine (2:1–11), which anticipated his later declaration, "I am the true vine" (15:1). This first sign, which occurred in Cana in Galilee, set the stage for the second sign – the healing of the official's son (4:43–54) – which was also performed in Cana in Galilee. These signs were important for Nathanael, who was from Cana in Galilee (21:2), especially since he had initially doubted whether anything good could come from Nazareth (1:46).

The third (5:1–15) and sixth (9:1–7) signs focus on the theme of healing. In the former incident, Jesus healed an invalid by the pool of Bethesda; in the latter, he healed a man born blind. Both signs took place near Jerusalem and provoked theological debates with the religious leaders, who questioned Jesus's identity as God's Son: Would a righteous man violate the Sabbath laws and command a paralyzed man to carry his bed and walk on the Sabbath? How could an unholy man heal a man born blind? While it is not clear whether the paralyzed man believed in Jesus (5:1–15), the blind man's progress in faith is apparent through his conversations with various groups (9:1–7).

The fourth (6:1–15) and fifth (6:16–21) signs have parallels with the works of Moses. Just as Moses provided manna in the wilderness, Jesus fed more than five thousand people with five loaves and two fish. While Moses gave the Israelites water from a rock, Jesus walked on water, demonstrating his power and authority over creation and revealing that he is greater than Moses.

The seventh sign (11:1–45) emphasizes Jesus's power to raise the dead and grant abundant life. It also foreshadowed his own imminent death and resurrection.

The signs in John's Gospel function dynamically, contributing semantically to its narrative framework. Jesus turned water into wine at a wedding to resolve an immediate situational issue faced by a family (2:1–12). He healed the son of a royal official, and the man made gradual progress in his journey of faith (4:43–54). The healing of the invalid symbolizes Jesus's generosity even toward strangers (5:1–18). In these two accounts (4:43–54; 5:1–18), the dialogue takes place at the time of the sign. The feeding of the five thousand demonstrates Jesus's compassion for the hungry (6:1–15), while walking on water reveals his power and authority over nature (6:16–21). The healing of the man born blind shows how a sign can lead to the development of personal faith

> (9:1–41).² Finally, the raising of Lazarus emphasizes Jesus's concern for the community of God's people (11:1–45).
>
> These signs proleptically direct the reader's attention toward the grand sign of the Gospel: the resurrection of Jesus (20:1–18). As Jesus carried out the mission of God, he used signs as tools to reveal his identity. In the Asian context, these signs can inspire faith in Jesus and bring hope – especially to the poor and marginalized.

---

1. Paul N. Anderson, *From Crisis to Christ: A Contextual Introduction to the New Testament*, (Nashville: Abingdon, 2014), 144–46.
2. Johnson Thomaskutty, *The Gospel of John*, 237–38.

2:12 DAY SEVEN

The narrator notes that Jesus went down from Cana to Capernaum, accompanied by his mother, brothers, and disciples (2:12). The mother of Jesus is first mentioned at the beginning of his public ministry; she reappears only at the climax of his ministry (19:25–27). After the events of the previous six days, Jesus rested with his family and disciples – recalling the creation story, where God rested after his six days of work (Gen 2:3).

John's *Prologue* – with themes such as "in the beginning," "life," "light," "darkness," and the incorporation of the seven-day motif in 1:19–2:12 – guides the reader toward a "new Genesis" motif.[34] The narrator introduces Jesus as "the Messiah" (1:41), "the Lord" (1:23), one who comes after John but is superior to him (1:27), "Lamb of God" (1:29, 36), "God's Chosen One" (1:34), "the one Moses wrote about in the Law" (1:45), "Jesus of Nazareth, the son of Joseph" (1:45), "Son of God" (1:49), "king of Israel" (1:49), and "the Son of Man" (1:51). The new wine motif symbolizes the gift of salvation. This section (1:19–2:12) reveals the glory of Jesus,[35] who manifests God's glory in the world, and this dramatic development of events over a seven-day period invites the reader to believe in Jesus.

---

34. Also Beasley-Murray, *John*, 34.
35. Thomaskutty, *Dialogue in the Book of Signs*, 45–92.

JOHN 2:13–25
CLEANSING THE TEMPLE AT JERUSALEM

While the synoptic evangelists place the story of Jesus cleansing the temple toward the end of Jesus's public ministry (Matt 21:12–13; Mark 11:15–17; Luke 19:45–46), John places it right at the outset of his Gospel (2:13–25). This relocation serves as a headline that proclaims the meaning of Jesus's ministry.[1] While the Cana event takes place during a wedding banquet (2:1), the temple event unfolds at the national religiopolitical headquarters (2:13). Whereas the event in 2:1–12 is set in Galilee, the event in 2:13–25 occurs in Judea. The Cana event takes place on the third day of Jesus's journey from the Transjordan area to Galilee, while the temple event is set in the context of the approaching Passover Festival of the Jews. While the event in 2:1–12 ends with the comment that Jesus "went down" (2:12), the event in 2:13–25 begins by saying that Jesus "went up" (2:13). Some well-known Asian temples are located on mountaintops, where pilgrims ascend in search of salvation. Thus Asian readers can relate to Jesus going up to the temple. The text unfolds through a situation of conflict in Jerusalem (2:13–15), a dialogue between Jesus and the Jews (2:16–20), the realization of the disciples (2:21–22), and a transition to the next passage (2:23–25).

The story begins with a chronological indication – "time for the Jewish Passover" (2:13a) – and a geographical reference – "Jerusalem" (2:13b). It forms an *inclusio* with the words "Passover" and "Jerusalem" in verses 13 and 23. In the temple, Jesus found people selling cattle, sheep, and doves, and money changers seated at their tables (2:14).[2] Cattle, sheep, and doves were sold for sacrificial offerings, and the sellers and money changers would have exploited the poor pilgrims who came to worship in the temple.

Greco-Roman religious centers usually had restaurants, merchandise, and other social associations. The Corinthian temples, for instance, were known for extra-religious activities such as dining, drinking, trading, and even temple

---
1. Beasley-Murray, *John*, 38–39; also Blomberg, *Historical Reliability of John's Gospel*, 88.
2. *Hieron* refers to the temple precincts while *naos* refers to the holy place or sanctuary proper. They were changing Roman money into Tyrian money so that people might pay the Temple tax with coins not bearing effigies. Beasley-Murray, *John*, 38; Moloney, *Gospel of John*, 76.

prostitution.[3] Similarly, commercialization was also prevalent in the Jewish temple precincts. Jesus drove them all out with a whip of cords[4] – foreshadowing the flogging he would later receive (19:1). His actions demonstrated his zeal against abuse of the temple.[5] Jesus's cleansing of the temple connects back to the Word "tabernacling" or dwelling among people (1:14).

The dialogue between the Jews and Jesus begins with Jesus's command to the sellers of doves: "Stop turning my Father's house into a market!" (2:16). In the Greek text, the word "house" occurs twice: my Father's "house" and the "house" of merchandise, clearly distinguishing between the secular (non-spiritual) and the sacred (spiritual). Jesus's strong language and stern actions make the scene a radical one.[6] He removed the barriers to true worship and purified the temple to facilitate proper worship. His disciples remembered the words of Psalm 69:9: "Zeal for your house will consume me" (2:17). Jesus's attitude toward the temple and worship should shape our view and approach to worship today. Asian religious institutions are often in the grip of class and caste hierarchies. This, too, is improper worship that needs purification. The temple cleansing also serves as a paradigm for all commercialized religious institutions around the world. The church, as God's community, must practice divine virtues such as justice, righteousness, equality, and communion.

The Jews demanded a sign to justify that Jesus had authority to do the things he was doing, including cleansing the temple (2:18). This is the second reference to a "sign" (*sēmeion*) in John, the first being in 2:11. The sign at Cana, which occurred during a feast, was not as offensive to the Jews as Jesus's actions in the temple precincts. Therefore, they demanded proof of his authority. The narrator uses the term "signs" to refer to the visible revelation of Jesus's "glory" (2:11), but the Jews demanded a "sign" as a form of authentication. Jesus's response – which refers to the ultimate sign of the resurrection – is the climax of the story: "Destroy this temple, and I will raise it again in three days" (2:19). His statement was misunderstood by the Jews, who thought that this referred to the physical temple, which had taken 46 years to build. They were skeptical when Jesus said that he would build the temple in three days (2:20).

The narrator clarifies the matter by stating that Jesus was speaking of the temple of his body (2:21). After Jesus's resurrection, the disciples realized

---

3. George Renner and Mark Shaw, *Ten Great Ideas from First Corinthians* (Eugene: Wipf & Stock, 2021), 109.
4. Moloney, *Gospel of John*, 81.
5. Moloney, 77.
6. Beasley-Murray, *John*, 39.

that he had been speaking about his body, not the physical temple. Just as the temple cleansing had reminded them of a psalm (2:17), they later remembered his metaphorical reference to his body as the temple that would be raised in three days – a reference to the resurrection – and believed both the Scripture and the words of Jesus (2:22). Beasley Murray comments,

> The "scripture" which the disciples believed after the resurrection is presumably Psalm 69:9, mentioned in verse 17, which enabled them to relate the temple cleansing to the death of Christ; the "word" of Jesus is that of verse 19, which enabled them to grasp the significance of his resurrection in relation to the temple.[7]

In this episode, Jesus travels to the temple at Jerusalem (2:13), cleanses the temple (2:15–16), fulfills prophecy (2:17), identifies himself as the new temple (2:19–21) and performs signs (2:23).[8]

Verses 23–25 conclude this episode and set the scene for the next. The narrator continues the theme of signs (2:11, 18), mentioned for the third time in verse 23 – this time in relation to belief. Jesus did not entrust himself to people because "he knew all people" (2:24),[9] an expression that points to his all-knowing power. Verse 25 states that Jesus had no need of human testimony to understand what was in human hearts (2:25),[10] another indication that Christ transcends all human boundaries, traditions, and institutions with his all-knowing power.

The narrator describes Jesus as one zealous for the Father's house, whose symbolic action in the temple leads to a dialogue, whose passion and resurrection are referred to metaphorically, and whose disciples came to faith after his resurrection.[11] In contexts where unrighteousness prevails, justice is denied, the disparity between rich and poor increases, women are dehumanized, people are marginalized based on caste or race, and old hierarchies prevail, this passage

---

7. Beasley-Murray, *John*, 41.
8. Thomaskutty, *Dialogue in the Book of Signs*, 103.
9. A derivative of *pisteuo* [believe] is used to indicate about his committing or entrusting on people. Beasley-Murray comments, "The comment in v. 24 indicates the inadequacy of the faith of those who believed in Jesus solely because of 'signs': 'Jesus did not trust them.'" Beasley-Murray, *John*, 47.
10. Blomberg, *Historical Reliability of John's Gospel*, 91.
11. Bruce J. Malina and Richard L. Rohrbaugh, *Social-Science Commentary on the Gospel of John* (Minneapolis: Fortress Press, 1998), 72–79; Dwight Moody Smith, *John*, Abingdon New Testament Commentary (Nashville: Abingdon Press, 1999), 88–91.

presents a powerful lesson. In contrast to the "old temple," a "new temple" and a message of liberation resonates among the people (2:19–22).¹² This message can serve as a bridge to reach Dalits (untouchables and scheduled castes), tribals (scheduled tribes), and Adivasis (indigenous people) in India. In Asia, where a people-centered and context-oriented approach to mission and ministry is essential, churches should embrace a liberative and transformative mission.¹³

---

12. J. Maniparampil, *Reading the Fourth Gospel: A Textbook for Students of Gospel according to John* (Bangalore: Claretian Publications, 2004), 200–203.
13. Johnson Thomaskutty, "A Polyvalent Hermeneutic of John 2:13–25: Theoretical and Exegetical Considerations," *HTS Theological Studies* 79/1, (2023): 1–7.

JOHN 3:1–21
JESUS AND A RELIGIOUSLY ELITE PERSON

The episode in John 3:1–21 begins as a religious dialogue between Jesus and Nicodemus (3:1–10) and then shifts into a monologue (3:11–21). Religious dialogues and discourses (or monologues) are widely used across Asia in interreligious dialogues among Hindus, Christians, Muslims, Buddhists, and Sikhs. In 1893, Swami Vivekananda's groundbreaking speech at the World Parliament of Religions in Chicago introduced Hinduism to America and called for religious tolerance.[1] Similarly, John's dialogue in 3:1–21 can be read as a reformative framework that introduces Jesus's new ideology to the world.

Through 2:24–25, the narrator conveys Jesus's all-knowing power to understand human nature. This attribute of Jesus is exemplified in his encounter with Nicodemus (3:1–21).[2]

Nicodemus was a Pharisee and a leader of the Jews. A Nepali reader might identify Nicodemus with a high-caste Hindu priest or Buddhist monk seeking to understand Jesus.[3] Nicodemus's socioreligious status as a Jewish elite closely resembles that of Indian Brahmins or Nepali Bahuns. Unlike many characters in the Gospel who remain unnamed (4:1–45; 5:1–18; 9:1–41), Nicodemus is introduced by name. His coming to Jesus "by night," Beasley-Murray says, "is less likely to be due to fear than to desire for uninterrupted conversation. If 'night' has a symbolical overtone (see especially 11:10 and 13:30), it hints of the darkness in which Nicodemus stood."[4]

The Chinese philosophy of *Yin-Yang* puts the story in perspective. Jyoti Sahi comments,

> In the Yin-Yang pattern, which is meant to represent the interplay of opposing forces in nature, the dark section has a point of

---

1. Swami Vivekananda, *Swami Vivekananda's Chicago Speech* (Kolkata: Edition Next, 2015).
2. Jesus's conversation begins with the conjunction *de* ("now," 3:1), connecting the former and this pericope.
3. Thomaskutty, "Reading John's Gospel in the Nepali Context," 5–21.
4. Beasley-Murray, *John*, 47.

light at its base, whereas the light section has a dark point at its apex, signifying that there is something of light in the darkness and something of dark in the lightness. The light of the world and the darkness of Nicodemus are in dialogue.[5]

In verse 2, Nicodemus reveals his knowledge of Jesus by addressing him as "Rabbi." As a representative of the Jewish leadership, Nicodemus acknowledged Jesus as a teacher who had come from God and in whom God's presence dwelled.[6] This acknowledgment reveals the light within Nicodemus himself. As presented in John, the church today should engage in dialogical mission.

As a teacher of Israel, Nicodemus attempted to understand Jesus on his own terms (3:10). When Jesus told him that the kingdom of God required birth from above, Nicodemus misunderstood this teaching.[7] He asked, "How can someone be born when they are old?" and wondered whether someone had to reenter their mother's womb and be born a second time (3:4). Jesus explained that a person must be born of water and the Spirit to enter the kingdom of God (3:5). His responses reflect both the enigmatic nature of his utterances and the perplexity of his interlocutor. When people born from above – "born of water and the Spirit" – they can see and live out God's kingdom values and virtues in the world. While being born of water is an explicit reference to ritual water baptism, being born of the Spirit emphasizes the experience of being in union with the One who comes from above.

Jesus said that "flesh gives birth to flesh, but the Spirit gives birth to spirit" (3:6). Jesus, the one who was Spirit-endowed (1:33) and had descended from above (3:2; 13:3), is presented as a truly spiritual human being. In John's Gospel, this is the only instance where the Spirit-flesh contrast appears.[8] There is a clear dualistic distinction between being born from above and being born from below. Being children of God requires both believing (1:12) and being born from above (3:7).

Jesus used the metaphor of wind to illustrate the work of the Holy Spirit. Humans cannot determine or control the work of the Holy Spirit. Just as the

---

5. Jyoti Sahi, "An Artist Looks at the Fourth Gospel," *India's Search for Reality and the Relevance of the Gospel of John*, eds. Christopher Duraisingh and Cecil Hargreaves (Delhi: ISPCK, 1974), 78.
6. Moloney says, "The plural is used to indicate Nicodemus's representative status." Moloney, *Gospel of John*, 97.
7. Moloney, *Gospel of John*, 98.
8. Beasley-Murray, *John*, 49.

wind bypasses all hindrances, finds an opening, and plunges into it,[9] the Spirit enters a person and directs their paths.

Nicodemus's perplexity is once again revealed through his question: "How can this be?" (3:9). While Jesus had earlier affirmed Nathanael as a true Israelite (1:47), he now notes Nicodemus's inability to grasp spiritual truths despite being a teacher of Israel (3:10). Nicodemus's position in the dark shadow of realities (3:2) and his inability to understand are significant considering that he was a member of the Jewish ruling council. Asian readers will appreciate this irony since teachers in Asian cultures are highly regarded as those who alleviate darkness and bring light to people's lives. While Nicodemus acknowledged Jesus as a teacher sent from God (3:2), Jesus regarded him as a teacher who could not understand spiritual truths (3:10).[10]

The dialogue between Jesus and Nicodemus falls into the category of interreligious dialogue.[11] In the Gospel of John, dialogue is often used as a literary tool to show how Jesus's mission advances. In this story, two rabbis engage in a pedagogical dialogue, with Jesus affirming a kingdom perspective and inviting Nicodemus to accept his call.[12] This kind of dialogue is significant in the multireligious and pluralistic contexts of Asia.[13]

The dialogue between Jesus and Nicodemus (3:1–10) transitions into a monologue in verses 11–21. First, Jesus affirmed that, he spoke truth: "Very truly I tell you, we speak of what we know, and we testify to what we have seen, but still you people do not accept our testimony" (3:11). Second, Jesus said that he had spoken of earthly teachings but Nicodemus had not believed. He asked, "How then will you believe if I speak of heavenly things?" (3:12). Basically, belief is needed to understand the Lord's earthly and heavenly teachings.[14]

Nicodemus, despite being a teacher, seemed unable to grasp heavenly realities. The ascending and descending motif of the Son of Man (3:13) points to Jesus's control over both the earthly and the heavenly realms. His descent from heaven to earth, his journeys in the world, his return to heaven, and his promise of a future return highlight his migrant status in the world. Jesus

---

9. Christine Devin, *Hanuman or the Way of the Wind* (New York: Discovery Publisher, 2020), cover page.
10. Thomaskutty, *Dialogue in the Book of Signs*, 115.
11. Thomaskutty, 107–23.
12. Johnson Thomaskutty, "Reading John's Gospel in the Nepali Context," *Journal of Asian Evangelical Theology* 20/1 (March 2016): 5–21.
13. Thomaskutty, "Reading John's Gospel in the Nepali Context," 5–21.
14. Moloney, *Gospel of John*, 100.

functions as the ladder between heaven and earth, and earth and heaven (1:51). Although he was the creator of the universe, he lived as a migrant on earth.

Because the world has not accepted Jesus, injustice and unrighteousness have been, and continue to be, rampant in the world. Asia is a land of great diversity, with migrant workers from different parts of the world. It is the responsibility of host communities and countries to accept these migrants and treat them with justice and righteousness. Beasley-Murray comments, "The descent is mentioned in verse 13 as the presupposition of the ascent (via the cross) for the salvation of humankind."[15] Having promised Nathanael earlier that he would see heaven opened and the angels of God ascending and descending upon the Son of Man (1:51), Jesus now testifies that no one had gone to heaven except he who had descended from heaven (3:13).[16] In verse 14, Jesus was referring to Numbers 21:8–9 as a key text to affirm his messianic and salvific role in the world. Just as Moses had lifted up the bronze serpent for the deliverance of Israel, the Son of Man would be lifted up for the salvation of all who believe (3:15).

In China and India, the lifting of flagpoles and flags during temple festivals is a moment of communal joy and religious hope.[17] Similarly, the lifting of the bronze serpent in the wilderness and the lifting of the Son of Man are socioreligious symbols of hope and deliverance.

Jesus's discourse emphasizes the aspects of seeing, believing, and transformation. Furthermore, Jesus spoke in the context of growing tension between the Jewish community and the emerging community of believers.

The term "lifted up" (3:14) is connected with "be glorified" (12:23; see also 13:31).[18] Moloney says,

> There is a close relationship between what Moses did with the serpent and what *must* happen to the Son of Man. The parallel runs into verse 15. As the Israelites gazed upon the elevated serpent to be returned to health, so also the one who believes in the

---

15. Beasley-Murray, *John*, 50.
16. Moloney, *Gospel of John*, 100.
17. Wang Gungwu, *Chinese Overseas: History, Literature, and Society* 12 (Leiden: E. J. Brill, 2018), 21.
18. Beasley-Murray, *John*, 50.

revelation of God (3:13) that takes place on a cross (3:14) will have eternal life.[19]

The lifted-up Son of Man assures eternal life to all who believe (3:15). The essence of this message is restated in verse 16: "God so loved the world that he gave his one and only Son, that whoever believes in him shall not perish but have eternal life." Vandana states, "Christ is the giver of life and the *conqueror of death*."[20] Jesus himself is life – life-giver, Word of life, light and life, knowledge and life, belief and life, and truth and life. Life is associated with and synonymous with the Word, light, knowledge, belief, and truth.

The Father–Son relationship in the NT can be understood in light of the Abraham-Isaac relationship in the OT (Genesis 21–22). God's everlasting love for the world is revealed through Jesus's salvific work in the world. In his ministry, Jesus emphasized love as the greatest commandment (15:9–17).

While the Synoptic Gospels use the *political* term "kingdom of God," John prefers relational language – "eternal life." God sent his Son not to condemn the world but to save it (3:17). While John the Baptist, chosen from the earth, was *sent* by God, Jesus was *sent* from the world above. In John's terminology, liberation comes through believing in Jesus and continuing in faith. Asians are generally "god" believers. John invites people to believe in the true God and his Son.

Those who are condemned are judged because they have rejected the light and have chosen to remain in darkness (3:19). The expression "people loved darkness instead of light" (3:19a) draws readers back to the *Prologue*, where the narrator contrasts light and darkness (1:5). Since Jesus himself is introduced as the light, people are called to follow the light through faith in him. The expression "because their deeds were evil" (3:19b) links unbelievers with the powers of darkness. While injustice prevails in the world, many pursue unrighteousness, disrupting the harmony of society. Those who do evil hate the light and do not approach it because the light will expose their evil deeds (3:20). In contrast, those who practice truth are not afraid to come into the light so that their actions might be seen as having been done "in the sight of God" (3:21). John's dualistic concepts are presented in salvific terms.

---

19. Moloney says, "Both the physical lifting up of Jesus on a stake as Moses lifted up the serpent and the theological meaning of 'exaltation' must be involved in the interpretation of v. 14." Moloney, *Gospel of John*, 101.
20. Vandana, "From Death to Life," *India's Search for Reality and the Relevance of the Gospel of John*, eds. Christopher Duraisingh and Cecil Hargreaves (Delhi: ISPCK, 1974), 29.

John

John associates darkness with evil powers and light with the power from above. While darkness is connected to *hiding* ("fear that their deeds will be exposed"), light is associated with *revealing*. Similarly, there is great emphasis on belief (3:12 [x2], 15, 16, 18 [x3]) as against unbelief. As in John 1:14 and 1:18, Jesus is introduced as the "one and only Son" (3:16). The legal vocabulary used in this passage is also significant: "we speak of what we know" (3:11), "we testify to what we have seen" (3:11), "our testimony" (3:11), "condemn the world" (3:17–18), salvation (3:17), and "the verdict" (3:19). Following the witness and testimony of John the Baptist (1:7–8, 15, 19, 32–34), Jesus testified to the truth (3:11). The episode takes the form of a dialogue (3:1–10) and a monologue (3:10–21).

Asian pastors and interpreters stand uniquely at the crossroads of multiple realities and ideological pluralities. At this intersection, John's pedagogical style serves as a powerful literary model. John emphasizes believing as a key step toward liberation and following Jesus as an ongoing, transformed way of life. The narrative of John 3:1–21 invites the reader to engage multiple emotional senses.[21] This process evokes a new *rasa* (aesthetic emotion) and creates different *bhāvas* (emotional states) in the reader, shaped by various Asian contexts.

---

21. G. Ayyaneth, *Indian Poetics (Kavya Sastra) and Narratology towards the Appreciation of Biblical Narrative*, SBL, vol. 165 (New York: Peter Lang, 2016), 208–30.

JOHN 3:22–36

FINAL DECLARATION OF JOHN THE BAPTIST

Rivers were attractive locations for ancient civilizations. The most notable examples are the Mesopotamians in the Fertile Crescent along the River Euphrates and the River Tigris, the Ancient Egyptians on the River Nile, the Ancient Chinese on the Yellow River, and the Indus Valley civilization in Ancient India.[1] In John's Gospel, the missions and ministries of Jesus and John the Baptist develop along the banks of the River Jordan (1:28; 3:22–23, 26).

With the narrative expression "after this," the narrator introduces the emerging countryside mission of Jesus and his disciples (3:22–36). After the temple cleansing and the discourse with Nicodemus in the city of Jerusalem (2:13; 3:1), the scene shifts to a rural area. John the Baptist was baptizing at Aenon near Salim, a place known for its abundant water.[2] Jesus also entered this region, and both his disciples and the Baptizer were baptizing.[3] This scene is a flashback, indicated by the narrator's note, "This was before John was put in prison" (3:24).[4] These initial remarks – which explain the geographical setting and introduce the protagonists – lead into the main discussion (3:25–30) and the narrator's commentary (3:31–36).

There arose a debate about Jewish purification between John's disciples and a certain Jew (3:25). The narrator does not give details about this discussion, but, instead, refers to concerns over Jesus's growing popularity and influence (3:26). Jesus had already spoken to Nicodemus about the necessity of being born of water and the Spirit (3:3, 5). Perhaps these baptisms were follow-up actions to that discussion. The expression "everyone is going to him" points to

---

1. Rebecca Craft Rector, *The Early River Valley Civilizations: The First Humans and Early Civilizations* (New York: Rosen Publishing, 2017). Also, https://courses.lumenlearning.com/suny-hccc-worldcivilization/chapter/river-valley-civilizations/.
2. The name "Aenon" is from the Aramaic plural of the word for "spring," while "Salim" reflects the Semitic root for "peace." Bennema says, "John appears to move freely in the wilderness along the Jordan valley, between Bethany in Perea (1:28; 3:26; 10:40) and Aenon in Samaria (3:23)." Bennema, *Encountering Jesus*, 23; Beasley-Murray, *John*, 52.
3. The narrator clarifies that Jesus himself did not baptize but his disciples did, 4:1–3.
4. Synoptics says Jesus's ministry takes place after John's arrest (Mark 1:14; Matt 4:12).

the rapid growth of Jesus's following and the resulting frustration or anxiety among the Baptizer's followers.[5]

The Baptizer responded that Jesus's authority was given from heaven. In contrast, he had already testified that he himself was not the Messiah but the one sent ahead to pave the way for Jesus's ministry (3:27–28; compare 1:19–28). There was no rivalry between Jesus and the Baptizer. This principle remains relevant for ministry today: Jesus must always increase, not us. Like the Baptizer, Asian missionaries are also called to develop Christ-centered missional and ministerial strategies.

The Baptizer used an image familiar to his hearers: a wedding, with the bride, the groom, and the friend of the groom. He compared himself to the friend of the groom, rather than to the groom. The bride belongs to the groom, not to the friend. The friend's role is to rejoice, which is what the Baptizer was doing. When people expressed concern over the growth of Jesus's mission, the Baptizer rejoiced saying that the bride belonged to the bridegroom, not the friend who attends the bridegroom, implying he was just the friend, not the bridegroom (3:29).[6] He, as the friend, rejoiced at the voice of the bridegroom, Jesus. Asian readers will relate well to this imagery. In Asian cultures, weddings are opportunities for social harmony as people from diverse backgrounds gather to bless the couple. The Baptizer used this image to convey the idea of religious and social harmony between his disciples and the followers of Jesus.

The theme of joy runs throughout the Gospel of John. Earlier, Jesus had transformed a potentially shameful situation at a wedding into a joyous celebration (2:1–12); now, the bridegroom's voice brings joy to his friend (3:29).[7] The Baptizer then stated his life motto: "He must become greater; I must become less" (3:30). With this statement, he receded into the background, allowing Jesus's ministry to flourish.[8] The Baptizer's mission was to find joy in fulfilling God's mission and purpose. His life vision can be a paradigm for us today – and all missionary movements in Asia – standing in contrast to the prevailing factional, denominational, and communal divisions that hinder the growth of the church.

---

5. Moloney, *Gospel of John*, 109.
6. Beasley-Murray states, "The 'voice of the bridegroom' is thought to be 'the triumph shout by which the bridegroom announced to his friends outside that he had been united to a virginal bride.'" Beasley-Murray, *John*, 52–53.
7. Moloney, *Gospel of John*, 110.
8. Blomberg, *Historical Reliability of John's Gospel*, 95.

Verses 31–36 continue the Baptizer's teaching. His speech is framed in dualistic terms, contrasting characters from the world above with those from the world below, reflecting clear spatial and ideological dualism. Jesus comes from above and is above all; those who are of the earth belong to the earth and speak about earthly things (3:31). Jesus's identity from above enables him to control the entire universe (compare 1:1–5).

Just as the Baptizer bore testimony to Jesus, Jesus testified to God based on what he had seen and heard from the Father (3:32a). Although his testimony is true, some reject it (3:32b; compare 1:10–11); but those who accept this testimony affirm that God is truthful (3:33). Jesus spoke the words of God as a representative from above and became the channel through whom God gives the Spirit unconditionally and without limit (3:34). The Father loves the Son and has placed all things into his hands – a reference to the Son's omnipotence and sovereignty (3:35).[9] Therefore, anyone who believes in the Son has eternal life. The refusal to listen to and abide by God's words prevent people from enjoying life; instead, they will face God's wrath.[10] This is an important and relevant message for Asian readers: To believe in Jesus is to have life. As the Baptizer warned, Christians must proclaim this liberating and transformative message of God.

The contrasts are clear: "from above" and "from the earth," heavenly and earthly, acceptance and rejection, believing and disbelief, and eternal life and God's wrath. Within these contrasts is the triune God: Father, Son, and Spirit. Jesus's messiahship and his superiority over the Baptizer are affirmed.[11] The Baptist was a witness, with a unique mission to guide people to Jesus. The same call goes out to Asian Christians and churches: exalt Jesus and draw others to the one who is the author of eternal life. The Baptizer's motto, "He must become greater; I must become less" (3:30), must become ours.

---

9. Moloney, *Gospel of John*, 112.
10. Blomberg, *Historical Reliability of John's Gospel*, 97–98.
11. Thomaskutty, *Dialogue in the Book of Signs*, 133.

JOHN 4:1–42
JESUS AND A DOWNTRODDEN WOMAN

Some Asian cultures view women as inferior beings and treat them unjustly, which aligns with a hermeneutical framework that dehumanizes the marginalized.[1] Jesus, however, patiently discussed theology with the Samaritan woman, just as he had earlier discussed spiritual matters with Nicodemus, a religious Jew.

The episode in John 4:1–42 can be divided into three sections: Jesus and the Samaritan woman (4:1–26); Jesus and the disciples (4:27–38); and Jesus among the Samaritans (4:39–42).

4:1–26 JESUS AND THE SAMARITAN WOMAN

Jesus's departure from Judea and return to Galilee via Samaria form the background for this story (4:1–3). He left Judea because of the Pharisees' jealousy over his popularity (4:1). The narrator emphasizes that Jesus himself did not baptize but that his disciples did (4:2; compare 3:22, 26). Many religions have a baptism ritual. In India, for example, Hindus take holy baths in the River Ganges in Varanasi.

This was the second time Jesus traveled to Galilee. Earlier, he had been in Bethany, across the River Jordan (1:28–29), then went to Galilee (1:43) – where he attended a wedding in Cana (2:1, 11) and then proceeded to Capernaum (2:12) – and after that, to the Jerusalem temple. It was at Jerusalem that Jesus had a conversation with Nicodemus (3:1–21). Thereafter, Jesus went into the Judean countryside, and his disciples performed baptisms in the area close to where John the Baptist was also baptizing people (3:22–23). Now, in John 4, Jesus leaves the Judean countryside for Galilee. Jesus's pilgrimage to Jerusalem reflects a practice common in Asia. His vertical descent from the Father and his horizontal travels across various regions of Israel influenced his followers,

---

1. Elizabeth Schüssler Fiorenza, *But She Said: Feminist Practices of Biblical Interpretation* (Massachusetts: Beacon, 1992), 134–37.

who also became involved in both pilgrimages and migration motivated by missionary purposes.[2]

Jesus traveled from Judea to Galilee through Samaria. It was unusual for a traditional Jew to take this route since Samaria was considered a morally polluted land. As a reformer, Jesus crossed traditional boundaries and ancestral practices. The expression "now he had to go through Samaria" suggests that compelling reasons lay behind his decision to travel through this restricted region (4:4).

Jesus came to a Samaritan city called Sychar, "near the plot of ground Jacob had given to his son Joseph" (4:5).[3] Earlier, the narrator had alluded to Jacob's dream (1:47b–51); here, he refers to Jacob explicitly (4:5–6). Jesus reached Jacob's well around noon (4:6). His thirst at noon (4:6) is echoed by his thirst on the cross – "it was about noon" (19:14) and "I am thirsty" (19:28). As he traveled through this mountainous region, Jesus would have been physically tired and thirsty. His travel, tiredness, and thirst are marks of his identification with the harsh realities of the world in which he became flesh (1:14). His physical tiredness reflects his identification with the world from below.[4] His itinerant ministry, with its rural and urban focus, that involved long walks and treks through hills and along the seashore, enables readers to understand Jesus as a human and also a lover of his creation, a model that Asian churches can also adopt in their missional and ministerial engagements in the world.

While Nicodemus had come to meet Jesus by night (3:2), Jesus came to Jacob's well at noon with a purpose. The first six verses set the stage for the dialogue between Jesus and the Samaritan woman (4:7–16).[5] This divine-human encounter took place amid the ordinary circumstances of life, showing that God meets human beings in their ordinary life situations.[6]

Jesus's dialogue with the woman centered on Jewish and Samaritan religious practices. Jacob appeared as a common figure in both religious traditions (4:12).

---

2. Sam George, "*Motus Dei* (The Move of God): A Theology and Missiology for a Moving World," *Pharos Journal of Theology* 102 (2021): 1–12.
3. The Old Testament doesn't refer to Jacob giving a well to Joseph, but it speaks of Jacob living in Shechem, which is Sychar (Gen 33:19). Blomberg says, "Sychar probably corresponds to modern-day Askar, while Jacob's well is one of the best-attested archaeological sites in Israel." Blomberg, *Historical Reliability of John's Gospel*, 99.
4. Blomberg, *Historical Reliability of John's Gospel*, 99.
5. Blomberg, 99.
6. Joseph Lalfakmawia, *Re-reading the Gospel of John from Indian Perspective* (Kolkata: SCEPTRE, 2013), 130.

After establishing the setting, the narrator introduces Jesus as the main speaker. To the woman who came to draw water, Jesus said, "Will you give me a drink?" (4:7). A Jewish man and a Samaritan woman met at Jacob's well, and the weary Jesus asked for a drink.[7] The narrator's note implies Jesus might also have been hungry (4:8). But Jesus's spiritual thirst for the woman's soul drove him to speak to her. Lalfakmawia writes, "It was rather a symbolic and expressive of a spiritual thirst, the thirst for getting entry into the life of the Samaritan woman with the living water."[8]

The woman responded in light of her status as a socially marginalized and subjugated person (4:9a). How could a Jew ask for water from a Samaritan? The woman viewed Jesus with the usual Samaritan prejudice toward the Jews and thus could not recognize who he really was. The narrator notes, "For Jews do not associate with Samaritans" (4:9b). The woman recognized that Jesus's behavior was radically countercultural.[9] A village woman from the deserts of Rajasthan in India, who walks miles to fetch water for her daily use, will be able to relate deeply to this story.

Jesus responded unexpectedly, inviting the woman into a deeper dialogue (4:10). He spoke of the "gift of God,"[10] her failure to recognize him, and his ability to provide her "living water."[11] Jesus offered her liberation – God's gift and living water.[12]

Just as Nicodemus had responded with earthly and human logic when Jesus told him he had to be born from above (3:4), the woman made a common-sense observation: "Sir . . . you have nothing to draw with, and the well is deep" (4:11). Her earthly understanding limited her thinking to matters concerning a bucket, a well, and its depth. Jesus used the well to introduce the idea of living water (compare 7:37–39), but, like Nicodemus, she failed to grasp the spiritual connection.

The woman also had a moral and religious query: How could Jesus be greater than Jacob, who had given the Samaritans this well? (4:12). The well had been a gift from her ancestor Jacob to her community. Jacob, his sons (the patriarchs), and their flocks had drunk from it. Was this "gift of God"

---

7. Moloney, *Gospel of John*, 116–17.
8. Lalfakmawia, *Re-reading the Gospel of John from Indian Perspective*, 130.
9. Beasley-Murray, *John*, 60.
10. Moloney, *Gospel of John*, 117.
11. Beasley-Murray, *John*, 58.
12. The metaphorical use of water is common in the OT (Ps 36:9; Prov 13:14; 18:4; Isa 55:1; Jer 2:13; 17:13; Ezek 47:1–12; Zech 14:18). Blomberg, *Historical Reliability of John's Gospel*, 100.

that Jesus spoke of greater than Jacob's gift? Could the "living water" Jesus offered be better than the water from Jacob's well? "Are you greater than our father Jacob?" (4:12).

Jesus made it clear that the water from Jacob's well could not permanently quench people's thirst (4:13). While the woman's identity was rooted in Jacob's well, Jesus invited her to depend on the well of God. The inferiority and insufficiency of Jacob's water is contrasted with the superiority and sufficiency of the water Jesus provides: "Whoever drinks the water I give them will never thirst. Indeed, the water I give will become in them a spring of water welling up to eternal life" (4:14). Wright comments, "It will become a spring bubbling up inside you, refreshing you with the new life which is coming into the world with Jesus and which is the life of the whole new world God is making (4:14)."[13] This conversation highlights the contrast between the transient nature of Jacob's gift and the intransient nature of Jesus's gift.

This story has some striking similarities to a story from Buddhist tradition. Jesus, who came to a Samaritan village and asked a woman for water, parallels Ananda, a famous disciple of Buddha, who asked a Matanga caste woman for water at a well.[14] The social distancing between communities is evident in her question: "How do you ask water of me, an outcaste who may not touch thee without contamination?" (compare John 4:9).[15] Ananda replied, "My sister, I ask not of thee thy caste, I ask for water to drink" (compare John 4:10, 14–14). By drinking the water, he broke through sociocultural and religious barriers.[16] This girl, attracted by the defiant action of this Buddhist bhikshu, followed his footsteps and entered the Buddhist Sangha Viharam (Ashram).[17] In caste-oriented cultures, a person from a higher caste would refuse to drink water offered by someone from a lower caste. Though the water itself is pure, it is considered impure when offered by someone of a lower caste. But we must regard all people as God's children, created in his image and worthy of respect and dignity. Viewing people in this way enables us to reach them in their humiliation and offer them the gift of salvation – Jesus.

---

13. Tom Wright, *John for Everyone: Part I, Chapters 1–10* (Delhi: ISPCK, 2002), 42.
14. Biju Chacko, "Samaritan Woman, Chandalabhikshuki, and a Third Space of Hermeneutics: Reading the 'Well-Encounter' in John 4 from an Intercultural Perspective" (academic paper, Senate of Serampore College, Kolkata, 2018), 3.
15. P. Lakshmi Narasu, *The Essence of Buddhism* (New Delhi: Gautam, 2009), 84.
16. Thomaskutty, "The Gospel of John," 149–50.
17. Chacko, "Samaritan Woman," 3. Also George M. Soares-Prabhu, *The Dharma of Jesus*, ed. Francis X. D'Sa (Maryknoll: Orbis, 2003).

The theme of eternal life continues in the narrative (4:14; compare 3:15–16, 36). Initially, the woman misunderstood Jesus's statements, thinking of the water Jesus offered as a "hand-to-mouth" kind of water like the water from Jacob's well (4:15). She was unable to distinguish between material and spiritual needs. She imagined a different physical well from which she could draw water instead of coming to Jacob's well.[18] For the tribal women in the Nuapada District of Odisha, clean water is a rare commodity. The region suffers from erratic rainfall, long dry spells, and drought-like conditions every other year. For the tribal population, who are dependent on rainfall to support their life-sustaining agriculture and forestry, existence has become extremely difficult.[19] Like the Samaritan woman, they also do not have access to "living water" – God's spiritual gift. Indian Christians can support such village communities by helping them to find both clean water to sustain physical life and spiritual water for eternal life.

While the woman initially identified Jesus as a Jew (4:9), she later addressed him as "Sir" (4:11, 15, 19)[20] – expressing a change in her attitude toward Jesus, perhaps because of the kindness and respect he showed in conversing and discussing theology with her. This is the power of good interreligious dialogue: It can foster mutual respect and help to lead the spiritually thirsty to salvation.

The narrator never indicates whether the woman actually offered Jesus water or whether he drank it, although we are told that he refused to eat the food the disciples brought (4:31–32), demonstrating that God's word is more important than even physical food (Deut 8:3; Matt 4:4). Food and drink often distract people from spiritual truths. The living water – the Spirit given by Jesus – gives life and satisfies our deepest human longing in a way that no earthly water ever could.[21]

Jesus then shifted the focus from water to the woman's personal life (4:16–18). He told her to go and call her husband, and when she denied having a husband, he affirmed her response and prophesied about her life: "You are right when you say you have no husband. The fact is, you have had five husbands, and the man you now have is not your husband. What you have

---

18. Beasley-Murray, *John*, 61.
19. https://www.culturalsurvival.org/publications/cultural-survival-quarterly/tribal-womens-struggle-water-india.
20. The Greek word is *kyrios*, which can mean "Lord" (6:68; 11:21) and "sir" (4:19; 4:49).
21. Lalfakmawia, *Re-reading the Gospel of John from Indian Perspective*, 130.

just said is quite true" (4:17–18).[22] This woman had a painful and messy past and an illegal present. As a Samaritan woman, she was a vulnerable person. Lalfakmawia writes, "Jesus brings her forcibly to face the truth. He tells her that he knows her thoroughly. Her life is crystal clear before his penetrating revelatory light."[23] She stands out as a person of dishonor. Neither the five men who had lived with her in the past nor the one she was living with in the present bore the shame that she did. She might have been a widow who had been subjected to a levirate marriage (compare Gen 38:6–10) or an immoral woman who had lived with different men. It was not to rebuke her that Jesus revealed her true situation but to show her that he was greater than Jacob and that he was the prophet foretold by Moses (compare 4:19; Deut 18:15, 18).[24] Jesus gently led her to acknowledge her past, giving her hope for her future.

Having identified Jesus as a prophet, the woman then brought up the topic of worship (4:20). She assumed that, as a Jew, Jesus would promote worship in Jerusalem (if only she knew of his cleansing of the temple!). However, as a Samaritan, she worshiped on Mount Gerizim – "this mountain." In Moses's time, when the Israelites recited the law before entering the promised land, six tribes stood on Mount Ebal and proclaimed the curses for failing to keep the law, while six tribes stood on Mount Gerizim and proclaimed the blessings that would accompany obedience to the law (Deut 11:29; 27:12–13). When the Samaritans separated from the Jews, they chose Mount Gerizim as their place of worship. Jesus and the woman were in the vicinity of that mountain when she raised the question about the proper place of worship.

Jesus responded with compassion, addressing her as "woman" (4:21) – the same term he had used earlier to address his mother (2:4) – and explaining a key truth about the worship the Father desired (4:21–24). He explained that although historically Jerusalem was the center of worship (4:22), a time was coming – and had already come – when neither Mount Gerizim nor Jerusalem would be the place of true worship (4:21).[25] Instead, true worship would be as

---

22. Moloney states, "Much is made of the five husbands, a number beyond the possibilities allowed by Jewish practice, as a possible symbolic use of the number five to refer to the five gods of Samaria (compare *Ant.* 9.288), or the five books of the Samaritan Pentateuch, or the five foreign cities that brought their gods with them (compare 2 Kings 17:27–31)." Moloney, *Gospel of John*, 131–32.
23. Lalfakmawia, *Re-reading the Gospel of John from Indian Perspective*, 130.
24. The Samaritans, unlike the Jews, believed only the Pentateuch was God's word, a reason for Jesus alluding to Moses.
25. Beasley-Murray comments, "Jesus champions neither Jerusalem nor Gerizim, for 'the hour is coming'– the eschatological hour, initiating the new age of the kingdom of God – when

the Father desires – "in the Spirit and in truth" (4:23). This is because God is Spirit and seeks worship that is spiritual, not worship that is tied to a particular physical location such as Jerusalem or Gerizim (4:24). The "time" referred to by Jesus emphasizes the inauguration of eschatological worship here and now (4:21, 23). Worship "in the Spirit and in truth" is the mark of this already inaugurated but eternally continuing worship.[26] Human beings engage in worship to maintain communication with God and as a bridge between the visible and invisible realms. This passage in John 4 speaks of such a personal relationship that is grounded in love and devotion.

Jesus's answer propelled the woman toward a new conviction about him: Could he be the Messiah? She said, "I know that Messiah . . . is coming. When he comes, he will explain everything to us" (4:25).[27] This intelligent and informed woman knew about Jacob, the coming prophet, and the Messiah. Could Jesus, who had already shown himself to be a prophet by revealing everything about her life, be that person?

Jesus declared, "I, the one speaking to you – I am he" (4:26). Whatever doubts she had were gone. He told her plainly who he was, and she believed (4:28–29). Jesus's words convey a subtle hint of his oneness with God (1:1) as the Greek phrase for "I am he" parallels the divine "I AM" of Exodus 3:14. Her understanding of Jesus's identity had grown exponentially: a Jew (4:9), Sir (4:11, 15, 19), someone greater than Jacob (4:12), a prophet (4:19), the Messiah (4:25–26), and now, someone like "I AM" (4:26).

The personal and moral aspects of the woman's life (4:16–18) are sandwiched between the discussions on living water (4:1–15) and worship (4:19–26). The dialogue moves from a contrast between well water and living water to a contrast between Jacob's gift and God's gift. It concludes with Jesus revealing himself to her as both a prophet and the Messiah.

In this encounter, Jesus elevated the role and status of a woman. In the previous episode, he spoke with a male religious leader from Jerusalem; now, he engaged in a theological discussion with a woman from a people group the Jews had no interactions (4:9). While Nicodemus enjoyed a high social status, this woman was socially marginalized because of her past and present

---

worship of the Father will be tied to no place (compare Rev 21:22)." Beasley-Murray, *John*, 61.
26. Blomberg, *Historical Reliability of John's Gospel*, 101.
27. Blomberg comments, "The Samaritans actually looked for a 'teacher,' 'restorer' and 'converter' figure called the *Taheb*." Blomberg, *Historical Reliability of John's Gospel*, 101. She understands that teacher to be the Messiah. This explains her great understanding of the Scriptures.

circumstances. Jesus crossed religious, ethnic, and gender barriers to redirect her Samaritan religiosity toward worship "in the Spirit and in truth" (4:24).[28]

In contemporary Asia, women need empowering because they are often poorly educated, powerless in politics, voiceless in religion, and culturally ostracized.[29] In contexts where polygamy is prevalent, Jesus's gentleness toward a woman with multiple husbands invites us to follow the same path. Jesus accepted the Samaritan woman as she was, enabling her to see him as he was. His work can serve as a model for the mission of liberation.[30] Raj Irudaya writes, "Jesus's enabling and liberative interaction with the Samaritan woman is a prototype of the liberation of Dalit women, who, though more oppressed in today's society are also seen as the agents of liberation."[31]

The story of the Samaritan woman continues to fascinate and inspire artists as well as women striving for emancipation, freedom, respect, and leadership in society. Jyoti Sahi, an Indian art theologian, captures the image of the Samaritan woman within an Indian context, portraying Jesus as one who walks the roads of India.[32] A reader's specific background, sensibilities, and life experiences will shape their creation of a "semantic network" where the message of the text intersects with the recipient's ideological domain. Themes such as water, the role and status of the woman, worship, the well of Jacob, the well of God, eternal life, and spiritual thirst may serve as shared concepts that can initiate interreligious dialogue and draw people to Christ.

---

28. Johnson Thomaskutty, "Reading John's Gospel in the Bangladeshi Context," *Journal of Asian Evangelical Theology* 21/1–2 (March-September 2017): 53–72.
29. R. Jahan, "Women in Bangladesh," *Women for Women: Bangladesh 1975* (Dhaka: Women for Women Research and Study Group, 1975), 1–30.
30. Thomaskutty, "Reading John's Gospel in the Bangladeshi Context," 53–72.
31. Raj Irudaya, *The Gospel according to John. The Gospel according to John*, Dalit Bible Commentary: New Testament, vol. 4 (New Delhi: Centre for Dalit/Subaltern Studies, 2009), 71.
32. Gudrun Löwner, *Intercultural Dialogue in Art and Religion* (New Delhi: Manohar Publishers, 2018), 43–52.

JEWS AND SAMARITANS

During NT times, the Samaritans were a significant religious group inhabiting parts of the central hill country of Samaria, which lay between Galilee to the north and Judea to the south.[1] The name "Samaritan" is derived from the term *šāměrîm*, which means "keeper [of the law]."[2]

The split between the Samaritans and the Jews began in the eleventh century BCE during the time of Eli (1 Samuel 1–4). Later, around mid-fifth century BCE, the Samaritans split from the Jerusalemites and established Mount Gerizim as a rival place of worship.[3] The term "Samaritan" (Heb. *haššōměrōnîm*) appears only once in the OT – in 2 Kings 17:29, where it is associated with idolatry. The Samaritans insisted that they were the "original" and "true" Israelites and the direct descendants of the northern Israelite tribes of Ephraim and Manasseh, who had survived the Assyrian destruction of the northern kingdom in 722 BCE.

Orthodox Jews, however, viewed the Samaritans as a mixed people whose religion had been corrupted when the Assyrians settled foreigners in the former kingdom of Israel in the eighth century BCE. These diverse populations, living together side by side, eventually intermingled and formed a new people who became known as the Cutheans or Samaritans. While the Samaritans regarded the Jews as a misguided community, the Jews viewed the Samaritans as a racially and religiously contaminated group.

James A. Montgomery views the Samaritans as the earliest Jewish sect.[4] Jewish accounts, such as 2 Kings 17 and Josephus (*Ant* 9.277–291), claim that the Samaritans were descendants of foreign colonists brought into the region of Samaria by the Assyrians from other conquered territories, including Cuthah.[5] This is the origin of the Jewish designation of the Samaritans as Cutheans (*Ant* 9.290). Ezra 4, the earliest source of information on relations between Jews and Samaritans during the Persian period, reports Samaritan opposition to both the rebuilding of the temple (Ezra 4:4–5, 24) and the rebuilding of the walls of Jerusalem (Ezra 4:17–23).[6] The initial breach between the two communities occurred during the time of Nehemiah, in the fifth century BCE, in connection with the rebuilding of the city wall.[7] While the southern Jews regarded the Samaritans as impure, racially inferior, and religiously and politically "other," the Samaritans actively resisted these discriminatory attitudes.

The *Kitab al-Ta'rikh*, the work of a fourteenth-century CE chronicler named Abu'l-Fath ibn Abi al-Hasan al-Samiri al-Danafi, claims that Zerubbabel and Sanballat became the leaders of the Jewish and Samaritan communities respectively. According to Josephus, Sanballat – whom he refers to as a "Cuthean" – was appointed as a political leader by Darius. Sanballat subsequently promised his son-in-law, Manasseh (a Jew who had married a Samaritan woman) that he would build a temple.[8] The first phase of this construction took place in the mid-fifth century BCE during the Persian period.[9] It was rebuilt during the period of Alexander the Great, and the complex was expanded later during the Hellenistic period.[10]

The temple continued to function until it was destroyed by the Maccabees in 110 BCE.[11] Therefore, the absence of any reference to the Mount Gerizim temple in the NT is not surprising since the temple had been destroyed long before the NT was written.[12] As a remnant group and subaltern community, the Samaritans continue to live in Israel today. Throughout history, they have usually managed to resist the hegemony of their Jewish neighbors. In the first century CE, courageous and committed individuals – such as the Samaritan woman and her fellow Samaritans – became the backbone of the Johannine community (John 4:1–45).

---

1. H. G. M. Williamson, "Samaritans," *DJG*, eds. Joel B. Green, Scot McKnight, and I. Howard Marshall (Downers Grove: InterVarsity Press, 1992), 724–28.
2. R. J. Coggins, *Samaritans and Jews* (Atlanta: John Knox Press, 1975), 10–12.
3. Reinhard Pummer, *The Samaritans: A Profile* (Grand Rapids: Eerdmans, 2016), 9.
4. James A. Montgomery, *The Samaritans, the Earliest Jewish Sect, Their History, Theology and Literature* (Philadelphia: University of Pennsylvania, 1907), 1–10.
5. Magnar Kartveit, *The Origin of the Samaritans* (Leiden/Boston: E. J. Brill, 2009), 17–44.
6. Jacob M. Myers, *Ezra, Nehemiah: Introduction, Translation and Notes*, The Anchor Bible 14 (New York: Doubleday, 1965), 36–39.
7. Mervin Breneman, *Ezra, Nehemiah, Esther*, The New American Commentary: An Exegetical and Theological Exposition of Holy Scripture NIV Text, Vol. 10 (Nashville: B&H Publishers, 1993), 98–99.
8. See Michael Walzer, Menachem Lorberbaum, and Noam J. Zohar, eds., *The Jewish Political Tradition*, vol. 2 (New Haven: Yale University Press, 2003), 351.
9. Abram Spiro, "Samaritans, Tobiads, and Judahites in Pseudo Philo," *PAAJR* 20 (1951): 279–355.
10. Robert T. Anderson and Terry Giles, *The Samaritan Pentateuch: An Introduction to its Origin, History and Significance for Biblical Studies* (Atlanta: Society for Biblical Studies, 2012), 17.
11. Kartveit, *The Origin of the Samaritans*, 56–58.
12. Gary N. Knoppers, *Jews and Samaritans: The Origins and History of their Early Relations* (Oxford/New York: Oxford University Press, 2013), 2.

4:27–38 JESUS AND THE DISCIPLES

A major shift takes place in John 4:27, when the disciples return from the city, where they had gone to buy food (4:8). Although they were astonished[33] to see Jesus speaking with a Samaritan woman, they refrained from voicing the questions that were probably burning within them: "What do you want?" and "Why are you talking with her?" (4:27). This reflects the disciples' anxiety about their honor in this honor-shame society.

Meanwhile, the woman left her water jar and returned to her city. Her actions reflected her leaving behind the worldly water to proclaim the message about the giver of living water (4:28).[34] In many parts of Asia and Africa, women stand in queues with their water pots to fetch water from public wells and pipelines. A woman carrying her water pot and walking through the streets may symbolize her role as a nurturer, providing for her family. The Samaritan woman's action in leaving behind her water jar may represent a reordering of priorities and an expansion of responsibilities. Her focus had shifted from merely caring for her own household to spreading the message about the Messiah to the whole city.

The woman testified to the people in her city about this man called Jesus who had told her everything she ever did. Her invitation was missional (compare 1:39, 46). She asked, "Could this be the Messiah?" (4:29). Contrary to popular belief, she might have been an influential figure who was able to draw their attention since many responded by going with her to meet Jesus (4:30).

Meanwhile, the disciples urged Jesus to eat something (4:31), but his response confused them (4:32). Just as a discussion about water and thirst had developed between Jesus and the woman (4:7–15), a discussion on food and hunger now develops between Jesus and the disciples. He had food from heaven – the words of his Father. The disciples misunderstood: "Could someone have brought him food?" (4:33). Jesus clarified: "My food . . . is to do the will of him who sent me and to finish his work" (4:34).[35] When they continued to be mystified, he responded with the metaphor of the harvest.[36] While crops usually took four months to yield fruit, the spiritual harvest in

---

33. Moloney uses the word "dumbfounded" for *thaumadzein* in verse 27. Moloney, *Gospel of John*, 134.
34. Moloney says, "The jar is a sign that she will return to the story." Moloney, *Gospel of John*, 135.
35. Moloney, *Gospel of John*, 143.
36. Harvest as an eschatological symbol occurs in Isa 27:12; Joel 4:13; Mark 4:1–9, 26–29; Matt 13:24–30; Rev 14:14–16.

Samaria was already ripe, meaning that the people were ready to accept Jesus as their Messiah (4:35). Jesus turned the disciples' attention from the material harvest – that would take at least four months – to the spiritual harvest that was possible now. He invited the disciples to look around and see the approaching Samaritans. The sowing and growing were over; the disciples were now called to begin the work of harvesting.

Jesus spoke of salvation in terms of sowing, reaping, and harvesting (4:36). The disciples were reaping what they did not sow (4:37).[37] Jesus had sent the disciples to reap a harvest they had not labored for (4:38). This is the way God works, and the focus here is people's labor in the mission of God.

Metaphors such as "food" and "hunger" – like "water" and "thirst" – direct our attention to spiritual realities. We usually hunger and thirst for material things, but the Lord wants us to hunger and thirst for spiritual things. Just as sowing, reaping, and harvesting are necessary for physical existence, spiritual sowing, reaping, and harvesting are vital for eternal life.

4:39–42 JESUS AMONG THE SAMARITANS

The narrative then focuses once more on the Samaritans. The woman's testimony in her hometown – especially her testimony that Jesus knew everything about her – led many to believe in Jesus (4:39). The Samaritans invited Jesus to remain with them, and he stayed for two days. During this time, many more believed in him (4:40–41). The story concludes with the Samaritans acknowledging, "This man really is the Savior of the world" (4:42).[38] Through the testimony of the woman and the words of Jesus, the Samaritans believed in the Savior.

---

37. Paul uses a similar metaphor in 1 Cor 3:6: Paul planted the seed, Apollos watered it, but God has been making it grow.
38. Beasley-Murray, *John*, 64–65.

INTERCULTURAL COMMUNICATION

In a globalized world, we regularly interact with people of different religions and cultures. In Asia, various linguistic, religious, cultural, ideological, and symbolic diversities exist. How can we share God's good news in this pluralistic context? Jesus's discussion with the Samaritan woman at the well gives us some basic principles for intercultural communication (4:4–43).

First, Jesus was intentional: "He had to go through Samaria" (4:4). The usual route from Judea to Galilee was through the Jordan valley, avoiding the mountainous region of Samaria. But Jesus chose this route for a specific purpose: the salvation of this Samaritan woman and her village.

Second, Jesus established common ground. He went to Sychar, "near the plot of ground Jacob had given to his son Joseph" and waited by "Jacob's well" (4:5–6; see also 4:12). Both Samaritans and Jews held Jacob in high regard. Thus, by meeting the woman at a place that was significant to both communities, Jesus created a point of connection between them.

Third, Jesus initiated a conversation aimed at overcoming cultural animosity. Jews did not typically associate with Samaritans, yet Jesus asked the Samaritan woman for a drink (4:7). His humility in asking her for help shocked her – "You are a Jew and I am a Samaritan woman. How can you ask me for a drink?" (4:9) – but also opened the door to a meaningful dialogue about spirituality.

Fourth, Jesus focused the conversation on a basic human need: water. By asking for a drink (4:7), he was able to introduce spiritual concepts: "If you knew the gift of God and who it is that asks you for a drink, you would have asked him and he would have given you living water" (4:10). His offer of water – the very thing she had come to get – and his reference to the "gift of God" opened the way for a deeper conversation. The woman pointed out practical problems – he did not have anything to draw water with and the well was deep – and posed the question, "Where can you get this living water?" (4:11). Thereafter, intrigued by Jesus's offer of living water, she said, "Sir, give me this water so that I won't get thirsty and have to keep coming here to draw water" (4:15). Originally, Jesus had asked her for water; but now, she was asking him for living water. Their dialogue merged around a common theme.

Fifth, Jesus gave her a directive relating to her personal life and revealed his prophetic insight: "Go, call your husband and come back" (4:16). When she replied that she had no husband, Jesus affirmed her honesty but also went deeper: "You have had five husbands, and the man you now have is not your husband" (4:17–18). This revelation led to her acknowledgment of him as a prophet (4:19).

Sixth, Jesus and the Samaritan woman engaged in a deep spiritual dialogue about worship (4:19–24). Although Jesus made it clear that the Samaritans worshiped incorrectly (4:22), he also pointed toward a new reality: "A time is coming when you will worship the Father neither on this mountain nor in Jerusalem" (4:21). He did not demand that she abandon or deny her cultural identity and embrace Jewish traditions; instead, he redefined true worship as being centered on the Father and "in the Spirit and in truth" (4:23).

Seventh, at the end of their conversation, Jesus revealed his true identity. When the woman expressed her faith that the coming Messiah would explain everything (4:25), Jesus declared, "I am he" (4:26).

Just as Jesus used a constellation of words and ideas common to both Samaritans and Jews, Asian Christians can find points of commonality in their dialogues before engaging in evangelism. Crossing traditional boundaries is crucial in biblical interpretation and evangelism. An interpreter should begin by attempting to understand differences in caste, religion, language, and ethnicity before proceeding to share the gospel. What is needed in Asia is a deeper understanding of "otherness" – recognizing and respecting how people differ from us. Jesus crossed traditional boundaries of gender, race, and culture to engage in a meaningful conversation with the Samaritan woman; we must do the same in our own contexts.

Although Jesus engaged with the woman in a local setting – by Jacob's well, where she came to draw water – the dialogue unfolded into a universal metaphor – water – that pointed to deeper spiritual realities. Jesus used what is called *dynamic localization* – taking a local element (water) and giving it a heavenly significance (the Holy Spirit). Ultimately, Jesus offered the woman eternal life. If we follow these principles of intercultural communication, rooted in respectful dialogue, people will come to Jesus to drink the living water and receive eternal life.

JOHN 4:43–54

JESUS AND A ROYAL OFFICIAL

In the next episode, Jesus returns to Galilee (4:43–54; compare 2:1–12). Jesus had traveled through Judea (2:13–3:36), Galilee (2:1–12), and Samaria (4:1–42). Now, after his two-day stay in a Samaritan town, he returned to Galilee (4:43–54). His intercultural mission is evident in his movements across these regional borders. Jesus was culturally sensitive as he interacted with people from varied backgrounds. Although a prophet was typically without honor in his own country, the Galileans welcomed Jesus because they were aware of what he had done in Jerusalem during the Passover Festival (4:43–44).

Before concluding this chapter, the narrator makes it clear that Jesus's popularity was growing daily in all these three provinces. His visits to the temple during the various festivals and his widespread appeal were significant. But now he returns to Galilee, a region where he frequently ministered. In Indian culture, Scripture (*Vēda*), experience (*anubhava*), inference (*anumāna*), and community (*sangha*) are regarded as important authorities (*pramāṇa*) in a person's religious experience.[1] Similarly, both Jews and Samaritans came to recognize Jesus's divine identity as the Messiah through their Scriptures, their personal experience, and their community involvement.

The story of the royal official begins in verse 46. The passage is structured as follows: the setting of the story (4:46); the royal official's initial request (4:47); Jesus's mild rebuke of the crowd (4:48); the official's repeated request (4:49); Jesus's response and subsequent events (4:50–53); and a conclusion (4:54).

Jesus came again to Cana in Galilee (4:46; compare 2:1, 11), where he had earlier changed water into wine. This time, a royal official from Capernaum came to Jesus because of his son's illness. The official must have been aware of Jesus's ability to perform miracles since Cana and Capernaum were both in Galilee, and Cana was just about a day's journey – about twenty-seven

---

1. Babu Immanuel, *Acts of the Apostles: An Exegetical and Contextual Commentary*, India Commentary on the New Testament, ed. Brian C. Wintle (Bangalore: Primalogue, 2016), 19–20.

kilometers – from Capernaum.² The story expresses a meeting point of two travelers: Jesus traveled from Samaria to Cana, while the royal official traveled from Capernaum to Cana, where they met face-to-face and engaged in a conversation.

The royal official held a position of authority and enjoyed a high social status. Bennema writes, "If he is a Gentile (compare the parallel story in Matt 8:5–13; Luke 7:1–10), he would be despised by the Jewish populace. If he is a Jewish nobleman, he would be similarly shunned by the populace since the Jewish aristocracy and Herodians often collaborated with the Romans."³ Like the religious leader Nicodemus (3:1–2), the royal official also came to meet Jesus (4:46–47). While elites like Nicodemus and the royal official sought out Jesus, Jesus went out to the Samaritan village (4:1–42) and to the invalid at Bethesda (5:1–18). Climbing the mountainous terrain from coastal Capernaum to Cana would have been difficult for the royal official. Yet he did so because of his love for his son – a love that may dimly reflect the love of God for his beloved Son.

Hearing that Jesus was in Cana, the royal official sought him out and begged him to come and heal his son, who was at the point of death (4:47). The expression "when this man heard that Jesus had arrived in Galilee from Judea" implies that the official had been searching for Jesus. His begging shows his desperate need and humility.⁴ In an honor-shame culture, the act of begging means surrendering one's prestige and honor before the other. The official's recognition of Jesus's superiority is obvious. Since Cana is a hilltop city and Capernaum a coastal area, his invitation to Jesus to "come down" (4:47b, in the Greek) is understandable.

In response – and perhaps somewhat frustrated – Jesus addressed the crowd and rebuked them:⁵ "Unless you people see miraculous signs and wonders . . . you will never believe" (4:48). It was their reliance on signs and wonders that was being judged. This is also a warning to us all: our faith should not rest on signs and wonders but on God and Christ who perform them. Belief based on signs and wonders is an immature faith. Jesus demands faith that does not demand signs and wonders.

---

2. Bennema, *Encountering Jesus*, 95.
3. Bennema, 94.
4. The verb *ērōta* can mean "to ask," "interrogate," "inquire of," "request," or "beg." The force of the language here is "begging."
5. The second plural verbs in the Greek text show that he was not addressing the royal official. That is why the NIV has "you people."

The royal official repeated his plea to Jesus: "Sir [Lord], come down before my child dies" (4:49). He addressed Jesus as Lord (*kyrios*), just as the Samaritan woman had done earlier (4:11). This shows that the royal official regarded Jesus as superior to himself. When the royal official left his home, his son was "close to death" (4:47); now, he was afraid that his son would die (4:49).

Jesus said, "Go . . . your son will live" (4:50a). The royal official believed in the words of Jesus and departed, demonstrating his remarkable faith (4:50b). As an official accustomed to giving orders and being obeyed, he recognized Jesus's authority and obeyed promptly. On his way home, his servants met him and reported that his son was alive (4:51). Upon questioning them about the exact time of his son's recovery, he was told that it had happened at "one in the afternoon" the previous day (4:52). The official realized that this was the very hour that Jesus had said, "Your son will live" (4:53). This realization led this father and his household to believe in Jesus.[6] The hour of the healing was "one in the afternoon" – which is the seventh hour, paralleling Jesus's conversation with the Samaritan woman at "about noon" (4:6), which is the sixth hour.

The narrator says, "This was the second sign Jesus performed after coming from Judea to Galilee" (4:54). This sign parallels the first miracle Jesus performed in Cana in Galilee – turning water into wine (2:1–11). Together, these two miracles form a parenthesis around three key events: the cleansing of the temple, the discussion with Nicodemus about new birth, and the offer of living water to the Samaritan woman and her village. Through these encounters, Jesus presented himself as Lord, teacher, Messiah, prophet, healer, and Savior of the world. This is the message we are called to proclaim to the world, beginning in Asia. Christians in Asia should stand as "pointers" to God and Christ so that they may participate in the healing of a wounded world.

---

6. Thomaskutty, "'Healing' and 'Life' in the Fourth Gospel," 21–27.

JOHN 5:1–47

JESUS AND THE INVALID BY THE POOL

Jesus returned to Jerusalem for a Jewish festival (5:1). There he met a man who had been an invalid for thirty-eight years – symbolizing Israel's forty years of wilderness wandering – and healed him (5:2–9). The man by the pool of Bethesda was marginalized even among the marginalized people. While ostracized communities are often silenced and voiceless, Jesus purposefully reaches out to them.

This episode can be divided into three parts: a dialogue between Jesus and the invalid (5:1–18); the authority of Jesus (5:19–30); and witnesses concerning Jesus (5:31–47).[1]

5:1–18 DIALOGUE BETWEEN JESUS AND THE INVALID

After a successful ministry in Samaria (4:1–42) and Galilee (4:43–54), Jesus returned to Jerusalem. The expression "some time later" (5:1) connects the events of 4:43–54 and 5:1–47.[2] Although the festival is not named, it was probably not the Passover[3] since the narrator mentions Jesus's attendance at previous Passover festivals (2:13, 23; 4:45). Had this been a Passover, he would probably have mentioned it.

This is the second mention of Jesus's presence in Jerusalem during a Jewish festival. The setting of the story is the pool at Bethesda, which was near the Sheep Gate and surrounded by five porticoes. The sick – the blind, the lame, and the paralyzed – lay there, longing for healing (5:2–3). These were people who were regarded as burdens by their society. They were unwanted, abandoned, and cast out, living without proper shelter, clothing, and food. Bethesda means "house of mercy" – and these sick people were awaiting divine mercy. In India, Hindu temples usually have pool and fortified structures, where beggars and physically handicapped people gather, hoping for the mercy of pilgrims.

---

1. Thomaskutty, *Dialogue in the Book of Signs*, 181–205.
2. The same style is found in 3:22.
3. Moloney states, "The narrator speaks generally of 'a feast' and many have attempted to resolve which particular feast is in question. Suggestions are Tabernacles, Passover, Pentecost, Purim, and Rosh Hashanah." Maloney, *Gospel of John*, 171.

JOHN

Although verse 4 is missing in some translations, others include an explanation: "For an angel went down at a certain time into the pool and stirred up the water; then whoever stepped in first, after the stirring of the water, was made well of whatever disease he had" (NKJV). Whether original or a later addition, this verse explains why the sick might have been waiting by that pool – it was because they believed the waters had magical healing power.

Jesus focused on one man – "one who was there . . . for thirty-eight years" (5:5). This long period of waiting must have frustrated the man and left him feeling hopeless, much like the hopelessness experienced by the unemployed, poor, and marginalized in Asia.[4] Seeing the man and knowing that he had been paralyzed for a long time, Jesus said to him, "Do you want to get well?" (5:6). Thirty-eight years is almost as long as the period the people of Israel spent wandering in the wilderness (Num 32:13; Deut 29:5). Most ancient religions believed that bad *karma* – arising from immoral actions – was the cause of disability. Even Job's friends assumed that his suffering was due to his sins (Job 4:7–8).

Instead of saying, "Yes, I want to get well," the paralyzed man gave the reason for his inability to obtain healing: "Sir . . . I have no one to help me into the pool when the water is stirred. While I am trying to get in, someone else goes down ahead of me" (5:7). The man had no one to help him, he required help from others, he was abandoned, neglected, and marginalized, and others always got ahead of him. The pool, which was believed to have magical healing power, was out of his reach. Jesus recognized the invalid's vulnerability, understood his marginalization, and approached him. The one who offers living water to anyone who thirsts (7:37–38) does not need a magical pool to heal.

The irony of the passage is that although the man had lain by the healing waters of the pool for so long, he was not able to access it. This reflects the plight of many marginalized communities in Asia. Although they live in lands rich in resources, ninety percent of the continent's wealth is owned by the ten percent who make up the dominant class. For example, though the Dalits are the majority community in India, they are not able to access the rich resources of the country.[5] Although India is considered a nation of sacred rivers, the Dalits are viewed as impure. The story of the invalid in John's Gospel reflects

---

4. Arvind P. Nirmal, *Heuristic Explorations* (Chennai: Gurukul/Christian Literature Society, 1990), 1–81.
5. V. V. Thomas, *Dalit and Tribal Christians of India: Issues and Challenges* (Nilambur: Focus India Trust, 2014), 85–128.

the honor-shame dynamics of the Jewish context, where disease was linked with sin, poverty was considered a curse, and the downtrodden were marginalized.

The man's helpless situation persuaded Jesus to say to him, "Get up! Pick up your mat and walk" (5:8). The three verbs here are progressive and symbolic: The person lying down is commanded to stand up, a call to overcome his prolonged situation of illness;[6] the person standing up is told to take up his mat, prompting him to bend down and hold the mat in his hands; and the person carrying the mat in his hands is invited to walk, enabling him to move on as a whole person. Vallianippuram writes, "Just as in the book of Genesis, God commands, 'let there be . . . and there was,' so here Jesus commands with the three imperatives (rise, take up and walk) and immediately it happens."[7] The word used for "get up" (*egeire*) in verse 8 is also used of Lazarus being raised from the dead in John 12:9 (*ēgeiren*) – a picture of his liberation from a death-like situation to life. The man obeyed Jesus's command (5:9) – no longer lying down, he stood up, bent down and picked up his mat, and moved forward.

This healing took place on a Sabbath, prompting a confrontation between the Jewish leaders and the healed man (5:9b–13). Jewish law prohibited carrying objects on the Sabbath. The man's action in carrying his mat and walking on the Sabbath might have implied his protest against a system that had showed no care for his lifelong frustration. The Jewish authorities were not concerned about the man's life situation or his years of suffering; their sole concern was the violation of religious rules and regulations imposed upon the common people (5:10). The power of the oppressed becomes evident only when the liberated stand against corrupt systems.[8] The healed man testified about the man who had cured him (5:11). Although he did not know the healer's identity, he remembered his exact words. Both he and the Jewish leaders were unable to figure out the identity of the healer; but both were familiar with the words he had spoken and the miracle he had performed (5:12). They did not know his identity because Jesus had slipped away into the crowd soon after healing the man (5:13). The strict religious rules and regulations practiced by the Jews – Sabbath observances, circumcision, and purity laws – are, in many ways, reminiscent of the caste-based religious observances and fundamentalist spiritual attitudes prevalent in the Indian context.

---

6. Beasley-Murray, *John*, 74.
7. T. Vallianippuram, *New Society in John's Gospel* (Aloor: Biblia Publications, 2008), 181.
8. Arul Raja, "New Exorcism and Dalit Assertion," 346–56.

Later, Jesus found the man in the temple and told him, "Stop sinning or something worse may happen to you" (5:14). Jesus's statement was a call to the man to begin a new lifestyle in Christ; it was also a warning that failure to do so would lead to further suffering.[9] Jesus's words were an invitation to the man to believe in him and follow him. Jesus affirmed that the man had been liberated from his dehumanized situation and that he should, therefore, identify himself with Christ and the community of God. Similarly, marginalized communities in Asia can find a new identity through the person and work of Christ.[10]

Without heeding Jesus's warning, the man told the Jewish leaders that it was Jesus who had made him well, thereby putting Jesus in danger (5:15–18). Jesus's loss of anonymity and the disclosure of his identity led to his persecution by the Jewish leaders, who also intensified their plots to kill him (5:16, 18).

The Jewish leaders regarded Jesus as a violator of religious laws – especially the Sabbath regulations (5:16b) – and a blasphemer who equated himself with God (5:18). Jesus's response reveals his identity as one who is always working, just as the Father is always at work (5:17). Jesus had earlier said that his food was to do the will of the Father and to finish his work (4:34); similarly, since the Father was working to bring healing to people, Jesus would also work (5:17).

5:19–30 THE AUTHORITY OF JESUS

The dialogue of verses 1–18 shifts into a monologue of Jesus in verses 19–47. The first part of this monologue focuses on Jesus's authority (5:19–30); the second part focuses on various witnesses of Jesus (5:31–47). The entire section is an elaboration of Jesus's statement in verse 17 that he and his Father are working.

The section begins by explaining the functional dynamism between the Father and the Son and Jesus's dependence on the Father – Jesus does not act on his own (5:19). The Father's love prompts him to show all his works to the Son, and he would show even greater works that would amaze the people (5:20). One of those "greater works" would be giving life: "Just as the Father raises the dead and gives them life, even so the Son gives life to whom he is pleased to give it" (6:21). Just as the official's son was brought back from a death-like illness, the invalid was liberated from a death-like situation, and Lazarus would be raised from the dead, those who believe in Jesus will receive

---

9. Beasley-Murray, *John*, 74.
10. Nirmal, *Heuristic Explorations*, 52–60.

eternal life. In the Asian context, marginalized communities are in a death-like situation, voiceless and ostracized. But when they encounter Jesus and his liberation, they can stand up, move forward, and speak up.[11] The functional dynamism between the Father and the Son is heavenly, and this dynamism actualizes God's plan through the Son and initiates God's mission in the world.

However, this involves a judgment based on how people honor the Son (5:22–23). The Son makes this judgment, not the Father. The Jews rejected the Son, but the Father wishes to honor the Son. Not honoring the Son is an insult to the Father who sent him (5:23). Respect and honor of the Father are measured by how people respect and honor the Son. We cannot honor God without honoring Jesus. The Father's ultimate concern is that the world would accept, honor, and believe in the Son.

In contrast, those who hear Jesus's word and believe in the Father who sent him will have eternal life – they have already crossed over from death to life (5:24). Jesus's words invite people to believe in God, and if they do, they pass from death to life. The theme of Jesus as the giver of life (1:4; 4:43–54) is once again brought to the foreground here. The realized nature of Johannine eschatology is evident through the use of the present tense: "Whoever *hears* my word and *believes* him who sent me *has* eternal life" (5:24, emphasis added). This means that eternal life is a present reality for those who hear Jesus's words and believe in God. The Gospel of John emphasizes that eternal life is not limited to a future age but is accessible "here and now" for those who believe in Jesus (3:15–18, 36; 5:24).[12]

The expressions "a time is coming," "the dead will hear the voice of the Son of God," and "those who hear will live" (5:25) point to the future eschatological era when the hour of God will be fully revealed to the people of God.[13] The tension between realized and future eschatology is evident through the use of both present and future tenses.[14] For the narrator, both realized and future eschatology coexist. The dynamic relationship between the Father and the Son extends to how they give life (5:26). The Father has given the Son authority to execute judgment in the world because he is the Son of Man (5:27).[15] Jesus,

---

11. Azariah, *A Pastor's Search for Dalit Theology*, 16–27.
12. D. H. Johnson, "Life," *DJG*, eds. Joel B. Green and Scot McKnight (Downers Grove: InterVarsity Press, 1992), 469–71.
13. Beasley-Murray, *John*, 76.
14. Moloney, *Gospel of John*, 180.
15. There are links between the Son of Man and judgment in 1 Enoch 49:4; 61:9; 62:2–3. The reference to the coming bodily resurrection of just and unjust (vv. 28–29) finds its clearest OT parallel in Dan 12:2.

the Son of Man, appears as an eschatological figure to bring order and peace in a chaotic world.

On the one hand, the people will be astonished by Jesus's works (5:20); on the other hand, they should not be amazed by the events that will happen (5:28) because these are the works of the Son of Man. When he returns, those in their graves will hear his voice and rise to live. Those who have done evil will rise to be condemned (5:29). Verse 29 describes two categories of resurrection: Those who have done good will enjoy the resurrection of life, but those who have done evil will experience the resurrection of condemnation. Since Jesus will make these judgments in unity with the Father and in full obedience to him, these judgments will be just (5:30). Jesus will execute judgment as directed by the Father and in accordance with his will, and the will of the Father and the Son are one and the same.

5:31–47 WITNESSES CONCERNING JESUS

The emphasis shifts from Jesus's authority (5:19–30) to witnesses of Jesus (5:31–47), and the Son's dynamic relationship with the Father is once again affirmed in this section. According to Jewish law, a truth had to be established by more than one witness (Deut 19:15), and this legal principle is the basis for this section, which presents multiple witnesses to Jesus. Martin Asiedu-Peprah describes this discourse as a "two-party juridical controversy," with multiple witnesses authenticating a truth.[16]

The monologue begins with Jesus saying, "If I testify about myself, my testimony is not true" (5:31). But Jesus's testimony was validated by many other sources: John the Baptizer (5:32–35), the works commissioned by the Father (5:36), the Father (5:37–38), the Scriptures (5:39), and Moses and the law (5:45–47). Yet, the people refused to believe in Jesus and his words (5:40–44).

The first witness was John the Baptizer (5:32–35), and his testimony concerning Jesus is true (1:6–9, 15, 19–36; 3:22–30). Just as Jesus Christ embodies truth (1:17), John's testimony was also trustworthy (5:33).[17] Jesus did not need human testimony because the Father himself was his greatest witness. But he mentioned the testimony of the Baptizer for the sake of the Jews, for whose salvation he was concerned (5:34). Jesus explained John's significance as a witness: "John was a lamp that burned and gave light" (5:35).

---

16. Martin Asiedu-Peprah, *Johannine Sabbath Conflicts as Juridical Controversy*, WUNT 132 (Tübingen: Mohr Siebeck, 2001), 24–27.
17. Wright, *John for Everyone*, 66.

The Baptizer was the first lamp, but Jesus was the greater light of the world (8:12; 9:5). The Jews rejoiced for a while in the light of John's lamp; but after John's death, they sought to kill the light of the world, Jesus.

The second witness was Jesus's works (5:36). Jesus completed the works the Father had given him to do. Fulfilling those works confirmed that he had truly been sent by the Father. Lozada writes, "If 'the Jews' are suspicious of John, Jesus's works, as the second witness, prove that Jesus is God's emissary" (5:36).[18]

The third witness was the Father (5:37–38). Sadly, the people were deficient in their religiosity. Although they claimed to know God, they had never heard the Father's voice or seen him; although they boasted about their religious heritage and religiosity, they did not have the word of the Father abiding in them because they failed to believe the One sent by the Father.

The fourth witness was the Scriptures. The Jews diligently searched and studied the Scriptures, thinking that these contained eternal life (5:39). But, ironically, they failed to understand that these Scriptures testified about Jesus. By rejecting Jesus and refusing to come to him, the Jews rejected life itself. Although the Scriptures testify to Jesus, the Jews did not recognize the life-giving character of Jesus (5:40).[19]

Before presenting his final witness, Jesus declared that he did not require human testimony or glory: "I do not accept glory from human beings" (5:41). He has his own glory (1:14), he had manifested his glory (2:11), and the Father would soon glorify him (8:54). He rejected their glory because the Jews refused to glorify him and because they did not have the love of God in their hearts (5:42). Malina and Rohrbaugh say, "When Jesus claims the love of God is not in (or, among) his opponents, he is challenging their loyalty to God."[20] The Jews accepted others who came in their "own name" but rejected the Son who came in the Father's name (5:43). Jesus concluded with this question: "How can you believe since you accept glory from one another but do not seek the glory that comes from the only God?" (5:44). Jesus criticized their false religiosity based on self-centered glory. Jesus's glory was based on his vertical and horizontal love relationships – his love and loyalty toward the Father and his sacrificial love for suffering humanity. Similarly, the Asian church must seek

---

18. Francisco Lozada, "Contesting an Interpretation of John 5: Moving Beyond Colonial Evangelism," *John and Postcolonialism: Travel, Space and Power*, eds. Musa W. Dube and Jeffrey L. Staley (London: Sheffield Academic Press, 2002), 88.
19. Asiedu-Peprah, *Johannine Sabbath Conflicts*, 27–28.
20. Malina and Rohrbaugh, *Social-Science Commentary on the Gospel of John*, 121.

glory and honor through love for a suffering world and through fulfilling the works of God in the world.

The fifth and final witness was Moses and his writings – the Pentateuch (5:45–47). Earlier, Jesus had referred to the Scriptures as a whole as his witness (5:39), but now the reference is specifically to Moses's writings. The Jews claimed to honor Moses, the lawgiver, but their actions revealed the opposite. Although Moses's writings pointed to Jesus, they rejected Jesus (5:45–46). They took pride in studying the law and imposed it on others, but they themselves "do not believe what he [Moses] wrote" (5:47). If they had believed what Moses wrote, they would have believed in Jesus's words.

Moses gave them the law; Jesus brought them grace and truth (1:17). Moses lifted up a bronze serpent to bring healing to those who had been bitten by serpents and faced imminent death; Jesus was lifted up to bring eternal life to those facing eternal death (3:14–15). Philip, unlike the Jewish religious leaders, recognized Jesus as the one Moses had written about, followed him, and found life (1:45).

The monologue concludes with a question: "How are you going to believe what I say?" (5:47). This clarion call to repentance and faith in Jesus continues today. But how can people believe what Jesus said unless they first hear it and then see these truths lived out in the lives of his followers? Churches often prefer to construct massive buildings and sustain their status quo in the world rather than emphasize the liberating mission of God. The Scriptures challenge Christians to be actively involved in the *missio Dei* – the mission of God.

JOHN 6:1–71
JESUS IS THE BREAD OF LIFE

John 6:1–71 consists of four sections: the feeding of the five thousand (6:1–15), walking on water (6:16–21), the bread of life discourse (6:22–59), and the response of Jesus's disciples (6:60–71). The entire chapter centers on the theme of Jesus as the bread of life. These events and discourses are particularly significant in Asia, where many people live in vulnerable situations and are concerned with both physical and spiritual nourishment.

6:1–15 JESUS FEEDS A MULTITUDE

Chapter 6 begins with a narratorial note: "Some time after this, Jesus crossed to the far shore of the Sea of Galilee (that is, the Sea of Tiberias)" (6:1). While such expressions usually connect to previous events, this scene in John 6 is not directly connected to the events in John 5, which took place in Jerusalem (5:1). This has led some scholars to question John's chronology. Schnackenburg, for example, says,

> 6:1 follows badly from Chapter 5, but easily from 4:54. The remark "After this Jesus went to the other side of the Sea of Galilee, which is the Sea of Tiberias," is out of place if Jesus was previously in Jerusalem because it refers to a journey from one side of the Sea to another, not a journey from Jerusalem to Galilee.[1]

However, the narrator's purpose does not seem to be chronological or sequential. John has been alternating between Jesus's presence in Galilee and Jerusalem – the latter during festival seasons. Even within Galilee, Jesus is depicted as moving between cities: Cana (2:1–11), Capernaum (2:12), and then Cana again (4:43–54). The geographic note alerts the reader to the fact that the story takes place in a new location, a place many pilgrims were passing through on their way to the "Jewish Passover Festival" (6:4). The setting of the story, with its references to rivers, seas, and other topographical and geographical details, may evoke a sense of nostalgia among Asian readers,

---

1. Schnackenburg, *The Gospel according to St. John*, vol. 2 (London: Burns & Oates, 1980), 5.

helping them to connect the narrative in John with the realities of their own world. Jesus's itinerant movements through rugged terrain resonate with the everyday experiences of many Asians, especially those from village settings.

The feeding of the multitude appears in all four Gospels (Matt 14:13–21; Mark 6:30–44; Luke 9:12–17; John 6:1–15). The narrator states that a large crowd followed Jesus because "they saw the signs he had performed by healing the sick" (6:2). "Signs" play a key role in this Gospel, occurring seventeen times.[2] The narrator has already mentioned three of Jesus's sign miracles: two in Cana and one in Capernaum, both Galilean cities (2:11; 4:54; 5:1–18). As he often did, Jesus went up a mountain and sat down with his disciples (6:3). The narrator introduces the setting of the story: "The Jewish Passover Festival was near" (6:4).[3] Jesus had already attended a Passover Festival in Jerusalem, where he had cleansed the temple (2:13, 23).[4]

In Asia, religious festivals and pilgrimage are common. These include Ramadan, Diwali, Holi, Onam, Pongal, Makara Sankranti, Ganesh Chaturthi, Christmas, and Passion Week. Many Indian people view these festival seasons as opportunities to serve others, extend hospitality to strangers, and foster interreligious harmony. Since Asian festivals are closely tied to people's religiosity, Asian readers can easily situate themselves within the narrative framework of John's story. Whereas Jesus had been in Jerusalem during the previous Passover Festival (2:13, 23), he was now in Galilee (6:1–15) – although he might have gone to the festival later.

The expression "Jesus looked up and saw a great crowd" makes the reader aware that people were flocking to Jesus (6:5a). Seeing the great crowd, Jesus asked Philip, "Where shall we buy bread for these people to eat?" (6:5b).[5] The narrator explains that Jesus's question was intended to "test" Philip (6:6a). The phrase "for he already had in mind what he was going to do" (6:6b) reveals Jesus's foreknowledge and his intention to perform a miracle.

When Jesus posed this test question, Philip responded by describing the enormity of the task: "It would take more than half a year's wages to buy enough bread for each one to have a bite!" (6:7).[6] It is unclear whether Philip

---

2. 2:11, 18, 23; 3:2; 4:48, 54; 6:2, 14, 26, 30; 7:31; 9:16; 10:41; 11:47; 12:18, 37; 20:30.
3. James L. Resseguie, *Narrative Criticism of the New Testament*, 87, 98, 113–14.
4. Whether the Passovers indicated in 2:13 and in 6:4 are the same is difficult to postulate. But from the narrator's point of view, this Passover happened later than the earlier one.
5. In Matthew and Luke, the disciples take initiative; in Mark and John, Jesus takes initiative (Matt 14:15; Luke 9:12; Mark 6:34; John 6:5).
6. The Greek text says, "two hundred denarius of bread," which the NIV editors have estimated.

was concerned about the cost, their lack of money, the difficulty of purchasing such a large quantity of bread, or all three. Although Philip had been at the wedding in Cana and seen how Jesus resolved the shortage of wine (2:1–11), he does not seem to have believed that Jesus could do something about their present food shortage. Philip's response reflects the typical reasoning of the human mind, highlighting the contrast between the mind of Jesus (from above) and the mind of Philip (of this world) – the divine perspective in contrast to the human viewpoint. Philip viewed the countryside, the mountainous place, and the large crowd from a human perspective. As a man of this world, he responded based on what seemed possible or impossible. From his perspective, the financial resources available were not sufficient to feed such a large crowd.[7] This situation is reminiscent of Asian realities: a large crowd (6:2), many possibly sick (6:2), a scarcity of food (6:5–6), and an economic crisis (6:7).[8] When faced with existential struggles, we, like Philip, often assess situations based on human calculations of what is possible or impossible.

Andrew, Simon Peter's brother, joined the discussion between Jesus and Philip (6:8). The narrator has already indicated that Peter, Andrew, and Philip all hailed from Bethsaida (1:44).[9] Both Andrew and Philip had introduced others to Jesus: Andrew introduced Peter, his brother, and Philip introduced Nathanael (1:40–41, 45). So it makes perfect sense that Andrew should point to a boy with five barley loaves and two fish. Andrew also raised a pertinent question: "But how far will they go among so many?" (6:9). Philip had expressed the idea of complete *impossibility* (6:7); Andrew, while drawing attention to *availability*, also emphasized the *impossibility* of the situation (6:9b).[10] Earlier Jesus had healed a boy who was close to death (4:49); now, a boy offers his lunch to feed a hungry crowd (6:7). The boy's willingness to share his food reflects the ethos of the poor in Asia, who often share what little they have.[11]

Jesus instructed his disciples to seat with the people so that they might rest from their pilgrimage and prepare to eat (6:10a). This might have created a moment of suspense, causing the people to wonder, "Why are we sitting

---

7. Donald A. Carson, *The Gospel according to John* (Leicester: IVP; Grand Rapids: Eerdmans, 1991), 269.
8. Johnson Thomaskutty, "Jesus is our benefactor and our helping hand (6:1–21)," *Barnabas Today*.
9. Carson, *The Gospel according to John*, 268–71.
10. While John refers to Philip and Andrew, the synoptic evangelists refer to the disciples without mentioning names.
11. Earlier the narrator refers to the boy as *paidion* "a child," but now he refers to the boy as *paidarion* "little child" (the *-arion* ending shows it's a diminutive form, "little").

down on a mountainside when we could be hurrying to Jerusalem to find food?" Nevertheless, they sat on the grassy mountainside. The narrator notes that "about five thousand men were there" (6:10b), but it is likely that they were accompanied by their wives and children (Matt 14:21), thus forming an even larger crowd.

Jesus "took the loaves," "gave thanks," and "distributed to those who were seated" – echoing the pattern of the Lord's Supper that he would soon establish (Luke 24:30), a sacrament that churches worldwide continue to practice (1 Cor 11:23–32). Philip had worried that even more than half a year's wages could not buy enough food "for each one to have a bite" (6:7), but the people now eat "as much as they wanted" (6:11). In Cana, Jesus had provided an abundance of the best wine – twenty to thirty gallons (2:6); now, he provides an abundance of bread and fish for people to eat as much as they want, with plenty of leftovers!

Jesus was not wasteful. He instructed the disciples to gather the leftovers: "Let nothing be wasted" (6:12). This demonstrates the sacred nature of the event.[12] The disciples obeyed and gathered the leftovers, filling twelve baskets (6:13) – twice the number of wine jars in Cana and corresponding to the number of disciples.

The witnesses to this sign were also the beneficiaries of the event. The Johannine theme of signs leading to belief (2:11, 23; 4:45–46) continues here (6:14). The people began saying, "Surely this is the Prophet who is to come into the world" (6:14b), which is the second time Jesus's prophetic ministry was acknowledged. Earlier, the woman at the well acknowledged Jesus as a prophet (4:19); now, the pilgrims do so. This contrasts with John the Baptizer's vehement denial that he was the long-awaited prophet (1:21, 25). The eschatological prophet who would perform signs and wonders, and heal and feed the nation, had come (6:14b).[13] Realizing this, the people intended to forcefully make him their king (6:15a). Jesus's ability to draw large crowds, perform signs and wonders, and meet their physical needs prompted the people's desire to make him their king. Once again, they were thinking from an *earthly* point of view. But since it was not yet Jesus's time, and the Father *above* had not told him to declare himself a king, Jesus withdrew by himself to a mountain

---

12. Morris, *Gospel according to John*, 305.
13. Andreas J. Köstenberger, *John*, BECNT (Grand Rapids: Baker Academic, 2004), 203; Herman Ridderbos, *The Gospel according to St. John* (Grand Rapids: Eerdmans, 1997), 215–16.

(6:15b). Mark Stibbe observes, "This quiet disappearance will be a frequent occurrence from now on."[14]

Like Jesus, churches and Christians today should be at the forefront of feeding the hungry, clothing the naked, sheltering the homeless, and comforting the abandoned. Many Asian countries have a large population of poor people. The 2020 *Human Development Report* by the United Nations Development Program ranked the Philippines 107th out of 189 nations. Around 2.7 million Filipino families experienced hunger during the first quarter of 2023. In such situations, the church as a whole – along with individual Christians – has a vital role to play in feeding the hungry and comforting the afflicted.

6:16–21 JESUS WALKS ON THE WATER

The pericope begins with a narratorial note that includes both temporal and spatial details: it is evening, and the disciples go down to the lake, get in a boat, and set off across the lake for Capernaum (6:16–17a).[15] These details suggest that the narrator may have been an eyewitness or gathered information from eyewitnesses. As the disciples rowed their boat across the lake, it became dark, but Jesus had not yet joined them (6:17b). Earlier, when the people had tried to make Jesus their king by force, he had withdrawn by himself to be alone (6:15) – and he was still not back.

As the disciples continued their journey, the waters grew rough because a strong wind was blowing (6:18). The Sea of Galilee faces such natural disturbances from time to time.[16] Although the disciples were experienced fishermen, who were familiar with this lake, the darkness, strong wind, rough waters, and Jesus's absence alarmed them. The Asian continent is rich in natural beauty – mountains, seas, lakes, and rivers – but also vulnerable to natural calamities such as rough seas, river floods, earthquakes, and soil erosion. As such, Asian readers will readily identify with the disciples' apprehension.

After rowing three to four miles, the disciples saw Jesus walking on the lake and approaching the boat. They were terrified because although Jesus had not accompanied them, they now saw him walking on the water despite

---

14. Mark W. G. Stibbe, *John's Gospel: New Testament Readings* (London: Routledge, 1994), 21.
15. Although the Greek text refers to the "sea" (*thalassa*), the NIV editors have changed it to a "lake" because of its relatively small size. It is approximately 53 kilometer in circumference.
16. E. A. Blum, "John." *The Bible Knowledge Commentary: New Testament* (Hyderabad: Authentic, 1983), 294.

the darkness around, the roughness of the sea, and the powerful winds.[17] The rough waters coupled with the darkness would have prevented them from recognizing Jesus – all they could have seen was a ghost-like figure.[18] The Chinese believe that the spirits of those who have drowned – called *Shui Gui* (meaning "water ghost") – linger in the place where they died.[19] In many primal religions, people believe that aquatic spirits and ghosts – both benevolent and malevolent – hover over the surface of the waters. The Jews regarded the depths of the sea as the abode of demonic forces. Malina and Rohrbaugh comment, "In antiquity, winds and seasons of the year were personified or attributed to certain invisible cosmic forces or powers . . . Jesus's ability to walk on the sea is evidence of his place in the hierarchy of cosmic powers."[20] The rough waters, the darkness around, the powerful winds, and the unexpected presence of Jesus walking on the water terrified the disciples.

Jesus comforted them, saying, "It is I; don't be afraid" (6:20). Earlier, he had used the same "I am" formula to reveal his identity as Messiah to the woman at the well (4:26). Now, he uses it to comfort the disciples and encourage them not to fear. Burge comments,

> More difficult are passages where Jesus says, "I am" and we are left uncertain if we are to supply a predicate or if the phrase is being used for self-identification. For example, in John 6:20 the frightened disciples are comforted when Jesus says, "*egō eimi* [I am], do not be afraid."[21]

We should probably supply the predicate as the NIV does: "It is I." The disciples' recognition of Jesus strengthened their confidence, making them willing to take him into the boat (6:21a). The fact that the boat reached the shore as soon as Jesus stepped into it (6:21b) may also be considered a sign. Although this passage is best known for the sign of Jesus walking on water (6:19), it also emphasizes their instant arrival at their destination (6:21).[22]

---

17. Craig S. Keener, *The IVP Bible Background Commentary: New Testament* (Downers Grove: InterVarsity Press, 1993), 279.
18. Matthew (14:26–27) and Mark (6:49–50) suggest that.
19. Theresa Bane, *Encyclopedia of Spirits and Ghosts in World Mythology* (Jefferson: McFarland & Company, 2016), 110.
20. Malina and Rohrbaugh, *Social-science Commentary on the Gospel of John*, 128.
21. Gary M. Burge, "'I AM' Sayings," *DJG*, eds. Joel B. Green, Scot McKnight, and I. Howard Marshall (Downers Grove: InterVarsity Press, 1992), 354–55.
22. Thomaskutty, *Dialogue in the Book of Signs*, 220.

Once again, Jesus had surpassed Moses, who gave their ancestors water to drink in the wilderness. Jesus walked on water. Earlier, he had given them bread – as much as they could eat – just as Moses had done. Furthermore, Jesus led them above the water, just as Moses had led the Israelites through the water when they crossed over to the wilderness.[23] Both the exodus community and Jesus's disciples were under the divine presence and guidance of Jesus. In that sense, a "new exodus" motif lies at the heart of this story. Asians typically read and interpret the book of Exodus as a story of hope and liberation. The "new exodus" motif in this event in John's Gospel calls us to a life of liberation and transformation. Jesus's presence in life's chaotic situations and his miraculous deliverance from dangerous situations offer hope and confidence to Asians who are poor, hungry, diseased, or marginalized. Jesus always says, "It is I; don't be afraid."

6:22–59 JESUS'S BREAD OF LIFE DISCOURSE

The setting now shifts to Capernaum (6:24), with the expression "next day" providing a natural transition from the story of Jesus walking on the water (6:16–21).[24] The crowd that had stayed on the other side of the lake realized that only one boat had been there (6:22a). The crowd must have camped at the place where Jesus had fed them. They knew Jesus had not got into the boat with his disciples (6:22b). The crowd, the boats, the waters, and the natural surroundings will seem familiar to readers from regions like Kerala in South India. Kerala is known for regular gatherings of people on various occasions, the use of boats by fisherfolk in coastal areas – sometimes even for boat races – its many rivers and lakes, and its coastal, mountainous, and hilly areas.

The crowd was aware of Jesus's withdrawal (6:15) and knew that he had not got into the boat with the disciples (6:22). However, they did not know about his walking on water and then joining the disciples in the boat (6:19–21). This situation changed when boats from Tiberias, a city south of Capernaum, came ashore. The people in those boats must have informed the crowd that Jesus was in Capernaum. Immediately, they got into boats and went there in search of Jesus (6:24). The expression "the people had eaten the bread after the Lord had given thanks" (6:23) recalls the miraculous meal the people had eaten with Jesus (compare 6:11–12).[25] The absence of Jesus and his disciples

---

23. Wright, *John for Everyone*, 75.
24. Schnackenburg, *Gospel according to St. John*, vol. 2, 34.
25. Malina and Rohrbaugh, *Social-Science Commentary on the Gospel of John*, 129.

from the place where this miracle had taken place motivated the crowd to go to Capernaum looking for Jesus (6:24). This reference to the bread (6:23) and the miracle of the feeding of the five thousand set the stage for Jesus's "bread of life" discourse (6:25–59).[26]

The crowd found Jesus on the other side of the sea and asked him, "Rabbi, when did you get here?" (6:25). Their question was motivated by curiosity because they had seen him withdrawing to the mountain.[27] Jesus responded by emphasizing the following points: They sought him not because of the signs they saw but because they had eaten their fill and were satisfied (6:26); they were not to work for food that perishes but for the food that the Son of Man gives, which endures forever (6:27a); and God himself had placed his seal of approval on the Son (6:27b).[28]

This section presents two contrasts. First, the crowd was seeking Jesus not for his signs and miracles (faith events) but for bread to fill their stomachs (non-faith events). Second, Jesus warned them not to work for "food that spoils" but for "food that endures." These contrasts once again emphasize the *from earth* versus the *from above* perspectives.[29] Jesus did not diminish the value of food or mock these followers; rather, he emphasized true spirituality. Schnackenburg comments, "A true 'seeing of signs' means realizing the divine meaning of Jesus's actions."[30]

People work hard for food that perishes but often disregard the food that satisfies forever. Jesus's responses here are based on his sign of feeding the five thousand (6:1–15; compare 2:1–11; 4:31–38). The phrase "on him God the Father has placed his seal of approval" (6:27) refers to Jesus being empowered by the Spirit, and the early church viewed the Holy Spirit as God's seal (Eph 1:13; 4:30). In this way, the narrator includes all three members of the Trinity in this verse (6:27). As the one sealed by the Father, Jesus can provide spiritual food from above.

The crowd asked, "What must we do to do the works God requires?" (6:28), reflecting their desire to do what pleased God. Earlier, Jesus had said

---

26. Bartholomä says, "The Bread of Life Discourse contains 480 words of Jesus, which makes it the fourth longest cohesive speech in the Gospel of John." Philipp F. Bartholomä, "The Johannine Discourses and the Teaching of Jesus in the Synoptics: A Comparative Approach to the Authenticity of Jesus's Words in the Fourth Gospel," (PhD diss., Leuven, Evangelical Theological Faculty, 2010), 109.
27. Wright, *John for Everyone*, 79.
28. Schnackenburg, *Gospel according to St. John*, vol. 2, 35–36.
29. Blum, *John*, 295.
30. Schnackenburg, *Gospel according to St. John*, vol. 2, 35.

that his food was to do the work the Father had commissioned him to do (4:34), that reaping a harvest of souls is divine work (4:38), and that he was working on the Sabbath because the Father is always working (5:17). In case the crowd had missed those earlier teachings, he now explains what divine work is: "The work of God is this: to believe in the one he has sent" (6:29). Jesus equated work that pleases God with believing in Jesus.[31] It is that simple. They needed to believe in Jesus and believe his words. Doing so was doing God's work rather than living for food that perishes. In the Gospel of John, belief includes knowing, working, and following.

The crowd, failing to grasp Jesus's message, asked a familiar question: "What sign then will you give?" (6:30). Earlier, after Jesus cleansed the temple, the Jews had asked, "What sign can you show us to prove your authority to do all this?" (2:18). On the way to heal the official's son, Jesus had commented, "Unless you people see signs and wonders . . . you will never believe" (4:48). This time, they seek a sign even to believe: "What sign then will you give that we may see it and believe you? What will you do?" (6:30).

Before Jesus could say anything, they hinted at the kind of miracle they wanted to see: "Our ancestors ate the manna in the wilderness" (6:31a). Once again, they wanted bread, a clear indication that they had missed Jesus's message altogether. When they said, "He gave them bread from heaven to eat" (6:31b), they were citing Psalm 78:24, where the psalmist recollects how Israel ate manna every day during their wilderness wanderings (Exod 16:4–36).[32] The crowd was asking Jesus for a manna-like sign, similar to their forefathers' experience during their earthly life. They were comparing Jesus to Moses. Just as Moses had fed the people of Israel with manna in the desert, Jesus had fed them with bread on the mountainside (6:1–15). But this was not enough for the people; they wanted further signs – more food! Their expectation was not just a one-time meal but continual provision, just as Moses had provided food for forty years. In making this request, they ignored Jesus's statement that he could give them "food that endures to eternal life" (6:27). Eternal life is so much longer than forty years in the wilderness. Yet, they did not ask for spiritual food. Their materialistic mindset persisted. Often, people follow God not to worship him but to gain material blessings. Jesus was not condemning

---

31. Bartholomä, "Johannine Discourses and the Teaching of Jesus in the Synoptics," 109.
32. Ben Witherington, *John's Wisdom: A Commentary on the Fourth Gospel* (Louisville: Westminster John Knox, 1995), 156; Frances Taylor Gench, *Encounters with Jesus: Studies in the Gospel of John* (Louisville: Westminster John Knox, 2007), 42–43.

physical food but, rather, the people's lack of interest in spiritual matters and in him.

In their haste to cite Scripture, the crowd made a crucial mistake. In Psalm 78:24, the "he" who provided manna refers to God, not Moses: "He rained down manna for the people to eat, he gave them the grain of heaven" (Ps 78:24; see also Neh 9:15). Jesus corrected them: "Very truly I tell you, it is not Moses who has given you the bread from heaven, but it is my Father who gives you the true bread from heaven" (6:32a). They were wrong to attribute the Father's work to Moses. The expressions "the bread from heaven" (6:32a) and "the *true* bread from heaven" (6:32b, emphasis added) indicate two different things here.[33] While the bread from heaven (6:32a) refers to manna, the true bread from heaven is the spiritual food available through Jesus.[34] Although both are from heaven – which implies that they are given by God the Father – they differ in nature. The first – the manna – had to be eaten every day to satisfy physical hunger; the second, the true bread, "endures to eternal life" (6:27) and "gives life to the world" (6:33). Manna was God's provision to satisfy their physical hunger, while the true bread from heaven is the Father's eternal provision for his people. It is this true bread, Jesus, who can give life to the world (6:33). Just as Jesus is the "true light" (1:9), the true "Savior of the world" (4:42), and the "true vine" (15:1), he is also the "true bread from heaven" (6:32). Indians use the phrase "*Satyameva Jayate*," which means "truth alone triumphs." Only the true light, the true vine, and the true bread can give eternal life to the people of the world.

When Jesus offered living water to the woman at the well, she said, "Sir, give me this water so that I won't get thirsty and have to keep coming here to draw water" (4:15). The crowd now makes a similar request: "Sir . . . always give us this bread" (6:34). Their response indicates their spiritual openness to Jesus but also their misunderstanding of Jesus's words about the true bread. Just as their forefathers had eaten manna for forty years, they were asking for daily provision of bread in this life.[35] Just as Jesus redirected the people's attention from the material to the eternal, the Asian church should adopt hermeneutical

---

33. Wright, *John for Everyone*, 80.
34. Maurice Casey, *From Jewish Prophet to Gentile God: The Origin and Development of New Testament Christology* (Louisville: Westminster John Knox Press, 1992), 24–27. Also Bartholomä, "Johannine Discourses and the Teaching of Jesus in the Synoptics," 110.
35. Schnackenburg, *Gospel according to St. John*, vol. 2, 42–43.

principles that do not merely focus on people's material concerns but point them to eternal and universal truths.[36]

Reiterating what he had said earlier – "to believe in the one he has sent" (6:29) – Jesus declared, "I am the bread of life" (6:35a) and added, "Whoever comes to me will never go hungry" (6:35b). The *true* bread from heaven (6:32) that gives life to the world (6:33) is Jesus. Earlier, Jesus had told the woman at the well that he was the source of living water: "The water I give them will become in them a spring of water welling up to eternal life" (4:14b). That thought is continued here: "And whoever believes in me will never be thirsty" (6:35c). Those who believe in Jesus (6:29) will never hunger or thirst – for eternity.

"I am the bread of life" (6:35b). By his *egō eimi* ("I am") statement, Jesus made it clear that he is the true bread from heaven that satisfies people's spiritual hunger and prepares them for eternal life.[37] His *egō eimi* statements connect God's promised blessings to Israel with the rest of the world through Jesus's mission as the Christ.[38] Jesus, as the one who can provide physical bread (6:1–15), is now revealed as the spiritual and universal bread from heaven. Sadly, they did not believe. Knowing this, Jesus said, "You have seen me and still you do not believe [me]" (6:36). Although they asked for this bread (6:34), they were not willing to believe in Jesus and receive the *true* bread from heaven.

Jesus was not alarmed. Since he knew his Father's will and plan, he responded, "All those the Father gives me will come to me, and whoever comes to me I will never drive away" (6:37). Once again, this expresses the dynamic and functional relationship between the Father and the Son. Jesus is generous, he will not reject or drive away anyone who comes to him, regardless of where they come from.

Jesus resumed speaking about his mission. He had come down from heaven not to do his own will but that of the Father who had sent him (6:38). And this was the Father's will: "That I shall lose none of all those he has given me, but raise them up at the last day . . . that everyone who looks to the Son and believes in him shall have eternal life, and I will raise them up at the last day" (6:39–40). Jesus will not lose anyone who believes in him; instead, he will give them eternal life by raising them up on the last day. The will of the Father is

---
36. Johnson Thomaskutty, "Biblical Interpretation in the Global-Indian Context," *Fuller Magazine* 8 (Pasadena: Fuller Theological Seminary, 2017), 64–68.
37. Bartholomä, "Johannine Discourses and the Teaching of Jesus in the Synoptics," 121.
38. Paul N. Anderson, *From Crisis to Christ: A Contextual Introduction to the New Testament* (Nashville: Abingdon, 2014), 151.

fulfilled in Jesus's mission – not only in the existential struggles of the people but also in the consummation of the eschatological day (6:40).[39] This affirms both the present reality and the future eschatological resurrection.

While the crowd asked for bread (6:34), the Jews in the synagogue were unhappy with Jesus's statement – verse 59 tells us that Jesus was in the synagogue during the second part of this discourse. They grumbled because he had said that he was the bread that came down from heaven (6:41). For them, Jesus's claim to be from God and his claim of a dynamic relationship with the Father seemed blasphemous. Although Jesus revealed his identity, they misunderstood him. They argued about his identity as the son of Joseph, citing their familiarity with his parents (6:42). They reduced him to an earthly figure and rejected his claims about his heavenly origin.

Jesus told the Jews to stop grumbling (6:43) and continued to reveal truths about himself (6:44–51). He reiterated what he had said earlier: No one can come to him unless the Father draws that person, and anyone who comes to Jesus will be raised up on the last day (6:44). To confirm this truth that God the Father is involved in drawing people to Christ, Jesus quoted from the prophet Isaiah: "They will all be taught by God" (6:45; see Isa 54:13). Jesus interpreted this verse to mean that "everyone who has heard the Father and learned from him comes to me" (6:45b). The Jews did not believe in Jesus because they had not been taught by God; they had not heard the Father and learned from him. That is why they did not believe in Jesus. Once again, Jesus emphasized his unique relationship with the Father: "No one has seen the Father except the one who is from God; only he has seen the Father" (6:46).

Before concluding his discourse, Jesus reiterated what he had been saying: The one who believes in Jesus will have eternal life (6:47); Jesus is the bread of life (6:48; compare 6:35, 41, 51); their ancestors ate manna and died (6:49), but Jesus is the bread that came down from heaven, which anyone may eat and not die (6:50). He then introduced a new element in his teaching: "I am the living bread . . . This bread is my flesh, which I will give for the life of the world" (6:51). This statement foreshadows what Jesus would later say and do in the Upper Room by offering of his body on the cross for the salvation of the world (19:30).

Earlier, the Jews had grumbled (6:41); now, they entered into a sharp dispute among themselves, asking, "How can this man give us his flesh to eat?"

---

39. D. C. Allison, "Eschatology," *DJG*, eds. Joel B. Green, Scot McKnight, and I. Howard Marshall (Downers Grove: InterVarsity Press, 1992), 206–209.

(6:52).⁴⁰ The Jews had strict dietary rules, and the thought of eating human flesh – even if it were to give life – was strictly against kosher laws. Therefore, they were greatly troubled by Jesus's words.

Instead of softening his words to ease their discomfort, Jesus continued: "Very truly I tell you, unless you eat the flesh of the Son of Man and drink his blood, you have no life in you" (6:53). They must eat his flesh and drink his blood. When God permitted people to eat the flesh of animals, he had commanded, "But you must not eat meat that has its lifeblood still in it" (Gen 9:4). But now Jesus was saying that people must eat his flesh and drink his blood to have life (6:53). This statement has Eucharistic overtones. Eternal life would be made possible through the destruction of Jesus's body and the shedding of his blood; his death on the cross is essential.

Once again, Jesus reiterated what he had been saying: Those who eat his flesh and drink his blood will have eternal life, and Jesus will raise them up in the last day (6:54); his flesh is true food, and his blood is true drink (6:55);⁴¹ those who eat his flesh and drink his blood will remain in him, and he in them (6:56); he was sent by the Father, and he lives because of the Father, and those who feed on him will live because of him (6:57); he is the bread that came down from heaven – while their ancestors ate manna and died, those who eat the true bread from heaven will live forever (6:58). Jesus assured believers of abundant life, both in this age and in the coming age of salvation. Through the symbolic acts of eating the flesh of the Son of Man and drinking his blood, believers express total identification and oneness with Christ (6:56–58). Those who eat his flesh and drink his blood experience a mutual indwelling and a mystical union between them and Christ. Similarly, there is a mutual dependence of existence and shared life between the Father, the Son, and the believers.

The discourse began with Jesus in Capernaum (6:24) and concluded in the synagogue at Capernaum (6:59). Whereas the people wanted the living bread that Jesus offered (6:34), the Jewish leaders in the synagogue responded with grumbling (6:41) and sharp disagreements (6:52). They even insulted Jesus by referring to his humble birth to Joseph and Mary (6:42). Rather than

---

40. Even after seeing the sign of feeding the multitude and hearing his discourse, the Jews consider him as "this man" and express their disbelief plainly.
41. The adjective *true* in "my flesh is *true* food" and "my blood is *true* drink" goes in line with his previous expression "*true* bread from heaven" (v. 55; compare v. 32b).

addressing him as "Sir" or "Lord" – as many others did – they referred to him merely as "this man" (6:52).

This discourse reveals what true work is – to believe in Jesus and the Father, who sent him (6:29). Asian readers can draw several significant lessons from this discourse. While the Jews prioritized Moses's commandments and the equitable distribution of manna – that is, material provision – Jesus offers spiritual manna to anyone who comes to him through hearing the Father's words. Jesus fulfilled the people's need for food (6:1–15), initiated a "new exodus" (6:16–21), and assured the people of both eternal life in the present and future resurrection.

THE "I AM" SAYINGS

Jesus's "I am" sayings in John's Gospel can be broadly classified into two main categories: uncertain predicative statements and absolute predicative statements. The first category – termed "uncertain predicates" – consists of "passages where Jesus says, 'I AM' and we are left uncertain if we are to apply a predicate or if the phrase is being used for self-identification"[1] (see 4:26; 6:20; 8:18; 8:24, 28, 58; 9:9; 18:5, 6, 8). In the second category – termed "absolute usages" – the "I am" is followed by a specific predicate such as the bread, the gate, or the vine (see 6:35, 41, 48, 51; 8:12; 10:7, 9, 11, 14; 11:25; 14:6; 15:1, 5). There are seven such absolute statements.

In these seven "I am" statements, Jesus described himself using metaphors. He said, "I am the bread of life" (6:35, 48) soon after feeding the five thousand (6:1–15). He proclaimed that he was the "light of the world" during the festival of lights described in John 7–8. This metaphor of light was also the context in which Jesus healed a man born blind, restoring his physical sight while symbolizing that many remain in spiritual darkness and need his healing (9:1–41).

The statements "I am the gate for the sheep" (10:7, 9) and "I am the good shepherd" (10:11, 14) were uttered shortly after the healed blind man was expelled from the synagogue (9:34). Through these sayings, Jesus implied that although the Jewish leaders expelled people from their assemblies because of him, he was there to welcome and accept them as the "gate for the sheep." The Jewish leaders, who had failed to address the lifelong problems of a man who belonged to their own community, were compared to "hired hands," while Jesus was portrayed as the man's "good shepherd" (10:1–18).

Jesus's self-revelatory declaration that he was "the resurrection and the life" (11:25) came in the context of the raising of Lazarus. The one who claimed to be "the way and the truth and the life" (14:6) also promised to prepare a place in heaven for his followers (14:2) and to send the "Spirit of truth" to guide them (14:15–17, 25–26; 15:26; 16:12–13). The one who provided wine (2:1–12) also identified himself as the "true vine" (15:1–11). In each instance, Jesus's self-revelatory "I am" statements were accompanied by actions that reinforced their significance.

---

1. David Mark Ball, *'I AM' in John's Gospel: Literary Function, Background, and Theological Implications* (Sheffield: Sheffield Academic Press, 1996), 177–201.

6:60–71 RESPONSES FROM THE DISCIPLES

The discourse began with the crowd who had witnessed the feeding of the five thousand (6:22, 24), shifted to the Jews in the synagogue (6:41, 59), and concluded with a discussion between Jesus and his disciples (6:60–71). These disciples were not the inner circle of the Twelve but other disciples who were genuine followers of Jesus – we know this because, at the end of the pericope, some of the disciples turned away (6:66), but the Twelve chose to stay with him (6:67–71). This wider group of disciples could not accept Jesus's teaching. They declared, "This is a hard teaching. Who can accept it?" (6:60). Their struggle was mainly because of Jesus's claim to unity with the Father and his teaching about eating his flesh and drinking his blood (6:52–59). Like the Jews had done earlier (6:41), these disciples began to grumble (6:61). After asking if his teaching was offending them (6:61) – which it was – Jesus presented two new teachings to these disciples.

First, Jesus challenged them. If they found this teaching difficult, he asked what they would do if they saw the Son of Man ascend to where he was before (6:62). The expression "where he was before" refers to the abode of the Father in heaven. Earlier, Jesus had told Nicodemus that just as Moses had lifted the bronze snake in the wilderness, the Son of Man must be lifted up (3:14). Later, he said that when lifted up from the earth, he would draw all people to himself (12:32). This "lifting up" refers both to his death on the cross and his ascension to the Father's presence. If the disciples could not accept these teachings about eating Jesus's flesh and drinking his blood, they would have even greater difficulty understanding the significance of his death on the cross and his ascension.

Second, Jesus spoke about the Spirit. Like other key terms in John – "born again" or born from above, "wind" versus "Spirit," water versus "living water," "manna" versus "bread from heaven" – the word "Spirit," too, carries a double meaning here. The human spirit is empowered by the divine Spirit, and Jesus's words are "full of the Spirit and life" (6:63).

Jesus realized that even after clarifying these teachings – first to the crowd, then to the Jewish leaders, and now to the disciples – some still did not believe (6:64a). Although Jesus knew who would not believe in him and who would betray him (6:64b), he did not reveal their identities. This foreknowledge demonstrates Jesus's heavenly vision and omniscience. In John's Gospel, this is the first reference to Judas Iscariot, who did not believe and would later betray Jesus. Nevertheless, Jesus was not alarmed because, as he told the disciples, no one could come to him unless enabled by the Father to do so (6:65). So, Judas and any others who would betray Jesus did not believe because they were not drawn by the Father and had not believed in Jesus!

Surprisingly, many of Jesus's disciples decided to leave him (6:66) – although it is clear that this does not refer to the Twelve, who are mentioned in the next verse (6:67). But many among the wider group of disciples rejected Jesus and his teachings and "no longer followed him," choosing to follow their own convictions instead.

Turning to the Twelve, Jesus then asked, "You do not want to leave too, do you?" (6:67). He may have asked this because even some among the Twelve were considering leaving, like the crowd, the religious leaders, and the other disciples. Simon Peter answered, "Lord, to whom shall we go? You have the words of eternal life" (6:68). This is the first time Peter speaks in John's Gospel. Whether or not he understood Jesus's teachings, he declared his loyalty to Jesus. Like the woman at the well and the royal official, Peter addressed Jesus as *kyrios* (translated here as "Lord"). For Peter, Jesus was now more than just a "Rabbi" – the term used by Andrew, Nathanael, Nicodemus, the disciples at the well, and the crowd (1:38, 49; 3:2; 4:31; 6:25); he was *kyrios*, Lord, and the source of eternal life. Peter acknowledged that he and the Twelve could no longer exist without Jesus (6:68). Thereafter, Peter (as a representative of the Twelve) made a monumental confession: "We have come to believe and to know that you are the Holy One of God" (6:69). In the Synoptic Gospels, it is only evil or unclean spirits who acknowledge Jesus as the "Holy One of God" (Mark 1:24; Luke 4:34), and in those instances, Jesus immediately commands them to be silent. But when Peter made this confession, Jesus did not silence him. Peter's statement emphasizes Jesus's holiness, his begotten status, and his intimacy with God. In response, Jesus revealed that even among the chosen Twelve, one was "a devil" (6:70). The narrator explains that this refers to Judas, the son of Simon Iscariot, who would later betray Jesus (6:71). Later, Judas lost his identity as one of the "chosen" and became "a devil" because he betrayed the true bread from heaven. His actions showed that he did not believe Jesus or accept the Father's teaching. Thus Judas joined the company of the antagonists, while Peter declared the greatness of Jesus. Although churches in Asia face significant opposition – both from within and from outside – God raises up committed individuals who stand firm and proclaim his message. Many become "chosen" children of God, who hear God's voice and believe in Jesus.

JOHN 7:1–52

THE FIRST TABERNACLES DISCOURSE

John 7 and 8 outline speeches given by Jesus in Jerusalem while he was attending the Festival of Tabernacles. However, inserted between these two chapters is a curious episode, in which people bring a woman caught in adultery to Jesus to test him (7:53–8:11). Therefore, I refer to chapter 7 as "The First Tabernacles Discourse" and chapter 8 as "The Second Tabernacles Discourse."

The first Tabernacles discourse (7:1–52) unfolds in four stages: Jesus and his unbelieving brothers (7:1–9); Jesus at the Festival of Tabernacles (7:10–36); Jesus's prophecy concerning streams of living water (7:37–39); and divided opinions about Jesus (7:40–52). As Asians, we can appreciate the ongoing significance of festivals within John's Gospel since such occasions are considered joyous moments within our own communities.

7:1–9 JESUS AND HIS UNBELIEVING BROTHERS

The section (7:1–9) begins with the expression "after this" (7:1), a term that has been used before (2:12; 3:22; 5:1; 6:1).[1] In the previous section, Jesus had been in Galilee – specifically, by the Sea of Galilee and in Capernaum (6:1–71), but the narrator now states, "Jesus went around in Galilee" (7:1a). Since the narrator speaks about Jesus's family, Jesus might have been in Nazareth, where he grew up. He intentionally avoided going to Judea because the Jews were looking for an opportunity to kill him (7:1b). In Judea, the Jews were offended by Jesus's cleansing of the temple (2:13–22), the success of his ministry in the Judean countryside (3:22–36), and the Sabbath controversy (5:1–47). Even his interaction with the Samaritan woman (4:4–29) and the salvation of the Samaritans (4:39–42) would have infuriated them.

The narrator has already mentioned the Jewish Passover four times (2:13, 23; 4:45; 6:4). In between, he refers to an unnamed festival, simply calling it "one of the Jewish festivals" (5:1). Now, in verse 2, he refers to the Festival of

---

1. The NIV translates it differently: "After this" (2:12; 3:22; 7:1); "Some time later" (5:1); "Later" (5:14); and "Some time after this" (6:1).

Tabernacles or Booths (*Sukkôt*).[2] The Festival of Tabernacles is a harvest festival celebrated on the fifteenth day of Tishri in the Jewish lunisolar calendar. It is similar to the Rice Harvest festival in Bali or Indonesia (1 May to 30 June), the Mid-Autumn Festival in China, Taiwan, Singapore, and Vietnam (September–October), and the Pongal Festival in India (January). Jesus usually went to Jerusalem for the Jewish festivals. But this time, he chose to stay in Galilee because of growing opposition from the Jews. Unlike the Passover, it was not mandatory for Jewish men to go to Jerusalem for the Festival of Tabernacles.

Jesus's decision to stay in Galilee led to a dialogue between him and his brothers (7:3).[3] They urged him to go to Jerusalem for the Festival of Tabernacles – as he had done for other festivals – and demonstrate his signs and works to the disciples there (7:3). Their exhortation parallels Jesus's temptations in the wilderness (Matt 4:1–11; Luke 4:1–13). Their reasoning went like this: "No one who wants to become a public figure acts in secret. Since you are doing these things, show yourself to the world" (7:4). His brothers wanted him to act publicly in Judea and Jerusalem so that he might reveal himself to "the world."

In the honor-shame culture of his time, Jesus's role as a countercultural teacher and miracle-worker would have brought him both honor and shame – honor from those who welcomed his miracles and shame from those who opposed his ministry, especially the religious leaders in Jerusalem. Similarly, in many parts of Asia, individuals who convert from another religion to Christianity often face both honor and shame. They may face sarcasm, insults, the loss of employment or property, and sometimes even physical persecution. In such situations, Jesus's experience serves as a model for those facing such situations.[4]

The brothers' stance contrasts with that of the Samaritans. The Samaritans acknowledged Jesus as "the Savior of the world" (4:42), but the brothers said, "Show yourself to the world" (7:4b), a statement triggered by their lack of faith in their brother. As the narrator says, "Even his own brothers did not believe in him" (7:5). While the Samaritans believed without demanding any signs,

---

2. Wise says, "The underlying Hebrew is *sukkôt*, the reference being to the temporary 'huts' which were the hallmark of this festival. It is also known as 'the feast of Yahweh' (Lev 23:39), and was the most important and best attended of the pilgrimages to the sanctuary. In recognition of this importance, both within the OT (Ezek 45:25) and in postbiblical Hebrew and Aramaic it was sometimes called simply 'the feast.'" M. O. Wise, "Feasts," *DJG*, eds. Joel B. Green, Scott McKnight, and I. Howard Marshall (Downers Grove: InterVarsity Press, 1992), 237.
3. Mark lists their names as James, Joseph, Judas, and Simon (6:3).
4. Thomaskutty, "Reading John's Gospel as a Jewish-Christian Conflict Narrative," 157–60.

the brothers assumed that Jewish disciples needed to see works to believe (7:3). As Jesus declared earlier, "A prophet has no honor in his own country" (4:44).

While the brothers were indifferent to Jesus's ministry, his mother was not. She was with him at the wedding in Cana and believed that he could make it a joyous occasion (2:1–12). Later, she would stand at the foot of the cross (19:25–27). Perhaps this was why Jesus entrusted his mother to one of his disciples rather than to his brothers (19:25–27).

Jesus responded to his brothers, saying, "My time is not yet here; for you any time will do" (7:6). Throughout his ministry, Jesus spoke about his "hour" or his "time," which always aligned with the hour the Father wanted him to work (2:4; 4:21, 23; 5:25, 28). For Jesus, this was not yet the time or the hour to go to this festival. His brothers, however, were of this world and so, for them, "any time will do." Once again, the narrator points to the contrast between what is from *heaven* and what is from *earth*. To both his mother (2:4) and his brothers (7:6), Jesus explained the inner conflict he faced in performing miracles out of sync with the Father's will and timing. He worked as the Father directed – not at the request of his mother or brothers. This served as a mild rebuke to his family, reminding them that they could not involve themselves in his mission on their own terms or timing. In honor-shame cultures, changing one's religion or denomination can affect a family's social status and create conflict, which seems to have been the case here.

There was an ideological conflict between Jesus and his brothers. His brothers represent the world from below: they followed the timing of this world and conformed to worldly systems, and hence the world did not hate them. But Jesus represents the world from above: he followed his Father's timing, came to bring the world below in alignment with the world from above, and testified that the works of the world were evil, and hence the world hated him (7:7). Jesus's words were harsh but truthful. Although Jesus's brothers had witnessed his signs in Cana of Galilee and stayed with him in Capernaum after the wedding (2:12), they still did not believe in him (7:5).[5]

Jesus encouraged his brothers to go to the festival without him, explaining that he was unable to go "because my time has not yet fully come" (7:8). His "time" was the divine time – the time determined by the Father. Jesus did not rule out the possibility of attending the festival, but he waited for the Father's

---

[5]. After Jesus's resurrection and post-resurrection appearances, at least two of them become his followers and write sermons and letters that are included in the New Testament: James and Jude.

timing, which reveals that he worked according to appointed times and under the authority of the Father (7:8). After this conversation, Jesus remained in Galilee (7:9), and due to the growing opposition against him from the Jewish leaders (7:1), he was cautious.

In India, new converts to Christianity often face conflict within their families and society. They frequently experience isolation, marginalization, persecution, and mental stress because of their faith in Jesus Christ. These people can identify with Jesus, who also experienced such tensions within his family and the broader socioreligious context.

7:10–36 JESUS AT THE FEAST OF TABERNACLES

After his brothers had left for the festival, Jesus also went to Jerusalem – not publicly, but in secret (7:10). While his brothers went according to the timing of the world, Jesus moved according to the appointed time from above. The Jewish leaders, who had expected Jesus to be present at the festival and were watching for him, asked, "Where is he?" (7:11). Their intentions, however, were not as innocent as his brothers had suggested: "So that your disciples there may see the works you do" (7:3b). Instead, these religious leaders wanted to kill him (7:1). Their animosity toward Jesus had been growing steadily. Already, they had tried to kill him (5:18), grumbled against him (6:41), argued sharply with him (6:52), grumbled about him (6:61), and turned away from him (6:66). Now, once again, they were looking for a way to kill him (7:1). But it was not yet the Father's time for him to be killed in Jerusalem. That was why Jesus was hesitant to go to Jerusalem; and when he did go, he went in secret.

The crowd had contradictory views about Jesus. Some said, "He is a good man," while others said, "No, he deceives the people" (7:12). It seems likely that those who had experienced his healing and acceptance saw him as the Savior of the world (4:42). However, the disciples who had turned away from him might have seen him as a deceiver, and the religious leaders had already plotted to kill him over the Sabbath controversy (5:18). The narrator notes the growing fear among the crowd: "But no one would say anything publicly about him for fear of the leaders" (7:13). If the crowd was to publicly claim that "he is a good man," the Jewish leaders might have persecuted them and even stopped people from speaking about him.[6] On the other hand, if they

---

6. Jo-Ann Brant comments, "John uses a classic technique for creating suspense by describing fear and its effects but not the object of their fear (for example, Amos 2:14–16)." Brant, *John*, Paideia Commentaries on the New Testament (Grand Rapids: Baker Academic, 2011), 136.

called him a deceiver, those who had benefited from his miracles and signs might have protested, causing divisions and conflict. In many parts of Asia, revolutionary leaders and movements often face opposition, persecution, and even martyrdom.

The Festival of Tabernacles lasted for seven days. Halfway through the festival, Jesus went to the temple courts and began to teach (7:14). Jesus had no formal training under rabbis like Gamaliel. Yet his teachings were so different and thought-provoking that even the Jews were amazed and asked, "How did this man get such learning without having been taught?" (7:15).[7] Jewish rabbis typically acquired knowledge through years of study and training, but of Jesus proved more brilliant than many of the rabbis of his time.

Jesus's teachings were unique because of their source: "My teaching is not my own. It comes from the one who sent me" (7:16). While the Jewish rabbis acquired their wisdom through study and training, Jesus spoke with heavenly wisdom from above – wisdom from his Father. Yet his wisdom was not exclusive: "Anyone who chooses to do the will of God will find out whether my teaching comes from God or whether I speak on my own" (7:17). Those who genuinely seek to do the will of God will recognize that Jesus's teachings are from God and not just his own.

There are two kinds of glory. There is human glory that comes *from below* – "Whoever speaks on their own does so to gain personal glory" – and divine glory that comes *from above* – "he who seeks the glory of the one who sent him" (7:18a). Jesus made a clear distinction between human glory and divine glory. Unlike the religious leaders, who sought human praise and glory, Jesus sought the glory of "the one who sent him." That is what makes him "a man of truth" with "nothing false about him" (7:18b).

Once again, Jesus called upon Moses as a witness: "Has not Moses given you the law? Yet not one of you keeps the law. Why are you trying to kill me?" (7:19). Moses had commanded, "You shall not murder" (Exod 20:13; Deut 5:17). But since the Jewish leaders were looking for a way to kill Jesus (7:1, 19), they had failed to keep the law.

It is the crowd, rather than the religious leaders, who then respond. Seemingly unaware of the religious leaders' intentions (7:1), they said, "You are demon-possessed . . . Who is trying to kill you?" (7:20). The leaders had tried to kill Jesus for breaking the Sabbath and claiming equality with God (5:18), but the crowd did not seem to know this and attributed his fear to

---

[7]. Mark explains he taught with authority, unlike their teachers of the law (1:22).

the influence of a demon.[8] In truth, the leaders' desire to kill Jesus, thereby breaking Moses's commandment, was influenced by the evil one.

Jesus then reminded the crowd of the incident that had taken place near Jerusalem – the healing of the paralytic by the pool of Bethesda (5:1–18) – which had prompted the leaders to start plotting to kill him for breaking their Sabbath regulations and claiming equality with God. He said, "I did one miracle, and you are all amazed" (7:21). They were amazed not in a positive way but negatively, seeking to kill him because he had healed on the Sabbath, which they viewed as a violation of Moses's law. Jesus pointed out the inconsistency of their argument: If, as they claimed, Jesus had broken the Mosaic law by healing a man on the Sabbath, how could the Jews justify circumcising a boy on the Sabbath (7:22–23). Jewish male children were circumcised on the eighth day. Even if the eighth day fell on a Sabbath, the rabbis went ahead with the circumcision. So, how could they be angry with Jesus for healing a man's whole body on the Sabbath (7:23b)?[9]

A common belief at the time was that Moses had instituted the practice of circumcision among the people of Israel (see Acts 15:1). Jesus corrected this misunderstanding, reminding the Jews that circumcision originated with the patriarchs. Long before Moses, God had commanded their forefather Abraham to circumcise himself and all his male descendants as a sign of the covenant (Gen 17:10–14). If Jesus's act of healing on the Sabbath (5:1–18) was viewed as a violation of the command to keep the Sabbath holy, then so should the Jewish practice of circumcision on the Sabbath (7:22–23). The Sabbath was made for human beings and intended for their wholeness; it was not meant to be a burdensome religious obligation. While circumcision on the Sabbath involved cutting the human body and shedding blood, Jesus's healing activity made a human being whole (7:23). Instead of focusing on religious duties or dogmas, we are called to focus on actions that truly liberate people and fulfill God's mission.

Jesus introduced a paradigmatic shift in how people were to judge. The Jews judged things based on appearances, leading to partial and distorted judgments. Jesus said, "Stop judging by mere appearances, but instead judge correctly" (7:24). James L. Resseguie states, "Instead of accepting approval and honor from one another, Jesus advocates a different category of glory (5:44). Instead of evaluating other persons and activities according to human

---

8. Unlike the crowd, the Jerusalemites knew the leaders were trying to kill Jesus (7:25).
9. Ironically, while Jesus saved a life on a Sabbath, the Jews were attempting to take his life.

standards, he advocates correct judgment (7:24)."[10] Jesus criticized the dogmatic and ceremonial religiosity of the Jews.

The people of Jerusalem raised a question: "Isn't this the man whom they are trying to kill?" (7:25; compare 7:11, 19). From the tone of their speech, we can distinguish them from both the religious leaders, who were plotting to kill him, and the crowd at large, who were unaware of their leaders' intentions (7:20). These Jews knew about the leaders' plot and were amazed at Jesus's boldness: "Here he is, speaking publicly, and they are not saying a word to him" (7:26a). They went on to wonder, "Have the authorities really concluded that he is the Messiah?" (7:26b). Their curiosity suggests that they were anticipating the arrival of the Messiah. Earlier, the Jewish religious leaders had asked John the Baptizer if he was the Messiah (1:19–20) and if he was not, why he baptized people (1:25). Andrew, a disciple of John, had told his brother Peter, "We have found the Messiah" (1:41). The Samaritan woman, too, had awaited the arrival of the Messiah. She said, "'I know that Messiah' (called Christ) 'is coming. When he comes, he will explain everything to us'" (4:25) and later wondered if Jesus was the Messiah because he prophesied about her life (4:29). The Jerusalemites were certainly anticipating the arrival of the Messiah, especially after John the Baptizer's declaration: "I am not the Messiah but am sent ahead of him" (3:28). Yet they were unwilling to accept Jesus as the Messiah because of their beliefs about his origin – "where this man is from" (7:27). Earlier, when Jesus claimed to be the bread that "came down from heaven" (6:41), they responded, "Is this not Jesus, the son of Joseph, whose father and mother we know? How can he now say, 'I came down from heaven'?" (6:42). What they knew of his origin, his parents, and his birthplace led them to question how he could be the Messiah because their tradition taught that "when the Messiah comes, no one will know where he is from" (7:27b).

"The view of these people regarding the Messiah that *no one will know where he comes from* reflects the idea that the origin of the Messiah is a mystery. In the Talmud (*b. Sanhedrin* 97a) Rabbi Zera taught: "'Three come unawares: Messiah, a found article, and a scorpion.' Apparently, OT prophetic passages like Mal 3:1 and Dan 9:25 were interpreted by some as indicating a sudden appearance of Messiah. It appears that this was not a universal view: The scribes summoned by Herod at the coming of the Magi in Matt 2 knew that the Messiah was to be born in Bethlehem. It is important to remember that

---

10. James L. Resseguie, *The Strange Gospel: Narrative Design and Point of View in John*, BINS 56 (Leiden: Brill, 2001), 117.

Jewish messianic expectations in the early 1st century were not monolithic."[11] Since these Jerusalemites believed that the Messiah's origin would be unknown, they struggled to accept Jesus as the Messiah.

Jesus acknowledged that their understanding of his birthplace and his parents was accurate: "Yes, you know me, and you know where I am from" (7:28a).[12] But that was only part of the truth. They did not recognize his authority or know the one who had sent him (7:28b). In contrast, Jesus knew him because he was "from him" and was sent by him (7:29). Jesus argued that although these people knew his human origin and background, they did not know the Father who had sent him. Wright says, "Often people look at Jesus and draw conclusions about him based on faulty ideas of God and the world."[13] The Jerusalemites saw only his earthly connections and failed to recognize his heavenly origin, a tendency that continues today and often leads to misinterpretations of the person and work of Christ.

While the crowd was afraid to speak publicly about Jesus because of the religious leaders (7:13), the Jewish leaders were afraid to act publicly against Jesus because of the people (7:26). At the same time, the Jerusalemites were unable to seize Jesus even though they wanted to because the divine hour had not come yet (7:30).

Although many opposed Jesus, many others believed in him (7:31a). They had expected the Messiah to perform signs, and they saw Jesus performing such signs (7:31b). His signs – turning water into wine (2:1–11), healing the royal official's son (4:46–54), healing the invalid (5:1–18), feeding the five thousand (6:1–15), and walking on water (6:16–21) – convinced many in the crowd to believe that Jesus was indeed the Messiah (7:31). Belief in Jesus as the Messiah came through hearing about him or personally witnessing his signs.

The narrator's focus now shifts to the Pharisees. The Pharisees had earlier questioned John the Baptizer about his identity (1:24–25). Later, Nicodemus, who was a Pharisee, had visited Jesus seeking answers (3:1). When Jesus heard that the Pharisees were concerned about his growing influence, he left Judea and returned to Galilee (4:1). From this point in the narrative, the Pharisees begin to play a more prominent role in challenging Jesus (8:13), drawing conclusions about his identity (9:16), and, ultimately, being instrumental in his arrest and death (18:3). Here, in John 7, when the Pharisees heard that some

---

11. The NET Bible, footnote.
12. The narrator says Jesus cried out, informing the readers it was a passionate speech.
13. Wright, *John for Everyone*, 102.

had come to believe in Jesus because of his miracles and signs, they joined forces with the chief priests and sent temple guards to arrest Jesus (7:32). Their shift in strategy – from wanting to kill Jesus to attempting to arrest him – was because of Jesus's growing popularity among the people.

Jesus persistently proclaimed his divine origin and oneness with the Father: "I am with you for only a short time, and then I am going to the one who sent me" (7:33). Jesus would reiterate this message later when speaking to his disciples (16:16–28), emphasizing the contrast between his eternal presence with the Father (1:1) and his temporary presence on earth (1:14). This "short time" refers to his earthly and incarnational life of nearly 33 years. After his departure to the Father, they would search for him but not find him (7:34a). Furthermore, they could not go where he was going unless they believed (7:34b). Jesus offered the Jews, the Jerusalemites, and the Pharisees an opportunity to experience God's presence. If they rejected this opportunity, they would lose it forever.

As usual, "the crowd, however, interprets the riddle incorrectly – at a literal level."[14] They assumed that Jesus was going to the Greeks to teach them. Blum writes, "'Greeks' means not only just people of Greece or Greek-speaking peoples but generally non-Jews or heathen (compare 'Greek' and 'Jew' in Col 3:11)."[15] Since the crowd was not willing to recognize Jesus as someone sent from the Father, they were unable to understand that he was going back to the Father. Instead, they assumed that he must be going to the Greeks – a people group they usually avoided – and that this was why they would not be able to see him or go where he was going (7:36). The Jews evaluated Jesus according to worldly standards; therefore, they misunderstood his heavenly origin. Jesus was continually misunderstood and unjustly targeted by the Jewish leaders, the crowd, the Jerusalemites, and the Pharisees. But some continued to believe in him, acknowledging that he had come from God and was going back to the Father.

Christians today continue to face opposition and various forms of persecution attempts to silence their voices, hatred, false accusations, unjust judgments, death threats, and even arrest. Like the Lord Jesus, they are called to stand firm, knowing that they do not belong to this world but to the world above and trusting that their heavenly Father cares for them.

---

14. Stibbe, *John's Gospel*, 23.
15. Blum, *John*, 301.

7:37–39 PROPHECY CONCERNING STREAMS OF LIVING WATER

The temporal setting is the last day of the festival. On that day, Jesus said, "Let anyone who is thirsty come to me and drink" (7:37). Earlier, Jesus had given the same invitation to the Samaritan woman at the well (4:7–15). Now he addresses the Jews in Jerusalem. On the last day of the Festival of Tabernacles, the Jews observed a ritual called *Simchat Beit HaShoeivah*, during which the priests went in procession to the Pool of Siloam, drew water, brought it back to the temple, and poured it on the altar.[16] That water was temporal, and this ritual had to be repeated every year, just as the Samaritan woman had to return daily to the well to draw water. In contrast, Jesus invites people to come to him and drink the living water that he alone can give.

What Jesus said next has been hotly debated, resulting in two opposing views. The first and most common view – known as the "Eastern Interpretation" – sees the believer as the source of the rivers of living water. This view is reflected in the NIV translation: "Let anyone who is thirsty come to me and drink. Whoever believes in me, as Scripture has said, rivers of living water will flow from within them" (7:37–38). This interpretation is supported by Eastern church fathers like Origen and Athanasius, as well as by contemporary scholars like Carson, Lightfoot, Lindars, and Morris. Leon Morris writes, "When the believer comes to Christ and drinks, he not only slakes his thirst but receives such an abundant supply that veritable rivers flow from him."[17]

The second view – known as the "Western Interpretation" – sees Jesus as the source of the rivers of living water. The NET reflects this view: "If anyone is thirsty, let him come to me, and let the one who believes in me drink. Just as the scripture says, 'From within him will flow rivers of living water.'" Western church fathers like Justin, Hippolytus, Tertullian, and Irenaeus, along with contemporary scholars like Beasley-Murray, Brown, Bullinger, Bultmann, Dodd, and Dunn, support this view.

Those who hold the first view cite John 4:14 and 14:12 in support. Jesus said, "The water I give them will become in them a spring of water welling up to eternal life" (4:14). He also said that those who believe in him would do even greater work than he did (14:12). Those who hold the second view refer to John 7:39 and argue that it is extremely difficult to see believers as

---

16. Alfred Edersheim, *The Temple, Its Ministry and Services* (Peabody, MA: Hendrickson 2006), 220–27.
17. Morris, *Gospel according to John*, 424–25.

the "source" of the Spirit for others and that Jesus alone is the source of both living water (4:10) and the Spirit (14:16; 20:22):

> The frequency of Exodus motifs in the Fourth Gospel (paschal lamb, bronze serpent, manna from heaven) leads quite naturally to the supposition that the author is here drawing on the account of Moses striking the rock in the wilderness to bring forth water (Num 20:8 ff). That such imagery was readily identified with Jesus in the early church is demonstrated by Paul's understanding of the event in 1 Cor 10:4. Jesus is the Rock from which the living water – the Spirit – will flow.[18]

Perhaps a compromise is possible. Jesus is the true source of both the living water and the Holy Spirit. But those who believe in Jesus become secondary sources through whom others hear the gospel, believe, and receive the Holy Spirit. Regardless of which view we adopt, Jesus's call was for people to believe in him so that they may receive the living water.

Jesus's promise of living water redirects his audience from the Jewish ablution rites to the eternal purification and satisfaction he offers (7:38). Jesus used the metaphor of water to refer to the experience of the Holy Spirit. Those who believe in him will receive such a spiritual experience (7:39a).[19] In this way, Christology (the study of Christ) and pneumatology (the study of the Spirit) are interwoven to explain the experience of salvation.

The narrator does not fully explain the experience of the Holy Spirit until John 14–16. However, he says that believers will receive the Holy Spirit when the Son of Man is glorified (7:39b). Since Jesus had not yet been glorified, the Spirit had not yet been given to anyone (7:39c). The outpouring of the Holy Spirit, which is predicted here, will be described in greater detail in chapters 14–16. As in the Festival of Tabernacles, many Asian religions also use water in their sacred rituals. This story can be retold in such contexts to draw people of other faiths toward Christ, who is the true living water.

---

18. See NET footnote a, for this passage, via BibleGateway, https://www.biblegateway.com/passage/?search=John%207%3A38-40&version=NET.
19. Wright, *John for Everyone*, 105.

John

7:40–52 DIVIDED OPINIONS ABOUT JESUS

The final section of John 7 reveals diverse opinions that existed among the people about Jesus. His invitation to believe in him and receive the living water (7:37–38) prompted them to express these views.

The first group affirmed Jesus's identity, saying, "Surely this man is the Prophet" (7:40). They were convinced that Jesus could be trusted and that he was the prophet they had been waiting for.

The second group affirmed, "He is the Messiah" (7:41a). Like the Samaritan woman, who initially saw Jesus as a prophet (4:19) but later identified him as the Messiah (4:25), these Jews, too, linked the coming of the prophet with the coming of the Messiah. Since they already regarded John the Baptizer as a prophet, perhaps they were inclined to view Jesus as the Messiah.

The third group were skeptical: "How can the Messiah come from Galilee?" (7:41b). Unlike the first two groups, who accepted Jesus as the eschatological prophet or the Messiah, the third group had considerable difficulty in accepting him as the Messiah. In Asia, many consider Jesus an ideal teacher, one among many gods, a good man, a social reformer, or a liberator – but not the Son of God or the only Redeemer. Similarly, the third group did not accept Jesus as their Messiah. They put forward a scriptural argument: "Does not Scripture say that the Messiah will come from David's descendants and from Bethlehem, the town where David lived?" (7:42). Evidently, they were not aware that Jesus had been born in Bethlehem and was a descendant of David, assuming instead that he was a Galilean from Nazareth. That was also how Philip introduced Jesus to Nathanael (1:45), and how those in the Garden of Gethsemane would later refer to him (18:5). Although they knew he was the son of Joseph (6:42), they did not know that both Joseph and Jesus were David's descendants.

In this way, the people were divided over Jesus (7:43). But even though some wanted to seize him, they hesitated to lay a hand on him (7:44). The repeated attempts to arrest and kill Jesus anticipate the events leading to his crucifixion.

Meanwhile, the temple guards returned to the chief priests and the Pharisees without arresting Jesus (7:45a). When asked, "Why didn't you bring him in?" (7:45b), they replied, "No one ever spoke the way this man does" (7:46). Their response reveals that Jesus's speech was persuasive and drew the attention of many. The Pharisees' retort – "You mean he has deceived you also?" – implies that they considered Jesus a deceiver who could fool even the temple guards (7:47). They also concluded that none of the Pharisees or religious rulers believed in Jesus and that only the mob – who did not know the law and were, therefore, considered accursed – believed in Jesus (7:48–49). In the eyes of the Pharisees, not only was Jesus a deceiver, but those who believed in him were under the curse of the law.

At that moment, Nicodemus – who was also a Pharisee – spoke up (7:50). Nicodemus had previously visited Jesus and engaged in a discussion with him (3:1–21), and that discussion might have left him uncertain about the Pharisees' claim that Jesus was a deceiver. Nicodemus, citing their own law, appealed for a fair hearing for Jesus: "Does our law condemn a man without first hearing him to find out what he has been doing?" (7:51). This was the very reason Nicodemus had gone to Jesus earlier – to find out what he had been doing. Now, he urged the rest of the Pharisees to do the same. The Jewish authorities were attempting to arrest Jesus, and even kill him, without following the proper legal process. This violated both Jewish and Pharisaical laws.

Nicodemus's speech in favor of Jesus infuriated the Jewish authorities. Although they knew that Nicodemus was not from Galilee as Jesus was, they insulted him: "Are you from Galilee, too?" (7:52a). This echoes Nathanael's words: "Nazareth! Can anything good come from there?" (1:46). The Pharisees then stated their theological position: "Look into it, and you will find that a prophet does not come out of Galilee" (7:52). But this was untrue – Jonah, for example, had been from Galilee. But they were unwilling to accept that God could raise up a prophet, far less the Messiah, from this despised region.

Asian Christians can learn several lessons from the first Tabernacles discourse (7:1–52). First, like Jesus, we should operate within God's timing, not on our own. Second, Jesus is not a deceiver but the Savior of the world. Third, in all we do, we should not work for our own personal glory but for God's glory. Fourth, we should focus on doing good rather than unquestioningly following traditions such as Sabbath observances. Fifth, Jesus alone reveals the Father to the people. Finally, Jesus offers living water – that is, the Holy Spirit – to all who believe in him.

JOHN 7:53–8:11
JESUS AND THE ADULTEROUS WOMAN

The story of Jesus and the adulterous woman can be approached on two levels: the text of John 7:53–8:11 and the interpretation of that text. Asian readers may understand the adulterous woman's role and status as a symbol of dehumanized womanhood. The story invites the reader to reflect on the marginalization of Asian women from a liberative perspective.[1]

7:53–8:11 THE TEXT OF JOHN

Scholars agree that John wrote the passage known as the *Pericope Adulterae* (7:53–8:11) for the following reasons: first, some of the some of the earlier and most reliable manuscripts of John do not contain it (example, P^{66}, P^{75}, ℵ, B, 053, 0141, and 0211); second, those manuscript that do include it often mark it with asterisks or obeli to suggest doubt; and third, the passage is placed in five different locations in different manuscripts (after 7:36; 7:44; 7:52; 21:25; and after Luke 21:38).[2]

Wright draws a comparison between this passage and the story in 1 Kings 3:16–28. Just as King Solomon revealed his remarkable wisdom in a seemingly impossible situation, Jesus demonstrated his wisdom when faced with a difficult dilemma.[3] Johannine narratives often taken the form of long discourses, except in the case of the Cana events (2:1–11; 4:46–54) and this *Pericope Adulterae*. Gail R. O'Day observes, "John 7:53–8:11 is a story without a time or place, a story to be read on its own terms without sustained reference to its larger literary context."[4] If viewed in this way, John 7:53–8:11 appears to be

---

1. For a postcolonial interpretation of the text, see Leticia A. Guardiola-Sáenz, "Border-crossing and its Redemptive Power in John 7:53–8:11: A Cultural Reading of Jesus and the Accused," *John and Postcolonialism: Travel, Space and Power*, eds. Musa W. Dube and Jeffrey L. Staley (London: Sheffield Academic Press, 2002), 129–52.
2. A more detailed discussion about the text and the content of John 7:53–8:11, see Chris Keith, *The Pericope Adulterae, the Gospel of John, and the Literacy of Jesus* (Leiden/Boston: Brill, 2009).
3. Wright, *John for Everyone*, 111.
4. Gail R. O'Day, "John 7:53–8:11: A Study in Misreading," *Journal of Biblical Literature* 111 (1992): 631.

a story without context – that is, it neither flows naturally from the previous passage or leads smoothly into what follows.

However, some scholars suggest that the *Pericope Adulterae* continues the theme of Jesus as "judge" (5:19–47; 7:16–24) and introduces the themes of Jesus as the "light of the world" (8:12; 9:5) and the "good shepherd" (10:1–18).[5] In the immediate context of 7:53–8:11, Jesus brought conviction to the hearts of the Pharisees (8:9, 41) and invited them to acknowledge his identity as "the light of the world" (8:12). There seems to be a logical progression in the sequence of themes in this section: living water (7:37–39), merciful judge (7:53–8:11), light of the world (8:12–9:41), good shepherd (10:1–18), and life-giver (11:1–54).[6] Although such an interpretation of the pericope is possible within the framework of the narrative, we cannot simply dismiss the absence of this passage in the earliest manuscripts, the marking of the text with asterisks or obeli to indicate doubt, and its placement in five different locations. Blum argues, "Both the textual evidence and stylistic data in the passage indicate that this is non-Johannine material."[7] Asian readers may understand the story as a narrative of liberation, a pericope empowering women, and an encounter that illustrates Jesus's attitude toward both the sinful and the self-righteous.

AN INTERPRETATION OF THE TEXT

The events of John 7:10–52 took place in and around the temple. Thereafter, Jesus retired to the Mount of Olives in the evening and returned at dawn to the temple courts, where he sat down to teach (8:1–2). The setting for the story of the woman caught in adultery is the temple courts. Jesus's posture in sitting down to teach and the gathering of people around him demonstrate his popularity as a rabbinic figure. Jesus's opponents devised several strategies to take him into custody, but they were unsuccessful. Factors such as his popular support among the crowd, his prophetic image, the signs he performed, his elusive nature, and the timing of his "hour" prevented them from arresting Jesus.

While Jesus was teaching, the teachers of the law and the Pharisees brought before him a woman caught in adultery.[8] They made her stand before Jesus

---

5. Maniparampil, *Reading the Fourth Gospel*, 273.
6. Maniparampil, 274.
7. Blum, *John*, 346.
8. Ridderbos comments, "'The scribes and Pharis' is common in the Synoptics; John does not have it and in such contexts speaks rather of 'the Pharis.' 'Scribes' refers to a class; 'Pharis' to a party." Ridderbos, *Gospel of John*, 287.

(8:3) and asked a question to trap him: "Teacher, this woman was caught in the act of adultery. In the Law Moses commanded us to stone such women. Now what do you say?" (8:4–5). Their intention was to trap him (8:6a), not to uphold the law of Moses (Lev 20:10–21; Num 5:11–31; Deut 22:22–24). Just as some Indian movies feature dramatic duels between protagonists and antagonists, this pericope reflects the dramatic tension between Jesus and the religious leaders.

If Jesus agreed with their interpretation of the law, they could punish the woman according to their tradition. But if Jesus did not condemn her to death, they could accuse him of failing to abide by Moses's law and seek to have him killed. Either way, one person could be put to death. Testing can be positive, as when Jesus tested the disciples with the intention of strengthening their faith (6:6). But Jesus's opponents were testing him with evil intentions (8:6a).[9] They were trying to use this woman's case to build a charge against Jesus. Jesus ignored them, bent down, and wrote on the ground with his finger (8:6b) – an action that recalls God writing the Ten Commandments with his finger (Exod 31:18; Deut 9:10). The content of Jesus's writing is uncertain.

The teachers of the law and the Pharisees were persistent and continued to provoke Jesus with their questions. Jesus faced this challenging situation with boldness, standing straight and facing his opponents. He challenged their integrity with a provocative command: "Let any one of you who is without sin be the first to throw a stone at her" (8:7). Moses had commanded that those guilty of adultery be stoned, and the Jews were prepared to fulfill that command. But Jesus effectively argued that the accusers also deserved punishment since they, too, were sinful (8:7b).[10] Jesus's challenge is obvious: "Do you dare to stone her?" He then returned to stooping down and writing on the ground (8:8).

Surprisingly, upon hearing Jesus's words, the accusers began to leave "one at a time, the older ones first, until only Jesus was left, with the woman still standing there" (8:9). Their leaving reveals that they were challenged by Jesus's speech. They left because they recognized that they, too, were lawbreakers like the woman. They left beginning with the oldest, implying that even the religious leaders – who were usually the elders in the community – recognized the truth of Jesus's statement. At that time, Judaism was corrupt from

---

9. Keener, *The IVP Bible Background Commentary*, 284.
10. Gench, *Back to the Well: Women's Encounters with Jesus in the Gospels* (Louisville: Westminster John Knox Press, 2004), 136–59.

top to bottom, and the religious leaders were often mere teachers rather than practitioners of the Mosaic law. The statement "only Jesus was left, with the woman still standing there" is ironic. It intended to contrast the sinless Jesus with the sinful woman.

Although the opponents targeted Jesus and used the woman to trap him, Jesus's knowledge and application of the law defeated them, leaving Jesus and the woman alone. According to Katrina Meynes, "Throughout Korean history, a woman's self-worth and honor were measured by her chastity and adherence to men. Females have consistently been expected to be obedient, fertile, impalpable, and above all, sexually subsistent."[11] Men, on the other hand, could be promiscuous. The *Pericope Adulterae* depicts Jesus as exercising justice and mercy, placing all sinners on equal footing so that all may seek mercy.

Just as Jesus had straightened up to speak to the Jewish leaders (8:7), he now straightened up to address the woman (8:10a). Just as he had spoken boldly with the men, he now spoke directly to the woman: "Woman, where are they? Has no one condemned you?" (8:10b). Jesus's concern was to engage the woman in conversation and leave her with a lesson. In Asia, Christians should stand against atrocities committed against the marginalized, while engaging them in conversation and empowering them to achieve self-actualization. The woman's response – "No one, sir" (8:11a) – conveys her relief in being freed from condemnation and punishment (8:10b). Jesus said, "Then neither do I condemn you . . . Go now and leave your life of sin" (8:11b). The Jews were unable to punish the woman, and Jesus refused to condemn her. Just as the Jews were commanded to stop sinning before judging others, the woman was commanded to stop sinning. This pericope calls us to practice justice, mercy, and truthfulness regardless of people's caste, class, or gender. It is a powerful paradigm against discrimination and marginalization.

---

11. Katrina Maynes, "Korean Perceptions of Chastity, Gender Roles, and Libido; From Kisaengs to the Twenty First Century," *Grand Valley Journal of History* 1, no. 1 (2012), article 2, https://scholarworks.gvsu.edu/gvjh/vol1/iss1/2.

JOHN 8:12–59
THE SECOND TABERNACLES DISCOURSE

The second Tabernacles discourse (8:12–59) contains four speeches by Jesus: he presents himself as the light of the world (8:12–20), foretells his death (8:21–30), speaks about true discipleship and the freedom found in him (8:31–38), and teaches that he existed before Abraham (8:39–59). The theme of light is particularly significant in Asia, where several religious festivals incorporate the symbolism of light.

8:12–20 JESUS IS THE LIGHT OF THE WORLD

On the last and greatest day of the Festival of Tabernacles, Jesus spoke about being the source of living water (7:37). If John 8:1 – where the narrator speaks of Jesus going to the Mount of Olives and returning to the temple courts at dawn the next day – is authentic, then this discourse took place the day after the Festival of Tabernacles. If John 8:1 is not authentic, then this discourse took place on the same day – the last and greatest day of the festival. Regardless, we will treat this passage as part of the "Second Tabernacles Discourse" because Jesus's discourse on light parallels his earlier discourse on water.

Jesus declared, "I am the light of the world. Whoever follows me will never walk in darkness but will have the light of life" (8:12). This echoes his earlier call: "Let anyone who is thirsty come to me and drink. Whoever believes in me . . . rivers of living water will flow from within them" (7:37–38). The Festival of Tabernacles was associated with two symbols – water and light. Jesus's claim to be the source of living water fulfilled the symbolic water-pouring ceremony since he alone is able to purify people's hearts (7:37–38). Similarly, the second symbol associated with the festival – light – also finds its eschatological fulfillment in Jesus.[1] During this feast, one of their most significant national festivals, Jews illuminate their houses and streets with various lights. Jesus's presence in the temple during the festival and his declaration that he is the light of the world drew the people's attention away from the festival toward himself as the universal and eternal light who tabernacled among

---

1. Teresa Okure, "John," *The International Bible Commentary*, ed. William R. Farmer (Bangalore: Theological Publications in India, 1998), 1551.

the people (1:9, 14). While the Jewish festival was bound to a specific time and space, Jesus, as the light of the world, transcends all chronological and geographical limitations. Whoever follows Jesus will never walk in darkness but will have the light of life (8:12; compare 1:4). The contrast between light and darkness and the identification of light with life were already introduced in the *Prologue* (1:4–5).

This is Jesus's second "I am" saying. The first was "I am the bread of life" (6:35, 48, 51). Implied here is also the message that he is the source of the living water, which he also offered the Samaritan woman (4:10–13) and the Jerusalemites (7:37–38).

Previously, Jesus had argued that he was not his own witness (5:31) but that John the Baptizer, Jesus's own works, and the Father were his witnesses. The Pharisees now return to this topic: "Here you are, appearing as your own witness; your testimony is not valid" (8:13). The Pharisees were unwilling to accept the testimony of Jesus, but Jesus insisted that his testimony was true because he knew where he came from and where he was going (8:14a). Sadly, the Pharisees did not know where Jesus came from or where he was going (8:14b), which was why they did not accept his testimony or understand his identity. The Pharisees judged people by human (*from below*) standards; but Jesus's judgment is neither hasty nor based on human standards (8:15). When he does judge, his judgment comes *from above* because he does not judge by himself but in collaboration with the Father (8:16). Just as the Son shares glory, grace, and truth in full measure with the Father (1:14–17), he also shares in divine judgment. Jesus referred to their "own Law," given by God, which affirms that "the testimony of two witnesses is true" (8:17). As though this were a legal setting, Jesus presented two witnesses: his own testimony as the Son of God – whom they had rejected – and the testimony of the Father who sent him (8:18).

Once again, the Pharisees challenged Jesus: "Where is your father?" (8:19a). Their rejection of the Son had led to their failure to recognize the Father who had sent him. Jesus made it clear that they knew neither him nor his Father and affirmed that knowing Jesus means knowing the Father (8:19b). It is only through the Son that people can come to know the Father.

Jesus's teaching took place near the temple treasury (8:20a). Although he was in the temple courts, no one seized him because his hour had not yet come (8:20b). The themes of arrest and the approaching hour continue throughout the Gospel.

John 8:12–59

8:21–30 Jesus's Foretelling of His Death

Yet again, Jesus spoke to the Jewish authorities about his departure from this world. He invited them to search for him before his departure. As they themselves could not go to the place where Jesus was going, they could not be set free from their sin (8:21). Their categorical neglect of the Son of God and their unfamiliarity with the Father would lead to eternal damnation. When Jesus healed the invalid, he had warned him to "stop sinning" (5:14). Similarly, he warned the Jews that they would die in their sin if they did not accept and believe in him (8:21).

Jesus had already declared his departure (7:34). At that time, the crowd misunderstood him, thinking he was going to the dispersed or Greek-speaking Jews (7:35). Here again, the Jews misunderstand him, thinking he was going to kill himself (8:22). Jesus spoke eternal truths from an all-knowing perspective, but the Jews were trapped in misunderstanding. Realizing their confusion, Jesus declared, "You are from below; I am from above. You are of this world; I am not of this world" (8:23). Once again, the *from below* and *from above* contrast is evident. Jesus also said, "I told you that you would die in your sins; if you do not believe that I am he, you will indeed die in your sins" (8:24). Jesus was their Redeemer or Savior, as the Samaritans had already acknowledged (4:42). But if the Jews failed to believe him, they would remain in their sins and, ultimately, die in their sins. True belief required recognizing him as equal to their "I am" God. Witherington says, "Here at 8:24 we have the absolute use of *ego eimi* [I am he], which likely is drawing on Isaiah 41:4–6 and on God's designation, involving a possible play on the manner God revealed himself to Moses in Exodus 3:14."[2] The salvation Jesus offers can only be attained through believing in him. Those who neglect the Savior will die in their sins. People are given the choice either to believe in Jesus and be delivered from death or to reject him and embrace death. Those who reject the messenger and the message of salvation will continue to remain in bondage to sin.

The dialogue continued, and they asked, "Who are you?" (8:25a). Since Jesus had repeatedly told them who he was, he said, "Just what I have been telling you from the beginning" (8:25b). Although the "I am" had spoken to them, they were unable to recognize him. When Jesus said that he had much to say in condemnation of them, he was offering them an opportunity to repent and believe in him (8:26a). Jesus has every right to condemn the world since he possesses authority from above, but he remains patient because he

---

2. Witherington, *John's Wisdom*, 175.

longs to see the salvation of the world. Jesus went on to say that his judgment would be a declaration of the trustworthy Father who had sent him and that what he heard from the Father, he would proclaim to the world (8:26b). As he had been saying all along, he was not operating on his own but repeating what he saw and heard from the Father; even judgment came from the Father, not from Jesus alone.

Once again, the Jews did not understand that Jesus was talking about the Father (8:27). Jesus then described his death on the cross: "When you have lifted up the Son of Man, then you will know that I am he and that I do nothing on my own but speak just what the Father has taught me" (8:28). The reference to being "lifted up" foretold his crucifixion. At that time, they would realize that he was who he claimed to be and that he had spoken only what the Father had taught him. The Jews would then realize that Jesus acted not on his own authority but according to the Father's instructions.

Once again, Jesus expressed the Father–Son relationship in convincing terms: the Father was with the Son; he had not left the Son alone; and the Son always did what was pleasing to the Father (8:29). Jesus was the manifestation of the heavenly Father, sent to establish the divine will in the world and to glorify God's name. Although the Son was in the world *from below*, because of his integral relationship with the Father, all his actions were attuned to the world *from above*. As Jesus spoke these words, many believed in him (8:30). Somehow, they began to understand and opened their hearts to Jesus and his teachings.

8:31–38 TRUE DISCIPLESHIP AND FREEDOM IN CHRIST

This section summarizes the dialogue between Jesus and the Jews who believed in him (8:31–32) and Jesus and the Jews who did not believe in him (8:33–38).

To the Jews who believed in him, Jesus said, "If you hold to my teaching, you are really my disciples. Then you will know the truth, and the truth will set you free" (8:31–32). This was an exhortation to keep believing in him, even amid persecutions they might face from other Jews who did not believe in him. As the book of Acts reveals, many believers even lost their lives because they believed in Jesus. So the Lord encouraged them to remain faithful regardless of what they faced.

Those who did not believe in Jesus missed his teaching on true discipleship and knowledge of the truth. Instead, they focused on the issue of freedom: "We are Abraham's descendants and have never been slaves of anyone. How can you say that we shall be set free?" (8:33). Had they forgotten the enslavement in

Egypt and the exodus? Had they forgotten the two major exiles to Assyria and Babylonia? Yet they boldly claimed they had never been enslaved to anyone.

Jesus countered their claim: "Very truly I tell you, everyone who sins is a slave to sin" (8:34). Not only had they been slaves to various nations in the past, they were also slaves to sin in the present. But that slavery could be transformed into sonship or a familial relationship: "Now a slave has no permanent place in the family, but a son belongs to it forever" (8:35). Slaves are not permanent members of a household; they can be dismissed at will. But sons and daughters belong in any household, especially in God's household. Only the heavenly Son can grant true freedom: "If the Son sets you free, you will be free indeed" (8:36). Jesus made it clear that only he could free them from the grip of sin and slavery.

Their sin was apparent: They wanted to kill Jesus. He said, "I know that you are Abraham's descendants. Yet you are looking for a way to kill me, because you have no room for my word" (8:37). Abraham acted in obedience to the word of God, but Abraham's descendants had no place for Jesus's word and attempted to kill the Son of God. As Stibbe notes, "Jesus uses *paradeigmata* (examples) from Jewish history (Abraham, 8:33–58) and everyday life (for example, the short parable in 8:35) to support his argument."[3] Their murderous intentions and plans proved that they remained in their sins and were still slaves. Their freedom would only come if they stopped plotting to kill Jesus.

Jesus then revealed how he knew that they were still in their sin and slavery: "I am telling you what I have seen in the Father's presence" (8:38a). In other words, Jesus was declaring the things that he had witnessed in the Father's presence, and he declared these heavenly truths in earthly terms. Although the Jews had been commanded to do things according to the word of God, they were acting on what they had heard from their "father" (8:38b) – whom Jesus would soon reveal to be the devil (8:44). While Abraham listened to the voice of God, his descendants neither heard the word of God – spoken through Jesus – nor believed in Jesus.

8:39–59 "BEFORE ABRAHAM WAS BORN, I AM"

The unbelieving Jews once again asserted that Abraham was their father (8:39a). Jesus had already acknowledged their physical lineage but also pointed out the inconsistency in their actions (8:37). Now, he returns to this same topic: "If you were Abraham's children . . . then you would do what Abraham did. As it

---

3. Stibbe, *John*, 102.

is, you are looking for a way to kill me . . . Abraham did not do such things" (8:39–40). Ridderbos comments, "Jesus persists in asserting a connection between 'fatherhood' and 'works' and now declares openly that their appeal to Abraham would be valid only if they did 'the works of Abraham.'"[4] If they were Abraham's children, they would have done what Abraham did. Since they were not doing the works of Abraham, they had no moral right to claim that they were descendants of Abraham.

Abraham was obedient and self-sacrificing. He had been willing to offer his own son, Isaac, as a living sacrifice to God. But his descendants were attempting to murder the one who had spoken the truth he had heard from God himself (8:40a). Their actions demonstrated the contrast between Abraham and themselves.[5] While Abraham was obedient to the word of God, his descendants were disobedient and sought to shed the blood of the Savior. Jesus concluded, "You are doing the works of your own father" (8:41) – who he identified as the devil (8:44). The devil was prompting their actions, and that was the reason for their anger against Jesus.

When heavenly truths were described, these Jews were slow to understand; but they were quick to grasp earthly matters. When accused of doing the works of their father, they retorted that they were not "illegitimate children" since God himself was their Father (8:41b), thus implying that Jesus was an illegitimate child and casting doubt on Mary's innocence. In India, legitimate children have legal rights to citizenship and to inherit their father's property, while illegitimate children are denied such rights. The Jews would have understood Jesus's statements as a direct challenge to their identity as citizens of Israel and children of Abraham and of God.

Jesus elaborated on their claim that God was their Father: "If God were your Father, you would love me, for I have come here from God. I have not come on my own; God sent me" (8:42). To please God, the Jews needed to understand the dynamic relationship between the Father and the Son. Their misunderstanding and inability to hear and understand what Jesus said arose from the fact that they belonged to another father – the devil – who had been a murderer from the beginning; and they wanted to carry out their father's desires, which was why they sought to murder Jesus (8:43–44a). Jesus revealed that their father was neither Abraham nor God but the devil himself. In an honor-shame culture, a person's parenthood and paternal relationship matters a

---

4. Ridderbos, *Gospel of John*, 312.
5. Witherington, *John's Wisdom*, 177.

great deal. While the Jews accused Jesus of illegitimacy at birth, he challenged their fatherhood.

The devil was not only a murderer – whom they were imitating – but a liar: "Not holding to the truth, for there is no truth in him. When he lies, he speaks his native language, for he is a liar and the father of lies" (8:44b). They lied by not believing the truth – that is, Jesus, who spoke the truth (8:45). In contrast to the devil, the father of lies, Jesus positioned himself as the speaker of truth and invited his opponents to believe in him. No one could convict Jesus of sin because he spoke divine truth (8:46a). Why didn't they believe him? Because their father was the father of lies. The urgency to believe in Jesus is further emphasized in this passage.

Jesus then reaffirmed that they did not belong to God: "Whoever belongs to God hears what God says. The reason you do not hear is that you do belong to God" (8:47). He identified himself as one who hears what God says and his opponents as those who do not hear what God says. Their claims to be "children of Abraham" and "children of God" were refuted by their sinful actions, their neglect of God's word, their devilish nature, and their attempts to kill Jesus. Unless they listened to the voice of God's Son and believed in him, they could not rightfully make such claims. When people do not practice what they proclaim in public, they become advocates of lies.

The Jews responded by accusing Jesus of being a Samaritan and demon-possessed (8:48). The narrator had earlier stated that the Jews did not associate with Samaritans (4:9), probably because they viewed them as descendant of people of low status. The Jews would have been aware of Jesus's visit to Samaria and his stay with them for two days (4:40). Since they regarded the Samaritans as illegitimate children due to their mixed heritage as half-Jews, they also considered Jesus illegitimate and labeled him a Samaritan.[6] Moreover, calling him demon-possessed was an insult in that culture, and such people were often ostracized from society and even confined to live among the tombs. Jesus rejected their accusation (8:49a), affirming his relationship with the heavenly Father, whom he honored. In contrast, they dishonored Jesus and, by implication, dishonored God (8:49b). Keener comments, "One who rejects a person's appointed agent also insults and rejects the one who

---

6. Tite Tiénou, "The Samaritans: A Biblical-Theological Mirror for Understanding Racial, Ethnic and Religious Identity?" *This Side of Heaven: Race, Ethnicity and Christian Faith*, eds. Robert J. Priest and Alvaro L. Nieves (Oxford: University Press, 2007), 216.

sent that agent."[7] While Jesus addressed the Jews as children of the devil, they accused him of being a Samaritan and demon-possessed. This harsh language and exchange of insults demonstrate the acute tension between the Jewish community and Jesus.

Jesus went on to affirm that while he did not seek his own glory, the Father sought to glorify Jesus (8:50a). Unlike the Jews who sought Jesus's death, the Father sought the Son's glory. Furthermore, the Father is the judge (8:50b), which implies that what he seeks – his Son's glory – is right and just. Jesus promised that those who obey his words, which are true, will never see death (8:51). Whereas the Jews were seeking ways to kill Jesus, Jesus was offering them a way to live forever.

Instead of believing Jesus, the Jews said, "Now we know that you are demon-possessed! Abraham died and so did the prophets, yet you say that whoever obeys your word will never taste death. Are you greater than our father Abraham? He died, and so did the prophets. Who do you think you are?" (8:52–53). Their false knowledge was once again revealed through their response. The Jews thought that Abraham and the prophets were dead, but Jesus said that those who keep his words will never taste death. Abraham and the prophets are still alive because God is not the God of the dead but of the living: "'I am the God of Abraham, the God of Isaac, and the God of Jacob' . . . not the God of the dead but of the living" (Matt 22:32). These Jews did not understand God and his power. Although the Pharisees believed in the resurrection (Acts 23:8), these Jews did not. They were ignorant of even the basic teachings of Scripture.

Jesus returned to the theme of glorification: "If I glorify myself, my glory means nothing. My Father, whom you claim as your God, is the one who glorifies me" (8:54). The Father glorifies the Son. Yet these Jews rejected the Son. Their actions proved that they neither knew God nor had a proper relationship with him (8:55a).

If Jesus denied knowing the Father, he would have been a liar like them. But he insisted, "I do know him and obey his word" (8:55b). Jesus contrasted his knowing with the unknowing of his opponents. Their father was the devil, who is himself a liar (8:44), but Jesus's Father is the God who seeks to glorify the Son. Furthermore, even Abraham, whom they claimed as their father, looked forward to the day of Jesus's coming and rejoiced (8:56), which refers to Abraham's faith in God's promise to send a Redeemer.

---

7. Keener, *The IVP Bible Background Commentary*, 287.

Once again, the Jews were reasoning from an earthly perspective. They said, "You are not yet fifty years old . . . and you have seen Abraham!" (8:57). Jesus had said that Abraham saw his day, but they twisted this, saying, "You have seen Abraham," and wondered how someone who was not even fifty years old could have seen Abraham. Jesus responded, "Very truly I tell you . . . before Abraham was born, I am!" (8:58). This absolute "I am" statement echoes God's utterance in Exodus 3:14. Jesus existed before Abraham – this was his *from above* statement. As the narrator has already stated, "In the beginning was the Word, and the Word was with God, and the Word was God" (1:1). Jesus existed long before Abraham.

Jesus's statement angered the Jews and "they picked up stones to stone him" (8:59b). Jesus had already exalted himself above Moses (1:17; 3:14; 6:32), Jacob (4:12–15), and Abraham (8:52–59). As the saying goes, this last claim "broke the camel's back" – and they picked up stones to kill him. Once again, Jesus slipped away from the temple grounds because it was not yet his time to be arrested and killed.

While the Jews believed in God, they failed to demonstrate this belief by following Jesus. While Abraham had welcomed divine messengers (Gen 18:1–15), the Jews rejected the messenger sent by God – Jesus. Jesus's dialogue with the Jews revealed a series of misunderstandings. This episode features two of Jesus's authoritative and revelatory "I am" sayings: "I am the light of the world" (8:12) and "Before Abraham was born, I am!" (8:58). The narrator uses courtroom language to stress Jesus's identity. The Jews responded in various ways as Jesus challenged their worldview and theological positions, accusing him of being a deceiver (7:12), a Samaritan (8:48), and demon-possessed (7:20; 8:48, 52; 10:20). Despite these accusations, Jesus repeatedly offered them the opportunity to believe in him and receive eternal life.

JOHN 9:1–41
A MAN BORN BLIND RECEIVES SIGHT

The events following the Festival of Tabernacles continue in John 9:1–41. The narrator creatively introduces "life" or "eternal life" as a central theme to address concerns about faith and discipleship among Jesus's followers. The story of the man born blind shows how the stigma of disability remains attached to him even after his healing. Swinton writes, "Without the hermeneutical voice of people living with disabilities, the revelation that God desires to impart to us remains lacking . . . Disabled human bodies can carry powerful messages of redemption just-as-they-are. To see such things we need to read Scripture in a quite particular way."[1]

John 9 unfolds through seven dramatic and ironic scenes: Jesus and the man born blind (9:1–7); the man and his neighbors (9:8–12); the man and the Pharisees (9:13–17); the Pharisees and the parents (9:18–23); the man's expulsion from the synagogue (9:24–34); Jesus's encounter with the healed man (9:35–38); and a concluding theological message (9:39–41). An individual's social acceptance as an able-bodied person does not necessarily reflect true ability. The Pharisees considered themselves physically, religiously, economically, and socially "able," while viewing the man born blind as physically disabled, religiously sinful, economically poor, and socially marginalized. This story centers on the theme of ability and disability within a socioreligious context.

9:1–7 JESUS AND THE MAN BORN BLIND

As a continuation of the previous two chapters (John 7–8), the events of John 9 also take place during the Festival of Tabernacles. The previous chapter ends with Jesus "slipping away from the temple grounds" (8:59), and this chapter picks up the story, saying, "As he went along, he saw a man blind from birth" (9:1). The fact that Jesus noticed the man's congenital disability emphasizes his identity as the light of the world (9:5) from whom nothing is hidden – just as nothing is hidden from the sun's rays.

---

1. John Swinton, "Foreword: The Strange New World within the Bible: Some Reflections on the Hermeneutics on Disability," *The Bible and Disability: A Commentary*, eds. Sarah Melcher, Mikeal C. Parsons, and Amos Yong (London: SCM Press, 2018), vii.

Jesus's disciples asked a theological question based on the prevailing assumption that infirmities were the result of sin or demonic activities: "Rabbi, who sinned, this man or his parents, that he was born blind?" (9:2).[2] If diseases were considered demonic and sinful, the disabled would probably have been considered terrible sinners. Today, approximately four percent of the world's blind population live in Pakistan. Of these 1.7 million people, many have limited access to eye care.[3] Christians must not conclude that these people's sins caused their blindness and ignore their needs. Jesus told the disciples, "Neither this man nor his parents sinned . . . but this happened so that the works of God might be displayed in him" (9:3). Divine ability would be manifested in human disability. Although the blind man was suffering, this was not because of either his own or his parents' sinfulness. By attributing his disability to sinfulness, people added to the burden of his suffering, reducing him to a downtrodden and untouchable figure in the public square. In Asia today, people with disabilities are often considered a burden to their families and societies. Even churches sometimes fail to accept and honor them as valued members of the body of Christ. In 1976, India launched the National Programme for Control of Blindness with the aim of reducing the prevalence of blindness to 0.3 percent by the year 2020. Such initiatives must be encouraged.

Jesus continued teaching the disciples: "As long as it is day, we must do the works of him who sent me. Night is coming, when no one can work" (9:4). Within the dualistic framework of "day" and "night," Jesus taught that as long as God was working, Jesus and the disciples should also work. God's work involves ministering to those with disabilities. But a time would come when no one could work. Jesus was in the *world below* as an agent of God to accomplish the works given to him. This time is described as "day," when all can work for the glory of God; but a future "night" time would come when no one would be able to work for God's glory. This hints at Jesus's own suffering and death, as well as the suffering of the disciples in the future.

In Scripture, the creation of the universe is presented as one of God's greatest works. Jesus's reference to "work" in this passage pointed to something similar to the divine work of creation. This would be actualized in the healing of the blind man. Christians are called to seize every appropriate opportunity

---

2. Ben Nworie, ed., *Integrating Faith and Special Education: A Christian Faith Approach to Special Education Practice* (Eugene: Wipf & Stock, 2016), 30.
3. For more details see, Seva.org, "Pakistan Fact Sheet," 2, http://www.seva.org/pdf/Seva_Country_Fact_Sheets_Pakistan.pdf.

to participate in God's creative mission in the world. Asian Christians in particular can serve as agents of mission by ministering among the disabled and other vulnerable groups.

God's new creation work continues because Jesus is in the world as God's light (9:5), just as the first creation began with the creation of light and the separation of day and night (Gen 1:3–5). Jesus said, "While I am in the world, I am the light of the world" (9:5). The period of Jesus's earthly life was a time of "light," while his departure from this world ushered in a time of "darkness." The man born blind, who had lived his life in darkness, could understand the value of light and, therefore, the significance of Jesus as the light of the world. Jesus's repeated identification of himself as the "light of the world" during the Festival of Tabernacles was intentional because rituals involving both water and light played significant roles at that festival.

Having taught the disciples, Jesus set about performing the miracle: "He spit on the ground, made some mud with the saliva, and put it on the man's eyes. 'Go,' he told him, 'wash in the Pool of Siloam'" (9:6–7a). In contemporary times, such actions may appear unclean and unsanitary. In any event, the blind man would have been used to insults. This method is not uncharacteristic of the way Jesus healed people with other disabilities (compare Mark 7:33; 8:23). The Pool of Siloam held religious significance because it was the place to where the priests came in procession to draw water on the final day of the festival.[4] "Siloam" means "sent," symbolizing Jesus being sent by the Father (9:4), the blind man being sent by Jesus (9:7a), and the later sending of the disciples by Jesus to continue his work. Hearing Jesus, "the man went and washed, and came home seeing" (9:7b). His actions demonstrate his obedience; his washing symbolizes a sacramental act; his return home symbolizes his missional work; and his seeing marks the starting point of holistic vision.

This encounter resembles the story of Naaman, who immersed himself seven times in the River Jordan to be healed from leprosy (2 Kgs 5:1–14). It also echoes the exodus event, where the people of Israel crossed the Red Sea and were delivered from slavery in Egypt (Exod 14:21–22). Jesus crossed the Sea of Galilee and offered the people bread from heaven (6:16–59), and in this episode, the blind man went to Siloam and began to experience divine sight through the true light of the world. Jesus's seeing of the man born blind (9:1) and his identity as the "light of the world" (9:5) emphasize the oneness of his

---

4. Edersheim, *Temple, Its Ministry and Services*, 220–27.

human and divine nature – "the Word became flesh" (1:14) – through which he restored a man with disabilities and offered him new life.

9:8–12 THE MAN AND HIS NEIGHBORS

The neighbors and others who had formerly seen the man begging for a living – a view *from below* – continued to see him from this *below* perspective: "Isn't this the same man who used to sit and beg?" (9:8). They did not see him, as Jesus had seen him, from an *above* perspective (9:1). Their opinions were divided. While some claimed he was the same person, others said, "No, he only looks like him" (9:9a). They were spiritually blind, failing to truly see the blind man even though he insisted, "I am the man" (9:9c). This is the only place in the Fourth Gospel where the dramatic phrase "I am" appears on the lips of anyone other than Jesus. Clark-Soles states, "Use of *egō eimi* ['I am'] on his part associates him with Jesus and is a bold expression or identity."[5] People with disabilities often have great inner strength and potential, but they need the support of others. For the man's neighbors, his healing was beyond their imagination: How could someone born blind now see?

The characterization of the blind man reveals that people with disabilities may possess great mental strength even though their physical condition may make them immobile. Although the man could now see, he was still viewed by others as one someone with disabilities. He continued to be marginalized because of the social stigma attached to his blindness and the religious judgment of him as a sinner. Despite being able to see, he was relegated to the periphery. People around him – who claimed that they could see – failed to recognize him, insisting that "he only looks like him" (9:9b). The narrator gradually develops the characterization of the man and the ideological irony between those who claimed to see and the man who claimed, "I am the man" (9:9c). Thus, the story draws the attention of the reader to the broader issues of ability and disability.

The neighbors asked the man, "How then were your eyes opened?" (9:10). Without hesitation, the man recounted what had taken place: "The man they call Jesus made some mud and put it on my eyes. He told me to go to Siloam and wash. So I went and washed, and then I could see" (9:11). In the words of Amos Yong, the world is gripped by "normal biases," and when people

---

5. J. Clark-Soles, "John, First-Third John, and Revelation." *The Bible and Disability: A Commentary*, eds., Sarah Melcher, Mikeal C. Parsons, and Amos Yong (London: SCM Press, 2018), 348.

approach those with disabilities, they do so with their own unexamined prejudices and assumptions.[6] While the people around failed to correctly perceive the blind man, Jesus saw the man with heavenly vision and led him to holistic sight. Just as Jesus guided the man forward, Asian churches must take a special interest in people with disabilities.

There are both differences and similarities between this miracle and the one described in John 5. First, while Jesus's command to the man by the pool was to pick up his mat and walk (5:11), his command to the blind man was to go to the pool and wash (9:11). Second, while the paralyzed man did not know the identity of the person who had healed him (5:13), the blind man knew Jesus by name (9:11). Third, while the paralyzed man's healing was instantaneous – he got up, picked his mat, and walked (5:8–9) – the blind man's healing was progressive and involved various steps: Jesus spitting on the ground, making mud, applying it on the blind man's eyes, and instructing him to go to the pool and wash (9:6–7). Fourth, while Jesus warned the paralyzed man to stop sinning lest something worse happen to him (5:14), he insisted that the blind man's blindness had not been caused by sin (9:3). Fifth, both men faithfully obeyed Jesus's command. Sixth, both men had suffered for many years – the paralyzed man for thirty-eight years and the blind man since birth. Seventh, both healings occurred on a Sabbath, provoking opposition from the religious leaders. Eighth, both miracles took place during the Festival of Tabernacles and form bookends that figuratively highlight Israel's spiritual paralysis and blindness that kept them from drinking the living water and receiving the light of the world.

The neighbors' interrogation continued. They asked, "Where is this man?" (9:12a). The blind man replied that he did not know. Duke says, "The newly sighted man, like the one in Mark 8:24 who at first saw people as moving trees, confesses what he does not yet perceive."[7] Although the blind man knew Jesus's name and had been a recipient of his healing, he did not know Jesus's whereabouts.

9:13–17 THE MAN AND THE PHARISEES

The neighbors and those who had seen the man as a beggar (9:8a) brought him to the Pharisees (9:13). They brought the man to "men of mature judgment

---

6. Amos Yong, *The Bible, Disability, and the Church: A New Vision of the People of God* (Grand Rapids: Eerdmans, 2011), 10.
7. P. Duke, *Irony in the Fourth Gospel* (Atlanta: John Knox Press, 1985) 119.

who can examine the case and arrive at definite conclusions."[8] The day Jesus made mud and opened the man's eyes was a Sabbath (9:14). The people's intention in bringing the blind man before the Pharisees becomes clear: They wanted both the blind man and Jesus to be punished for Sabbath violations. When the Pharisees interrogated the blind man about how he had received his sight, he repeated what he had already told his neighbors (9:15). So far, these events have been narrated three times in this passage (9:6–7, 11, 15), and the consistency of the three accounts attests to the truthfulness of the story. Miracles may prompt people to remember the giver of supernatural gifts. The man born blind had a disability, but he had passed from disability to ability through Jesus's healing. This empowered him to boldly witness to Christ despite opposition from people who possessed sight and power.

The Pharisees were divided in their assessment of Jesus. Some concluded, "This man is not from God, for he does not keep the Sabbath" (9:16a). The law clearly prohibited work on the Sabbath, but Jesus was working – healing the paralyzed and the blind. Therefore, they concluded that he was a lawbreaker and that such a lawbreaker could not have come from God. Other Pharisees countered, "How can a sinner perform such signs?" (9:16b). Earlier, Nicodemus – also a Pharisee – had said, "Rabbi, we [plural] know that you are a teacher who has come from God. For no one could perform the signs you are doing if God were not with him" (3:2). The Pharisees knew that true miracles originated from God and that God's messengers – such as Moses and Elijah – performed such signs. Therefore, they reasoned that perhaps Jesus, too, was from God – and not a sinner – and that was why he performed miracles (9:16b). While the Pharisees asserted that Jesus was not from God, he performed divine works. While they considered him a sinner, he saved people. Despite their claim he was a Sabbath-breaker, he made people whole. The blind man had endured several Sabbaths as a man with a disability, but no one had helped him. Jesus healed the man, taking him from disability to ability, but the Pharisees were not pleased with this divine intervention. Jesus was accused of dishonoring God and Sabbath-breaking, which was serious sin under Jewish law.

The Pharisees interrogated the man further, as though they were not convinced by his earlier response: "What have you to say about him?" (9:17a). The blind man made a profound statement: "He is a prophet" (9:17b). Like the Pharisees, he knew that only those in close communion with God – such

---

8. Martyn, *History and Theology in the Fourth Gospel*, 31.

as prophets – could perform miracles of this kind. Earlier, the woman at the well had concluded that Jesus was a prophet because he knew and exposed her secrets (4:19). Similarly, the pilgrims who ate the multiplied bread and fish declared, "Surely this is the Prophet who is to come into the world" (6:14). Jesus's disclosure of truth and his miracles confirmed his identity as a prophet, just as in the case of the prophets of old. The Samaritan woman and the pilgrims understood this basic truth, but the Pharisees failed to do so. The blind man's faith and his assessment of Jesus grew from "the man they call Jesus" (9:11) to "he is a prophet" (9:17b). While the paralyzed man's understanding of Jesus had remained static (5:13–15), the blind man's faith deepened, and he now saw Jesus as a prophet. His understanding surpassed that of the Pharisees, who, as those supposedly well-versed in religious matters, should have been able to recognize a prophet by his works. Clark-Soles states, "To call Jesus a prophet is to ascribe him religious authority; recall that Moses, Elijah, and Elisha all performed healing miracles."[9] The blind man grew in his understanding of divine truths, while the Pharisees were spiritually short-sighted.

9:18–23 THE PHARISEES AND THE PARENTS

The Pharisees did not believe that the man born blind had received his sight through Jesus's miracle (9:18a). Despite their disbelief, lack of recognition, and failure to understand, they were still regarded by the people as those with rightful religious authority, empowered to make rulings about people's beliefs, to discern God's work in people's lives, and to determine whether someone was a prophet or the Messiah. While the blind man progressed from disability to ability, the Jewish leaders' discernment diminished. Unable to recognize the truth of what had taken place, they summoned the man's parents to confirm the facts (9:18b). They asked the parents, "Is this your son? . . . Is this the one you say was born blind? How is it that now he can see?" (9:19). These questions clearly reveal their unwillingness to accept and believe the things that had been publicly demonstrated.

The parents replied, "We know he is our son . . . and we know he was born blind. But how he can see now, or who opened his eyes, we don't know. He is of age; he will speak for himself" (9:20–21). Their response suggests that they wanted to escape a potentially dangerous situation. The parents' testimony confirms that the man had been suffering from a congenital disability – he had been born blind. Although the Pharisees had not asked them who healed their

---

9. Clark-Soles, "John, First-Third John, and Revelation," 349.

son (9:19), they offered the information that they did not know "who opened his eyes" (9:21a). They were probably aware that the Pharisees had interrogated their son (9:17a) and that his reply that Jesus was a prophet (9:17b) had irritated the Pharisees. The parents' frustration is evident in their statement: "He is of age; he will speak for himself" (9:21b). The man was an adult and a firsthand witness. He did not need his parents' testimony.

The parents must have felt trapped. If they, like their son, identified Jesus as a prophet or as the Messiah, they would get into trouble. They were afraid of the Jewish leaders, knowing that the religious authorities had "already had decided that anyone who acknowledged that Jesus was the Messiah would be put out of the synagogue" (9:22b).[10] The themes of prophet and Messiah run throughout the Gospel. While the blind man openly acknowledged Jesus as a prophet, his parents may have wondered if Jesus was the Messiah. However, since the religious leaders had threatened to expel from the synagogue anyone who made such a confession, the parents remained silent despite their conviction. The Jewish leaders' ruling and its penalty was widely known, prompting the parents to say, "He is of age; ask him" (9:23; see also 9:21b).[11] Even the parents concealed the truth to adapt to the demands of their context.

Ironically, although the religious leaders claimed to have sight and were respected members of the synagogue, Sabbath keepers, and people of influence, they lacked wisdom.[12] Duke comments, "Here we are told that belief in Jesus will result in expulsion from a cherished community, and that disbelief in him will require deliberate blindness to the undeniable works of God."[13] Although the blind man had suffered from a congenital disability, been marginalized by society, and silenced in religious assemblies, he demonstrated progress – moving from a single disability to multiple abilities.

9:24–34 THE MAN'S EXPULSION FROM THE SYNAGOGUE

For the second time, the Pharisees summoned the healed man for an interrogation. The religious authorities did not recognize Jesus as a prophet, the Messiah, or God's Son. Instead, they viewed him as a sinner who violated Sabbath regulations and blasphemed God's name. Earlier, they had accused

---

10. The Greek word *aposunagōgos* means casting somebody out of the synagogue (9:22, 34; 12:42–43; 16:2).
11. Leo Zanchettin, ed., *John a Devotional Commentary: Meditations on the Gospel according to St. John* (Ijamsville: The Word Among Us Press, 2000), 100–105.
12. Clark-Soles, "John, First-Third John, and Revelation," 349.
13. Duke, *Irony in the Fourth Gospel*, 121.

Jesus of being demon-possessed and mentally insane (7:20; 8:48–52; 10:20). Now they told the blind man, "Give glory to God by telling the truth . . . We know this man [Jesus] is a sinner" (9:24). If the man acknowledged Jesus as a prophet – as he had done earlier (9:17b) – he would also be labeled a sinner and a blasphemer. The religious authorities invoked God's name to pressure the man into denying God's work. They commanded the man to speak the truth, but they themselves were closed to the truth. Although they claimed to possess knowledge, they proved their ignorance. Jesus had said that the Son shared in the glory of the Father, but the Jews refused to give glory to the Son. Jesus had performed a sign (9:1–7, 16b) that glorified the Father's name, but the religious authorities neither accepted the Son nor gave him glory; instead, they considered him a sinner.

The blind man declared that he did not know whether or not Jesus was a sinner; what he did know was that he had once been blind but now could see because of Jesus (9:25).[14] Earlier, Jesus had said that neither this man nor his parents had sinned; now, the Pharisees labeled Jesus a sinner. The one who came to save sinners was labeled a Samaritan, demon-possessed, and a sinner. According to labeling theory, people use labels to control people and classify them as deviant. The Pharisees used their power and authority to secure their own position and suppress other people. Here, the irony of ability and disability is striking: the authorities, who were supposed to protect the rights of vulnerable people, exploited them, and the legal system, which was supposed to safeguard marginalized, was used to dehumanize them.

The Pharisees realized that although they were able to silence the man's parents, they were unable to silence the healed man. Their attempts to discredit the Messiah and deny his miracles utterly failed in the face of the blind man's testimony. Despite this, they repeated the same questions (9:26), hoping to intimidate him with their threats. But the blind man's passionate testimony frustrated their aim. The blind man bravely questioned the religious authorities. His ability rose above their ability. He did not appreciate their tactic of erasing the event of enabling him and their persistent questioning and threats. He questioned them with a mix of realism and sarcasm: "I have told you already and you did not listen. Why do you want to hear it again? Do you want to become his disciples too?" (9:27). Brown comments, "The courageous sarcasm of the man's answers strikes a warm chord in the reader's heart; obviously here

---

14. This phrase becomes a part of John Newton's "Amazing Grace": I once was lost but now am found. Was blind, but now I see.

we have a character very different from the timid paralytic of John 5."[15] In a sense, the paralytic had betrayed Jesus by revealing his name to the Jewish leaders (5:15). In contrast, the blind man challenged the Pharisees, expressing his support of Jesus as someone worth following (9:27). His response reflects the mind of a determined follower. It is as if he himself were a disciple, inviting them to join him and others in following Jesus.

As the man moved from physical disability to ability, he also demonstrated spiritual growth. By interrogating the religious authorities, he frustrated them and rendered them speechless. Again, the irony of ability and disability reaches unexpected heights. In many Asian contexts, when those in authority lack the courage to face and respond to questions raised by ordinary people, they often resort to various tactics to suppress dissenting voices.

The Pharisees became harsh and abusive: "They hurled insults at him and said, 'You are this fellow's disciple! We are disciples of Moses!'" (9:28). They made a sharp distinction between Jesus's disciples and Moses's disciples. They accused the blind man of being a sinner's disciple, while claiming that they were disciples of Moses, the lawgiver. Earlier, the blind man had asked them, "Do you want to become his disciples too?" (9:27b); now, they accused him of being a disciple of Jesus.

The Pharisees proudly identified as disciples of Moses. They said, "We know that God spoke to Moses" (9:29a) and then attacked Jesus's legitimacy: "As for this fellow, we don't even know where he comes from" (9:29b). Earlier, they had said, "We are not illegitimate children" (8:41), implying that Jesus was illegitimate; now, they claimed ignorance of his origin or place of birth. But their knowledge was imperfect because Moses himself had pointed to Jesus. As Jesus had told the Jews, "If you believed Moses, you would believe me, for he wrote about me" (5:46). They claimed to be Moses's disciples but failed to understand Moses's words!

The healed man again insulted the Pharisees because they did not know Jesus's origins: "Now that is remarkable! You don't know where he comes from, yet he opened my eyes" (9:30). Once again, the blind man's personal testimony is contrasted with the Pharisees' superficial understanding of Scripture and tradition. The man born blind had progressed from his lifelong disability to strength, ability, and superior knowledge.

The blind man then spoke on behalf of all true disciples: "We [plural] know that God does not listen to sinners. He listens to the godly person who

---

15. Brown, *Gospel and Epistles of St. John*, 74.

does his will" (9:31). His statement implies that Jesus is not a sinner but a godly person who does God's will. The blind man viewed Jesus as a prophet from God who heals people – that is, does the works of God the Father. What a bold assertion! The blind man did not speak from the perspective of a passive observer but as a person who had experienced the presence of God through Jesus. While he spoke as a firsthand witness to the power of God in his life, the Pharisees argued from their biased religious perspectives. While they argued from their own "knowing" and, ironically, ended up being "unknowing," the blind man moved from his "unknowing" to become a "knowing" person. What convinced him was Jesus's miracle: "Nobody has ever heard of opening the eyes of a man born blind. If this man were not from God, he could do nothing" (9:32–33). His words echo what Nicodemus – also a Pharisee – had said earlier (3:2) – a truth that the other Pharisees refused to acknowledge. The blind man's "knowing" extended to acknowledging Jesus as someone coming from the Father. As someone who had been born blind but then experienced God's healing touch, he challenged the religious leaders. In that sense, he was a believer par excellence. His spiritual sight increased as his understanding of Jesus progressed – from "the man they call Jesus" (9:11) to "a prophet" (9:17) to a man "from God" (9:33). He reasoned that Jesus must be from God because he had performed a universally convincing miracle, to which the blind man was a living witness. His formerly disabled life situation was transformed into one of holistic ability, spiritual knowledge, and a new theological outlook. Similarly, in India, the witness of Christians has moved many Dalits, Tribals, and Adivasis toward wholeness and spiritual knowledge. God's liberative power continues to work among vulnerable communities in different parts of Asia.

The story has now come full circle. Earlier, the disciples had asked whether it was the man's sin or his parents' sin that caused him to be born blind (9:2). Now, the Pharisees concluded, "You were steeped in sin at birth" (9:34a). Perhaps they also considered him a sinner because he associated with Jesus, whom they regarded as a sinner and lawbreaker. Then, they attacked his intellect: "How dare you lecture us!" (9:34b). After all, it was they – rather than blind beggars – who were the teachers of the law. Finally, they threw him out (9:34c) – probably from the synagogue, in line with the decree that had already intimidated the man's parents (9:22). Even at this stage, the Pharisees continued to think of the blind man as diseased and sinful.

John 9 depicts the man as openly and progressively growing in loyalty to Jesus (9:11, 17, 33). As Martyn writes, "A member of the *Am ha-Aretz* [People of the Land, a term for the Jews] has failed to recognize the halakic [Jewish law] authority of the Gerousia [the council of elders, of which the Pharisees were members] in regard to a most sensitive matter [that is, Sabbath regulations]."[16] The blind man's disability, the interrogations following his healing, and the religious leaders' attempts to silence him form the core of the narrative framework. The man's theological vision and bold Christian witness serve as a powerful paradigm for followers of Jesus in Asia.

9:35–38 JESUS'S ENCOUNTER WITH THE HEALED MAN

Jesus seeks out those he heals until they are fully restored. He had looked for the paralyzed man in the temple and revealed his identity to him (5:14); now, he finds the man born blind, who had been thrown out of the synagogue (9:35). As someone expelled from institutional Judaism, the healed man would have lost all privileges, especially the identity associated with his synagogue membership. But Jesus expressed solidarity with him. He searched for him, and when he had found him, he asked, "Do you believe in the Son of Man?" (9:35b). The man had already fulfilled the basic requirements of a believer through his confessions and loyalty to God's Son. Jesus gave him the opportunity to truly see him for the first time. As Martyn says, "They stand face to face in the street."[17] Jesus once again referred to himself by the title "Son of Man" (see 1:51; 3:13–14; 6:27, 53, 62; 8:28; see also 12:23, 34; 13:31).

Even after hearing Jesus's voice and seeing him, the healed man struggled with recognition (9:36a). Nevertheless, he expressed his willingness to believe in the Son of Man (9:36b). He was ready to take further steps in his faith journey. Once labeled disabled, marginalized, and sinful within Jewish society, he was now able, saved, and possessed a new identity in Christ. Although the doors of the synagogue were closed to him, Jesus appeared before him as the "gate for the sheep" (10:7). The man's vision expanded as he saw Jesus for who he truly was.

Jesus told the man, "You have now seen him; in fact, he is the one speaking with you" (9:37), echoing his declaration to the Samaritan woman: "I, the one speaking to you – I am he" (4:26). Jesus revealed his identity as the Son of Man to the healed man (9:37). Perkins says, "Jesus's coming to find the man may also be an enactment of Jesus's saying in 6:37: 'Everyone the Father

---

16. Martyn, *History and Theology in the Fourth Gospel*, 35.
17. Martyn, *History and Theology in the Fourth Gospel*, 35.

gives me will come to me, and the one comes to me, I will not cast out.'"[18] While the Jews had cast out this man from their assembly, Jesus received him.

In response, the blind man confessed, "Lord, I believe" and immediately worshiped Jesus (9:38). The man's confession and his posture of worship demonstrate the highest level of his loyalty to Jesus. Having earlier referred to Jesus as "the man they call Jesus" (9:11), "a prophet" (9:17), and a man "from God" (9:33), this man – now an expelled Jew – accepted Jesus as "Lord" and expressed his willingness to believe in him. His confessions about Jesus and his willingness to believe in him were expressed through an act of worship (9:38b). Just as the Samaritan woman – a member of a community rejected by the Jews – learned the true nature of worship (4:20–24), this blind man – who was also rejected by his community – understood and entered into true worship.

As a person with disabilities, the man had been denied justice, thrown out of the synagogue, unfairly judged, and regarded as a lifelong sinner. All these details reflect the harsh treatment of disabled persons in Jewish society, but the blind man overcame these challenges. In contrast to the Jews who saw the Savior with their physical eyes but neither believed in Jesus nor developed spiritual insight, the blind man saw his healer with his physical eyes and attained the highest level of spiritual insight.

9:39–41 A CONCLUDING THEOLOGICAL MESSAGE

The blind man's confession brought the Lord back to the core of what he had been teaching. Earlier, Jesus had said, "The Father judges no one, but has entrusted all judgment to the Son, that all may honor the Son just as they honor the Father. Whoever does not honor the Son does not honor the Father, who sent him" (5:22–23). Now, addressing the healed blind man, Jesus said, "For judgment I have come into this world, so that the blind will see and those who see will become blind" (9:39). Jesus's judgment is double-edged. While the man born blind received both physical sight and spiritual insight, the Jews who claimed to have knowledge and sight proved that they lacked spiritual insight. While the man gained both physical sight and spiritual insight, the Jews – though physically able to see – descended to the level of blind guides. They claimed a relationship with God but were unable to recognize the Son

---

18. Pheme Perkins, "The Gospel according to John," *The New Jerome Biblical Commentary*, eds. Raymond E. Brown, Joseph A. Fitzmyer, and Roland E. Murphy (Bangalore: Theological Publications in India, 2001), 968.

of Man – the Lord who stood in their midst. They claimed to be disciples of Moses but failed to accept the one about whom Moses wrote.

Some of the Pharisee overheard Jesus's words and asked, "What? Are we blind too?" (9:40). Jesus was speaking about holistic sight, which includes both physical sight and spiritual insight. But they took his words literally, interpreting them to mean that they were blind. Jesus answered, "If you were blind, you would not be guilty of sin; but now that you claim you can see, your guilt remains" (9:41). Jesus challenged the Jews. First, although they had physical sight and could see Jesus, they did not acknowledge him as God's Son. If they had truly been blind – that is, unaware of the truth – they would not have been guilty of sin. Second, though they saw the Messiah – the Son of Man – with their physical eyes, they did not follow him as the healed man did. As such, while seeing, they remained sinful. Duke says, "Their [Pharisees'] disease, quite different, is an illusion of sight, which has led them to a far deeper darkness than they know."[19] Without spiritual insight, their sight was deficient. Their spiritual shortsightedness and shortcomings made them incapable of fulfilling their religious responsibilities, and this is also true of all religious extremists, fundamentalists, and terrorists.

At the beginning of the story, Jesus clearly stated, "Neither this man nor his parents sinned"; and his final statement to the Jews is this: "If you were blind, you would not be guilty of sin." At the beginning of the narrative, the man is seen as blind and sinful by those around him; but by the end of the story, the Jews are portrayed as blind and sinful. The Pharisees dismissed Jesus as a sinner (9:24) and the blind man as one "steeped in sin at birth" (9:34). Clark-Soles states,

> Jesus, the light, has come into the world and is shining in the faces of the religious leaders. They hate the light and want to do the evil deed of disabling Jesus through death. The man born blind sees the light and does the work of God by believing in Jesus.[20]

Neither Jesus nor the man born blind were sinners, but the people who claimed to be children of Abraham, disciples of Moses, and, ultimately, the people of God remained in sin because of their willful ignorance. The Pharisees interpreted the Scriptures dogmatically but failed to practice it. Jesus's life and ministry demonstrate what it means to "walk the talk" as the people of God.

---

19. Duke, *Irony in the Fourth Gospel*, 124.
20. Clark-Soles, "John, First-Third John, and Revelation," 351.

Christians are called to focus on areas such as restoring wholeness to those with physical and spiritual disabilities, the poor, the underprivileged, and the oppressed. Churches should be open to people with disabilities, sex workers, underprivileged children, the poor, and those who are ostracized.

In Asia, the categories of ability and disability continue to dominate in the socioreligious and political-economic contexts. Ghai says, "Within the dominant cultural ethos, labels such as 'disability,' 'handicap,' 'crippled,' 'blind,' and 'deaf' are used synonymously."[21] Ability is associated with physical wellness, ignoring the more holistic aspects of human capacity. Similarly, disability is defined narrowly, based solely on physical impairments. Prabhu comments,

> [The narrative of the man born blind] invites us to read the Gospel of John with truly Indian eyes, for in this story of the blind man enlightened by his encounter with Christ, endowed with an insight into the really real, made conscious of his oneness with the Lord, and abandoning all things to cling to him alone, we sense those elements of the unity of being, of the duality of the real and the unreal, and of the symbolism of the world, which, we have been told, are the skeletonic structures of Indian thought.[22]

At the personal, ecclesiastical, and societal levels, we must ensure that no one is judged based on disabilities. Abilities and disabilities are part of our human existence. While physical disabilities should be diagnosed and cared for with compassion this does not mean that those without physical disabilities are somehow superhuman. We all need one another's love, care, protection, and appreciation. We are called to treat all people with love, regardless of their abilities or disabilities, remembering that the God of all ability entered and accommodated a world of disabilities to embrace a disabled humanity – all who fall short of the glory of God.

---

21. Anita Ghai, *Rethinking Disability in India* (London: Routledge, 2015), xix.
22. George M. Soares-Prabhu, "The Man Born Blind: Understanding a Johannine Sign in India Today," *India's Search for Reality and the Relevance of the Gospel of John*, eds. Christopher Duraisingh and Cecil Hargreaves (Delhi: ISPCK, 1975), 76.

JOHN 10:1–21
GATE FOR THE SHEEP AND THE GOOD SHEPHERD

John 10 concludes the narration of events that followed the second Tabernacles discourse (John 8) and is closely connected to the healing of the man born blind (John 9). The pericope in 10:1–21 can be divided into two sections: Jesus as the gate for the sheep (10:1–10) and Jesus as the good shepherd (10:11–21).

10:1–10 JESUS IS THE GATE FOR THE SHEEP

Jesus's discourse in 10:1–21 does not stand apart from the previous episode. As in 5:1–47, where a story and a dialogue led to a monologue, the story and dialogue in 9:1–41 flows into a monologue in 10:1–18, followed by the community's response in 10:19–21. We know that this is still part of the blind man's story because of the bookend in 10:21: "These are not the sayings of a man possessed by a demon. Can a demon open the eyes of the blind?" This verse serves as an appropriate conclusion to the story of the man born blind.

Jesus began this monologue with yet another truth statement, directed particularly at the Pharisees: "Very truly I tell you Pharisees, anyone who does not enter the sheep pen by the gate, but climbs in by some other way, is a thief and a robber" (10:1). The old city of Jerusalem was fortified with several gates. India has some amazing historical gates. For instance, the Buland Darwaza at Fatehpur Sikri – built in 1602 CE as a victory arch to commemorate Akbar's Gujarat campaign – is 54 meters (177 feet) high and ranks among the largest in the world.[1] India Gate – a monumental sandstone arch in New Delhi is 42 meters (138 feet) high and serves as a memorial to the troops of British India who died in wars fought between 1914 and 1919.[2] The Gateway of India in Mumbai – an arch monument built during the twentieth century – commemorates the landing of King George V and Queen Mary at Apollo

---

1. "Fatehpur Sikiri," Taj Mahal, https://www.tajmahal.gov.in/fatehpur-sikri.aspx.
2. Its official name is Delhi Memorial, originally called All-India War Memorial, https://www.britannica.com/topic/India-Gate.

Bunder when they visited India in 1911.³ All these gates symbolize welcome, hospitality, security, protection, and openness to the world. In Jesus's day, since shepherds would have entered the city of Jerusalem through its various gates, the metaphor of the gate would have been familiar to both Jews and early Christians. Jewish shepherds protected their sheep pens within fortified spaces so that they could guard their sheep from wild animals and thieves.

In contemporary Saudi Arabia, shepherds camp with their sheep in deserts or mountainous areas, sometimes risking their lives to protect the sheep during sandstorms, thunderstorms, or extreme weather. Deaths of shepherds due to inadequate protection from extreme weather and other natural disasters are regularly reported in Saudi Arabia. These shepherds sacrifice their lives to protect the sheep. Sheep stealing is also a serious issue. Since shepherding is one of the oldest occupations in Asia – where sheep are kept for their milk, meat, and wool – Asian readers can readily identify with the imagery in Jesus's parable, which contrasts faithful and unfaithful leadership.

The contrast is clear: While thieves and robbers enter the sheep pen by illegal means (10:1), the shepherd of the sheep enters through the gate (10:2). The gatekeeper recognizes the shepherd and opens the gate for him (10:3a). The sheep hear and respond to the shepherd's voice (10:3b).⁴ The shepherd calls his sheep by name and leads them out (10:3c). These details reflect the relationship between the sheep, the shepherd, and the gatekeeper. The reference to knowing the sheep and calling them by name reveals the intimate relationship between the sheep and the shepherd.

When leading the sheep out to pasture, the shepherd walks ahead of them while talking to them (10:4a), "and his sheep follow him because they know his voice" (10:4b). It is the shepherd's task to lead the sheep to pasture and then bring them back safely. Because of his loving relationship and regular communication with the sheep, they recognize his voice and follow him. However, the sheep will never follow a stranger (10:5a), and "in fact, they will run away from him because they do not recognize a stranger's voice" (10:5b). Sheep are often regarded as dumb animals, but they are intelligent enough to follow only the shepherd and not a stranger.

The bond between the sheep and the shepherd is made clear through reference to the shepherd knowing each sheep's name and the sheep's recognition

---

3. Mumbai City District, "Gateway of India," https://mumbaicity.gov.in/tourist-place/gateway-of-india/.
4. In Asia, shepherds use sounds that only their sheep can understand.

of their shepherd's voice. In the Arabian wilderness, travelers may notice long lines of sheep following their shepherds, responding to familiar signals and commands of the shepherd. These sheep do not follow strangers but flee from them.

The narrator then notes that "Jesus used this figure of speech, but the Pharisees did not understand what he was telling them" (10:6). This Greek word for "figure of speech" is *paroimia*, which occurs only in John's Gospel (10:6; 16:25 [2x], 29) and in 2 Peter 2:22. It can be translated as a parable, a maxim, or a figure of speech. Jesus used metaphorical language – sheep, shepherd, sheep pen, gate, thief, robber, gatekeeper, and strangers – to communicate spiritual truths in the next few verses (10:7–10). But the Pharisees did not understand, once again revealing their ignorance while boasting about their knowledge.

Because of the Pharisees' lack of understanding – and for the benefit of the ordinary people – Jesus explained his figure of speech. He began by saying, "Very truly I tell you, I am the gate for the sheep" (10:7), just as he had earlier declared himself the "bread of life" (6:35) and the "light of the world" (8:12). This is the third of Jesus's "I am" statements. According to Swami Abhishiktananda, this pronounced "I" of Jesus is nothing less than the divine "I" revealed in the OT.[5] Jesus is the gateway to life. This access is exclusively for his sheep – that is, those who believe in Jesus and follow him.

Jesus acknowledged the reality of false messiahs or false teachers who had preceded him: "All who have come before me are thieves and robbers" (10:8a). These people had not come in through the gate but climbed in by other means because they were thieves and robbers (10:1b). But their efforts were useless since the sheep did not listen to them because they did not recognize their voice (10:8b). Jesus alone is the gate (10:9a) – the only way – and any sheep entering through this gate will be saved: "They will come in and go out and find pasture" (10:9b). Sheep cannot be saved unless they enter through Jesus, the gate. Access to the *world above* and to the Father is possible only through Jesus, affirming that Jesus is the only mediator between God and humanity (Acts 4:12; 1 Tim 2:5; Heb 8:6; 9:15; 12:24). In Asia, while thieves are regarded as harmful, the police are supposed to shepherd and protect the people. However, in some instances, these "shepherds" neglect the cries of

---

5. Abhishiktananda, *Hindu-Christian Meeting Point*, Übersetzt von Sara Grant (New Delhi: ISPCK, 1976), 93. Also Basker, *Interpreting Biblical Texts*, 74.

the marginalized and align with the elite classes. Jesus's imagery stands as a corrective paradigm in such contexts.

The intentions of the thieves are made clear: They come "only to steal and kill and destroy" (10:10a). They are selfish and feed on the sheep and destroy the flock. In contrast, Jesus came so that the sheep "may have life and have it to the full" (10:10b). Jesus was drawing a contrast between himself and the Pharisees and other religious leaders. Earlier, the Pharisees had cast out the blind man instead of protecting him (9:34) – they had shown no care for this sheep. But Jesus found the man and welcomed him into the community of faith. Jesus offers the sheep life in its fullness.

10:11–21 JESUS IS THE GOOD SHEPHERD

Jesus then modified the metaphor slightly. Earlier, he referred to himself as the gate through which the sheep entered safety (10:7). Now, he says, "I am the good shepherd" (10:11a). This is the fourth of the "I am" sayings, following the earlier declarations, "I am the bread of life" (6:35), "I am the light of the world" (8:12), and "I am the gate for the sheep" (10:7). Whereas thieves and robbers come to steal, kill, and destroy (10:10), the good shepherd "lays down his life for the sheep" (10:11), protecting the sheep even at the cost of his own life. Jesus demonstrated this sacrificial love on the cross.

Another character is then introduced – the hired hand (10:12a). Hired hands were not regular shepherds but day workers who were hired due to a shortage of shepherds. Unlike a true shepherd, the hired hand neither owned nor cared for the sheep and did not know them personally. Therefore, "when he sees the wolf coming, he abandons the sheep and runs away. Then the wolf attacks the flock and scatters it" (10:12b). Hired hands would not risk their own life to protect the sheep (10:13). They cared more for their own lives than for the lives of the sheep because they were neither the owners nor the shepherds of the sheep but worked only for wages. While Jesus, the good shepherd, "lays down his life for the sheep," the hired hands run away to save themselves, abandoning the sheep and leaving them vulnerable to attack by the wolves. This prompts us to reflect on how we shepherd the flock God has entrusted to us: Are we good shepherds who lay down our lives for the sheep, or hired hands who run away, leaving the sheep to the wolves?

In contrast to the hired hands who worked only for wages, Jesus, as the good shepherd, risked his life for the sheep. The good shepherd knows his sheep, and they in turn know him in (10:14). The relationship between the shepherd and the sheep is one of intimacy and affection. Historically, the

Bedouin shepherds from the nomadic Arab tribes of the desert regions of the Arabian Peninsula and Mesopotamia have exemplified such dedication to their sheep.

Jesus then revealed the spiritual truth behind this relationship: "My sheep know me – just as the Father knows me and I know the Father – and I lay down my life for the sheep" (10:14b–15). This mutual knowing – which has already been established through expressions like "the sheep listen to his voice" and "he calls his own sheep by name" (10:3) – also reflects the intimate "knowing" that exists between the Father and the Son. The Father is yet another character introduced in this story, and the triangular relationship between the Father, the Son, and the sheep is a divine bond. Later, in response to Philip's request, "Lord, show us the Father and that will be enough for us" (14:8), Jesus would say, "Don't you know me, Philip, even after I have been among you such a long time? Anyone who has seen me has seen the Father. How can you say, 'Show us the Father'?" (14:9). Similarly, the sheep know Jesus, just as the Father knows the Son and the Son knows the Father (10:15a). Furthermore, the Son – the good shepherd – will lay down his life for the sheep (10:15b). This relationship between the shepherd and the sheep is not merely expressed in words but also demonstrated through practical action: The shepherd lays down his life for the sheep (10:11, 15b), and the sheep obey the shepherd (10:3–4, 16, 27). These repeated references highlight Jesus's intimacy with the sheep.

Jesus then introduces yet another character – "other sheep" – saying, "I have other sheep that are not of this sheep pen. I must bring them also. They too will listen to my voice, and there shall be one flock and one shepherd" (10:16). These "other sheep" would include people like the Samaritan believers and the Greeks who would later come seeking Jesus (12:20–22). Jesus will bring them in as well. Jesus's words also point to the future union of Jewish and Gentile believers. As Paul writes, "For he himself is our peace, who has made the two groups one and has destroyed the barrier, the dividing wall of hostility" (Eph 2:14). This foretold unity should challenge us to pursue oneness that transcends caste, class, and gender.

Not only will the sheep be united, but they will also all have just one shepherd. Jesus is the ultimate shepherd of both Jews and Gentiles. Ezekiel prophesied that one day, God himself would directly shepherd his people and that they would have one shepherd (Ezek 34:14; 37:24). Jesus now declares that he is that good shepherd – that one shepherd who unites all his sheep. The relationship between the one shepherd and the sheep is a mystical and inseparable union.

Once again, the love relationship between the Father and the Son is central: "The reason my Father loves me is that I lay down my life – only to take it up again" (10:17). Jesus's self-giving – in laying down his life and taking it up again – reflects his sacrificial nature as a shepherd, which causes the Father to love him even more. This is a clear indication of Jesus's imminent death and resurrection, through which God's love would be manifested.

Jesus made it clear that no one could take his life from him but that he would lay it down voluntarily: "No one takes it from me, but I lay it down of my own accord. I have the authority to lay it down and authority to take it up again. This command I received from my Father" (10:18). It is at the Father's command and through the Father's power that Jesus was empowered to do all good things. Neyrey comments, "The reason for Jesus's death lies entirely in his own hands: he can both 'lay it down' and 'take it up.' It would be fair to say that he dies voluntarily and is unvanquished and unconquered, which are marks of a noble death."[6] The contrast between the good shepherd and the hired hand becomes even more evident after the healing of the man born blind. The Jewish religious authorities and the synagogue leaders acted like hired hands in failing to care for the man in his helplessness. But Jesus, the good shepherd, sought him out and healed him. This passage underlines the nobility of the good shepherd's sacrificial death and supernatural resurrection, expressed through the language of laying down and taking up his life for the sake of the sheep.

As in Jesus's earlier discourses, his words once again gave rise to division among the Jews (10:19; see also 6:52; 8:57–59; 9:39–41). Many said, "He is demon-possessed and raving mad. Why listen to him?" (10:20). Earlier, the people had accused Jesus of being a Samaritan and demon-possessed (8:48); here, the claim was that he was out of his mind because he was possessed by a demon (10:20b; compare Mark 3:22). On the previous occasion, Jesus himself had refuted their claim (8:49); in this instance, another group defended him:[7] "These are not the sayings of a man possessed by a demon. Can a demon open the eyes of the blind?" (10:21). Jesus's words did not carry the power of demonic forces but, rather, power from above. The second group made a statement – "These are not the sayings of a man possessed by a demon" (10:21a) – and asked a rhetorical question: "Can a demon open the eyes of

---

6. J. H. Neyrey, "The 'Noble Shepherd' in John 10: Cultural and Rhetorical Background," *JBL* 120, no. 2 (2001): 285.
7. Beasley-Murray, *John*, 172.

the blind?" (10:21b). The healing of the blind man remained a central topic. What began in John 9:1 continues through to John 10:21. The healing led to a broader theological discourse, in which Jesus revealed himself as the gate and the good shepherd. Through Jesus, people enter into safety, and he lays down his life to protect them. That was exactly what the blind man experienced – though his own people rejected him, Jesus saved him.

In Asian contexts, the metaphor of "shepherd" has great significance in relation to leadership. Jesus's identity as the "good shepherd" offers a radical paradigm for all leaders, both sacred and secular. Jesus offers mercy, protection, and life to all: women, the paralyzed, the blind, Samaritans, Galileans, Judeans, Greeks, and others. In a world where people's striving for power and wealth often leads to individualism and corruption, Jesus's sacrificial model of leadership transcends all levels of management and leadership in Asia. His roles as the gate and the good shepherd offer transformative models for Asian Christians to follow.

JOHN 10:22–42
JESUS DURING THE FESTIVAL OF DEDICATION

The setting of the story shifts abruptly to the Festival of Dedication, also known as *Hanukkah* or the Feast of Lights, which took place in Jerusalem, during winter, in Solomon's Portico (10:22–23). Celebrated on Kislev 25 – a month in the Hebrew calendar – this festival commemorates the cleansing and rededication of the temple by Judas Maccabaeus in 165 BC, following its desecration by Antiochus Epiphanes, the king of Syria, in 167 BC. According to Willard M. Swartley, "The festival's light symbolism links it to the earlier Feast of Tabernacles; chapters 7–10 cohere as one long unit, even though other divisional markers within these chapters are evident."[1] The light symbolism in Judaism provides a point of connection with many Asian religions, which also place a strong emphasis on lights.

Jesus, the walking teacher, entered Jerusalem and the temple – the center of Jewish worship. The Jews gathered around him and asked, "How long will you keep us in suspense? If you are the Messiah, tell us plainly" (10:24). They thought that Jesus was intentionally keeping them in suspense by not revealing his identity. Although they suspected that Jesus might be the Messiah, their disbelief kept them from accepting him as such. This suspense, misunderstanding, and lack of knowledge was because of their rejection of Jesus, whose messianic identity had already been revealed publicly on several occasions (5:36). Once again, the pattern of misunderstanding, ignorance, and rejection by the Jews comes into play. Jesus told them that he had already made it clear that the works he did in his Father's name testified to his identity (10:25; compare 5:17, 36). The fault did not lie with Jesus for he had not hidden the truth from them. They did not believe because they were not his sheep (10:26). Belief cannot be actualized until a person adopts the ethos of the community and becomes part of it. Believing in Jesus qualifies a person to belong to the community

---

1. Willard M. Swartley, *John: Believers Church Bible Commentary* (Harrisonburg: Herald Press, 2013). See his discussion in "Time and Location of Discourse: Feast of Dedication." Josephus called it *phōta*, "the festival of lights" (*Ant.* 12.325).

of God's flock. Parananda contends that even in the original etymological sense, "belief" and "believing" were understood as "love" and "to love."[2] The Johannine community is depicted as an inclusive community of equals. Jesus reiterated what he had already said: "My sheep listen to my voice; I know them, and they follow me" (10:27; compare 10:1–18). But the Jews – who neither heard the voice of Jesus nor followed him – were not accepted into the community of believers. In contrast, those who believe belong to Jesus, follow him, and receive eternal life; they will neither perish nor be snatched out of the hand of the shepherd (10:28).

In the Fourth Gospel, it is only when someone denies themselves and embraces Christ that they are said to be truly "believing" and "following." The metaphorical language – "no one will snatch them out of my hand" – emphasizes the protection and eternal security promised to the sheep. In Northeastern India, tribal communities must hear and obey the voice of their chieftains and may remain in the community only if they have their leader's acceptance.[3] This mirrors the ethos of the Johannine community, where functional aspects are implemented with an emphasis on the principles of love and inclusivity.

Jesus declared that the Father, who had given him all these sheep, is greater than all things (10:29a). In this way, he acknowledged his submission and servitude to the Father. The expressions "no one will snatch them out of my hand" (10:28b) and "no one can snatch them out of my Father's hand" (10:29b) point to the unity of the Father and the Son in their salvific mission. The word "snatch" can mean to seize something quickly in a rude or eager way, to steal something, or to kidnap someone by suddenly seizing or grabbing them. To snatch from the hand of the Son is to snatch from the hand of the Father, and vice versa, underscoring the impossibility of seizing the sheep from the hands of these two mighty shepherds.[4]

The unity between Father and Son comes full circle in Jesus's declaration, "I and the Father are one" (10:30). The revelation that Jesus and the Father are one is one of the most profound statements in this Dedication Discourse.[5] The motif of oneness that runs through the Fourth Gospel functions as a

---

2. Sri Parananda, *An Eastern Exposition of the Gospel of Jesus according to St. John. being an interpretation thereof*, ed., R. L. Harrison (London: William Hutchinson and Co., 1902), 127. Compare Basker, *Interpreting Biblical Texts*, 14.
3. Yangkahao Vashum, ed., *Tribal Theology and the Bible: A Search for Contextual Relevance*, Tribal Study Series 19 (Jorhat: Tribal Study Center, 2011).
4. The following passages portray the Father or Yahweh as the shepherd of his people (Gen 48:15; 49:24; Pss 23:1; 28:9; 80:1).
5. Craig S. Keener, *The Gospel of John: A Commentary* (Peabody: Hendrickson, 2003), 1:825–26.

paradigm for building unity among believers. Mystical union with Christ is organic, reciprocal, and transformative. But the Jews were unable to connect the Son with God. Jesus's demonstration of unity with the Father and his call to the sheep to mirror that unity has great significance for Asian Christians, who often find themselves in denominationally competitive or doctrinally divided contexts. The declaration that no one can snatch the sheep out of the hands of either the Son or the Father reveals that even though believers' lives may be under threat, they are protected. Just as the Johannine community found safety in Christ, persecuted Christians in Asia can also place their trust and hope in him.

Once again, the Jews opposed Jesus's teachings and picked up stones to kill him (10:31). Unlike the Synoptic Gospels – Matthew, Mark, and Luke – which show opposition to Jesus arising later in his ministry, John's Gospel presents such opposition as taking place throughout Jesus's ministry. Stoning was a punishment reserved for serious moral offenses (compare 7:53–8:11) or blasphemy. Even today, some Islamic countries – such as Iran, Afghanistan, Pakistan, the United Arab Emirates, Qatar, and Yemen – practice stoning for sexual crimes. This execution method is rooted in ancient Greece and in the Judeo-Christian religious texts. Although Jesus had shown his opponents many good works from the Father, they attempted to stone him purely because of their misunderstanding and ignorance. Ironically, while Jesus did the good works of the Father, the people of the world failed to act according to God's expectations (10:32; compare 5:17).[6] They attempted to stone him not because of his works but because of his words. They had witnessed his signs but were unwilling to acknowledge them. They had heard his messianic utterances but misunderstood these. They had conditioned themselves not to accept either his works or his words. Out of misunderstanding, they accused Jesus of blasphemy: "We are not stoning you for any good work . . . but for blasphemy, because you, a mere man, claim to be God" (10:33). In Islam, blasphemy refers to insulting God, Prophet Muhammad, or other revered figures, and Islamic law condemns those who are guilty of apostasy or blasphemy. Similarly, Judaism also rejects apostasy and blasphemy. Although John claimed – and the early Christians believed – that God became human in the person of Jesus Christ and dwelled among them, the Jewish leaders rejected this claim, viewing Jesus as merely a human being who claimed divinity. The situation in Asia is often

---

6. Archibald T. Robertson, *The Fourth Gospel/The Epistle to the Hebrews*, Word Pictures in the New Testament 5 (New York: Ray Long & Richard R. Smith, Inc., 1932), 187.

similar, where many are willing to accept Jesus as a moral teacher or, at most, as one *deva* among many gods.[7] But accepting Jesus as God and acknowledging his words as divine often remains beyond the bounds of comprehension.

Jesus responded by quoting from their own Scriptures: "Is it not written in your Law, 'I have said you are "gods"'?" (10:34). This is a quote from Psalm 82, which portrays God as presiding over the great assembly and rendering judgment among the "gods" (82:1). He calls Israel "gods" and "sons of the Most High" (82:6). The believing Israelites, "to whom the word of God came" (10:35), were considered "gods" – that is, God's sons and daughters. They were called "gods" because they judged people righteously, just as God is an impartial judge. They stood in the place of God to execute judgment. Kings, high priests, and prophets functioned as divine voices in the world, speaking on behalf of God and revealing God's will to the world. Everyone to whom the word of God came (10:35a) was regarded as "gods" – his sons and daughters. God's word – that is, Scripture – cannot be set aside (10:35b) or considered false. Citing Scripture, Jesus used a lesser-to-greater argument: If God viewed all Israel as his sons and daughters, then "what about the one whom the Father set apart as his very own and sent into the world?" (10:36). Jesus's uniqueness in being set apart and sent into the world surely qualified him to be called God's own Son.

In India, outstanding figures such as sports stars or national heroes are often referred to as "gods." For example, Sachin Tendulkar is often called the "god of cricket." Such titles may be given because of extraordinary contributions, benevolence to the poor, commitment to righteousness, or advocacy for justice on behalf of the voiceless. In comparison, Jesus – who was set apart by God and sent into the world – is truly God and the Son of God.

Jesus directly asked on what grounds they accused him of being a blasphemer (10:36b). The Father had set him aside and sent him, and Jesus's own works testified that he is "God's Son." Blomberg comments, "The Hebrew for 'gods' (*ĕlōhîm*) could refer to various exalted beings beside Yahweh, without implying any challenge to monotheism, so if Jesus acknowledges that the Father has appointed him to be the divine Messiah, it is no crime to confess it."[8] Through his works, Jesus proved that he was and is the Son of God who manifested God in the world, but his opponents ignored these works.

---

7. *Deva* is a member of a class of divine beings in the Vedic period, which in Indian religion are benevolent.
8. Blomberg, *Historical Reliability of John's Gospel*, 163.

Similarly, even today, Christian missionaries who serve in the world as "gods" representing the heavenly God are often opposed and rejected by the world.

Jesus challenged them further: "Do not believe me unless I do the works of my Father" (10:37). This echoes what Nicodemus had said earlier: "Rabbi, we know that you are a teacher who has come from God. For no one could perform the signs you are doing if God were not with him" (3:2). Jesus's works testified that he had been sent from God, and his works reflected the Father's works. If they acknowledged the works of the Father manifested among them, they could not avoid believing in the Son. He continued, "If I do them, even though you do not believe me, believe the works, that you may know and understand that the Father is in me and I in the Father" (10:38). Jesus's life and ministry were dynamically interconnected and interwoven with the Father's life and work. Therefore, Jesus was entitled to call himself God or Son of God.

In Asia, many claim divine status based on self-exaltation. In ancient Israel, when the people obeyed God's word, they were considered "gods" – sons and daughter of God. But Jesus is the unique Son of God. He alone is one with the Father, who sent him to reveal God's love to all people. Jesus is not a human being who was exalted to divine status but a divine being who took on humanity. In a context where numerous gods are venerated and worshiped, Jesus stands apart as the true God of heaven and one whose origin is from above. The connection between this "God" of heaven and the "gods" of the earth (that is, believers in God) enables God's people to live in communion with God, hear his voice, and be equipped to serve as "gods" – God's representatives – on earth among mortals. This vertical and horizontal relationship between God, his people, and the rest of the world makes the earth a place where divine virtues flourish. In Asian contexts, the human and divine nature of Jesus has led to his recognition as a "sanctified teacher,"[9] "indwelling God,"[10] "purusha," "sannyasi,"[11] and "satpurusha."[12]

Once again, Jesus's revelation about his dynamic relationship with the Father provoked his opponents; they attempted to seize him, but he escaped (10:39).

---

9. Parananda, *Eastern Exposition of the Gospel of Jesus*, 30.
10. Appasamy, *Christianity as Bhakti Marga: A Study of the Johannine Doctrine of Love* (Madras: Christian Literature Society, 1930), 34–52. Also Basker, *Interpreting Biblical Texts*, 30.
11. Bede Griffiths, *The Marriage of the East and West: A Sequel to the Golden String* (London: Collins, 1982), 70, 189; Bede Griffiths, *A New Vision of Reality: Western Science, Eastern Mysticism and Christian Faith*, ed. Felicity Edwards (New Delhi: Harper Collins, 1989), 127; Bede Griffiths, *Return to the Centre* (London: Collins, 1976), 93.
12. Swami Abhishiktananda, *Saccidananda: A Christian Approach to Advaidic Experience* (New Delhi: ISPCK, 1974), 77–82.

John

Jesus then crossed the River Jordan to the place where John had been baptizing and remained there (10:40). Once again, this Gospel highlights Jesus's elusive nature – his sudden disappearance, his reappearance in an entirely different geographical location, and people's persistence in searching for him – which adds to the sense of mystery surrounding Jesus.

On one side of the river – that is, in Jerusalem – Jesus was rejected; but across the river, people flocked to him and believed in him (10:41–42). This parallels today's situation, where the global Christian center has shifted from the traditional Western and Northern regions to Eastern and Southern regions – especially Africa and Asia.

Those across the Jordan compared Jesus to John the Baptizer: "Though John never performed a sign, all that John said about this man was true" (10:41b). Unlike John, Jesus performed many signs. The people remembered John's revelation and confessed, "All that John said about this man was true." The forerunner had revealed the truth about Jesus. As a result of John's work, those across the Jordan believed in Jesus – unlike those in Jerusalem, who had rejected his works and his identity.

While "many" (10:20) in Jerusalem rejected Jesus, "many" (10:41a) across the Jordan accepted him and recognized his superiority to John the Baptizer. While many in Jerusalem stood against him, rejected his words, attempted to stone at him, and even tried to arrest him, many across the Jordan affirmed their faith in him (10:42). Just as Jesus offered himself as the true light during *Sukkoth* (7:1–10:21) – that is, the Festival of Booths or the Festival of Tabernacles – he again offered himself as the true light during *Hanukkah*, the festival of lights. Jesus, as the light of the world, exposed the dark side of his opponents.

Christians in Asia can reflect this true light and bring light to a world in darkness. Just as the light symbolism of the Festival of Dedication made it an appropriate occasion for Jesus to reveal his identity as the true light and his unique relationship with the Father, Asian festivals offer great opportunities to present Jesus as the true light to those seeking light. Jesus's revelation during the Festival of Dedication emphasized his unity with the Father, and this unique relationship of Father and Son was manifested in the public arena through the unique mission and ministry of Jesus. As the gospel spreads across the continent of Asia, the dualism of light and darkness can be used to explain the gospel by creating bridges between Christianity and other religions in Asia. Such bridge-building can be a powerful hermeneutical tool for communicating the biblical message in Asian contexts.

JOHN 11:1–57

JESUS RAISES LAZARUS FROM THE DEAD

This episode (11:1–57) describes the final sign performed by Jesus in the *Book of Signs*. It has six subsections: a concern of Mary and Martha (11:1–6); Jesus and the disciples (11:7–16); Jesus and Martha (11:17–27); Jesus and Mary (11:28–37); Jesus raises Lazarus (11:38–44); and antagonism against Jesus (11:45–57). The themes in this story – such as friendship, resurrection, and life – hold deep significance for Asians.

11:1–6 A CONCERN OF MARY AND MARTHA

The event begins in narrative form with Lazarus of Bethany, Mary, and her sister Martha as the main characters (11:1). The narrator employs a storytelling style reminiscent of the familiar "Once upon a time . . . there was a place . . . three people lived there." In ancient India, *katha* (or *kathya*) was a storytelling format used in oral traditions to recount stories of India's history or religious narratives. In Hinduism and Sikhism, the priests functioned as the storytellers. John uses a similar style. The narrative expressions "a man named Lazarus" and "the village of Mary and her sister Martha" reveal that the village was associated with the names of the sisters, not Lazarus. He is introduced in relation to his sisters, which suggests that the narrator is telling the story mainly from the sisters' perspective. Just as the city of Kolkata is often referred to as the city of Mother Teresa and Kedgaon is considered the village of Pandita Ramabai, Bethany is portrayed as the village of Mary and Martha. Somehow, John's audience seemed to have been more familiar with the sisters than with their brother.

Lazarus – whose name means "God helps" – was sick (11:1–4, 6). Although these verses refer to him being sick (*asthenia*), they do not tell us the nature of the sickness – only that it resulted in his death.

The narrator adds one more piece of background information: "This Mary, whose brother Lazarus now lay sick, was the same one who poured perfume on the Lord and wiped his feet with her hair" (11:2). Although these words give the impression that this anointing had already taken place, the narrator reports this event only in the next chapter (12:1–8). In this way, he leaves readers anticipating the story. Although scholars have tried to harmonize this account with similar stories in the Synoptic Gospels (Matt 26:6–13; Mark 14:3–9; Luke 7:36–50), such attempts have been unsuccessful due to both similarities and differences in these accounts. For instance, Matthew, Mark, and John place the events in Bethany. Matthew and Mark say it happened in the house of Simon the leper, while Luke places it in the house of one of the Pharisees and John in Lazarus's house. Luke presents the woman in the story as someone "who lived a sinful life," while John refers to her as Mary, the sister of Lazarus and Martha. Matthew, Mark, and Luke refer to an alabaster jar containing a very expensive perfume; similarly, John mentions "a pint of pure nard, an expensive perfume." Matthew and Mark refer to the woman anointing Jesus's head, while Luke and John say that she poured the perfume on Jesus's feet and wiped his feet with her hair. One possible solution is that these were two separate events. Nevertheless, the fact that all four Gospel writers seem to refer to this incident suggests that this was a historical event, perhaps retold to fit each writer's overall theme. For John, these two stories involving the two sisters and their brother conclude the *Book of Signs* and prepare for the *Book of Glory* through Mary's act of anointing Jesus in preparation for his death. From a storytelling perspective, their back-to-back placement makes good sense.

Knowing the severity of Lazarus's illness, the sisters sent a message to Jesus: "Lord, the one you love is sick" (11:3).[1] Their message affirms that Lazarus was a beloved disciple of Jesus or that they were close family friends. Perhaps Jesus had stayed in their home whenever he passed through Bethany.

The Korean *Minjung* theology is a theology of the people that emerged from the people's struggles for social justice in South Korea. Similarly, other cultures and religions also recognize divine intervention in human affairs during times of crisis. This story reflects both divine-human interaction and family dynamics among the sisters, their brother, and their friend. Readers will understand that Lazarus's illness greatly troubled the sisters, prompting them to seek help from Jesus – a family friend known to be a miracle worker. The setting and characterization in the narrative resonate with the realities of many Asian villages, where communities are often plagued by illness, epidemics, and death, leaving people deeply concerned about their loved ones.

Upon hearing about Lazarus's sickness, Jesus said (perhaps to his disciples): "This sickness [*asthenia*] will not end in death. No, it is for God's glory so that God's Son may be glorified through it" (11:4). This response is reminiscent

---

1. John Painter, *The Quest for the Messiah: The History, Literature and Theology of the Johannine Community*, 2nd ed. (Nashville: Abingdon, 1993), 367–73.

of what he had earlier told his disciples about the man born blind: "Neither this man nor his parents sinned . . . but this happened so that the works of God might be displayed in him" (9:3). Once again, the narrator highlights the connection between suffering and glory. While this theme of glory continues to develop at *micro-level* (see 11:40), at a *macro-level*, the ultimate glory would be seen in Jesus's death on the cross and his resurrection, which this story of Lazarus anticipates.[2]

The narrator emphasizes Jesus's love not only for Lazarus (11:3) but also for Martha and Mary (11:5). Initially, Martha is described as Mary's sister (11:1), but now Mary is referred to as Martha's sister (11:5). The alternating focus on Lazarus, Martha, and Mary suggests that each of them is important to the narrative and that Jesus loved them equally, regarding all three as his friends.

Nevertheless, Jesus's love for his friends did not lead him to rush to Bethany: "When he heard that Lazarus was sick [*asthenia*], he stayed where he was two more days" (11:6). He did not hurry because he knew that this sickness was not meant to end in death (11:4). Jesus was in a remote place, far from the Jewish authorities, since opposition against him was growing.

Jesus's ministry in both villages and cities serves as a helpful model for us. Missional and pastoral activities are often carried out in large and prominent cities, neglecting rural and village areas. This tendency is widespread among missionaries and pastors in different parts of Asia. Jesus had earlier been in Jerusalem, the capital city, but now he was in Bethany, which was a two-day journey from Jerusalem. Mahatma Gandhi once shared this vision: "The future of India lies in its villages."[3] Centuries earlier, Jesus practiced this principle by ministering in villages and valleys just as much as in cities and mountains.

Furthermore, Asian churches must not ignore the ministry of women. In this Gospel, Jesus taught the Samaritan woman about the importance of worship (John 4). Later, Mary Magdalene would become the first witness to Jesus's resurrection (John 20). In John 11, Martha would learn the significance of resurrection, and both Mary and Martha would witness their brother being raised from the dead. In John 12, Mary would anoint Jesus in preparation for his death. Similarly, women in Asia play a key role in understanding who Jesus is, accepting him, witnessing to his resurrection, and proclaiming

---

2. R. Alan Culpepper, *Anatomy of the Fourth Gospel: A Study in Literary Design* (Philadelphia: Fortress Press, 1983), 140–42.
3. Dhiru Thadani, "The Future of India Lies in Its Villages," Planetizen, https://www.planetizen.com/node/50694#.

his gospel message of deliverance and acceptance. Therefore, Asian churches should actively affirm their courage, ministry, and significance in the growth of Christianity.

11:7–16 JESUS AND THE DISCIPLES

Initially, the Lord had remained two extra days in a remote place after hearing of Lazarus's sickness; now he tells the disciples, "Let us go back to Judea" (11:7), prompting a dialogue between Jesus and the disciples (11:7–16).

"Back to Judea" implies that they had previously left Judea, perhaps ministering near the Judean boundary or in Samaria or Galilee. The Jews' attempt to stone Jesus (10:31), their efforts to arrest him (10:39), Jesus's crossing over to region of Jordan (10:40), and his decision to go back to Judea (11:7) must be read together. The Jews' rejection had driven Jesus out of Judea; now, Lazarus's death drew him back. This highlights Jesus's love for Lazarus and his sisters and symbolizes God's unwavering love for Judea and its people.

The disciples responded, "But Rabbi . . . a short while ago the Jews there tried to stone you, and yet you are going back?" (11:8). Recalling the Jews' antagonism toward Jesus and his disciples and their escape from danger (10:31, 39–40), they were troubled by Jesus's decision to return to the place where he had been accused of violating the Sabbath and blasphemy. As eyewitnesses to these events, the disciples were surprised by Jesus's decision to return to Judea. This incident reveals two attitudes toward mission: boldness to witness in the face of persecution and fear of persecution. Jesus's commitment to his mission in dangerous circumstances serves as a paradigm in the Asian context today.

In verses 9–10, Jesus spoke metaphorically to his disciples, distinguishing between the twelve hours of daylight and the twelve hours of night. While those who walk during the day do not stumble because they see the light of the world, those who walk at night stumble because the light is not in them. The dualism between light and darkness is widely used in Asian religions like Zoroastrianism. While Zoroastrianism emphasizes a pure dualism, John's Gospel presents a modified dualism in which God remains in control of everything even amid tensions and conflicts. Jesus used the metaphors of day and night, and light and darkness, to communicate the importance of the present moment for fulfilling God's will, emphasizing that his time on earth was limited and warning of a time when witnessing would become even more difficult. Stumbling or not stumbling would depend on whether the disciples walked in light or in darkness. Indian roads are usually safe during the day, but those who travel at night often face difficulties due to poor road conditions, overflowing gutters, robbers, and wild animals.

Jesus continued to speak metaphorically: "Our friend Lazarus has fallen asleep; but I am going there to wake him up" (11:11). But taking his words literally, the disciples responded, "Lord, if he sleeps, he will get better" (11:12). Jesus was referring to Lazarus's death, but the disciples missed his point yet again, and so Jesus stated it plainly: "Lazarus is dead" (11:13–14). In religious discourse, metaphor often plays a significant role. Jesus used the "sleep" metaphor to express the divine perspective: Believers are not truly dead, only asleep. Christians in Asia can use such metaphorical language to communicate truth in culturally relevant ways. Since the Asian thought-world is metaphorical and figurative, interpreters of the Gospel of John should pay attention to these dynamics in their interpretative endeavors.

Jesus's absence from Bethany and Lazarus's death were necessary to reveal God's glory through Jesus. Later, Jesus's own death would glorify the Father who had sent him. At the same time, this pericope also illustrates the disciples' lack of faith and misunderstanding. They were fearful of returning to Jerusalem and its surrounding region, including Bethany.

Thomas appears in the narrative for the first time here. He will later feature prominently in several pericopes, including the well-known incident where he asked for evidence of Jesus's resurrection (20:24–28; see also 14:5; 21:2). Thomas said, "Let us also go, that we may die with him" (11:16). In *Sati* (also known as "suttee") – which was one of India's most controversial practices – a widow was expected to die alongside her deceased husband to prove her chastity. However, this practice never extended to dying alongside one's deceased teacher. While Thomas affirmed his willingness to die with his teacher, he would not have realized the prophetic nature of his statement: The Lord would soon die in Jerusalem, and his disciples would later die elsewhere as his witnesses. Thomas's attitude stands in sharp contrast to Judas Iscariot's betrayal and Peter's denial. His devotion to Jesus and his loyalty to his master's mission are clear in his bold declaration.

Thomas had a nickname or a family name – "Didymus" – that meant "twin." Whether or not he was a biological twin, Thomas may be considered Jesus's spiritual "twin." While the other disciples tried to discourage Jesus from returning to Jerusalem due to the growing hostility, Thomas boldly expressed his willingness to die with Jesus. Thomas's statement shifts the attention of the reader from the *micro-story* of Lazarus to the *macro-story* of Jesus. In the Gospel of John, dramatic stories are told with twists, ironies, and misunderstandings. Thomas's bold statement introduces a new twist within John's narrative framework.

Thomas is highly venerated and respected as the "Apostle to the East," and Indian Christians believe that he came to India and was martyred there.[4] Thomas's willingness to die with Jesus serves as a powerful paradigm for Christians in Asia, where persecution of Christians remains rampant and many still die as martyrs.

11:17–27 JESUS AND MARTHA

When Jesus and the disciples arrived in Bethany, they found that Lazarus had already died and been in the tomb for four days (11:17; compare 11:14). Bethany was less than two miles from Jerusalem (11:18), and as was the custom, many Jews had come to console Martha and Mary on the loss of their brother (11:19). In Asia, comforting and consoling the bereaved family is an important social custom. Neighboring families usually take the initiative to provide food and other necessary assistance to the bereaved families. In the Thar Desert region of Rajasthan, India, women from lower castes were once hired to mourn at funerals on behalf of privileged upper-caste women, who were expected to maintain their composure and dignity. In Vietnam, professional mourners are hired to take the attention of family members so that they can handle other responsibilities.[5] These practices show that communal mourning is a significant part of funerals in Asian cultures.

When Jesus arrived in Bethany, Martha went out to meet him, while Mary stayed at home (11:20). Martha expressed her confidence that if Jesus had been there, Lazarus would not have died (11:21).[6] As a close friend of the family and a miracle worker, Jesus could have healed his friend. But Jesus had not been there, and Lazarus had died. Despite this, Martha viewed Jesus as someone commissioned and sent by God and with access to God, and she expressed confidence that God would give Jesus whatever he asked (11:22). Martha's words reveal her faith in Jesus's identity and his privileged relationship with the Father. In John's Gospel, women are portrayed as exercising great faith. Similarly, women continue to demonstrate great faith and to serve as witnesses to Jesus across Asia. Martha's faith stands in contrast to the disciples'

---

4. Thomaskutty, *Saint Thomas the Apostle*, 15–34.
5. Michelle FlorCruz, "The Hysterical World of Professional Funeral Mourners," Asia Society, 24 February 2016, https://asiasociety.org/blog/asia/hysterical-world-professional-funeral-mourners.
6. Keener, *Gospel of John*, 2:842–44.

fear of entering Jerusalem and the religious leaders' intent to kill Jesus. Jesus responded to Martha's statement by assuring her that her brother would rise again (11:23). The raising of Lazarus – like the healing of the official's son's (4:46–54) – foreshadowed Jesus's own resurrection. Believers will rise again.

Martha, like Nicodemus and the Samaritan woman, misunderstood the spiritual meaning behind Jesus's words. Connecting Lazarus's resurrection with the eschatological resurrection, she said, "I know he will rise again in the resurrection at the last day" (11:24). As a devout Jew, she believed in the eschatological resurrection of all Israel.[7] However, despite her belief that Lazarus would not have died if Jesus had been there and her acknowledgment "I know that even now God will give you whatever you ask" (11:22), she did not expect Jesus to raise Lazarus from the dead. Her theology, combined with the painful reality that her brother had been buried for four days, left her confused but also hopeful.

Jesus declared, "I am the resurrection and the life" (11:25a). This is the fifth "I am" statement in John's Gospel, the others being, "I am the bread of life" (6:35, 48; see also 6:51), "I am the light of the world" (8:12), "I am the gate" (10:9), and "I am the good shepherd" (10:11–14).[8] Jesus was not talking about the future eschatological resurrection of all people but a present resurrection hope for her brother, Lazarus. He would soon prove this by raising Lazarus from the dead, even though the body had already been in the tomb for four days. Jesus's "I am" declaration flowed from the intimate Father-Son relationship.[9]

As the embodiment of this present resurrection hope, Jesus said, "The one who believes in me will live, even though they die" (11:25b). Jesus's resurrection life extends to his followers. Believing in Jesus is the basic requirement for enjoying life in abundance (compare 20:31). This invitation was not just for Martha but is universal. Jesus connected belief with life, stating that for those who believe, the eschatological age of salvation begins now (11:26). True life begins by believing in Jesus and living in accordance with that faith. In

---

7. G. H. C. MacGregor, *The Gospel of John*, Moffat New Testament Commentary (London: Hodder & Stoughton, 1928), 248.
8. This list doesn't include statements like "I am" to the Samaritan woman's inquiry who was the Messiah (4:26) or "I am" to the frightened disciples on the Sea of Galilee (6:20). Similarly, it doesn't include Jesus's statements, "I am one who testifies for myself" (8:18), "When you have lifted up the Son of Man, then you will know that I am he" (8:28a), or "Before Abraham was born, I am!" (8:58b).
9. Abhishiktananda, *Hindu-Christian Meeting Point*, 59. Also Basker, *Interpreting Biblical Texts*, 73.

this way, the present and future resurrections converge – the eschatological age has already begun.

Martha believed in a future resurrection at the end of the world; but Jesus invited her to believe in him and experience resurrection life in the present. He asked, "Do you believe this?" – meaning, would she believe in more than a future eschatological resurrection of all people? She confessed, "Yes, Lord . . . I believe that you are the Messiah, the Son of God, who is to come into the world" (11:27). Previously, Martha had believed that Jesus's presence would have saved her brother's life (11:21); now, she confessed him as the long-anticipated Messiah, God's Son. Martha's faith moved through several stages, revealing perplexity, confusion, and, finally, trust in Jesus. Her experience reflects the journey of many Asian believers, who begin their faith journey by leaving behind their gods and even their families. Faith is not instantaneous but an ongoing lifestyle of believing in Jesus and living for him.

Jesus, as both a spiritual shepherd and a friend of the family, demonstrated his care for his friends during a crisis. Asian believers expect their spiritual leaders to be present during both joyful and sorrowful situations in their lives. For example, Japanese pastors are well-known for their role in hospice care – ministering to the dying and their families.[10] Jesus's compassionate approach to Martha's concerns enabled her to understand new spiritual truths. Just as Martha affirmed her friendship, confidence, and trust in Jesus, many Asians place their confidence and trust in their spiritual leaders during life's critical moments.

Jesus's death and resurrection have been used as a "picture" for other revolutions. After the assassination of Mahatma Gandhi in 1948, Sarojini Naidu delivered a speech titled "My Father, Do Not Rest" on All India Radio. In her speech, she said,

> Like Christ of old on the third day he [Gandhiji] has risen again in answer to the cry of his people and the call of the world for the continuance of his guidance, his love, his service and inspiration. And while we all mourn, those who loved him, knew him personally, and those to whom his name was but a miracle and a legend, though we are all full of tears and though we are full of sorrow on this third day when he [Gandhiji] has risen from his

---

10. Timothy O. Benedict, "Practicing Spiritual Care in the Japanese Hospice," *Japanese Journal of Religious Studies* 45, no. 1 (2018): 175–200.

own ashes, I feel that sorrow is out of place and tears become a blasphemy.[11]

Naidu's speech offered metaphorical hope to a nation heartbroken by the assassination of the one they had trusted for their deliverance. Yet this pales in comparison to the hope expressed by Martha, who believed in Jesus as the resurrection – not merely a metaphorical hope but a present and living reality. That same hope is available to anyone in Asia – and elsewhere –who believes in Jesus and lives a life of faith.

11:28–37 JESUS AND MARY

After her profound declaration (11:27), Martha returned home and called her sister, Mary, saying, "The teacher is here . . . and is asking for you" (11:28). Although the narrator makes no mention of the fact that Jesus had asked Martha about Mary, Martha's words imply that he had done so, revealing Jesus's care for both sisters. The narrator's style of abbreviating dialogue is at work here. Mary, one of the story's central characters, who was introduced in verses 1–3, now makes an appearance. As Martha's words indicate, it was Jesus's call that prompted Mary to go to Jesus. Her response indicates it is evident that she was unaware of Jesus's return to Bethany. At Martha's statement, Mary immediately went to meet Jesus (11:29). Her prompt response reveals her love and affection for Jesus. Perhaps Mary believed that Jesus's presence would bring comfort to the family. In honor-shame cultures in Asia, while women are expected to express their agony and despair when there has been a death in the family, they are also expected to act with restraint in their interactions with the opposite sex. But both Martha and Mary showed no hesitation in rushing to meet Jesus and openly expressing their grief and despair to him.

The narrator notes that Jesus was still at the place where Martha had met him – outside the village of Bethany (11:30). When Mary suddenly left, the Jews who had come to console the sisters followed her, assuming that she was going to the tomb to mourn. These details emphasize the emotional intensity of the situation and the communal nature of mourning within the Jewish community. Similar practices can be seen in many Asian cultures. In Tibet, for example, Buddhists gather to mourn a person's death for forty-nine days. During this period, the family makes clay figures and prayer flags, allowing for

---

11. Sarojini Naidu, "My father, Do Not Rest," 1 February 1948, Comprehensive website of the life and works of Mahatma Gandhi, https://www.mkgandhi.org/Selected%20Letters/Sarojini/broadcast.htm.

a collective expression of grief. In Hindu tradition in India, extended family and friends come together to support the grieving family in an elaborate thirteen-day ritual.[12] The Jewish community also observed several socioreligious customs, including public expression of sorrow, burial rituals, accompanying the bereaved family, covering the body with burial clothes, and placing the dead body in a tomb.

The confessions of Martha (11:21) and Mary (11:32) are identical in meaning but differ in their structure in the Greek text. Whereas Martha says, "Would not have died the brother of mine," Mary says, "My would not have died brother" – with the placement of the verb "died" between "my" and "brother" visually representing the separation caused by that death. Similarly, their body language is also different: Mary "fell at his feet" as she spoke (11:32). Earlier, Mary had sat at the Lord's feet and listened to his words, with no thoughts of food, hospitality, or helping her sister (Luke 10:39). Not long after, Mary would anoint and wipe Jesus's feet while he reclined at table with the resurrected Lazarus (11:2; 12:3). This repeated posture of being at Jesus's feet reveals Mary's love, adoration, deep emotions, and eagerness to learn. She also wept at Jesus's feet (11:33), and her grief led him to weep (11:35). While the sisters' words could be interpreted as a rebuke of Jesus for his absence and his failure to prevent Lazarus's death, their theology, presence with him, weeping, and posture convey their deep trust that he would act for the good of their family. Martha and Mary found in Jesus a family friend who shared in their sorrows, and they clung to him in their time of need. The same can be true of us today. Jesus may sometimes seem absent in our times of need, but he is never too late to comfort and heal.

Just as many people gathered at the wedding at Cana in Galilee (2:1–11), many gathered at Lazarus's home to comfort and console his sisters. This resonates with Asian cultures and challenges Christians to be present with both those who rejoice and those who mourn, thereby creating opportunities for people to experience Jesus's compassion and power.

People relate to Jesus in different ways. While Martha conversed with him about eschatological resurrection, Mary approached him with deep emotion, adopting a posture of humility and revealing her troubled soul. Both

---

12. John Frederick Wilson, "Death and Dying: How Different Cultures Deal with Grief and Mourning," The Conversation, 25 January 2023, https://theconversation.com/death-and-dying-how-different-cultures-deal-with-grief-and-mourning-197299.

approaches were acceptable to Jesus, and he met each woman where she was – an important lesson for us in our own ministries.

Mary's weeping and the weeping of those who accompanied her "deeply moved" Jesus's spirit and troubled him (11:33). His sorrow was not passive but stirred him to action. He asked, "Where have you laid him?" (11:34a), and they replied, "Come and see, Lord" (11:34b). Earlier, Jesus had invited the curious disciples to "come and see" where he lived (1:39). Similarly, Philip had invited Nathanael to "come and see" the one whom the prophets had written about (1:46). Now Mary, Martha, and the Jews invited Jesus to "come and see" where they had buried their beloved Lazarus.

At their summons, and seeing their sorrow, "Jesus wept" (11:35). The same Jesus who had made a whip and driven out the merchants from the Jerusalem temple, showing his zeal for his Father's house (2:13–22), now wept at the tomb of his friend Lazarus, showing deep tenderness (11:35).[13] These two seemingly contrasting emotions of Jesus reflect both the wrath and the mercy of the God of the OT.

The Jews who saw Jesus weeping exclaimed, "See how he loved [*phileō*] him!" (11:36). Although some scholars place great emphasis on the different Greek words used to describe love – *agapaō* for "divine" or "genuine" love and *phileō* for "brotherly" or "friendly" love – in John's Gospel, these terms are used interchangeably. For example, "The Father loves [*phileō*] the Son and shows him all he does" (5:20), "Anyone who loves [*phileō*] their life will lose it" (12:25), and "The Father himself loves [*phileō*] you because you have loved [*phileō*] me" (16:27). Earlier, when Lazarus was sick, the sisters had sent a message to Jesus, saying, "Lord, the one you love [*phileō*] is sick" (11:3); and the Jews who saw Jesus weep now said, "See how he loved [*phileō*] him!" (11:36). Certainly, Jesus's love [*phileō*] for Lazarus – like the Father's love for the Son or the Father's love for believers – is deeper than mere friendship or brotherly love.

While some marveled at Jesus's love for Lazarus, others questioned his power: "Could not he who opened the eyes of the blind man have kept this man from dying?" (11:37). Their references to the healing of the man born blind (John 9) recalls the decree that anyone who confessed Jesus's messiahship would be expelled. Up to this point, the antagonism of the Jewish leaders had been driven mainly by concerns over Sabbath violations (5:1–18; 9:1–41). But

---

13. Witherington, *John's Wisdom*, 203–4.

from this point on, the raising of Lazarus became the main focus, leading, ultimately, to Jesus's own death and resurrection.

11:38–44 JESUS RAISES LAZARUS

As he stood outside the village of Bethany, Jesus was "deeply moved in spirit and troubled" (11:33). Standing before the tomb of Lazarus, Jesus was "once more deeply moved" (11:38). In both references to "deeply moved," the Greek verb used is *embrimaomai*, which also referred to the snorting of horses, expressing Jesus's intense grief over Lazarus's death and his identification with the people's sorrow. The tomb was a cave [*spēlaion*], sealed by a stone lying across its entrance (11:38).[14] The same Greek word is used when Jesus accused the religious leaders of turning his Father's house into a "den [cave, *spēlaion*] of robbers" (Matt 21:13; Mark 11:17; Luke 19:46). Now, his beloved friend lay dead in a cave, waiting to be raised to life by Jesus.

Jesus stood at the entrance of the cave and commanded, "Take away the stone" (11:39a). As noted elsewhere, such stones were large and not easily moved (see Mark 16:3–4). In addition, there would have been the emotional and psychological trauma of viewing a decaying body. As Martha said, "But, Lord . . . by this time there is a bad odor, for he has been there four days" (11:39b). Crime detectives and medical examiners often describe the smell of a decaying human body as unforgettable. Anyone who has smelled decaying vermin can attest to this. Despite Martha's faith and her confession of Jesus's messianic identity (11:27), she had doubts: Would Jesus really be able to raise the decaying body of Lazarus?

Undeterred, Jesus reminded Martha, "Did I not I tell you that if you believe, you will see the glory of God?" (11:40). The theme of glory recurs here. Just as a man's blindness was for the glory of God, Lazarus's death was also to reveal God's glory, and Martha would soon see this with her own eyes. Jesus assured Martha that if she believed, she would witness the glory of God. Like Martha, we can witness divine glory when we put our trust in Jesus. This entire episode functions within the framework of a promise of glory (11:4, 40) and its actualization.[15] Jesus, who is greatly troubled when his friends suffer, continues to transform their sufferings into glorious moments.

---

14. In the Gospels, this noun, *spēlaion*, refers to a cave used for a tomb only here. Elsewhere, it occurs in Jesus's accusation that the religious leaders had made his Father's house into a "den [cave, *spēlaion*] of robbers" (Matt 21:13; Mark 11:17; and Luke 19:46).
15. Mary L. Coloe, *Dwelling in the Household of God: Johannine Ecclesiology and Spirituality* (Collegeville: Liturgical Press, 2007), 85.

In that culture, it would have been unthinkable to open a sealed tomb after four days. Yet at Jesus's insistence, the people obeyed and removed the stone (11:41a). Jesus then prayed, "Father, I thank you that you have heard me" (11:41b). Jesus's prayer affirms his intimate connection with the Father, his humility before the Father, and his belief that the Father always hears him. His prayer was not for his own benefit but for the people, that they might believe that God had sent him (11:42).

After his prayer, Jesus cried out in a loud voice, "Lazarus, come out!" (11:43). Elsewhere, Jesus used this same command "come" (*deuro*) to call a man bound by attachment to wealth to follow him (Matt 19:21; Mark 10:21; Luke 18:22). Here, the same command is issued to a man bound by humanity's greatest enemy – death. Jesus's cry was passionate and deeply emotional. In the face of unbelief, doubt, and even mockery, his command was also a confirmation of his power over death.

While the people referred to Lazarus as "this man" (11:37b), the narrator refers to him as "the dead man." The dead man came to life and emerged from the tomb with his hands and feet still wrapped with the strips of linen they had bound him with and a cloth around his face (11:44a) as was the burial custom of the Jews.[16] Jesus's command to "take off the grave clothes and let him go" (11:44b) symbolized Lazarus's release from all human bindings as well as from death's grip, setting him free to resume his normal life. This sign demonstrated Jesus's authority to give life and to liberate people from whatever binds them. Where sin, death, and the powers of darkness prevail, Jesus's resurrection power is both liberative and transformative. In this way, the rhetoric of the Johannine narrative speaks powerfully and persuasively to Asian readers. Just as Lazarus's sisters moved from utter despair and hopelessness to joy and hope, the resurrection life that Jesus gives brings hope to the hopeless in Asia.

11:45–57 ANTAGONISM AGAINST JESUS

The raising of Lazarus led many of the Jews who had accompanied Mary to believe in Jesus (11:45). As is typical in this Gospel, the author highlights the connection between signs and faith – seeing ("seen what Jesus did") and believing ("believed in him") are paired together.

While some believed, others acted as informants and reported Jesus's miracle to the Pharisees (11:46). Not all Pharisees were opposed to Jesus – Nicodemus, for instance, had sought out Jesus and engaged him in a theological

---

16. Brant, *John*, 177.

discussion (3:1). However, many of the Pharisees functioned as a kind of "theology police," questioning religious figures like John the Baptizer (1:24) and itinerant preachers like Jesus to ensure that their teachings were aligned with the Scriptures. Their intention was partly to protect the people from the wrath of the Romans should any unrest arise (11:48), and their opposition to Jesus was not solely on theological grounds but also because of political concerns.

Frustrated by their inability to silence Jesus, the chief priests and the Pharisees called a meeting of the Sanhedrin, the highest Jewish legal body (11:47). They complained, "What are we accomplishing . . . Here is this man performing many signs" (11:47). Although only a few miracles are recorded in John's Gospel, the narrator says, "Jesus performed many other signs . . . which are not recorded in this book" (20:30) and "Jesus did many other things as well. If every one of them were written down, I suppose that even the whole world would not have room for the books that would be written" (21:25). These signs of Jesus were the cause of the Pharisees' frustration.

The Jewish authorities feared that if they did not act to stop Jesus, "everyone will believe in him," resulting in a riot against Rome, and "then the Romans will come and take away both our temple and our nation" (11:48). They were afraid that local unrest would provoke Rome's anger.

Caiaphas – the high priest and a member of the Sanhedrin – challenged his colleagues, accusing them of failing to understand the situation. He declared, "It is better for you that one man die for the people than that the whole nation perish" (11:50).[17] Caiaphas's statement was not something new; earlier, Nicodemus – one of Pharisees and a member of the Sanhedrin – had defended Jesus: "Does our law condemn a man without first hearing him to find out what he has been doing?" (7:51). Caiaphas proposed that one man's (Jesus's) death would preserve the whole nation (11:50). His motivation was both political and religious: politically, Jesus should be killed to avoid possible unrest among the people that could lead to rebellion against Rome, resulting in the loss of the temple and the land; religiously, he viewed Jesus's death as a necessary sacrifice to safeguard the nation. The Jewish authorities began to plot against Jesus and the growing movement that had emerged under his leadership.

---

17. Most commentators follow Origen (c. 200 AD) and understand "that year" to mean something like "that fateful year in which Jesus died." Blomberg, *Historical Reliability of the Fourth Gospel*, 173.

The narrator makes it clear that Caiaphas did not speak these words on his own initiative, "but as high priest that year he prophesied that Jesus would die for the Jewish nation . . . [and] for the scattered children of God" (11:51–52a). Jesus's death would be a substitutionary sacrifice that would prevent the destruction of the whole nation. Caiaphas's prophecy would come true as Jesus did in fact die for the nation's sins, thereby rescuing the Jews within Judea and Galilee, as well as those scattered throughout the diaspora "to bring them together and make them one" (11:52b).[18] Non-biblical Jewish writings of the time also spoke of such a gathering of all Jews in Jerusalem.[19] Later, Paul would write about Jesus uniting both Jews and Gentiles (Eph 2:14–16). But the chief priests, the Pharisees, and the Sanhedrin did not view Jesus as a unifier of the national and dispersed Jews. Instead, they were consumed by fear that "the Romans will come and take away both our temple and our nation" (11:48). Therefore, from that day on, they made plans to kill Jesus (11:53). Through Jesus's death, they aimed to deliver the nation of Israel from the hands of Romans and gather the dispersed children of God. The irony is that, unknowingly, their actions contributed to the fulfillment of God's plan of salvation.

Knowing their plans – and because it was not yet his time to die – Jesus withdrew from public view. He left Judea and went with his disciples to the village of Ephraim, near the wilderness (11:54).

In the meantime, another Passover was approaching, and many Jews from the countryside went early to the temple to purify themselves (11:55). "They" – perhaps the religious leaders mentioned in this pericope or those who had witnessed the raising of Lazarus and reported it to the Pharisees in the previous pericope – searched for Jesus as they stood in the temple courts (11:56a). They wondered, "Isn't he coming to the festival at all?" (11:56b). This recalls an earlier occasion, during the Festival of Tabernacles, when Jesus initially avoided going to Jerusalem but later went there in secret (7:1–11). Then, too, "the Jewish leaders were watching for Jesus and asking, 'Where is he?'" (7:11). Jesus continually faced threats – stoning, arrest, and death – from his opponents. Just as the Jewish leaders had decreed that "anyone who acknowledged that Jesus was the Messiah would be put out of the synagogue"

---

18. Blomberg writes, "The 'scattered children of God' in John's mind could foreshadow the Christian mission to the Gentiles . . . But Caiaphas undoubtedly was thinking only of the restoration to Israel of literal Jews from the Diaspora." Blomberg, *Historical Reliability of the Fourth Gospel*, 173.
19. Josephus *Ant.* 11.327; 13.299; Josephus, *War* 3.352; Philo, *Spec. Laws.* 4.192. See Blomberg, *Historical Reliability of the Fourth Gospel*, 173.

(9:22b), the chief priests and Pharisees had given orders that "anyone who found out where Jesus was should report it so that they might arrest him" (11:57). Although Jesus came to save the nation of Israel and the world, he was treated as a wanted criminal.

This pericope again reveals the intimacy between the Father and the Son (11:41–42). It emphasizes Jesus's intense love and empathy for humanity, describing how he wept with those who were weeping (11:33–35). Lazarus, whose name means "God helps," received God's help through Jesus, who declared, "I am the resurrection" (11:25); and the good shepherd (10:3) called this particular sheep by name (11:43). Through the high priest, God prophesied that Jesus would die for the salvation of the nation (11:50).

JOHN 12:1–50
END OF JESUS'S PUBLIC MINISTRY

The first major section of the Gospel of John – the *Book of Signs* – concludes with this chapter, which can be divided into six subsections: Mary anoints Jesus (12:1–11); Jesus enters the city of Jerusalem (12:12–19); the Greeks come to meet Jesus (12:20–22); Jesus predicts his crucifixion (12:23–36); unbelief of the people (12:37–41); and postlude to the *Book of Signs* (12:42–50).

12:1–11 MARY ANOINTS JESUS

The event in 12:1–11 is a continuation of the story of Lazarus from John 11, where the narrator notes that Jesus withdrew to the village of Ephraim to avoid being caught before his time (11:54) and that "it was almost time for the Jewish Passover" (11:55). In John 12, he begins the narrative by saying, "Six days before the Passover, Jesus came to Bethany." Both chapters place Jesus at Bethany – at the home of Lazarus, whom he had raised from the dead (12:1). Perhaps the sisters of Lazarus had arranged a thanksgiving dinner "in Jesus's honor" (12:2a). In Asia, people organize dinner parties to celebrate memorable events. As in many Asian cultures, Lazarus reclined at the table with the guests (12:2b), while Martha – as on an earlier occasion – cooked and served (12:2a; compare Luke 10:38–42). Mary, however, sat at Jesus's feet (12:3; compare Luke 10:39).

This time, however, Mary was not listening to Jesus's teachings but "took about a pint of pure nard, an expensive perfume . . . [and] poured it on Jesus' feet and wiped his feet with her hair" (12:3a),[1] which was probably a gesture of gratitude. Elsewhere, when a woman poured perfume on his feet, Jesus said, "To whom little is forgiven, *the same* loveth little" (Luke 7:47 KJV). Mary might have been expressing gratitude both for her forgiveness – "one man die for the people" (11:50b) – and for her brother's restoration to life. Because of its purity, the perfume was so potent that "the house was filled with the fragrance

---

1. These sorts of perfumes would have been imported from Egypt, India, Mesopotamia, or the Far East, and thus costly. https://wysinfo.com/the-ancient-perfume-route/. Israel's connection with India from king Solomon's time would have helped the Israelites to import spices and perfumes from India.

of the perfume" (12:3b) – like the sweet aroma that arose from offerings and sacrifices (Gen 8:21; Exod 29:18; Lev 1:9). Mary's act of wiping Jesus's feet with her hair is strange and would have been regarded as scandalous in that culture, just as it would be in Asian cultures today. Simon the Pharisee certainly thought the sinful woman's actions disqualified Jesus as a prophet (Luke 7:36–39). Mary's action and her posture at Jesus's feet also demonstrated her humility. Earlier, John the Baptizer had declared himself unworthy to untie the straps of Jesus's sandals (John 1:27). Now, Mary adopted a lowly posture as she wiped Jesus's feet with her hair.

Instead of enjoying the perfume and appreciating the hospitality, Judas Iscariot criticized Mary's actions. Jesus had already foretold that Judas was aligning himself with the devil (6:70). Now, the narrator informs readers that Judas would soon betray Jesus (12:4). Judas's complaint focused on what he considered wasteful: "Why wasn't this perfume sold, and the money given to the poor? It was worth a year's wages" (12:5). But was Judas truly concerned about the poor? Was he really committed to charity? Absolutely not. The narrator notes that Judas was "a thief" and that "as keeper of the money bag, he used to help himself to what was put into it" (12:6). If Judas had taken just one-twelfth of the perfume's value, that would have amounted to one month's salary! In contrast to Mary's extravagant generosity toward Jesus, Judas sought ways to rob both Jesus and the poor. Sadly, this kind of exploitation is common across all cultures and religions.

Jesus openly rebuked Judas, saying, "Leave her alone," and explained her actions: "She has kept it for the day of my burial" (12:7 NET).[2] Either Mary demonstrated a prophetic imagination about Jesus's imminent death, or she had paid close attention to his repeated statements that he came to lay down his life for his sheep (10:11) and might even have heard of Caiaphas's declaration that one man must die for the nation. Whatever the source of Mary's insight, she knew that Jesus's death was imminent – and instead of waiting to anoint his body after death, she offered him the perfume while he was still alive. There is an important principle here: Instead of buying flowers for someone's grave, we can give them those flowers while they are still living. Mary foresaw Jesus's death, and Jesus foresaw the significance of Mary's act.

---

2. John's use of *hina* construction is ambiguous. That's why the NIV has translated, "She should save this perfume for the day of my burial," almost implying Jesus, too, thought her action was wasteful. The NET Bible's translation and explanation in the footnote are preferred.

Jesus's final statement serves as a punch line: "You will always have the poor among you, but you will not always have me" (12:8). Here, honoring Jesus is given precedence over acts of charity. This is not an attempt to diminish charity but challenges the attitude that glorifies charity above honoring Jesus. The disciples would have ample opportunities to serve the poor but limited opportunities to honor Jesus in the flesh, while he was still living among them (1:14). Once again, Jesus was foretelling his imminent death.

This episode presents a powerful contrast between Mary and Judas. While Mary's focus was a humble act of devotion (12:3), Judas's focus was on wealth and his words were harsh and critical (12:4–5). Mary's action filled the house with the fragrance of the perfume (12:3), but Judas's heart was full of evil (12:4–6). Mary spent 300 denarii (as the Greek text indicates) to honor her master (12:5), but Judas later sold Jesus for 30 silver coins (Matt 26:15–16). While Mary, as a "host," demonstrated superabundant generosity, Judas, as a "guest," criticized his host's actions. Mary anticipated Jesus's death and anointed him for his burial (12:7), but Judas betrayed his master and gave him up to his death. What a contrast between light and darkness! Mary's spirituality was authentic; Judas Iscariot's was a counterfeit spirituality. Asian Christians can learn important spiritual lessons from the lives of Mary and Judas Iscariot.

Meanwhile, a great crowd had learned that Jesus was at the house of Lazarus, and they gathered there not only because of Jesus but also to see Lazarus (12:9). Hearing of this large crowd (12:9, 11), the religious leaders became fearful (compare 11:48) and "made plans to kill Lazarus as well" (12:10). This foreshadows what would later happen to Jesus's disciples: The religious leaders would target them, capture them, and kill them (for example, Acts 7 and 12). Throughout history, persecution of Christians has continued in various countries, and Asian Christians must always be prepared to face such opposition and persecution.

We must also be mindful of our attitudes toward wealth. Mary honored the Lord with her wealth, but Judas sought personal gain. While many Christians in Asia generously and self-sacrificially use their resources to support missions and ministries, others exploit churches and the poor for their personal gain. Churches and Christian organizations, while encouraging charity, must teach that loving and honoring God is always the most important priority.

12:12–19 JESUS ENTERS THE CITY OF JERUSALEM

On the following day – that is, the day after Mary anointed Jesus with her costly perfume – the crowd, hearing that Jesus was coming to Jerusalem for the festival of the Passover (12:12), took palm branches and went out to welcome him (12:13a). Palm branches were typically used to welcome royal figures.[3] The crowd shouted "Hosanna!" – which means "save us." Their *makarism* ("declaration of blessedness") in verse 13b reflects their expectation of the coming Messiah (see Ps 118:25–26). Just as Nathanael had acknowledged Jesus as the "king of Israel" (1:49), the crowd now acclaimed him as someone who came in the name of the Lord.[4] Witnessing Jesus raising Lazarus from the dead had made people realize that the long-awaited *eschaton* ("last days") had come and that, perhaps, Jesus was indeed the long-awaited Messiah. Their hope was that such a kingly Messiah would stand against the imperial powers of Rome. From 42 BCE onward – when the Roman Senate had declared Julius Caesar "Divus Iulius" (Divine Julius) – the people regarded Roman emperors as divine beings. The Jews viewed Jesus as the Messiah who would challenge Rome. This event also fulfilled the prophecy of Zechariah 9:9, which speaks of a humble king entering Jerusalem riding on a donkey's colt. By linking Jesus's actions to this prophecy, the narrator implies that Jesus is truly the promised Messiah (12:14–15), while the expression "do not be afraid" (12:15) points to the comfort this Messiah brings. Jesus's arrival in Jerusalem as a royal figure signaled his divine power and his authority against the Roman Empire and its dehumanizing rule.

In ancient times, kings would usually enter their capital cities riding horses, which were symbols of power. In contrast, Jesus entered Jerusalem riding on a donkey's colt, pointing to the humble Messianic figure of Zechariah's prophecy. In the honor-shame context of the time – similar to many Asian cultures today – this act held deep theological significance, signaling that Jesus had not come to dominate but to save and serve humanity. The prophetic assurance, "Do not be afraid," emphasizes that he had come to dispel fear and proclaim peace.

Even though Jesus's disciples knew his teachings and had witnessed his signs and wonders, they had difficulty applying these Scriptures to Jesus. Their eyes were clouded until Jesus was glorified (12:16). Only after his death and resurrection did they fully grasp his identify as the Word who became flesh, God's Son, and the true Messiah.

---

3. C. H. Dodd, *The Interpretation of the Fourth Gospel* (Cambridge: University Press, 1960), 370–71.
4. Moloney, *Gospel of John*, 350.

The crowd that had witnessed the raising of Lazarus "continued to spread the word" about this miracle (12:17). The healing of the blind man had a great impact on the people (9:24–34; 11:45), but the raising of Lazarus made an even greater impact (11:45–48; 12:9–11; 12:17–19). This crucial "sign" in the Gospel of John (12:18) drew even more people to see both Jesus and Lazarus.

This growing admiration of Jesus infuriated the Pharisees. Unable to suppress Jesus's popularity among the masses, they began devising strategies to get rid of him. They said, "See, this is getting us nowhere. Look how the whole world has gone after him!" (12:19). Jesus had begun to attract not just Jews but even people from other nations. The visit of some Greeks (12:20–22) illustrates Jesus's popularity even among non-Jews. Today, in India, Christianity continues to grow among unexpected communities such as the Dalits.

12:20–22 THE GREEKS COME TO MEET JESUS

The Pharisees' fear that "the whole world has gone after him" (12:19) had begun to come true: "Now there were some Greeks among those who went up to worship at the festival" (12:20), and they wanted to see Jesus (12:21). The Pharisees were already troubled by Jesus's growing popularity, and the arrival of these Greeks must have caused them even greater concern. The fact that these Greeks had come to worship at the festival (12:20b) implies that they were "God-fearers" – uncircumcised Gentiles who believed in the God of Israel (Acts 10:2, 22; 13:26, 50) – rather than Hellenistic Jews – that is, ethnic Jews who spoke Greek and embraced Greek culture. John 1–3 focuses on Jesus's ministry in Judea and Jerusalem; John 4 describes his mission in Samaria; John 12:20–22 points, symbolically, to his mission to "the ends of the earth" – that is, the Greek world established by Alexander the Great. In this way, the visit of the Greeks anticipated Jesus's statement in Acts 1:8.

Philip and Andrew are brought to the forefront in this scene (compare 1:40, 43–50; 6:6–9). The narrator notes that Philip was "from Bethsaida in Galilee" (12:21; see also 1:44). Although Bethsaida was located within Galilee and not in the diaspora, it had become a highly Hellenized place, and both Philip and Andrew – who was also from Bethsaida (1:44) – would have spoken Greek. The Greeks, probably realizing this, approached Philip, who then spoke to Andrew – perhaps because Philip was more timid than Andrew or because Andrew was older, and age carried weight in that culture. The Greeks expressed their desire to "see" Jesus (12:21). Philip told Andrew about this, and then they both conveyed this request to Jesus (12:22). However, readers are not told about the outcome of this request.

A. J. Appasamy, a famous Indian theologian, suggests that the Greeks' longing to see Jesus can be regarded as their *bhakti* ("mystical love") for God[5] – they wanted to see him because they loved him. Just as Andrew and Philip – who were part of Jesus's inner circle – introduced the Greeks to Jesus, Asian Christians can be involved in cross-cultural and multilingual missions.

Jesus's mission extended to diverse groups in society: Jews from Judea and Galilee, Samaritans, and now Greeks. He ministered not just to the healthy and wealthy but also to invalids, the blind, and social outcasts. Similarly, the church in Asia must minister to the untouchable, the lowly, the outcasts, and anyone in need of uplifting, as well as to the wealthy and the socially mobile.

12:23–36 JESUS PREDICTS HIS CRUCIFIXION

It is unclear whether Jesus was speaking to the Greeks or the Jews in this section, which is yet another monologue in which Jesus explained divine truths using mysterious language. Here, for the first time, Jesus declared that his time had arrived: "The hour has come for the Son of Man to be glorified" (12:23). Until this point, he had repeatedly stated that his hour had not yet come (2:4; 4:21, 23; 5:25, 28; 7:6, 8, 30; 8:20). But now, his time had come, and Jesus affirmed this using a metaphor: "Very truly I tell you, unless a kernel of wheat falls to the ground and dies, it remains only a single seed. But if it dies, it produces many seeds" (12:24). Jesus's imminent death on the cross would produce much "fruit" – that is, new believers.

But this mission extended beyond Jesus to his followers: "Anyone who loves their life will lose it, while anyone who hates their life in this world will keep it for eternal life" (12:25). This may include martyrdom. Those who serve Jesus must follow him, which means that wherever he is, his followers must go as well. Since Jesus went to the cross, his followers are called to do the same. All the early disciples faced the possibility of martyrdom. Those who faithfully follow and serve Jesus are assured that they will receive "honor" from the Father (12:26).

The Western world frowns upon "honor killing." But honor-shame cultures view honor killing differently. Jesus was not calling his disciples to be suicide bombers who engage in violence; rather, he was calling them to love and value eternal life above temporary comforts and even their earthly life. The Pharisees wanted a comfortable life in the present. In contrast, Jesus called his followers to "hate" their present life to gain eternal life (12:25), promising

---

5. Appasamy, *Christianity as Bhakti Marga*, 163–68.

that God would honor such faithful sacrifice (12:26). The death of a seed is necessary for life to emerge through a sprout. Although the seed disappears, the sprout emerges and brings forth life in abundance. This image illustrates how the death of Jesus brought life to many. Asian communities, especially those in agrarian contexts, can easily understand the significance of Jesus's metaphor.

Jesus declared, "The hour has come for the Son of Man to be glorified" (12:23). But his soul was troubled (12:27a). Although he would have liked to escape this hour, Jesus affirmed that it was for this very hour that he came to this world: "What shall I say? 'Father, save me from this hour'? No, it was for this very reason I came to this hour" (12:27b). Knowing that death awaited him, Jesus prayed a simple prayer: "Father, glorify your name!" (12:28a). Immediately, he received an answer from the Father: "I have glorified it and will glorify it again" (12:28b). The crowd, however, did not hear the words the Father had spoken. Some thought it had thundered, while others thought an angel had spoken (12:29). But Jesus heard what the Father said and drew comfort from these words – not for himself but for his hearers: "This voice was for your benefit, not mine" (12:30). Although Jesus was clear about his identity and mission, he knew that the people needed reassurance.

Just as Jesus's coming created division between those who believe and those who do not, division exists between God – who is the ruler from above – and "the prince of this world" (12:31) – who is the ruler of this world. At the moment of Jesus's death and glorification, the prince of this world would be driven out (12:31b). When Jesus was "lifted up from the earth" – a reference to his crucifixion, where he hung on the cross, his feet no longer touching the earth – he would "draw all people to [himself]" (12:32). Jesus's death had a far greater impact than the religious leaders had anticipated. They thought that killing him would end the movement; instead, his death (and resurrection) inaugurated a movement that would reach out to "all people." This offer of salvation – that extended beyond the Jews – was made possible only through Jesus's cruel death: "the kind of death he was going to die" (12:33).

Once again, a miscommunication took place between Jesus and the people. They asked, "We have heard from the Law that the Messiah will remain forever, so how can you say, 'The Son of Man must be lifted up'? Who is this 'Son of Man'?" (12:34). This was a legitimate question. In Daniel, the Son of Man is promised an eternal kingdom (Dan 7:13–14). How then could this Son of Man be killed? Did this mean his kingdom would come to an end? Jesus responded with reference to the duality of light and darkness: "You are going to have the light [Jesus] just a little while longer. Walk while you have the light, before darkness overtakes you. Whoever walks in the dark does not know where they are going. Believe in the light while you have the light, so that you may become children of light" (12:35–36a). This echoes the words about Jesus in John's *Prologue*: "The light shines in the darkness, and the darkness has not overcome it" (1:5) and "The true light that gives light to everyone was coming into the world" (1:9). This same thought is now expressed in Jesus's own words. Jesus's – and the narrator's – vision for the people was that they might "believe in the light . . . [and] become children of light" (12:36), a call that persists today. We must present this light to a world in darkness, and we ourselves must live as children of light.

After he had said this, Jesus once again "hid himself from them" (12:36b; compare 8:59). His elusive nature can be understood in terms of the life of a sannyasi. As Griffiths notes, a sannyasi must disappear from the world once his mission is complete.[6] These *micro-level* disappearances of Jesus would come to an end after his return to the Father, which was a *macro-level* disappearance.

12:37–41 UNBELIEF OF THE PEOPLE

Despite witnessing numerous signs, the Jews categorically rejected Jesus's messiahship and publicly expressed their unbelief. In doing so, they fulfilled the prophecy of Isaiah: "Lord, who has believed our message and to whom has the arm of the Lord been revealed?" (12:38; see Isa 53:1). The answer to this rhetorical question is "no one." The narrator explains that the reason for this unbelief is that God himself "has blinded their eyes and hardened their hearts, so they can neither see with their eyes, nor understand with their hearts, nor turn – and [God] would heal them" (12:39–40; Isa 6:9–10). This prophecy of Isaiah is quoted five times in the NT (Matt 13:14–15; Mark 4:11–12; Luke 8:10; John 12:40; Acts 28:26–27), each time in the context of Israel's rejection of Jesus as the Messiah. Paul explains why God had blinded their eyes: "Israel has experienced a hardening in part until the full number of the Gentiles has come in" (Rom 11:25b). Even Israel's hardening was used to further God's plan of salvation. Without Jesus's death and resurrection, salvation would not have been possible for either Israel or the nations.

In true prophetic fashion, Isaiah foresaw these days of Jesus's glory: "Isaiah said this because he *saw* Jesus' glory and spoke about him" (12:41, emphasis added). As a prophet, Isaiah foresaw the glory of the preincarnate Jesus and

---

6. Bede Griffiths, *The Marriage of East and West: A Sequel to the Golden String* (London: Collins, 1982), 42–45.

anticipated the revelation of that glory among the people of Israel. Although many believed in Jesus as the Messiah, a large number of people continued in their unbelief – and this makes the distinction between "children of light" and "children of darkness" increasingly obvious to the reader.

12:42–50 POSTLUDE TO THE BOOK OF SIGNS

Paul says that "Israel has experienced a hardening *in part*" (Rom 11:25b, emphasis added), and the Gospel of John attests to this. While many refused to believe in Jesus (12:37b), "yet at the same time many even among the leaders believed in him" (12:42a). Nicodemus (7:50–52) and Joseph of Arimathea (19:38) are two such examples. But some leaders who believed "would not openly acknowledge their faith for fear they would be put out of the synagogue" (12:42b). Earlier, the blind man's parents had exhibited a similar fear because the Jewish leaders "had decided that anyone who acknowledged that Jesus was the Messiah would be put out of the synagogue" (9:22).

Although their fear is understandable, the narrator sees this as a spiritual fault: "They loved human praise more than praise from God" (12:43). A distinction is drawn between human glory – which comes from below – and divine glory, which comes from above. In India, for example, many people are willing to believe in Jesus as a *deva* (god) but are reluctant to leave their traditional religions due to socioreligious or political-cultural pressures. Although the church welcomes such people, existential issues – such as fear of expulsion from their community or loss of jobs or property – often prevent them from becoming full members of the church.

In Jesus's final public statement (12:44–50) – as recorded in the *Book of Signs* – he returned to the theme of his oneness with the Father: "Whoever believes in me does not believe in me only, but in the one who sent me" (12:44). Similarly, he said that whoever sees him also sees the one who sent him (12:45).[7] Philip would later echo this thought: "Lord, show us the Father and that will be enough for us" (14:8). Jesus replied, "Anyone who has seen me has seen the Father" (14:9). Jesus also declared that he was the light and that no one who believed in him would remain in darkness (12:46). Once again, the narrative focuses on Jesus as the light and emphasizes the dualistic contrast between light and darkness (compare 1:5; 8:12; 9:5). The Chinese believe in *yin* and *yang* as complementary and contrasting principles. In the Johannine narrative, light and darkness function in a similar manner: Jesus

---

7. Stibbe, *John*, 137–41.

is the light; those who reject him are in darkness, under the dominion of the devil (compare 6:70; 8:44; 13:2).

Jesus then turned to the theme of judgment. He declared that if someone hears his words but fails to obey, even though he might not judge that person (12:47a), they would still be judged: "There is a judge for the one who rejects me . . . the very words I have spoken will condemn them at the last day" (12:48). Jesus's mission was "to save the world" (12:47b). Although the Father had "entrusted all judgment to the Son" (5:22), Jesus came not to judge but to save.

Nevertheless, there are consequences for refusing to believe in Jesus: "There is a judge for the one who rejects me" and "the very words I have spoken will condemn them at the last day" (12:48). The reason is simple: Jesus's words were not his own but the Father's. As Jesus affirmed, "I did not speak on my own, but the Father who sent me commanded me to say all that I have spoken" (12:49). Just as under Mosaic law, obedience brought blessing and disobedience had consequences (Deut 28), judgment will come upon those who reject Jesus's words because his words are God's own words.

Those who obey the Father's words will experience blessing: "I know that [God's] command leads to eternal life" (12:50a). Therefore, people need to believe in Jesus's words. Unlike the prophets – who were merely God's mouthpiece – Jesus is the eternal Word through whom God speaks (1:1; see also Heb 1:1–2). Because Jesus speaks the Father's words (12:50b), those who disobey his words will be judged by those very words (12:48). Therefore, Christians and churches must take Jesus's words seriously, treating these as the words of God himself. As Jesus said, "Heaven and earth will pass away, but my words will never pass away" (Matt 24:35). His words will not pass away because they are the words that the Father commanded him to speak (12:50b).

With this, Jesus's public ministry – and the *Book of Signs* – came to an end. From John 13 onward, the Gospel of John focuses on Jesus's teaching and equipping of his disciples to take up his mantle after his ascension.

JOHN 13:1–38
FOOT WASHING AND THE
FORETELLING OF JESUS'S DEATH

Following the *Prologue* (1:1–18) and the first major part of the Gospel – the *Book of Signs* (1:19–12:50) – the narrator shifts to the second major division: the *Book of Glory* (13:1–20:31). While the *Book of Signs* presents Jesus's teachings and miracles in the public space, the *Book of Glory* focuses on his teachings and preparation of his disciples in private. The broader public – which included the people of Israel in general – did not hear these words unless they became believers and read this Gospel.

The *Book of Glory* can be divided into three parts: the Farewell Discourse of Jesus (13:1–17:26); the passion of Jesus (18:1–19:42); and the resurrection narrative followed by the Gospel's purpose statement (20:1–31). The Farewell Discourse and the resurrection narratives are private because the dialogues, discourses, narratives, and the prayer in this section took place in private, just between Jesus and the disciples – which included the Twelve as well as disciples like Mary Magdalene. However, the events surrounding Jesus's passion – his arrest, crucifixion, and death – took place in public, for everyone to see.

The Farewell Discourse (John 13–17) follow the literary style of ancient farewell speeches or testaments of prominent people.[1] They reflect some of the literary features of texts like *The Testament of the Twelve Patriarchs*, which contains the last words of each of the patriarchs to their people.[2] Moreover, John's Farewell Discourse also bears striking resemblances to the Greco-Roman symposium traditions.[3] Engberg-Pedersen describes the Farewell Discourse in John as *Paraklēsis* – "comforting words" that were intended to console the disciples who were struggling with all they had learned and seen during

---

1. R. F. Collins, *These Things Have been Written: Studies on the Fourth Gospel*, Louvain Theological and Pastoral Monographs 2 (Louvain: Peeters Press, 1990), 221.
2. G. R. Beasley-Murray, *John*, WBC 36, 2nd ed. (Dallas/Nashville: Thomas Nelson, 1999), 222–23.
3. Cornelis Bennema, *Excavating John's Gospel: A Commentary for Today* (Delhi: ISPCK, 2007), 140.

the past three years.[4] The Farewell Discourse features *hypodeigmata* – that is, teaching by example[5] – which is clearly seen in Jesus washing the disciples' feet and then saying, "I have set you an example that you should do as I have done for you" (13:15).

On the eve of his historic Dandi March in 1930, Mahatma Gandhi delivered a memorable speech at Sabarmati Sands at Ahmedabad. He said, "In all probability this may be my last speech to you. Even if the government allows me to march tomorrow evening, this will be my last speech on the sacred banks of the Sabarmati. Possibly these may be the last words of my life here."[6] In his "Quit India" speech to the British Empire in 1942, he issued a call to "Do or Die." Gandhi structured almost all his speeches as farewell speeches as he was prepared to die at any time. His speeches were powerful and motivational to the Indian masses struggling under British rule.

Teachers must facilitate dialogue with their students. Rather than using a hierarchical model in which the teacher imparts knowledge without engaging with students' questions, concerns, and curiosities, a good teacher engages in meaningful dialogue with students. Several ancient schools – including the peripatetic Greek school,[7] Confucius's Chinese school,[8] and the Indian gurukula school[9] – followed this approach, developing an interactive or one-on-one discourse methodology. Jesus, too, practiced this method when interacting with or responding to his disciples' questions in private settings. Similarly, today, teaching should not be limited to public instruction but must include personal mentoring that addresses students' questions, concerns, and curiosities.

13:1–20 JESUS WASHES THE DISCIPLES' FEET

The narrator of John centers his Gospel around the Passover festival. While the Synoptic Gospels (Matthew, Mark, and Luke) speak of just one Passover, the Fourth Gospel refers to several. The first Passover took place soon after

---

4. Troels Engberg-Pedersen, "A Question of Genre: John 13–17 as *Paraklēsis*," *The Gospel of John as Genre Mosaic*, ed. Kasper Bro Larsen (Göttingen: Vandenhoeck & Ruprecht, 2015), 283–302.
5. R. A. Culpepper, "The Johannine *hypodeigma*: A Reading of John 13:1–38," *Semeia* 53 (1991): 133–35.
6. Mahatma Gandhi, "Dandi March," Gandhi Ashram, https://gandhiashramsabarmati.org/en/the-mahatma/speeches/dandi-march.html.
7. Han Baltusen, *The Peripatetics: Aristotle's Heirs (332 BCE-200 CE)* (New York: Routledge, 2016), 1–5.
8. Britannica, "Confucius Summary," https://www.britannica.com/summary/Confucius.
9. "Gurukul Education System," Wings, 18 July 2025, https://leverageedu.com/blog/gurukul-education-system/.

Jesus turned water into wine in Cana of Galilee (2:13, 23; 4:45); the second was after the healings of the royal official's son and the paralyzed man by the pool (6:4); and the third Passover took place after the healing of the man born blind and the raising of Lazarus (11:55). Six days before that final Passover, Mary anointed Jesus for burial (12:1–7). Five days later, the night before Passover, Jesus shared a private meal with his disciples in an Upper Room in Jerusalem and revealed what would happen to him. The narrator begins this section saying, "It was just before the Passover Festival" (13:1). Since Passover was an annual festival, John's reference to three Passovers suggests that Jesus's ministry lasted over three years.

Jesus knew that, as the Father had revealed to him, "the hour had come for him to leave this world and go to the Father" (13:1a). He had already referred to this moment as his hour, the time of his lifting up, and the time of his glorification (12:23, 27–28). Before returning to the Father, Jesus wanted to leave his disciples with a powerful memory of himself and his teachings. He was motivated by a deep love for his disciples, which the narrator describes like this: "Having loved his own who were in the world, he loved them to the end" (13:1b). Jesus's love was endless. Having loved them from the day he called them to follow him, his love continued, with no wavering or partiality; he even loved Judas, who would soon betray him. In Asian countries, migrant workers often leave their home to work abroad so that they can support their families. Their departure does not diminish their love. Similarly, Jesus's departure would not change or lessen his love for the disciples; and on his last night before this departure, he demonstrated that love to them.

As the Passover meal progressed, "the devil had already prompted Judas, the son of Simon Iscariot, to betray Jesus" (13:2). Earlier, Jesus had said, "Have I not chosen you, the Twelve? Yet one of you is a devil!" (6:70). As Jesus had foretold, Judas became "a devil" – that is, he was influenced by the devil to betray Jesus unto death. Jesus remains the ultimate paradigm of love, while Judas exemplifies deception, hate, and murder. This same choice confronts us all: love or hate? The decision is ours.

Jesus was not driven by Judas's hate or betrayal but by his confidence in the Father: "Jesus knew that the Father had put all things under his power, and that he had come from God and was returning to God" (13:3). It was this awareness of his authority, origin, and destination that motivated Jesus to act as he did. In difficult times, keeping in mind our destination – going to the Father – will strengthen us to endure our struggles.

Confident of his authority, origin, and destination, Jesus humbled himself: "He got up from the meal, took off his outer clothing, and wrapped a towel around his waist . . . poured water into a basin and began to wash his disciples' feet, drying them with the towel that was wrapped around him" (13:4–5). In those days, this was the role of household slaves in both Jewish and Roman homes.[10] Jesus – the master, teacher, and Lord – humbled himself to serve as a slave to his disciples.

Although the other disciples allowed Jesus to wash their feet, Simon Peter resisted. When Jesus approached him, Peter asked, "Lord, are you going to wash my feet?" (13:6). In the honor-shame society of that time, it was unthinkable for someone of higher status to wash the feet of someone of inferior status. Similarly, in India, a high-caste person would never wash a Dalit's feet. But Jesus broke with tradition and washed his disciples' feet, an act that disturbed and shocked Simon Peter.

Peter frequently spoke his mind without restraint, a tendency that often got him into trouble. Here, he objected to the idea of Jesus washing his feet without even asking Jesus why he was doing this. Jesus responded, "You do not realize now what I am doing, but later you will understand" (13:7). Borchert says, "Jesus's response in 13:7 is a direct confronting of Peter's implied challenge which had been based on his confusion. Peter did not know what was in fact taking place at that time."[11] After Jesus's death and resurrection, Peter would understand the significance of this moment. But at that moment, Peter objected, saying, "No . . . you shall never wash my feet" (13:8) – words that came from a worldly perspective. But when Jesus said, "Unless I wash you, you have no part with me" (13:8b), Peter immediately changed his attitude, inviting Jesus to wash not just his feet but his hands and head as well (13:9), revealing his desire to remain united with Jesus. Although confused, Peter was a loyal disciple.

The Jews would go to Jerusalem "for their ceremonial cleansing before the Passover" (11:55). Therefore, the disciples and Jesus would have undergone ceremonial cleansing before they gathered to eat the Passover meal. Jesus told Peter, "Those who have had a bath need only to wash their feet; their whole body is clean" (13:10a). The temple cleansing had already purified them. But

---

10. Catherine Hezser, *Jewish Slavery in Antiquity* (Oxford: Oxford University Press, 2005), 121–48.
11. G. F. Borchert, *John 12–21*, The New American Commentary, vol. 25B (Nashville: Broadman & Holman Publishers, 2002), 2:81.

the foot washing by Jesus, their teacher, was intended to teach them a new lesson about humility. It modeled the way they were to serve their flock in the future, not by lording over them but by example (1 Pet 5:3).

However, the Passover washing ritual could not really cleanse everyone or ensure clean hearts: "You are clean, though not every one of you" (13:10b). While Peter was cleansed by the Passover washing ritual, Judas was not. Even after the foot washing, Judas chose to betray Jesus to the Jewish authorities – "that was why [Jesus] said not everyone was clean" (13:11b). Although physically clean, Judas's heart was darkened by the devil. Jesus knew all people (see 2:24–25), and he knew who would betray him. Yet, without showing any partiality, Jesus washed even Judas's feet. This act exemplifies true humility – honoring and serving even our "enemies."

When he had finished washing the disciples' feet, Jesus put on his outer garment and returned to his place at the table (13:12a). Then he began to teach them, asking, "Do you understand what I have done for you?" (13:12b). Jesus wanted to make sure that his disciples had understood that his actions symbolized his servanthood. The speech that follows (13:13–20) is a verbal exposition of his actions.

First and foremost, Jesus wanted his disciples to understand servanthood: "You call me 'Teacher' and 'Lord,' and rightly so, for that is what I am. Now that I, your Lord and Teacher, have washed your feet, you also should wash one another's feet" (13:13–14). Jesus set an example for the disciples to follow (13:15). Although "no servant is greater than his master, nor is a messenger greater than the one who sent him" (13:16), this does not prevent the master from serving the servant or the sender from serving the messenger. This was a radical new idea. Jesus introduced a new paradigm that was radically different from the servant-master and messenger-sender relationships familiar among the Jews. In the honor-shame context of the first century, the patron-client model was the prevailing social norm. In the Greco-Roman context, servants were considered inferior to their masters, and messengers were considered inferior to their senders.[12] But Jesus did not view servants as inferior to their masters or messengers as inferior to their senders.[13] Rather, he saw them as complementary, as in the Chinese concept of *yin* and *yang*. Instead of reinforcing the

---

12. Slaves or servants were considered as the lower strata of the society. Similarly, messengers were considered as the carriers of the royal charter to the public.
13. For more details, refer to John 13:35. John 13:16 closely resembles Matthew 10:24–25 and John 13:20 closely resembles Matthew 10:40.

existing hierarchical model, Jesus established a servant leadership model. He expects his disciples to follow his example of servanthood – "you will be blessed if you do them" (13:17) – setting aside traditional ideas about role and status.

Although Jesus exhorted all the disciples to follow his example, he knew that not all were clean (compare 13:10b), and so he said, "I am not referring to all of you; I know those I have chosen. But this is to fulfill this passage of Scripture: 'He who shared my bread has turned against me'" (13:18). Judas had knowledge but failed to act on what he knew by doing good works. Despite sharing bread with Jesus – a symbol of fellowship – he turned against him. But this betrayal was not unexpected for it was a fulfillment of Scripture. As David wrote, "Even my close friend, someone I trusted, one who shared my bread, has turned against me" (Ps 41:9). Similarly, Judas – who had shared meals, life, signs, and even money with Jesus – turned against him.

Judas's betrayal is portrayed as a fulfillment of Scripture (13:18; compare Ps 41:9). He had "lifted up his heel" against the Son of God (13:18) – meaning that although Judas was part of Jesus's inner circle, he had aligned himself with those who opposed Jesus. Jesus emphasized the importance of "doing" as a result of "knowing"; but what Judas "knew" did not shape his actions. Brown states, "In both verses 11 and 18 John makes clear that Jesus was perfectly aware that Judas had turned against him irrevocably."[14]

Jesus did not want his disciples to be taken unawares by what would happen, and so he said, "I am telling you now before it happens" (13:19a). He wanted them to have faith in him even when faced with the awful reality that one of their own had betrayed Jesus. He declared, "When it does happen you will believe that I am who I am" (13:19b). This "I am" statement differs from Jesus's previous "I am" statements such as "I am the good shepherd." Judas's betrayal was not just against Jesus but also against the Father. As Jesus said, "Very truly I tell you, whoever accepts anyone I send accept me; and whoever accepts me accepts the one who sent me" (13:20). Jesus extended this missional perspective to include his disciples and followers. In this sense, the Father, the Son, and the believers are united in their mission, a theme that Jesus would later expand on in his high priestly prayer (John 17). This unity is essential in every area of Christian living.

---

14. Brown, *Gospel according to John*, 571.

John 13:1–38

13:21–35 JESUS FORETELLS HIS BETRAYAL

Although it was a night of joy – remembering God's deliverance of the Israelites from slavery in Egypt through the celebration of the Passover – Jesus's spirit was troubled because he knew that one of his own was going to betray him (13:21; compare 13:11). This was the same kind of anguish he experienced when he saw Mary and the Jews weep over Lazarus's death (11:33).

Jesus's revelation also troubled his disciples. They "stared at one another, at a loss to know which of them he meant" (13:22). Even though Jesus had been talking about this (13:11), it still came as a surprise to his disciples – Judas's fellow disciples.

At that moment, "the disciple whom Jesus loved" (13:23a) – probably John, the son of Zebedee and brother of James – was reclining "next to him" (13:23b NIV) or "leaning on Jesus' bosom" (KJV), signifying their intimate friendship.[15] Simon Peter signaled to that disciple to ask Jesus about the identity of the betrayer (13:24). As on other occasions, the narrator places Simon Peter alongside the beloved disciple (see 20:2; 21:20–23). The beloved disciple then leaned back against Jesus and asked, "Lord, who is it?" (13:25). Jesus replied, "It is the one to whom I will give this piece of bread when I have dipped it in the dish" (13:26a). After saying this, he dipped a piece of bread and gave it to Judas, the son of Simon Iscariot (13:26b). The fact that Jesus was able to hand the bread to Judas implies that Judas was reclining close to Jesus. By presenting a reclining disciple and a betrayer side by side, the narrator invites the reader to decide: Will they choose intimacy with Jesus, or will they betray him? The same choice confronts us all.

Jesus's action echoes his earlier statement, "He who shared my bread has turned against me" – a prophetic utterance of David (Ps 41:9).[16] Jesus's words, followed immediately by his action, disclosed the identity of the betrayer – Judas, son of Simon Iscariot. Immediately after Judas took the bread, "Satan entered into him" (John 13:27). Although Jesus had earlier referred to Judas as being "a devil," this is the only time reference made to Satan entering him. The terms "devil" and "Satan" function as synonyms in John's Gospel. Like villains who gradually enter the scene in Indian movies, the narrator progressively

---

15. Other candidates are Thomas (James H. Charlesworth, *The Beloved Disciple*), Lazarus (https://medium.com/@alanrudnick/lazarus-not-john-was-the-beloved-disciple-a4723223a16a.), and Mary Magdalene (Ivonne Montijo, *Mary Magdalene: Beloved Wife, Beloved Disciple* [CreateSpace Independent Publishing Platform, 2017]).
16. E. F. F. Bishop, "'He that eateth bread with me hath lifted up his heel against me' — Jn xiii.18 (Ps xli.9)," *ExpTim* 70 (1958–59): 331–33.

reveals Judas's identity as the antagonist of the story. Judas chose to move away from the believing community and align with the company of unbelievers.

Realizing that his time – his hour – had come and that Satan has entered Judas, who would soon betray him, Jesus told Judas, "What you are about to do, do quickly" (13:27b). This statement demonstrates that Jesus willingly surrendered his life and allowed himself to be handed over to Satan's evil schemes, trusting that the Father was still in control. Earlier, he had said, "The Son of Man did not come to be served, but to serve, and to give his life as a ransom for many" (Mark 10:45). Now, Jesus wanted Judas to continue with what he had planned. God's will for Jesus and Judas's desire coincided to bring about Jesus's death. However, the other disciples, who had heard Jesus say, "What you are about to do, do quickly," did not understand his words (13:28). Since Judas was the disciple in charge of the money, they assumed that Jesus had told him to go and buy what was needed for the festival or perhaps to give some money to the poor (13:29), in whom he had expressed an interest (12:6). Once again, the narrator contrasts Jesus's knowing with the disciples' unknowing. The disciples thought that Jesus was telling Judas to buy the things for the festival so that he could give something to the poor, while Jesus permitted him to go and accept the betrayal money. Judas received the piece of bread and immediately walked away from Jesus and the other disciples (13:30a).[17] Judas left, "and it was night" (13:30b). This theme of "night" has symbolic significance in John's Gospel, which portrays Jesus as the light and those who reject him as walking in darkness. Judas's actions showed that he had aligned himself with the darkness. He was drawn by money, political connections of his world, and the mainstream religious ideologies of his time. In Asian countries like Vietnam, many Christians live in poverty and helplessness. Yet, unlike many around them who are drawn by greed – like Judas – these believers remain faithful, living godly lives despite their poverty and serving as a powerful model for all Christians.

Judas left the "insider" community of Jesus to embrace the "outsider" community of the world.[18] We see similar movements taking place even today, through forced reconversion,[19] *Ghar Wapsi*[20] (literally, "coming home") – a movement to bring back Hindus who had left that religion – and other forms

---

17. Morris, *Gospel according to John*, 558.
18. Brown, *Gospel according to John*, 576.
19. Edward P. Lipton, *Religious Freedom in Asia* (New York: Nova Science Publishers, 2002).
20. Wessly Lukose, "An Indian Pentecostal Reading on Conversion," *Religious Freedom and Conversion in India* (Bengaluru: SAIACS Press, 2017), 162–85.

of social pressure. In such contexts, Christians are called to stand firm for Christ.

Once Judas left, Jesus said, "Now the Son of Man is glorified, and God is glorified in him. If God is glorified in him, God will glorify the Son in himself and will glorify him at once" (13:31–32). The repetition of "glorified" emphasizes the significance of this moment. Jesus did not view his death on the cross as failure or defeat but as glorification or exaltation. Earlier, he had said, "Just as Moses lifted up the snake in the wilderness, so the Son of Man must be lifted up" (3:14), "When you have lifted up the Son of Man, then you will know that I am he and that I do nothing on my own but speak just what the Father has taught me" (8:28), and "I, when I am lifted up from the earth, will draw all people to myself" (12:32). For Jesus, Judas's betrayal would lead to the moment when the Son of Man would be glorified and God would be glorified in the Son and would, in turn, glorify the Son (13:31–32). Asian Christians who suffer because of their obedience to God's will view their suffering as glorious, despite its pain. Suffering, marginalization, persecution, and even martyrdom can be glorious, provided it is not the result of wrongdoing but is caused by faithfully doing God's will. The imminent glorification of Jesus on the cross represents God's ultimate intention. The glory of the Father and the Son are integrally connected. The theme of glorification through suffering and death holds great interpretative significance within the Asian context.

On a practical level, Jesus's time with the disciples was coming to an end. He said, "My children, I will be with you only a little longer. You will look for me, and just as I told the Jews, so I tell you now: Where I am going, you cannot come" (13:33). By addressing his disciples as "children," Jesus demonstrated his great affection for them, like a parent speaking to a child.[21] The expression "little longer" implies that there is only a short time left. He would be with them for just three more days and then appear among them intermittently during a forty-day period before ascending to the Father. His death, burial, resurrection, and ascension were imminent. Jesus's arrest, trial, and death can serve as a model and motivation for Asian Christians facing similar trials. All such trials bring glory to God's name.

Jesus then gave the disciples a new command: "A new command I give you: Love one another. As I have loved you, so you must love one another" (13:34). In a world that hated Jesus (7:7), the only way to show that they were children from above was to continue to love one another. The phrase "I

---

21. Beasley-Murray, *John*, 246.

have loved you" is sandwiched between the repeated call to "love one another" (13:34). The way Jesus demonstrated love to the disciples models how they are to love one another. Jesus loved the world even to the point of death on the cross. By loving one another with that divine love, disciples of Jesus demonstrate true love. As Jesus said, "By this [their love for one another] everyone will know that you are my disciples" (13:35). This call extends beyond the twelve disciples. Even today, when Christians love one another in this way, it testifies to the world that they are Jesus's followers. Despite denominational and theological differences, we are called to love one another and be united under the umbrella of Jesus's love so that the world will know that we are his followers. By loving one another and reflecting the love of Jesus, we become witnesses of Christ in this world.

13:36–38 JESUS PREDICTS PETER'S DENIAL

Peter's question – "Lord, where are you going?" (13:36a) – reveals that he was still confused by Jesus's statement, "Where I am going, you cannot come" (13:33b). Jesus responded patiently, repeating what he had earlier told the Jews: "Where I am going, you cannot follow now, but you will follow later" (13:36b; compare 7:33–34; 8:21). There is an important difference between Jesus's words to the Jews (7:33–34) and his words to his disciples (13:36b). While the Jews would never follow Jesus to the place where he was going, the disciples – though unable to follow him immediately – would eventually do so, emphasizing their privileged position.

Peter could not understand the intent of Jesus's words. He asked Jesus why he could not follow him and even expressed his willingness to die for him: "I will lay down my life for you" (13:37). Jesus responded, "Will you really lay down your life for me?" (13:38a). Jesus knew what was in Peter's heart. Despite Peter's confident affirmation, Jesus pronounced one of the saddest prophecies Peter could have heard: "Very truly I tell you, before the rooster crows, you will disown me three times!" (13:38b). In the Bible, animals sometimes function as God's messengers – for example, Balaam's donkey (Num 22:22–35) and Elijah's raven (1 Kgs 17:1–7). Here, Jesus used a rooster as his messenger – Peter would "disown" Jesus three times before the rooster crowed. Blum comments, "Jesus's prediction of Peter's defection (you will disown me three times) must have completely shocked the other disciples. They may have wondered if Peter was the traitor (compare, John 13:21–25)."[22] Having revealed Judas as

---

22. Blum, "John," 332.

the betrayer, Jesus foretold Peter's denial. Both betrayal and denial may come from those closest to us. This is why Christians and churches should stand firm with those they love and guard against denial or betrayal in any form.

In the first part of the Farewell Discourse, the narrator foregrounds some significant lessons for Jesus's followers. Jesus reversed the hierarchical teacher-student and master- servant models with his foot washing. This example of humbling oneself and exalting the other becomes a model for mission and ministry for all Jesus's disciples. His foretelling of the betrayer and the denier serves as a reminder that in life and ministry, we may encounter such people, even from among our circle of friends and family. The statement that "Jesus knew that the hour had come for him to leave this world and go to the Father" (13:1) highlights the cross-centered nature of Jesus's mission. Similarly, we should live as if each day were our last and love those around us deeply and sacrificially.

JOHN 14:1–31

JESUS IS THE WAY, THE TRUTH, AND THE LIFE

The Farewell Discourse, delivered by Jesus on the night before he died, is a collection of his teachings from throughout his ministry, now repeated as a reminder before his departure. In John 14:1–31, Jesus affirmed that he is the way to the Father, the truth, and the life.

The Lunyu (*Analects*) is a collection of oral and written teachings of Confucius, compiled by his disciples. Similarly, the teachings of Plato and Socrates were collected and compiled by their disciples. In the same way, the Farewell Discourse is a collection of Jesus's oral teachings, which his disciples later organized and recorded in the form of a written document.

John 15 can be divided into three subsections: Jesus as the way to the Father (14:1–14); the promise of the Holy Spirit (14:15–26); and Christ's offer of enduring peace (14:27–31).

14:1–14 JESUS AS THE WAY TO THE FATHER

After a moving introductory section (13:1–38), the narrator proceeds to the profound discourse sections. The discourse begins with an imperative: "Do not let your hearts be troubled" (14:1a). Since Jesus's words about his departure would have troubled the disciples, Jesus now comforted them. This message is particularly relevant today for Asian churches facing turmoil, persecution, and internal strife. As someone who experienced trouble in the world (11:33; 13:21), Jesus could can identify with the disciples' struggles. He told them that believing in God – and in Jesus himself – was the only way to overcome their troubles (14:1b).

Jesus then assured his disciples that his "Father's house has many rooms [*monē*]" (14:2a). At the end of this conversation, he would say, "Anyone who loves me will obey my teaching. My Father will love them, and we will come to them and make our home [*monē*] with them" (14:23). This literary book-end – that is, using the same Greek word *monē* – implies that Jesus was not speaking of literal rooms but of an abiding relationship between the Father and the believers. The phrase "if that were not so" affirms that such a dwelling place already existed in heaven (14:2a); but Jesus still had to "prepare a place" by his death and resurrection, which would open the way to the Father (14:2b). Jesus promised, "If I go and prepare a place for you, I will come back and take you to be with me that you also may be where I am" (14:3).[1] His ascension to the Father would be realized by way of the cross. Jesus's ascension and his promise to prepare a place for his disciples assures believers of his return. When he comes again, all those who believe in him will be taken to the place of God's presence to be with him (14:3c). This echoes Jesus's words to Nathanael: "Very truly I tell you, you will see heaven open, and the angels of God ascending and descending on the Son of Man" (1:51). This motif of ascending and descending offers Asian Christians hope for a place of transformation amid the existential struggles, dehumanization, and marginalization of this world. Faith in God, love for Jesus, and hope in the future are essential characteristics of the Christian life.

Jesus then told the disciples that they knew the way to the place where he was going (14:4) – back to the Father through his death, resurrection, and ascension. Although he had told the religious leaders, "I am going away, and you will look for me, and you will die in your sin. Where I go, you cannot come" (8:21), he had not told the disciples that they would not be able to follow where he was going. Later, many of them would follow in his way through martyrdom. While earthly paths are often frustrating, the "way" Jesus referred to is a vertical "way" that leads believers to the Father through the cross.

Thomas, who had earlier said, "Let us also go, that we may die with him" (11:16), once again revealed his willingness to follow Jesus even while expressing his confusion: "Lord, we don't know where you are going, so how can we know the way?" (14:5).[2] Jesus's teachings became clearer only after his resurrection. Thus, Thomas's question is understandable – he genuinely did not know where Jesus was going and, as such, did not know the way. The disciples' uncertainty and confusion recall the people's speculation about whether Jesus intended to go to the Greeks (7:35) or to kill himself (8:22). Jesus's use of the word "way" is mysterious – being both vertical, and cross-centric – and Thomas was unable to comprehend his master's enigmatic statement.

---

1. Qur'an has a similar picture: Allah promises to those who heed him mansions raised upon mansions high, beneath which running waters flow (Surat az-Zumar, 20). Most likely, Mohammad read portions of the Gospel to form that imagery.
2. He addresses Jesus as "Lord" and he acknowledges the honorable position of Jesus among them.

We then have Jesus's sixth "I am" statement: "I am the way and the truth and the life" (14:6a). Earlier, he had declared, "I am the bread of life" (6:35), "I am the light of the world" (8:12), "I am the gate for the sheep" (10:7), "I am the good shepherd" (10:11), and "I am the resurrection and the life" (11:25). Scholars argue that both "I am the resurrection and the life" and "I am the way and the truth and the life" combine several elements, thus making a total of nine "I am" statements. Regardless, Jesus made an exclusive claim: "No one comes to the Father except through me" (14:6b). This statement has important missional implications. In a world with many religions and many religious leaders, Jesus asserted that access to the Father is exclusively through the Son, which requires believing in Jesus and accepting him as Lord.

Jesus continued, "If you really know me, you will know my Father as well" (14:7a). Knowing the Son is the most significant requirement for knowing the Father. The conditional "if" implies that not all the disciples truly know Jesus – Judas being one example. But to those who knew and believed in Jesus, he said, "From now on, you do know him and have seen him" (14:7b). These are powerful statements. The *Prologue* affirms, "No one has ever seen God, but the one and only Son, who is himself God and is in closest relationship with the Father, has made him known" (1:18). The Gospel now revisits this theme. Seeing Jesus is the only way a person can see the Father. The intimate relationship between the Father, the Son, and the Holy Spirit is now extended to the believing community, drawing them into this oneness.

When Jesus invited Philip to follow him, Philip obeyed (1:43). Not long after, Philip told Nathanael about Jesus and invited him to "come and see" the one Moses had written about in the law (1:45–46). As Jesus prepared to feed a multitude, it was Philip who asked, "Where shall we buy bread for these people to eat?" (6:5), adding, "It would take more than half a year's wages to buy enough bread for each one to have a bite!" (6:7). When some Greeks sought an audience with Jesus, Philip acted as a mediator in that situation (12:20–22). Now, once again, we see Philip voicing a very practical question: "Lord, show us the Father and that will be enough for us" (14:8).[3] Jesus had said, "From now on, you do know him and have *seen* him" (14:7b, emphasis added). But Philip realized that he had not yet seen the Father in this way and wanted Jesus to show him the Father. Like Thomas (14:5), Philip was also a *satyagrahi* – a seeker of truth.

---

3. Like Thomas (v. 5), Philip addressed Jesus as "Lord" (v. 8).

Jesus answered Philip, "Don't you know me, Philip, even after I have been among you such a long time? Anyone who has seen me has seen the Father. How can you say, 'Show us the Father'?" (14:9). This echoes the words of the *Prologue*: "No one has ever seen God . . . [The Son] has made him known" (1:18). To see Jesus is to see the Father, just as knowing the Son is knowing the Father (14:7). For over three years, the disciples had experienced the Son who made the Father visible; yet they still struggled to grasp this truth, prompting Philip to ask to see the Father. Jesus continued, "Don't you believe that I am in the Father, and that the Father is in me? The words I say to you I do not speak with my own authority. Rather, it is the Father, living in me, who is doing his work" (14:10). In the OT, the angel of the Lord, speaking on behalf of God, would sometimes speak in the first person as if God himself were speaking. For example, the angel of the Lord said to the Israelites, "I brought you up out of Egypt and led you into the land I swore to give to your ancestors. I said, 'I will never break my covenant with you'" (Judg 2:1). But Jesus is far greater than the angel of the Lord – he is the incarnate Word who became flesh (John 1:1, 14) and who was both "with God" and "was God" (1:1). As Jesus declared, "I am in the Father . . . the Father is in me" (14:10a). Therefore, anyone who has seen Jesus has seen the Father. Even his words were not his own but the work of the Father (14:10b).

Jesus repeated these truths: "Believe me when I say that I am in the Father and the Father is in me; or at least believe on the evidence of the works themselves" (14:11). Much earlier, Nicodemus had made a similar assertion: "Rabbi, we know that you are a teacher who has come from God. For no one could perform the signs you are doing if God were not with him" (3:2). Jesus's miracles – healing the sick, giving sight to the blind, and raising the dead – were the works of God himself, testifying that Jesus had come from God and is God. Those who witnessed these signs were like the Israelites who saw God's presence manifested powerfully on Mount Sinai (Exod 19:16–19). Barrett says, "Throughout this gospel the *erga* [works] or *sēmeia* [signs] are presented as events which ought to and sometimes do elicit faith (for example, 2:11)."[4]

As Jesus prepared to depart, he left his disciples with a promise of great power: "Very truly I tell you, whoever believes in me will do the works I have been doing, and they will do even greater things than these, because I am going to the Father" (14:12). Although the disciples had performed miracles and cast out demons while Jesus was still with them (Luke 9:1–10), he now

---

4. Barrett, *Gospel according to St. John*, 384.

promised that they would do even greater works after his departure. This would become possible because he would be with the Father and would do whatever they asked in his name so that the Father would be glorified in the Son (14:12b–14). Just as Jesus mirrored the Father's works, he would empower the disciples to mirror his own works. In that sense, Jesus's departure was a good thing for the disciples – and for believers today. We can do great works for God, provided we ask in the name of the Lord Jesus and according to his will. In every generation, the church has witnessed divine miracles.

Mission should not be restricted to preaching and proclamation. Instead, the church must do far more. However, they cannot do such work on their own but only as Jesus allows, just as Jesus did only what he saw the Father doing. The Johannine narrative presents Jesus as carrying out his mission through discourses, dialogues, works, and signs. Similarly, Asian Christians must actively participate in liberative actions. The Son has power to do whatever people ask in his name because the Father glorifies the Son (14:13).[5]

In Japan, samurai were trained in strict self-discipline and taught to follow specific paths or ways prescribed by Confucius. Early missionaries used this concept of the "way" as a means to draw people to Jesus, who is the true way (14:6).[6] Similarly, in regions where Taoism is practiced, since *tao* means "way" or "path," missionaries communicate the gospel by using this concept to present Jesus as the ultimate *tao* or "way." Whatever missiological techniques we use should ultimately point people to Jesus because when they know Jesus, they will know and see the Father who sent him.

14:15–26 THE PROMISE OF THE HOLY SPIRIT

After comforting the disciples with the assurance of his presence that would enable them to do great works (14:1–14), Jesus spoke of the third person of the Trinity – the Holy Spirit – and his presence with the disciples (14:15–26). He began by saying, "If you love me, keep my commands" (14:15). Surprisingly, none of the disciples asked, "What are your commands [*entolē*]?" Earlier, the chief priests and the Pharisees gave the command [*entolē*] that "anyone who found out where Jesus was should report it so that they might arrest him" (11:57). In contrast, Jesus talked about the command [*entolē*] he had received

---

5. R. H. Lightfoot, *St. John's Gospel, St. John's Gospel: A Commentary* (Oxford: The Clarendon Press, 1956), 270.
6. Veli-Matti Kärkkäinen, ed., *Holy Spirit and Salvation: The Sources of Christian Theology* (Louisville: Westminster John Knox Press, 2010), 437.

from the Father: "No one takes it [his life] from me, but I lay it down of my own accord. I have the authority to lay it down and authority to take it up again. This command [*entolē*] I received from my Father" (10:18). Jesus also gave his disciples a command [*entolē*]: "A new command [*entolē*] I give you: Love one another. As I have loved you, so you must love one another" (13:34). Therefore, they already knew that Jesus's command was that they love one another.

Jesus then turned to the topic of the Holy Spirit: "I will ask the Father, and he will give you another advocate to help you and be with you forever – the Spirit of truth" (14:16–17a). The Father is always willing to give whatever the Son asks. Jesus assured the disciples that he would ask the Father for another advocate (*paraklēte*), who would stay with them forever. Though Jesus would be absent, the Holy Spirit would be present with them and guide them. The adjectival form used here is not *heteros* (of a different kind) but a derivative *allos* (of the same kind).[7] This means that the substance of both advocates – Jesus and the Holy Spirit – is the same. The substance of Jesus would be continued through the mission and ministry of the Holy Spirit. That was why Jesus referred to him as the "Spirit of truth." Whereas Jesus was the truth (14:6), the Spirit would be the Spirit of truth (14:17a), meaning that he would represent Jesus and his teachings.

Earlier, Jesus had told the woman at the well, "God is spirit" (4:24). Similarly, the third person of the Trinity is "the Spirit" of truth (14:17a). Only Jesus, the Word who "became flesh and made his dwelling among us" (1:14), has unique human properties. The author of Hebrews explains the reason for this: "Since the children have flesh and blood, he too shared in their humanity so that by his death he might break the power of him who holds the power of death – that is, the devil" (2:14). It was for our sake that the Word became a human being.

This does not, however, mean that the Father or the Spirit of truth cannot live with believers. Jesus said, "The world cannot accept him, because it neither sees him nor knows him. But you know him, for he lives with you and will be in you" (14:17b). Earlier, the narrator said that Jesus "was in the world, and though the world was made through him, the world did not recognize him" (1:10). The world does not recognize the Spirit either. In contrast, the disciples know him because he lives with and in them (14:17b). The presence of the Holy Spirit among the disciples is a special divine arrangement so that

---

7. Thomaskutty, *Gospel of John*, 104.

he may teach, comfort, and counsel them and be an advocate for them – and the word *paraklētē* conveys all these meanings.[8] Even now, when believers are suffering or persecuted, they are not alone for the Spirit of truth is with them to enable them to endure. As people live with a wounded psyche – due to floods, natural disasters, violence by the armed forces, wars, ecological devastation, and other situations of chaos – God's presence through the Spirit brings comfort (14:17a). Jesus promised that the Spirit would abide *with* the disciples and be *in* them. Earlier, he had affirmed, "The Father's is *in* me" (14:11, emphasis added). Now, he assured the disciples that the Spirit would be *in* them, which reveals a mystical oneness between the divine and the believer. Just as the Father is *in* Jesus, the Spirit is *in* the disciples.

The church must shift from seeing mission as "witness" to viewing it as "with-ness." Kaunda writes, "The with-ness missiology can help in the process of re-discovering the theological and missiological meaning of life in an ever-wounded world and alternative ways of intercarnating [becoming flesh] into one another for the sake of common basic good."[9] Believers, indwelt and empowered by the Spirit, are called to reach out to the world with renewed strength just as Jesus did, showing people the Father and glorifying the Son.

The world cannot experience or understand these mystical unions between the Father and the Son, the Son and believers, and the Spirit and believers. If only they could discern these unions by believing in Jesus, they would be different people. The Pentecostal movement, which emphasizes the presence and power of the Holy Spirit, continues to grow in many Asian and African countries. But the Holy Spirit is not merely a power that is confined to liturgical services but someone who draws believers into a mystical relationship with God all the time.

Jesus then assured his disciples that he would not leave them orphans (14:18a). The OT emphasizes God the Father's concern for orphans (Exod 22:22; Deut 14:28–29; Ps 68:5; Prov 23:10; Jer 7:6–7). God the Son was concerned not to leave the disciples orphaned. Therefore, he assured them, "I will come to you" (14:18b). The fact he was referring to his resurrection is evident in the next verse: "Before long, the world will not see me anymore, but you will see me. Because I live, you also will live" (14:19). The world,

---

8. The *paraclete* is also considered as a *Christomorph* [image of Christ], a person who perpetuates Jesus's mission on earth. Andreas Hoeck, "The Johannine Paraclete: Herald of the Eschaton," *J. Biblic. Pneumatological Res.* 4 (2012): 27–28.
9. Chammah J. Kaunda, "Mission as Withness," *The Expository Times* 134, no. 7 (October 31, 2022), 299.

having rejected faith, would not see the resurrected Jesus; but the disciples, who followed him in faith, would see him face-to-face. Just as Jesus had promised, the disciples did see him and enjoy fellowship with him after his resurrection (21:1–23). Their lives became intimately intertwined with his: "Because I live, you also will live" (14:19b). His resurrection guarantees their resurrection (1 Cor 15:17–19).

"On that day" – a reference to resurrection morning – "you will realize that I am in my Father, and you are in me, and I am in you" (14:20). Jesus underscored the integral connection and mystical union among the Father, the Son, and the disciples. Those who obey Jesus's commandments are the ones who truly love Jesus (14:21a), and they, in return, will be loved by the Father, and Jesus will manifest himself to them (14:21b). Asian Christians exemplify this kind of love in public spaces through educating the underprivileged, offering healthcare to the sick and suffering, and showing charity amid human vulnerability.

Throughout the Farewell Discourse, several disciples asked Jesus questions, addressing him with the title "Lord." Simon Peter asked, "Lord, are you going to wash my feet?" (13:6). John leaned toward Jesus and asked, "Lord, who is it [that will betray you]?" (13:25). Simon Peter also asked, "Lord, where are you going?" (13:36) and "Lord, why can't I follow you now?" (13:37). Thomas said, "Lord, we don't know where you are going, so how can we know the way?" (14:5). And Philip said, "Lord, show us the Father and that will be enough for us" (14:8). This dialogical way of learning can serve as a model for Christian teaching today.

Judas – not Judas Iscariot the betrayer but another Judas – then asked, "But, Lord, why do you intend to show yourself to us and not to the world?" (14:22). Luke refers to this Judas as "Judas son of James" and lists him together with "Judas Iscariot, who became a traitor" (Luke 6:16). Judas's question referred to Jesus's earlier words: "Before long, the world will not see me anymore, but you will see me" (14:19a). Since Judas did not anticipate Jesus's resurrection, his question stemmed from confusion. Yet even after the resurrection, the question remains puzzling for us as well: Why didn't the risen Jesus show himself to multitudes? Wouldn't such an appearance have led many more to believe, as in the case of Saul on the road to Damascus (Acts 9)?

Instead of answering Judas's question, Jesus responded by speaking about two different groups of people: those who love him and those who do not love him. Those who love him will obey his teaching (14:23a). Love is demonstrated through action. Jesus promised that those who love him by obeying his teachings will be loved by his Father and that both the Father and the Son will make their home [*monē*] with them (14:23b). Earlier in the discourse, Jesus said, "My Father's house has many rooms [*monē*]" (14:2). One might expect that going to heaven means entering a room in the Father's house. But Jesus clarified that this home [*monē*] is within the disciples' hearts, where the Father and the Son will take up residence (14:23). Earlier, Jesus explained that he had to die and be resurrected before people could occupy that *monē*. Now, we are told that disciples must love Jesus and obey his teachings before the Father and the Son make the disciples their *monē*.

In contrast, those who do not love Jesus will not obey his teachings – even though these teachings are not his but come from the Father who sent him (14:24). Although the Jews prided themselves on obeying the law God had given them, they rejected the teachings of Jesus – including his claim to be the Messiah and the Son of God. By rejecting Jesus's words, they were rejecting God's own words because it was the Father himself who had sent Jesus and instructed him to speak as he did. Previously, Jesus said, "The words I say to you I do not speak on my own authority. Rather, it is the Father, living in me, who is doing his work" (14:10b). He now reaffirmed this truth: As the divine agent of God, Jesus reveals the mysteries of the Father to those who obey and follow him.

Jesus then contrasted his earthly work and the work of the coming Advocate (*paraklētē*). During his ministry, Jesus taught his disciples (14:25). The Advocate has two tasks: He will teach new truths and bring to remembrance all that Jesus taught (14:26). Jesus identified this Advocate as the Holy Spirit – earlier described as "the Spirit of truth" (14:17) – "whom the Father will send in my name" (14:26). Just as the Father had sent the Son, he would send the Advocate in Jesus's name. In Jesus's absence, the Advocate would teach and remind believers of Jesus's teachings.

The Gospels and NT letters are examples of the Holy Spirit's work. The Spirit enabled the disciples to remember and record Jesus's life and teachings, which then became the Gospels. He also taught them new truths, which they recorded in the form of Letters or Epistles. The teachings of Jesus and the Holy Spirit continue. As the writer of Hebrews says, "In the past God spoke to our ancestors through the prophets at many times in various ways, but in these last days he has spoken to us by his Son" (1:1–2a). Today, the Holy Spirit continues to remind Asian Christians of Jesus's teachings and teach them new truths. Each generation of Christians faces its own ethical challenge, problems, and life situations that they must address with the help of the Holy Spirit. This process is often referred to as "contextualization." In our globalized and technologically advanced world – with new developments such as Artificial Intelligence (AI) and ChatGPT – it has become necessary to reinterpret the gospel in new idioms and semantics. The Holy Spirit helps Christians in this task.

The teachings about the Holy Spirit should not be confused with animistic religions and worldviews in Asia, which often teach that gods and spirits are found in everything and can be experienced by becoming one with nature. The biblical teaching that God is spirit and sends the Spirit of truth – the Holy Spirit – makes it clear that God cannot be reduced to a physical form or fashioned into an idol to be worshiped. He is not a physical object that can be represented or reproduced. Although the Son "became flesh and made his dwelling among us" (John 1:14), this does not make him inferior to the Father or the Holy Spirit. Instead, it demonstrates his love and sacrifice: "Since the children have flesh and blood, he too shared in their humanity" (Heb 2:14a).

14:27–31 JESUS'S OFFER OF ENDURING PEACE

Jesus began this discourse by saying, "Do not let your hearts be troubled" (14:1). Even if his teachings and the persecutions they had endured up to this point did not trouble them, the events that would unfold in the next few days – Jesus's arrest, trials, crucifixion, death, and burial – would greatly trouble them. And when he ascended to heaven, leaving them behind like orphans, this would also be troubling. That is why Jesus spoke about the coming of another advocate, who would always be with them and *within* them. Now, returning to the theme of "trouble," Jesus said, "Peace I leave with you; my peace I give you. I do not give to you as the world gives. Do not let your hearts be troubled and do not be afraid" (14:27). In this way, Jesus bestowed divine blessings on the disciples' future life and ministry. The peace that had sustained Jesus during his ministry – amid threats and violence from his opponents – would abide with them. Malina and Rohrbaugh state, "Here 'peace' is a virtual equivalent of 'truth,' 'light,' 'life,' and other terms in John's antilanguage that describe the group's quality of life."[10] Like Jesus, the disciples would face uncertainty and persecution, but they were not to be troubled or afraid because the Father, Jesus, and the Holy Spirit would be with them.

The peace Jesus gives is different from the peace the world gives. Worldly peace is temporary and lacks assurance. This is illustrated by the recent conflict

---

10. Malina and Rohrbaugh, *Social-Science Commentary on the Gospel of John*, 232.

between India and Pakistan – peace had existed for many decades before war suddenly broke out because of a terrorist act. Paul says, "While people are saying, 'Peace and safety,' destruction will come on them suddenly" (1 Thess 5:3). The peace that the world offers is temporary. But the peace of Jesus enables his disciples to stand firm in troubled situations without giving in to fear (14:27). The best model is Jesus himself, who remained calm even amid severe opposition. In Asia, mission and ministry can be conducted with this divine peace, which enables believers to serve as peacemakers (Matt 5:9). By humbling himself even to the point of death (Phil 2:5–11), Jesus established divine peace and reconciliation between God and the world (Col 1:15–20) and instructed his disciples to continue this mission in the world under the guidance of the Holy Spirit.

After offering peace to the disciples, Jesus once again announced his departure and return: "I am going away, and I am coming back to you" (14:28a). He was referring to his death ("going away") and resurrection ("coming back"), but this also points to his ascension to heaven and future return. The ascending and descending motif reappears. While Jesus's "going away" created perplexity in the disciples' minds, his "coming back" was a promise that offered them hope. The U-shaped structure of the Fourth Gospel is evident yet again: The Word was with God (1:1); the Word became flesh and lived among humanity (1:14); and the incarnate Word would return to the Father (14:28).

Jesus said that his return to the Father should not trouble the disciples. In fact, he said that if they truly loved him, they would be glad he was going to the Father because the Father is greater than Jesus (14:28b). Earlier, Jesus had said that it was only after returning to the Father that he could send another advocate who would always be with them and dwell within them. Now, he reminded them that by going to the Father, he was going to someone greater than himself – someone who would do whatever the disciples asked him in Jesus's name. Therefore, Jesus's return to the Father would be beneficial for the disciples. His return to the Father also guaranteed the coming of the Holy Spirit and the preparation of a place for believers. Asian believers who experience situations of great hardship and suffering in the world can draw great comfort and hope from these words of Jesus.

Earlier in the Gospel, the Samaritan woman recognized Jesus as a prophet because he told her everything about her life (4:19). Similarly, those who saw his signs confessed that he must be a prophet (6:14; 7:40; 9:17). Now, wanting the disciples to know that he was indeed a prophet, Jesus said, "I have told you now before it happens, so that when it does happen you will believe"

(14:29). Their faith in Jesus would become stronger when they experienced the fulfillment of his words. The glorification of the Son would reveal great truths and establish extraordinary faith in his disciples (14:29).

Sometimes, an author wants to say more but is prevented from doing so. The author of Hebrews could not say more because of the people's hardness of hearts (Heb 5:11). Similarly, Jesus explained that he could not continue speaking because "the prince of this world is coming" and went on to affirm, "He has no hold over me, but he comes so that the world may learn that I love the Father and do exactly what my Father has commanded me. Come now; let us leave" (14:30–31). Jesus referred to this "prince of this world" three times (12:31; 14:30; 16:11). This "prince" could symbolize the political or religious system of the day – the Roman Empire that would ultimately destroy Jerusalem or the religious leaders who opposed Jesus. Alternatively, this "prince" could refer to Satan. Either way, Jesus contrasted the heavenly Son with the prince of this world who opposed the Son. Although this prince would try to undo whatever Jesus accomplished, he has no hold over Jesus (14:30b). In fact, despite the antagonism of the prince of this world, the world would learn that the Son loved his Father and did exactly what the Father commanded him to do (14:31).

Jesus's words offered hope for the future to the Johannine community in the face of opposition and hostility. Similarly, Asian Christians can find the same kind of hope amid their sufferings, knowing that even though the prince of this world opposes them, he has no hold over them. Political powers and dominant religious ideologies often form alliances against the community of God. Just as the Roman Empire was antagonistic to the Johannine community, the new colonial powers in Asia persecute and marginalize the people of God. But just as Jesus assured his disciples that "[the prince of this world] has no hold over me," believers can be confident that these powers have no hold over them either.

At the end of the discourse, Jesus invited his disciples to leave the place where they were (14:31b). This narrative marker signals the conclusion of the discourse in John 14 and the introduction of a new discourse in John 15.

The discourse in John 14 highlights several important teachings. Jesus is the way to the Father. The Father and Jesus have prepared a place [*monē*] for believers and will abide [*monē*] with them and *within* them. Just as the Father is in the Son, so the Son is among his people, and his people are united with the Father. In Jesus's absence, another advocate – the Spirit of truth or the Holy Spirit – is sent. This Spirit teaches and reminds the disciples of Jesus's teachings. Jesus bestows his divine peace on the disciples. His departure to the Father is beneficial for them because he represents them before someone greater than he – that is, the Father – and whatever they ask the Father in Jesus's name, the Father will grant. These teachings offer great encouragement to Asian Christians. In contexts where multiple ideologies and religions co-exist, Christians can proclaim Jesus as the true way to the Father. They can take comfort in knowing that they are never alone because the Spirit and Jesus are with them and dwell within them. They enjoy enduring peace with the Father – a peace they can experience even when they go through struggles and persecution – and are empowered to become peacemakers in a troubled world.

JOHN 15:1–27

JESUS IS THE TRUE VINE AND A FRIEND

The previous discourse ended with Jesus saying, "Come now; let us leave" (14:31), which suggests that they were in a different location when Jesus began this next discourse. Since vine imagery features in this discourse, perhaps Jesus and the disciples were in a vineyard or near the Mount of Olives.

John 15:1–27 can be divided into four sections: the vine and the branches (15:1–14); Jesus as a friend (15:15–17); the world's attitude toward believers in Christ (15:18–25); and a second statement about the *paraklētos* or Advocate (15:26–27).

This section (John 15) is often regarded as the central discourse within John 13–17, where the mystical and relational unity among the Father, the Son, the Holy Spirit, and believers comes full circle.

15:1–14 THE VINE AND THE BRANCHES

In 15:1–14, Jesus began yet another discourse, opening with the words, "I am the true vine" (15:1). This is the last of the seven "I am" statements.[1] The mystical union among Jesus, the Father, and believers is explained using the imagery of the vine, the branches, and the gardener. Jesus identified himself as the true vine and his Father as the gardener (15:1). As the true vine, he had earlier turned water into a superior-quality wine (2:1–11).

The gardener – God – cuts off [*airō*] every branch of the vine that does not bears fruit (15:2a). This imagery raises a problem: How could branches "in me" – that is, in Christ – be cut off or removed? Therefore, scholars have proposed another translation for the verb *airō*: "lifted up." If a vine branch drags on the ground, it begins to rot. So, gardeners lift such branches using sticks so that they can bear more fruit. This latter translation aligns with Jesus's next words: "While every branch that does bear fruit, he prunes so that it will be even more fruitful" (15:2b). Bearing fruit is a hallmark of a Christian who is in Christ. While branches that bear no fruit go through extensive pruning

---

1. The others are "I am the bread of life" (6:35), "I am the light of the world" (8:12), "I am the gate for the sheep" (10:7), "I am the good shepherd" (10:11), "I am the resurrection and the life" (11:25), and "I am the way, and the truth, and the life" (14:6).

and lifting to make them fruitful, fruitful branches are pruned so that they may bear more fruit than before. Pruning is a gracious act of the gardener-God to make the branches more fruitful.

The text distinguishes between not bearing fruit, bearing fruit, and being even more fruitful. God's activity of pruning is intended to move the believer from the stage of not bearing fruit to the stage of becoming even more fruitful.

Jesus's next statement – "You are already clean" (15:3) – may seem out of place until we realize that the gardener who prunes the vine also purifies it by removing bird nests or cobwebs that hinder its fruitfulness. Similarly, he removes the weeds that grow around the vine because these drain the nutrients the vine needs to flourish. In this case, Jesus himself functions as the gardener because it was his word that had already cleansed them: "You are already clean because of the word I have spoken to you" (15:3).

Since branches must remain connected to the vine if they are to bear grapes, Jesus said, "Remain in me, as I also remain in you. No branch can bear fruit by itself; it must remain in the vine. Neither can you bear fruit unless you remain in me" (15:4). Just as the branch can only bear fruit if it aligns well with the vine, believers cannot bear fruit unless they remain in Jesus. The focus here is the inseparable union between Jesus and the disciples.

Jesus then repeated the imagery of the vine and the branches (15:5a). Although he omitted the word "true" in this second statement, the meaning remains unchanged. Christian life is life in Christ, and fruit-bearing is possible only through mutual indwelling. In fact, apart from Jesus, the disciples can do nothing (15:5b). Haenchen states, "When verse 5 says that we Christians can do nothing without him, that is not a declaration of bankruptcy, but an expression of the readiness for and confident hope in the fullness that the vine can furnish."[2]

Jesus then spoke of the fate of those who do not remain in him (15:6). Earlier, he foretold that one of his disciples would betray him (6:64, 70–71) and another would deny him (13:38). Like the rest of the Jews, at least two of his disciples would desert him as hung on the cross. So, he warned, "If you do not remain in me, you are like a branch that is thrown away and withers; such branches are picked up, thrown into the fire and burned" (15:6). Anyone who does not remain in Christ is like a thrown-away branch that withers and dies because it is disconnected from the vine (15:6a). A thrown-away branch is

---

2. Ernst Haenchen, *John 2: A Commentary on the Gospel of John Chapters 7–21* (Philadelphia: Fortress Press, 1984), 131.

destined to wither and be "picked up" for the unpleasant fate of being "thrown into the fire and burned" (15:6b). The message is clear: disconnectedness from Christ destines a person to spiritual death (15:6).

On the other hand, if the disciples continue to remain [*menō*] in Jesus, his words will remain [*menō*] in them, and whatever they ask of him will be done for them (15:7). The verb *menō* (meaning "remain") is related to *monē*, translated as "room" (14:2) and "home" (14:23). If the disciples remained in Christ, they would continue to have life in him, and he would answer their prayers. Believing, knowing, and obeying are important for living an abiding life. The Father is glorified not only through the Son but also through the believers' fruitfulness: "This is to my Father's glory, that you bear much fruit, showing yourselves to be my disciples" (15:8). In marriage, a man and woman are united and become one. But when the divine "from above" and a human "from below" are united in Christ, the divine-human union that results transcends earthly. In Paul's words, this is an "in Christ" experience of becoming a "new creation" (2 Cor 5:17).

Jesus then reaffirmed his love for the disciples: "As the Father has loved me, so have I loved you. Now remain in my love" (15:9). The love between the Father and the Son, and between the Son and the disciples, was the reason, motivation, and solid foundation for the disciples to remain in Jesus. When tempted to deny, betray, or abandon Jesus, they were to remember God love made visible and tangible through Jesus's love for them. The narrator began this second half of the Gospel, the *Book of Glory*, by saying, "Having loved his own who were in the world, he loved them to the end" (13:1). This love of the Father and the Son is what enabled the disciples to keep abiding in him. As the story moves forward, the denier, Peter, remained and accepted Jesus's challenge to keep on loving him (21:15–17), but the betrayer, Judas, cut himself off from the vine and died (Matt 27:5).

Remaining in this love relationship requires obedience. Just as Jesus obeyed the Father's commands and remained in his love, the disciples must obey Jesus's commandments in order to remain in his love (15:10). This obedience would lead to joy even amid persecution and suffering: "I have told you this so that my joy may be in you and that your joy may be complete" (15:11). Those who continually remain in this dynamic love relationship will enjoy the full measure of Jesus's joy (15:11).

This fullness of joy can only be found in loving one another as Jesus had loved them (15:12). Jesus was preparing the disciples for the coming days when he would be tortured and killed, and they would scatter in fear. Only by continuing to love one another and remembering Jesus's love for them would they be able to remain with him instead of abandoning him or betraying him as one of them would do. Later, when Simon Peter announced to his fellow disciples that he was going fishing, the rest replied, "We'll go with you" (21:3). Their love abided, and their fellowship with Jesus remained and was renewed (21:4–14).

The narrator emphasizes the theme of love among the Father, the Son, and the believing community. God extends this same love to the world (3:16). Today, this offer of love is extended to all who hear about Jesus. If they love him, they will be loved by the Father. If they love him, they will also love other Christians, as well as non-Christians. When Christians are united in love, they are sheltered from the world's hatred against them. Christian love must also extend beyond the church, reaching out especially to the poor, the dehumanized, and the ostracized. Examples of such love from Asia include Pandita Ramabai's missionary endeavors in Maharashtra, India, and Mother Teresa's ministry in Kolkata, India.

In summary, "Greater love has no one than this: to lay down one's life for one's friends" (15:13). The disciples were not to view Jesus's death as failure or an abandonment that left them orphaned. Instead, they were to understand that Jesus would willingly lay down his life on their behalf (15:13). Jesus exemplified his love on the cross, and they would continue their friendship with Jesus if they obeyed his command to love one another and remain united in difficult times (15:14). Jesus's invitation to friendship reveals how deeply he identified with them.

Jesus's incarnational and accommodative mission in John's Gospel is a powerful model for Asian communities seeking a paradigmatic figure to edify, transform, and emancipate people and systems. Asian churches can follow the example of Jesus, whose ministry was marked by service to humanity, friendship with the people of God, and servant leadership.

15:15–17 JESUS AS A FRIEND

Ancient cultures, like many Asian countries today, were characterized by power distance – for example, between masters and slaves, rich and poor, Hebrews and Greeks, male and female, and teachers and disciples (or students). In India, whenever a teacher enters a classroom, students stand up and remain standing until the teacher instructs them to sit. In caste-based societies, Dalits (sometimes called "untouchables") are not permitted to eat with Brahmins (the high caste). Such delineation between groups was common even in biblical times.

James condemned partiality in churches where the rich were given honorable seats while the poor were made to sit on the floor (Jas 2:1–4). Paul describes how although Cephas (Peter) ate with the Gentiles in Antioch, when Jews from Jerusalem arrived there, he withdrew from fellowship with these Gentiles (Gal 2:11–13). Similarly, the narrator of John's Gospel relates how Peter initially objected to Jesus washing his feet (John 13:8). Such power distances create barriers that are difficult to overcome.

But the Lord Jesus challenged these power distances between God and believers, and among believers themselves. For instance, when he washed their feet, he said, "You call me 'Teacher' and 'Lord,' and rightly so, for that is what I am. Now that I, your Lord and Teacher, have washed your feet, you also should wash one another's feet" (13:13–14). Jesus set aside the power distance between himself and the disciples and called them to do the same. Now, he returned to this same theme by saying that he considered his disciples "friends" – his equals, not his "servants" (15:15–17). Although modern translations often use the politically correct term "servants," Jesus used the words *kyrios* (master) and *doulos* (slave), which highlights the contrast.

Slaves do not understand the intricacies of their masters' business – where they buy their crops, how they invest, or what profit they make – but simply do whatever their masters tell them to do. However, Jesus did not call his disciples "slaves" but said, "I have called you friends, for everything that I learned from my Father I have made known to you" (15:15b). As friends of Jesus, the disciples knew his business – his dealings with the Father, which he had plainly explained to them. Haenchen states, "If he now rejects the designation 'servants' or 'slaves' (*douloi*) for his friends, he does so because the slave obeys blindly, without insight into the command of his lord and without the joyful understanding heart of a friend."[3] By revealing heavenly things to them, Jesus raised his disciples to a new level of intimacy and understanding.

Their selection by Jesus also reveals their importance: "You did not choose me, but I chose you and appointed you so that you might go and bear fruit – fruit that will last – and so that whatever you ask in my name the Father will give you" (15:16). In ancient cultures, the master (*kyrios*) did not choose the slave (*doulos*). Instead, the chief servant in the house bought lower-ranking slaves on behalf of the master. These chief servants were called *oikonomos* – a term derived from the words "house" (*oikos*) and "law" (*nomos*) – which means something like "house-lawyers." The NIV translates this as "manager" (Luke

---

3. Haenchen, *John 2*, 132.

12:42; 16:1–8), "director" (Rom 16:23), "those entrusted with" (1 Cor 4:1), "trustees" (Gal 4:2), and "stewards" (1 Pet 4:10). In contrast, masters would usually select their friends from among equals in business, status, and wealth. By choosing and commissioning the disciples to bear lasting fruit, Jesus established them as "friends" rather than "slaves." Therefore, whatever they asked in Jesus's name, the Father would give them, just as the Father granted Jesus's requests. They were not subservient slaves but friends of Jesus and the Father.

After establishing the disciples' status as friends, Jesus repeated the command he had emphasized all along: "Love each other" (15:17; compare 13:34; 15:12). Since the disciples were now equal in status – as friends of Jesus – they were called to love one another equally, without allowing power distance to create barriers between them.

A key literary feature of John's Gospel is repetition. This discourse section repeats various themes: the relationship or union among the Father, the Son, and believers; the importance of heaven-born love; the removal of power distance between God and people, and among people; and the role of Jesus as an intermediary. These are important lessons for Asian churches, where prejudice, racial tensions, caste discrimination, and gender-based discrimination persist. While political powers attempt to divide and rule by imposing human-made boundaries, Jesus's message of oneness, love, and friendship should be the paradigm followed by Christian communities and churches.

Indian poet N. Kumaranasan emphasizes the dictum *Snehamanakhilasaramoozhiyil* (which means "love is the essence of everything in the world").[4] This truth lies at the heart of John's Gospel.

15:18–25 THE WORLD'S ATTITUDE TOWARD BELIEVERS IN CHRIST

While Jesus regarded the disciples as his friends and loved them unconditionally, the world would not share the same sentiment. In fact, the world would hate them. This was true for Jesus's disciples then and remains true for his followers today.

Jesus warned the disciples about the world's hatred. Just as the world hated Jesus, his followers would also face hatred from the world. The disciples had witnessed the Jewish leaders' plots to arrest Jesus and even kill him. So, when

---

4. It is an expression from *Chandalabhikshuki*, a Malayalam poem written by N. Kumaranasan, a poet from Kerala. http://knanayam1.blogspot.com/2017/08/blog-post.html.

they faced the world's hatred, they were to remember that the world hated Jesus first (15:18).

If the disciples followed the world's values and principles, the world would not have hated them but loved them (15:19a). Barrett comments, "The disciples have been 'of the world' and they continue to be 'in the world' (17:11), but they have been chosen out of the world."[5] The disciples did not belong to the world but were chosen out of the world by Jesus (15:19b). The world would hate them because of their association with Jesus and their distancing from the world (15:19c).

Jesus, their master, was persecuted, and the world viewed the disciples as his slaves – even though Jesus saw them as friends. The world that lived by the philosophy that "a servant is not greater than his master" (compare 13:16) would treat the servants – the disciples – with the same contempt it showed Jesus. If the world persecuted Jesus, it would persecute his servants even more easily (15:20a). On the other hand, if the world obeyed Jesus's teaching, they would receive the disciples as Jesus's representatives and obey their words (15:20b).

The disciples would face hostility because of their association with Jesus – "because of my name" (15:21a). Although the narrator does not explain what this name is, he has already noted that "whoever does not believe stands condemned already because they have not believed in the name of God's one and only Son" (3:18b) and recorded Jesus as saying, "I have come in my Father's name" (5:43a). Paul writes more about this name: "Therefore God exalted him to the highest place and gave him the name that is above every name, that at the name of Jesus every knee should bow, in heaven and on earth and under the earth" (Phil 2:9–10). Kanagaraj says, "The name of Jesus is the name of God given to him to exhibit his glory to humanity . . . the world persecutes the church as it persecuted Jesus."[6] Because of their association with the name "Jesus," the disciples would face mistreatment and persecution. This remains true today. In many countries, Christians are hated because of their association and relationship with Jesus and their belief that he is God's one and only Son (3:18b). The world rejected Jesus because "they do not know the one who sent me" (15:21b). Their antagonism toward the disciples was due to their unfamiliarity with the Father (15:21b). This was a rebuke directed at the religious

---

5. Barrett, *Gospel according to St. John*, 400.
6. Jey J. Kanagaraj, *John*, New Covenant Commentary Series (Eugene: Cascade Books, 2013), 156.

leaders who prided themselves on their knowledge of God and his law but failed to recognize Jesus or the Father who had sent him.

The Oxford dictionary defines the proverb "ignorance is bliss" as follows: "If one is unaware of an unpleasant fact or situation, one cannot be troubled by it."[7] This was true of the Israelites and the world in Jesus's time: "If I had not come and spoken to them, they would not be guilty of sin; but now they have no excuse for their sin" (15:22). Jesus came to reveal the Father and himself, but the world rejected him. If Jesus had not come, they would have continued in blissful ignorance. But now that he had come, they were accountable for their sin of rejecting him and had no excuse. Their sin was great: "Whoever hates me hates my Father as well" (15:23). Jesus is not merely a good teacher or healer – he is one with the Father, the Father sent him, he is God's Word that became flesh and lived among humanity. To reject Jesus is to reject the Father who sent him. To hate him is to hate the Father who sent him.

They remained in their sin not only because they rejected Jesus but also because they ignored his signs and wonders. Although Jesus revealed himself and his Father through extraordinary miracles, the world hated both the Father and the Son (15:24). Earlier, Jesus had said, "I have testimony weightier than that of John. For the works that the Father has given me to finish – the very works that I am doing – testify that the Father has sent me" (5:36). Those works – his signs – had revelatory significance, revealing Jesus's identity as the Son of God. They were intended to draw people to both Jesus and the Father. The world's failure to respond resulted in their remaining in the sin of ignoring God's work among them.

Jesus saw the world's rejection and hatred as a fulfillment of a prophecy: "This is to fulfill what is written in their Law: 'They hated me without reason'" (15:25). This is a quotation from Psalm 69:4, a psalm of David. Its opening words, "Save me, O God, for the waters have come up to my neck. I sink in the miry depths, where there is no foothold. I have come into the deep waters; the floods engulf me" (Ps 69:1–2), indicate that it is a "lament" psalm. In verse 4, David says, "Those who hate me without reason outnumber the hairs of my head; many are my enemies without cause, those who seek to destroy me." This psalm is also alluded to in John 2:17 and 19:29. Jesus undoubtedly identified with his ancestor David, who was also hated. Not only was Jesus

---

7. Oxford Learners Dictionaries, "Ignorance," https://www.oxfordlearnersdictionaries.com/definition/english/ignorance, accessed on 21 July 2025.

hated by his own people without good reason, this hatred and persecution would extend to his disciples.

Sadly, such hatred against Jesus's followers has continued throughout the centuries. In 1999, Australian missionary and doctor Graham Staines and his two young sons (ages ten and six) were burned alive while they slept in their car – killed out of pure hatred for Christianity. In Sri Lanka, Buddhist nationalists view Christianity as a product of Western colonialism that threatens the country's Buddhist identity. Although Christians often humbly and faithfully serve people, anti-Christian movements remain prevalent across Asia. The world still hates Christians because it first hated their Lord.

15:26–27 SECOND STATEMENT ABOUT THE *PARAKLĒTOS*

In John 14:15–17, the narrator presents Jesus's first promise of the "Advocate" (*paraklētos*). He returns to this theme in the last two verses of this chapter (15:26–27). In this way, John 14 and 15 are interconnected even though these discourses might have been delivered in different locations, as suggested by 14:31: "Come now; let us leave."

Once again, the Advocate's role is seen as affirming the truth about Jesus (15:26). Jesus would be gone, and his signs and wonders would no longer take place among the people, but the Advocate whom Jesus would ask the Father to send would continue to testify about Jesus. As Jesus had said earlier, this second Advocate – who is the Spirit of truth and thus without falsehood – would faithfully bear witness to Jesus, teaching and reminding the disciples of everything Jesus had said. Just as Jesus was the first Advocate – sent by God, embodying truth, and testifying to the Father – the Spirit is the second Advocate, who also comes from the Father, is sent by the Son, is the Spirit of truth, and testifies about the Son.

Jesus concluded this section with a challenge. Not only would the second Advocate continue to testify about Jesus, the disciples were to do so too: "You also must testify, for you have been with me from the beginning" (15:27). This was why he had called them early in his ministry. They had witnessed his miracles and signs and heard the testimony of the Father and John the baptizer. Soon they would have another Advocate – the Holy Spirit – dwelling among and within them, who would continue to testify to Jesus's truthfulness. Therefore, they, too, should continue to testify to who Jesus is. Kanagaraj states, "The community of Jesus's disciples witnesses to Jesus not in its own strength, but by the power of the Spirit (15:26–27)."[8] Eleven disciples were obedient to Jesus's command. Even the Gospel of John is an example of faithful witnessing to Jesus as God's Son, the one sent by the Father, the way, the truth, and the life.

Asian Christians today face many difficult and hostile situations – for example, political oppression, personal trials, religious discrimination, poverty, and war. In all these circumstances, they must remain faithful, remembering that they are not slaves but friends of the Son, empowered by the Spirit of truth, just as the original disciples were. Therefore, they are called to abide in the true vine, bearing fruit and bearing witness to Christ, even in a world that hates them.

---

8. Kanagaraj, *John*, 157.

JOHN 16:1–33
JESUS'S WARNINGS, PROMISES, AND PROPHECIES

In the long discourse section of the Gospel of John (John 13–17) – often called the "Farewell Discourse" – Jesus prepared his disciples through various teachings. In John 13, he washed their feet and prepared them for servant leadership. In John 14, which begins, "Do not let your hearts be troubled," he reassured the disciples about the presence of the Father and the Son. In John 15, he used the imagery of the vine and its branches to emphasize the importance of the disciples continuing to abide in him in order to bear fruit. Now, in John 16, Jesus warned about the world's continued hatred toward the disciples, assured them of the constant presence of the second Advocate who would strengthen them, and foretold his imminent departure. His departure was the reason for the Farewell Discourse – Jesus wanted to prepare his disciples beforehand so that they would not be alarmed when his departure became a reality.

The discourse in John 16:1–33 can be divided into three sections: Jesus's warning of persecution (16:1–6); the third introduction to the *paraklētos* (16:7–15); and Jesus's teaching on his death and resurrection (16:16–33).

16:1–6 JESUS'S WARNING OF PERSECUTION

In the opening section of this chapter, Jesus explained that the reason he had been telling them all these things was "so that you will not fall away" (16:1). The Greek word used for "fall away" is *skandalizō*, which Jesus previously used when many of his disciples were offended by his teaching that he was the bread from heaven and grumbled about this (6:58–61). Jesus responded, "Does this offend [*skandalizō*] you?" He feared that, like the world, even his own disciples would be offended – as, in fact, Judas was – and did not want to lose the Twelve (compare 6:70). Therefore, he kept repeating these lessons to encourage them to persevere.

Jesus warned the disciples that life would only get more difficult: "They will put you out of the synagogue; in fact, the time is coming when anyone who kills you will think they are offering a service to God" (16:2). Just as the parents of the healed blind man feared being put out of the synagogue

(9:22) – and the man himself was, in fact, cast out (9:34) – the disciples were warned of possible expulsion from the synagogue. Even worse, they would be killed by those who believed their actions were a service to God (16:2b). Jesus predicted a "jihad" mindset – violence against people, or even killing them, in the name of God.

Those who would persecute the disciples in this way would do so because "they have not known the Father or me" (16:3). Their ignorance of the Father and the Son, as well as their relationship to the disciples, would blind them to the truth and lead them to persecute the disciples. Layang Seng Ja says, "If Christians remain faithful to their identity in Christ, different forms of discrimination and persecution follow as a consequence. Very often, Hindus attack Muslims and Christians in India, Muslims attack Christians in Pakistan, and conservative and nationalistic Buddhists attack minority Christians in Myanmar."[1] Christian communities across Asia suffer persecution to varying degrees because their persecutors do not know the Father or the Son.

Jesus had delayed revealing these truths to the disciples because he had been with them (16:4b). But now, as the time of his departure drew near, Jesus told them these things "so that when their time comes you will remember that I warned you about them" (16:4a). He did not want them to be surprised or alarmed when these evil things took place. Barrett comments, "When the time of persecution comes the disciples will remember that Jesus had foretold it, and it will therefore not weaken but strengthen their faith, because they will see in it the fulfillment of his word and the confirmation of his supernatural knowledge."[2]

After revealing these frightening truths, Jesus asserted that he was going to the Father who sent him (16:5a). Earlier, Thomas had said, "Lord, we don't know where you are going, so how can we know the way?" (14:5). But now, none of the disciples asked, "Where are you going?" (16:5b) because they were "filled with grief" by Jesus's words (16:6) – about his departure, as well as about impending persecution and even the possibility of death.

In August 2023, a mob in Punjab, Pakistan's most populated province, vandalized eight churches and several homes following false accusations of

---

1. Layang Seng Ja, "The Letters of Peter," *An Asian Introduction to the New Testament*, ed. Johnson Thomaskutty (Minneapolis: Fortress Press, 2022), 472.
2. Barrett, *Gospel according to St. John*, 404.

blasphemy against Islam.³ Yet many Christians in the region responded with resilient faith, demonstrating the steadfastness and perseverance that Jesus had urged his disciples to embody.

16:7–15 THIRD INTRODUCTION TO THE *PARAKLĒTOS*

Since the disciples were "filled with grief" about the things Jesus had said – especially about his departure – he again spoke of the Advocate (*paraklētos*). He reminded them that his going away was good for the disciples because he could only send the second Advocate to them after his departure (16:7). This clearly demonstrates the continuation of Jesus's ministry through the presence of the Advocate (*paraklētos*). Ngewa says, "In the context of redemption, the Holy Spirit's work would be built on Jesus's finished work. This work included his death, resurrection, and ascension. The Holy Spirit would then make Jesus's work effective in human hearts."⁴ Jesus's departure refers to two events: his imminent death on the cross and his ascension to the Father in heaven.

Jesus said that when the Advocate came, he would "convict the world" of its wrongdoings (ESV) or "prove the world to be in the wrong" (NIV) in relation to three things: sin, righteousness, and judgment (16:8). Thus far, Jesus had been talking about the Holy Spirit's ministry of teaching and reminding the disciples of all that Jesus had taught them. Now he was speaking of the Holy Spirit's ministry to the "world" – those outside the community of believers. First, the Spirit would convict them of their sin – specifically the sin of not believing in Jesus (16:9) – and they would be proved wrong for not believing him. Second, the Advocate would convict the world of righteousness – not on their own merits but based on Jesus's relationship with the Father – from whom he came and to whom he would return (16:10). Once again, those who questioned Jesus's origin and did not believe that the Father had sent him would be proved wrong. Third, the Spirit would convict the world of judgment – Jesus, as the righteous one and judge, would judge the prince of this world. Although Satan may appear victorious, on the cross, he was defeated and condemned. Those who align with him are aligning with a loser and will, ultimately, be proven wrong.

---

3. Sophia Saifi and Azaz Syed, "Eight churches set ablaze in Pakistan's Punjab province after accusations of blasphemy," dated 16 August 2023. https://edition.cnn.com/2023/08/16/asia/pakistan-punjab-churches-vandalized-blasphemy-intl/index.html.
4. Ngewa, *Gospel of John*, 309.

In this way, the Advocate continues the work of Jesus in the world, calling people to repentance just as Jesus did and as his disciples should be doing. Yet many will not listen, just as they did not listen to Jesus. But many will also believe, just as many – like the Samaritan woman – believed in Jesus. This has been evident throughout history. In modern times, more and more people in the Majority World are coming to faith in Jesus. The work of the Holy Spirit – the Advocate – among the people of the world is strong, convicting them of their sin, righteousness, and judgment, and bringing them to the Lord.

Jesus had much more to say, but the disciples could not bear it all at that moment (16:12). Therefore, Jesus promised them that when the Spirit of truth came, he would do two things. First, he would "guide [them] into all the truth" (16:13a). Second, he would "tell [them] what is yet to come" (16:13c), giving them prophetic abilities. The book of Revelation is one example of the Spirit of truth granting prophetic ability to the disciples. Just as Jesus did not speak on his own authority but only what he heard from the Father, the Spirit of truth "will not speak on his own; he will speak only what he hears" from the Son (16:13c–14). In doing so, Jesus said that the Spirit of truth "will glorify me because it is from me that he will receive what he will make known to you" (16:14). Jesus received words from the Father and communicated these to the disciples; now, the Spirit of truth would receive words from Jesus and communicate those truths to the disciples. The mission of the Holy Spirit is integrally connected to the mission that Jesus inaugurated and would continue through the Spirit. Just as the Son's mission was for the glory of the Father, the Holy Spirit's mission is for the glory of the Son. The Trinity's unity in mission and ministry offers a model for Christian unity in Asia.

The unity of the Father, the Son, and the Holy Spirit is further emphasized by the words, "All that belongs to the Father is mine. That is why I said the Spirit will receive from me what he will make known to you" (16:15). After the departure of Jesus – their rabbi – the Holy Spirit would become the teacher and guide for the disciples and the believing community. Kanagaraj states, "Just like the Father gave authority to the Son to speak his words, the Son has given authority to the Spirit to declare his words. The message of the Father, the Son, and the Holy Spirit is identical because they, being essentially one, hear one another in essential agreement."[5]

In a world divided by caste, class, color, denomination, language, and regional biases, the eternal unity of the Trinity offers a paradigm for the church to

---

5. Kanagaraj, *John*, 161.

follow. As a community of truth, called to be bearers of the truth of salvation, Asian Christians must stand firm as they establish truth and righteousness in the world.

16:16–33 JESUS'S TEACHING ON HIS DEATH AND RESURRECTION

After warning that the disciples would face persecution (16:1–6) and promising that the Advocate – the Spirit of truth – would be with them (16:7–15), Jesus returned to the theme of his imminent death and what would follow (16:16–33). He began by saying, "In a little while you will see me no more, and then after a little while you will see me" (16:16). Earlier, Jesus had said that the crowd would look for him and not find him (7:34; 14:19). Now, he said that even his disciples would experience his absence for a brief period: "You will see me no more, and then after a little while you will see me" (16:16). The repeated phrase "a little while" (Gk. *mikron*) stresses the shortness of time between his departure and his return. Since the disciples had not fully grasped the coming events – Jesus's crucifixion, death, and resurrection within three days – they wondered what he meant by "a little while" and "going to the Father" (16:17) and admitted, "We don't understand what he is saying" (16:18).

Jesus was aware of their confusion and addressed the matter directly (16:19). He said, "Very truly I tell you, you will weep and mourn while the world rejoices. You will grieve, but your grief will turn to joy" (16:20). At his death, they would weep and mourn the loss of their friend and Lord, while the world would rejoice over it. Blomberg comments, "The description of weeping and mourning (16:20) reflects standard Jewish behavior at funerals."[6] But the disciples' grief would soon be transformed into joy as they witnessed his resurrection and realized that their Lord was alive! In this way, Jesus clearly foretold both his going (death) and his coming (resurrection), both of which would take place in "a little while."

Jesus used the metaphor of a woman in labor to illustrate the briefness of the disciples' grief and the transformation of their sorrow into joy (16:21). Though a woman must endure intense labor pains when her time has come, this excruciating pain is short-lived. Once the baby is born, the mother forgets her anguish because of the great joy she finds in this new life that has come into the world. Time becomes relative. In the same way, the disciples' sorrow during Jesus's absence would be intense but would quickly turn to rejoicing

---

6. Blomberg, *Historical Reliability of John's Gospel*, 215.

when they saw the risen Jesus: "So with you: Now is your time of grief, but I will see you again and you will rejoice, and no one will take away your joy" (16:22). The time following Jesus's departure would be a time of grief as the disciples mourned his absence, but when he appeared to them after his resurrection, their sorrow would turn into great joy – joy that no one could take away.

After the resurrection – "in that day" – the disciples would no longer ask Jesus for explanations (16:23a) because everything would be clear to them. The Fourth Gospel has already testified to this: "After he was raised from the dead, his disciples recalled what he had said. Then they believed the scripture and the words that Jesus had spoken" (2:22). Jesus also assured them, "Very truly I tell you, my Father will give you whatever you ask in my name" (16:23b). After Jesus's resurrection, the disciples could pray to the Father in the name of Jesus (16:23). Blum comments, "The words 'in my name' are not a magical formula which enable the user to get *his* will done; instead, those words tied the requests to the work of the Son in doing the *Father's* will."[7] Like Jesus, the disciples would enjoy direct access to the Father and the right to present their requests to him in the name of Jesus.

Jesus elaborated: "Until now you have not asked for anything in my name. Ask and you will receive, and your joy will be complete" (16:24). While Jesus was with them, they had not needed to ask the Father for anything since Jesus had provided everything they needed. When the wine ran out, he provided. When a crowd of more than five thousand people needed food, he provided. He spoke to the Father on their behalf, and they received the blessing. But after Jesus's death and ascension, the disciples would be able to bring their requests directly to the Father, asking for whatever they needed in Jesus's name, and the Father – who delights in providing for his children – would answer, and their joy would be complete (16:24). Unlike the temporary joy the world offers, the disciples of Jesus are promised complete and lasting joy.

Jesus acknowledged that he had been using figurative language (16:25a) but assured the disciples that a time was coming – soon after the resurrection – "when I will no longer use this kind of language but will tell you plainly about my Father" (16:25b). It was only after the resurrection that the disciples enjoyed greater clarity (2:22). After his resurrection, Jesus revealed the Father more clearly, and the disciples recorded these truths in the Gospels and Epistles. The use of the expression "my Father" emphasizes Jesus's intimate relationship with God.

---

7. Blum, "John," 329.

Not only would the disciples come to know the Father more clearly (16:25), but they would also gain direct access to him – Jesus would no longer have to intercede on their behalf (16:26) because "the Father himself loves you because you have loved me and have believed that I came from God" (16:27). By this, the Lord Jesus was saying that the disciples would have direct access to the Father because they loved Jesus. Since his mission was complete, Jesus said, "I came from the Father and entered the world; now I am leaving the world and going back to the Father" (16:28), once again illustrating the Gospel's U-shaped structure – the motif of descent and ascent.

Either the minds of the disciples were enlightened, or the Spirit of truth had already started ministering to them, for the disciples said, "Now you are speaking clearly and without figures of speech" (16:29). They recognized that Jesus was speaking God's words, and they believed that he came from God (16:30). Jesus then asked, "Do you now believe?" (16:31). The implicit answer was "yes." However, they still had to overcome the challenges of that night – when one of them would betray him, another would deny him, and all of them would scatter, leaving Jesus alone on the cross. So, he said, "A time is coming and in fact has come when you will be scattered, each to your own home. You will leave me all alone. Yet I am not alone, for my Father is with me" (16:32). At his crucifixion, the disciples would scatter, abandoning Jesus at this critical juncture. Despite this, Jesus remained confident that his Father would never leave him alone.

However, the disciples should not be troubled by their scattering on the night of Jesus's crucifixion. Jesus forewarned them so that despite their fear and failure, they might still experience peace (16:33a). They would not only have trouble that night but thereafter, too: "In this world you will have trouble" (16:33b). Therefore, they were called to be courageous – "take heart!" – because, through his death and resurrection, Jesus had overcome the world (16:33c). As light overcomes darkness, Jesus declared that the puny powers of the world could not overpower him; he would be victorious, defeating death by his cross.

When the disciples faced persecution, they would find peace in Jesus. His repeated warnings about the suffering, persecution, and martyrdom of believers have become a reality throughout history, especially in contexts where Christianity is a minority religion. Just before being persecuted and crucified to establish God's peace on earth, Jesus exhorted his disciples to walk the same path that he did.

John

Jesus emphasized victory through suffering, crucifixion, and death. John's narrative assures readers that followers of Jesus are promised protection, guidance, and leadership in the name of Jesus. The promise of divine providence and sustaining grace is one of the greatest assurances for those who believe and follow Jesus.

In 2023, the Kuki Christian communities of Manipur experienced severe trials and persecution – being killed, paraded naked on the streets, or having their churches and organizations burned. Yet the world ignored their cries because they were a marginalized group. These communities faced the hardships Jesus had foretold for his followers; but they persevered – just as Jesus had promised.

JOHN 17:1–26
JESUS'S HIGH PRIESTLY PRAYER

The Farewell Discourse (John 13–17) spans five chapters, with each chapter dealing with a specific theme: servitude (John 13), encouragement (John 14), an exhortation to abide like branches of a vine (John 15), perseverance with the help of the Advocate during Jesus's absence (John 16), and, in the final chapter, Jesus's prayer (John 17).

The Farewell Discourse ends with Jesus's prayer, which scholars refer to as his "High Priestly Prayer." This prayer has four subsections: Jesus's prayer for himself (17:1–5); Jesus's prayer for the disciples (17:6–19); Jesus's prayer for future disciples worldwide (17:20–23), and Jesus's prayer for the Twelve (17:24–26). Since these prayers transcend time and space, they can be considered universal.

17:1–5 JESUS'S PRAYER FOR HIMSELF

Jesus began by praying for himself (17:1–5). This section focuses on the theme of glorification, with its repeated use of words like "glory" (2x) and "glorify" (3x). Adopting the traditional Jewish posture of prayer – looking toward heaven – Jesus prayed: "Father, the hour has come. Glorify your Son, that your Son may glorify you" (17:1). This prayer has the following structure:

> Request: "Glorify your Son" (17:1a)
>   Reason 1: That the Son may glorify the Father (17:1b)
>   Reason 2: The Father had already glorified the Son (17:2)
>   Reason 3: The Son has finished the work the Father had given him (17:4)
> Request: "Glorify me" (17:5)[1]

Jesus addressed the prayer to his Father in heaven, declaring aloud that "the hour has come." The Father already knew the appointed hour – this was not a reminder for him. Rather, this was Jesus's acknowledgment that his time had come.

---

1. "Glorify" (*doxason*) is the only imperative in the prayer, occurring twice (vv. 1 and 5).

His "hour" played an important role in Jesus's mission. When his mother wanted him to intervene when the wine ran out at the wedding in Cana, Jesus replied, "Woman, why do you involve me? . . . My hour has not yet come" (2:4). When the religious leaders tried to seize him, they could not do so because his hour had not yet come (7:30; 8:20). But as the final Passover approached, Jesus knew that his time had come – "The hour has come for the Son of Man to be glorified" (12:23) – and asked, "What shall I say? 'Father, save me for this hour?' No, it was for this very reason I came to this hour" (12:27). The opening statement in the Farewell Discourse also affirms that "Jesus knew that the hour had come for him to leave this world and go to the Father" (13:1).

Now, in this final high priestly prayer, Jesus acknowledged that "the hour has come" (17:1a) and made request of the Father: "Glorify your Son, that your Son may glorify you" (17:1b). Glorification, too, played an important role in Jesus's teachings. Earlier he had said, "If I glorify myself, my glory means nothing. My Father . . . is the one who glorifies me" (8:54). He had also prayed, "Father, glorify your name!" – and the Father had answered, "I have glorified it, and will glorify it again" (12:28). He had told the disciples, "If God is glorified in [Jesus], God will glorify the Son in himself and will glorify him at once" (13:32). And one of the ministries of the Holy Spirit is to glorify Jesus (16:14). Therefore, at this moment when his hour had come, when Jesus asked the Father to glorify him, this was not a selfish request. He wanted the Father to glorify the Son so that the Son, in turn, might glorify the Father (17:1c).

A second reason Jesus requested glorification was because of what the Father had already done for him: "You granted [me] authority over all people that [I] might give eternal life to all those you have given [me]" (17:2). The Father, who had commissioned and sent the Son, had granted him authority to give life to those the Father had given him. In the *Prologue*, the narrator said, "Yet to all who did receive him, to those who believed in his name, he gave the right to become children of God . . . [those] born of God" (1:12–13). Jesus's purpose in coming to the world was to give eternal life to all who believe in him.

Jesus defined eternal life as knowing the Father – the only true God – and Jesus Christ, whom the Father had sent (17:3). Throughout his ministry, Jesus explained that those who believe in him will have eternal life (3:15–16, 36; 4:14; 5:24; 6:47). Although we sometimes view eternal or everlasting life as life without end, the Lord Jesus explained it as a life of knowing the Father and Jesus Christ. Eternal life is intimate fellowship with the giver of life, the only true God.

Jesus, the Word, became flesh with the purpose of "finishing the work" the Father had given the Son to do (17:4b). That was why he told the disciples who urged him to eat, "My food . . . is to do the will of him who sent me and to finish his work" (4:34), and said to the religious leaders who questioned why he was working on the Sabbath, "My Father is always at his work to this very day, and I too am working" (5:17). Jesus came to finish the work the Father had given him (17:4b), thereby bringing glory to the Father (17:4a). On many occasions, when Jesus performed a sign or miracle, the people believed in him, and this brought glory to the Father (2:11; 4:39; 4:53–54; 7:31; 8:30; 11:45). This is the third reason Jesus asked the Father to glorify him – he had finished the work the Father had given him to do.

Once again, Jesus returned to his request, saying, "And now, Father, glorify me in your presence with the glory I had with you before the world began" (17:5). The Son existed with the Father even before the beginning of the world (1:1) and enjoyed a glory that was quite different from the glory that was revealed when "the Word became flesh" (1:14). Now, the Son wanted the Father to restore the glory he had before the creation of the world (17:5).

Ironically, this glorification would come through the cross. Jesus had to die and be buried before he was resurrected and ascended to the Father's presence. The cross is the apex of divine glory. Glorification includes suffering – an important lesson for believers worldwide. We must patiently endure suffering before God ultimately glorifies us.

17:6–19 JESUS'S PRAYER FOR THE DISCIPLES

The high priestly prayer of Jesus was for himself (17:1–5), for his disciples (17:6–19), for future believers worldwide (17:20–22), and for his present disciples (17:23–26). His request for himself was that the Father glorify him with the glory he had before the creation of the world.

Jesus then prayed for the disciples whom he had mentored over the past three years (17:6–19). As in the previous section, this prayer includes two requests: "Protect them" (17:11) and "Sanctify them" (17:17). The surrounding verses provide the context and reasons for these requests.

Jesus began by saying, "I have revealed you to those whom you gave me out of the world. They were yours; you gave them to me, and they have obeyed your word" (17:6). The coming of Jesus created a division in the world between those who follow him and those who do not. The disciples – the

Twelve, along with many others who truly believed in Jesus – belonged to the Father because they had obeyed the Father's word, given through Jesus. This called-out community belonged to the Father, who had given them to the Son. These disciples had obeyed the word of the Father, just as the Son obeyed the Father. The disciples realized that everything Jesus possessed was from the Father (17:7), including his words and teachings (17:8a). Therefore, they accepted these words (17:8b). Similarly, "They knew with certainty that I came from you, and they believed that you sent me" (17:8c). This conviction was what set them apart from the world. They recognized Jesus's authority, his origin from the Father, and his mission as the one sent by the Father.

Because the disciples belonged to the Father, Jesus prayed for them (17:9a). He was not praying for the world that had rejected him but "for those you have given me, for they are yours" (17:9b). Although Jesus had chosen them (15:16), he was aware that every one of those disciples first belonged to the Father. The Father and Jesus worked together in unity: "All I have is yours, and all you have is mine" (17:10a). Although people sometimes view the disciples as ignorant and burdensome to Jesus, he saw them as people through whom he received glory (17:10b). Even today, Jesus sees his followers not as burdens but as people through whom he is glorified.

Jesus then made his first request on behalf of the disciples (17:11). He began by explaining the reason for his petition: "I will remain in the world no longer, but they are still in the world, and I am coming to you" (17:11a). His departure would leave his disciples in a hostile world. Therefore, he prayed for their protection: "Holy Father, protect them" (17:11b). God alone can protect them "by the power of [his] name" – the same name that he gave Jesus – so that "they may be one" as the Father and Son are one (17:11c). While God's power would protect them, Jesus's ultimate desire for them was divine oneness: "that they may be one as we are one." Just as there was perfect harmony and unity among the Trinity – Father, Son, and Spirit – Jesus wanted his disciples to be united and share in this oneness. This was particularly significant on the night of his betrayal. One disciple would betray him, another would deny him, and all would scatter in fear. Only the power of the Father's name could bring them together and unite them. This prayer was answered – everyone came back together, except the betrayer. Even today, Christians are called to unite, transcending earthly divisions such as caste, color, race, and gender.

Jesus addressed the Father as "Holy Father," a title found nowhere else in Scripture. It is based on the holiness of the Father that Jesus made his second request: "Sanctify them" (17:17). Only a holy Father can sanctify others. Jesus then returned to the theme of the special name that the Father had, which had also been given to him. This name would keep the disciples protected. Brown says, "[The disciples] are to be both marked with and protected by the divine name that has been given to Jesus."[2] While the world would hate and mistreat them because of the name of Jesus (15:21), Jesus prayed that God would protect them because of this name (17:11). The name of Jesus provokes animosity from the world but invokes the protection of the Father.

Jesus did not have to make this request of the Father while he was with the disciples because he himself "protected them and kept them safe by that name you gave me" (17:12a). Whenever enemies attempted to seize, arrest, or kill them, Jesus protected them. As a result, he was able to say, "None has been lost except the one doomed to destruction so that Scripture would be fulfilled" (17:12b). Jesus knew ahead of time that eleven of his disciples would ultimately abide in him – returning to him after their initial fall, remaining united just as the Father and the Son are one, and bearing fruit. None would be lost except Judas, who would depart as the Scriptures had prophesied. In this way, Jesus's high priestly prayer for the disciples focused on two groups.

Jesus continued the theme of departure – "I am coming to you now" – and explained the reason for his prayer: "I say these things while I am still in the world, so that they may have the full measure of my joy within them" (17:13). Earlier, in the illustration of the vine and the branches, Jesus had said, "If you keep my commands, you will remain in my love, just as I have kept my Father's commands and remain in his love. I have told you this so that my joy may be in you and that your joy may be complete" (15:10–11). Similarly, using the illustration of a woman in labor, he had explained that although his departure (death) would bring grief, at his resurrection, they would rejoice greatly and forget their pain, just as a mother forgets her labor pains the moment she sees her newborn child (16:20–22). Now, he prayed that his disciples would experience the full measure of joy "within" them. Despite the troubles they would face in the world, they would have true joy within them.

Jesus then returned to the reason they needed protection: The world had hated them because they had received the Father's word, which Jesus had given them (17:14a). Their obedience to the Father's word made them "not of the world" just as Jesus was not of this world (17:14b). Although they were living in this world, their identity as the children of the Father caused the world to hate them. Frykenberg comments that the term "anti-national" has been used

---

2. Brown, *Gospel according to John*, 759.

"to implicate Indian Christians as being alien, anti-national, and unpatriotic, or subject to forces from outside of India."[3] Believers are no longer of the world, just as Jesus is not of this world; and they need the Father's protection because the world hates them.

Jesus did not, however, ask the Father to "take them out of the world" but, rather, to "protect them from the evil one" (17:15). The "evil one" here could refer to Satan, the world, the religious leaders, the Roman Empire, or anyone who stands against the Son of God and his followers. Jesus did not pray that the disciples be removed from the world to escape persecution; instead, he wanted them to remain in the world but with the Father's protection (17:15). They would need this protection because, like Jesus, they were in this world but not of this world (17:16). As those who had been born from above, they belonged to the Father and to the heavenly realm.

Jesus then returned to his second petition: "Sanctify them by the truth; your word is truth" (17:17). Only God's word – and Jesus himself – constitute divine truth. In the *Prologue*, the narrator says, "The Word became flesh and made his dwelling among us. We have seen his glory . . . full of grace and truth" (1:14), and "The law was given through Moses; grace and truth came through Jesus Christ" (1:17). To the Samaritan woman, Jesus said, "God is spirit, and his worshipers must worship in the Spirit and in truth" (4:24). Jesus told the crowd, "The truth will set you free" (8:32b). And in one of the seven "I am" statements, Jesus declared, "I am the way and the truth and the life" (14:6). Now, Jesus prayed that the Father would sanctify the disciples by the truth – God's own word (17:17). Even today, the only way believers can be sanctified – set apart for God – is by studying, meditating, and living by God's word.

Jesus then spoke of how he had commissioned the disciples to go into a hostile world: "As you sent me into the world, I have sent them into the world" (17:18). It was a dangerous world for Jesus, and it would be a dangerous world for the disciples. But they must go – just as he had come – to rescue others from peril. Even today, this is the reason missionaries and church members must enter the world and be witnesses for Jesus. This is the Father's commission – for Jesus, for his first disciples, and for the universal church.

---

3. Robert Eric Frykenberg and Alaine Low, eds., *Christians and Missionaries in India: Cross-Cultural Communication since 1500: With Special Reference to Caste, Conversion, and Colonialism*, Studies in the History of Christian Missions (Grand Rapids: Eerdmans, 2003), 7–8; quoted in Manohar James, *Religious Conversion in India* (Eugene: Wipf & Stock, 2022), 15.

To be witnesses of Jesus demands holiness: "For them I sanctify myself, that they too may be truly sanctified" (17:19). Jesus lived a sanctified life, serving as a living witness before them, so that they could see and imitate his example. Now, he wanted them to do the same – to live as sanctified people in an unholy world. That was the reason for his second request: "Sanctify them by the truth" (17:17). Jesus, as the Son of God, was sanctified by the Father's word and name, and he wanted this same sanctification for his disciples. Even today, it is only through our sanctified lives that people are drawn to Jesus and God. Our actions speak louder than our words. The maxim attributed to St. Francis of Assisi still holds true: "Preach the gospel at all times, and if necessary, use words."

Jesus's prayer for the disciples has many themes – his passion, crucifixion, death, and ascension, as well as their protection, sanctification, and oneness. This prayer remains relevant for Christians in Asia today. But the Lord did not pray just for the eleven disciples but extended his prayer to include all believers (17:20–23).

17:20–23 JESUS'S PRAYER FOR FUTURE BELIEVERS WORLDWIDE

In his high priestly prayer, Jesus prayed for himself (17:1–5), for the eleven disciples (17:6–19), and then "for those who will believe in me through [the disciples'] message" (17:20–26). This prayer (17:20–23) has no direct requests (or imperatives) but only desires or wishes, expressed using the phrase "may be" (*osin*) – "all of them *may be* one" (17:21, emphasis added), "*may* they also *be* in us" (17:21, emphasis added), "they *may be* one as we are one" (17:22, emphasis added), and "they *may be* brought to complete unity" (17:23, emphasis added).[4]

Jesus was confident that his disciples would make more disciples – that they would be fruitful. Anticipating their harvest, he prayed for future believers: "My prayer is not for them alone. I pray also for those who will believe in me through their message" (17:20). His desire for future believers was oneness with the divine oneness: "That all of them may be one, Father, just as you are in me and I am in you. May they also be in us so that the world may believe that you have sent me" (17:21). Once again, Jesus emphasized the mutual indwelling among the Father, the Son, and the believing community: Jesus is in the Father; the Father is in Jesus; and the disciples are in both the Father

---

4. Subjective mood of "I am." The italics are added.

and the Son. By seeing this intimately interwoven relationship, the world may come to believe in Jesus, the Son of God. This passage is about far more than unity among believers; it is also about oneness among the Father, the Son, and believers – an extension of the life of the Trinity, not in essence but in union, oneness, and mission.

This passage is also about their oneness or union in glory: "I have given them the glory that you gave me, that they may be one as we are one" (17:22). Just as the Father and the Son share divine glory, the disciples also share in this glory as they fulfill their mission in the world. Culpepper comments,

> The unity of the church is based on its common origin, at the cross. Ultimately, however, John insists that the unity of believers is rooted in Jesus's oneness with the Father, so that just as Jesus was one with the Father, 'his own' will find their unity through their unity with him.[5]

Jesus concluded this prayer by returning to the themes of union, unity, and love: "I in them and you in me [divine union] – so that they may be brought to complete unity [unity]. Then the world will know that you sent me and have loved them even as you have loved me [love]" (17:23). Future believers would testify to the union between the Father and the Son, demonstrate their unity amid suffering, and reflect on their privileged place as recipients of the Father's love. When believers embrace this unity of Father and Son, they enter a complete oneness based on the principle of love.

Jesus envisioned a glorious relationship among believers that would bear witness to the world – "so that the world may believe that you have sent me" (17:21) and "then the world will know that you have sent me and have loved them even as you have loved me" (17:23). Believers' union, unity, and love bear witness to the world and invite others into the shared love of the Father and the Son. This must be the mission and vision of Asian churches – to exemplify union, unity, and love in a way that draws people out of darkness and into the light.

17:24–26 JESUS'S PRAYER FOR THE TWELVE

Jesus's prayer for those who would believe in him because of the disciples' message (17:20–23) forms a "detour" within his broader prayer for the disciples,

---

5. R. Allan Culpepper, *Design for the Church in the Gospel of John: Collected Essays 1980–2020*, WUNT 465 (Tübingen: Mohr Siebeck, 2021), 72.

whom he referred to as "those you have given me" (17:9, 24). This section has a chiastic structure:

> Jesus's prayer for the disciples (17:6–19)
> > Jesus's prayer for those who believed because of the disciples (17:20–23)
>
> Jesus's prayer for the disciples (17:24–26)

Once again, Jesus addressed "the Father" and prayed, "I want those you have given me to be with me where I am, and to see my glory, the glory you have given me because you loved me before the creation of the world" (17:24). Just as he had asked to be restored to the glory he had shared with the Father before the creation of the world (17:5), he wanted the disciples also to be with him and see that glory that came from the Father's eternal love for him.

In the *Prologue*, the narrator says of Jesus that "he was in the world, and though the world was made through him, the world did not recognize him" (1:10). Now, Jesus said that the world did not know the "righteous Father" either (17:25a). In contrast, he knew the Father (17:25b), and the disciples knew that the Father had sent the Son (17:25b). Jesus had made the Father known to the disciples (17:26a), and he would continue to do so "in order that the love you have for me may be in them and that I myself may be in them" (17:26b). Jesus ministered among the disciples, continually revealing the Father to them, because he desired that the love the Father had for him would be in them and that he himself would dwell in them. He prayed for this divine oneness between the Father, the Son, and the disciples to become a reality.

Jesus's prayer is more an acknowledgment of realities than a series of "requests." It reveals truths about the intimate relationships between the Father and the Son, the Son and the disciples, the disciples and the Father, and between future believers – those who would believe because of the disciples' teachings – and both the Son and the Father. To reduce this prayer to a simple plea for unity is to water down the greater truth of oneness with the divine in fellowship, glory, love, and mission.

Jesus's prayer ended with several key concerns: He had made the Father known to the disciples and would continue to do so in the future; and he desired that the love the Father had for him might be in the disciples and that he himself might be in them. The final verse is a recapitulation of the entire prayer, emphasizing the mutuality among the Father, the Son, and the believers. In Asia's multidenominational and pluralistic contexts, these words challenge Christians to strive for oneness with the Father and unity among believers.

John

This oneness is to be understood as *koinōnia* – communion or fellowship – that is fulfilled through coming together, sharing, accepting differences, and honoring each person's distinctive identity and role.

Jesus's high priestly prayer concludes the extended Farewell Discourse (John 13–17). This is followed by the final section of John's Gospel: the trial, passion, crucifixion, and death of Jesus (18:1–19:42).

JOHN 18:1–19:42
THE PASSION OF JESUS

The second major section of John's Gospel – the *Book of Glory* – deals with three main topics: the Farewell Discourse (13:1–17:26), the passion of Jesus (18:1–19:42), and the resurrection of Jesus (20:1–31). The narrative unit in John 18:1–19:42 can be further divided into six subsections: Jesus's betrayal and arrest (18:1–14); Peter's three denials (18:15–27); Jesus before Pilate (18:28–40); Pilate's final attempt to release Jesus (19:1–15); the crucifixion of Jesus (19:16–30); and events following the burial of Jesus (19:31–42).

18:1–14 JESUS'S BETRAYAL AND ARREST

This pericope connects directly to the previous chapter by its opening phrase, "When he had finished praying" (18:1a). Whether Jesus and his disciples were still in the Upper Room or had moved to a vineyard, the event in this chapter follows Jesus's teachings in John 13–16 and his prayer in John 17. Jesus and the eleven disciples crossed the Kidron Valley[1] – which lay between Jerusalem and the Mount of Olives – and entered an area of the Mount of Olives where there was a garden (18:1b).[2] By this time, Judas had already departed (13:30).

The narrator says, "Now Judas, who betrayed him, knew the place, because Jesus had often met there with his disciples" (18:2). Because Judas knew where Jesus would go to pray after the Passover meal, he came to the garden with a group of soldiers, officials, chief priests, and Pharisees, who were carrying torches, lanterns, and weapons (18:3). The narrator again reminds readers that Judas was the betrayer (18:2; compare 6:64, 71; 12:4; 13:2). The alliance between the Jewish religious authorities and the Roman political system is obvious. The scene recalls a modern crime-thriller movie: the time is night, the surroundings are dark, influential Jewish authorities enter the garden,

---
1. Brown comments, "The Kidron, not mentioned by the Synoptics, is a wadi that has flowing water only in the rainy or winter season. John's use of the correct terminology for the Kidron is not necessarily a proof that the Gospel is authentic Palestinian tradition, for 'winter-flowing' is the usual designation of the Kidron in LXX (2 Sam 15:23; 1 Kgs 15:13)." Brown, *Gospel according to John*, 2:806.
2. From Matthew, we can surmise this was the Garden of Gethsemane (Matt 26:30, 36). The Garden of Gethsemane is situated at the bottom level of the Mount Olives. He would have gone there to pray.

accompanied by Roman army officials holding torches, lanterns, and weapons, with Judas guiding the group. In contemporary terms, the scene resembles an investigative team on a mission to catch a religious terrorist, an underground leader, or a fugitive. The presence of Roman troops shows that Jesus was treated as a political criminal who critiqued the authoritarian Roman imperial system of the first century.

Before the authorities could speak, Jesus himself initiated a dialogue by posing a question: "Who is it you want?" (18:4). They replied, "Jesus of Nazareth" (18:5a). Jesus answered, "I am" (18:5b, in the Greek). This statement – which is also repeated in 18:8 – is not usually included in the seven "I am sayings" of Jesus: "I am the bread of life" (6:35), "I am the light of the world" (8:12), "I am the gate for the sheep" (10:7), "I am the good shepherd" (10:11), "I am the resurrection and the life" (11:25), "I am the way and the truth and the life" (14:6), and "I am the true vine" (15:1). However, these words were powerful: "They drew back and fell to the ground" (18:6). Jesus's bold words frightened them.

The narrator says, "Judas the traitor was standing there with them" (18:5c). While Jesus demonstrated heroic courage before his enemies, Judas remained passive.

Once again, Jesus asked whom they wanted to see, and they responded as before, "Jesus of Nazareth" (18:7). Jesus replied, "I told you that I am he" and asked them to let the disciples go (18:8). As he had mentioned in his prayer, he had protected them while he was with them (17:12). The narrator explains, "This happened so that the words he had spoken would be fulfilled: 'I have not lost one of those you gave me'" (18:9). In doing so, Jesus demonstrated his identity as the good shepherd, protecting and saving his disciples. People in Asia, when they are in trouble or feel trapped, can remember Jesus's saving and protecting acts. His love, protection, and care can serve as a paradigm for mission and ministry in Asia, where many marginalized communities lack care, protection, guidance, compassion, and support.

At that moment, Peter drew his sword and struck the high priest's servant, cutting off his right ear (18:10). It seems unlikely that Peter was aiming for the ear – this was probably the best fisherman from Galilee, untrained in the use of weapons, could do. Jesus never encouraged his followers to carry weapons or engage in violence. Yet his opponents marched toward him as if he and his disciples were a militant group of Zealots. The presence of Simon the Zealot among Jesus's disciples might have led to such an assumption (Matt 10:4; Mark 3:18; Luke 6:15). Regardless of what they thought, Peter's act of violence might have confirmed their fears, or it might have disproved their suspicion because of his inefficient wielding of the sword. The narrator's mention of the servant's name, Malchus, serves as additional evidence of the historicity of the event.

Jesus rebuked Peter: "Put your sword away! Shall I not drink the cup the Father has given me?" (18:11). Although not intentionally, Peter was trying to hinder the fulfillment of God's plan and purpose in Jesus's life. Jesus had earlier said, "I lay down my life for the sheep" (10:15b), "I lay down my life – only to take it up again" (10:17), and "Greater love has no one than this: to lay down one's life for one's friends" (15:13). Drinking the "cup" that his Father had given him was the goal and climax of Jesus's mission in the world. Peter had forgotten this in his love and zeal for his teacher and Lord. Like Mahatma Gandhi, Martin Luther King Jr., Nelson Mandela, and Jesus himself, Christians in Asia can practice nonviolence and choose to quietly suffer for the sake of their mission.

Jesus then surrendered himself, and under the direction of the Jewish officials, the soldiers arrested and bound him (18:12). This marked the arrival of Jesus's "hour" (compare 2:4; 7;30; 8:20; 12:23, 27; 13:1; 17:1). Their binding (*deō*) of him recalls the incident where Lazarus was bound (*deō*) and Jesus commanded the people to "take off the grave clothes and let him go" (11:44), as well as the future binding (*deō*) of Jesus for his burial (19:40).

Jesus was arrested and bound as if he were a criminal. He was first taken to Annas, who, although he was not the high priest that year, was still influential. Annas was the father-in-law of the high priest, Caiaphas, "who had advised the Jewish leaders that it would be good if one man died for the people" (18:14) – an incident already recorded by the narrator earlier (11:49–52). Caiaphas had not said these words on his own; rather, as high priest that year, he unknowingly prophesied that Jesus would die for the Jewish nation and to unite the scattered children of God. The fact that they brought Jesus to Annas, who was not the high priest that year, highlights Annas's continued influence in society and over his son-in-law, Caiaphas.

The Jewish leaders had been wanting to kill Jesus for a long time (5:18; 7:1). Now, they had succeeded. Just as the Jewish religious authorities were determined to eliminate Jesus, religious and political powers in many parts of Asia today attempt to suppress Christianity and even kill Christians. John's Gospel reminds us that nothing can happen to God's people apart from his sovereign plan and purpose.

John

18:15–27 PETER'S THREE DENIALS

In this section, the narrator presents a sandwich (or chiastic) structure, with Peter's denials framing Jesus's trial before Annas: Peter's first denial (18:15–18), Jesus's trial before Annas (18:20–24), and Peter's second denial (18:25–27).

When Jesus was arrested in the garden, Simon Peter demonstrated his courage by drawing his sword (18:10). However, after that failed attempt to defend his master and Lord, he followed Jesus quietly (18:15a). Another disciple – probably John the son of Zebedee – who had also followed Jesus was known to the high priest. Therefore, he was able to enter the high priest's courtyard along with Jesus (18:15b), while Peter had to wait outside at the door (18:16a). The other disciple, using his influence, spoke to the servant girl on duty and arranged for Peter also to be let in (18:16b). This suggests that some of Jesus's disciples – such as Nicodemus (3:1–10; 7:50–52) – had connections in high places and were influential. Throughout the Gospel, the narrator maintains the anonymity of some disciples (1:37–40; 18:15–16). Perhaps it was to protect those who maintained a relationship with both Jesus and the Jewish priestly aristocracy – who had given orders to expel anyone who acknowledged Jesus as the Messiah (9:22) – that the narrator kept their names confidential. The image of Peter standing at the door has a touch of irony, recalling Jesus's earlier statement, "I am the gate" (10:9).

Perhaps this is a challenge to Asian Christians to build meaningful relationships and friendships with those holding political power so that they may influence decisions concerning religion and religious organizations. Paul told Timothy, "I urge, then, first of all, that petitions, prayers, intercession and thanksgiving be made for all people – for kings and all those in authority, that we may live peaceful and quiet lives in all godliness and holiness" (1 Tim 2:1–2). Christians should actively develop friendship with outsiders, not only to bring them to Christ but also to influence the welfare of all people.

The servant girl at the door seemed to have recognized Peter. She asked, "You aren't one of this man's disciples too, are you?" (18:17a). Peter replied curtly, "I am not" (18:17b). This "I am not" contrasts sharply with Jesus's "I am he" (18:5a, 6a, 8a) and his "I am" statements. This also parallels John the Baptizer's "I am not" responses (1:19–28). While John the Baptist's "I am not" sayings prepared the people for Jesus's "I am" sayings, Peter's "I am not" statements reflect disassociation and denial of Jesus.

Since it was cold, the servants and officials had built a fire and were standing around it to warm themselves (18:18a). Peter's presence at the door despite the cold demonstrated his commitment to Jesus – even though he would soon fail. We, too, may desire to follow Jesus but stumble when persecutions arise. By joining the servants and officials at the fire (18:18b), Peter symbolically identified with those who opposed Jesus. He concealed his relationship with Jesus (18:17) and chose to avoid danger by remaining in a secure place among those who opposed Jesus. Like Peter, Asian Christians are often caught between their faith and the surrounding world.

While Peter was in the courtyard warming himself, the high priest questioned Jesus about his disciples and his teachings (18:19). On the one hand, the authorities were perplexed by the rapid growth of Jesus's disciples; on the other hand, they disapproved of his teachings. Their questions must have implied that Jesus had been secretly spreading false teachings or causing divisions because he said, "I have spoken openly to the world . . . I always taught in synagogues or at the temple, where all the Jews come together. I said nothing in secret" (18:20). Apart from Jesus's private teachings to his disciples (John 13–17), he had spent the previous three years teaching publicly, especially in the temple courts and synagogues. He had not taught in secret or taught anything that contradicted the Scriptures or opposed God. Therefore, he asked, "Why question me? Ask those who heard me. Surely, they know what I said" (18:21). The people who had followed Jesus had heard his words and bore witness to his message. Jesus's teaching had already spread among the public through oral or perhaps even written traditions. Ironically, the religious leaders questioned him in private rather than in their temples or synagogues!

Jesus's bold response before the high priest provoked one of the officials to slap him in the face, saying, "Is this the way you answer the high priest?" (18:22). The official's action was both insulting and unlawful. In India, slapping someone in public is an assault under Section 351 of the Indian Penal Code. Jesus was slapped without a proper legal inquiry, and there is no indication that the high priest rebuked the official for this act. The official's question and action implied that the high priest was worthy of honor, while Jesus was not – and that Jesus could be slapped, just as an evil master might have slapped a slave in ancient times.

Jesus responded, "If I said something wrong . . . testify as to what is wrong. But if I spoke the truth, why did you strike me?" (18:23). Jesus demonstrated courage in the face of injustice. Like Jesus, when falsely accused or unjustly harmed, Asian Christians can also stand firm and respond courageously. Jesus revealed that he was a man with authority and power from above by demanding an explanation: "If I spoke the truth, why did you strike me?" (18:23). Unable to respond, Annas had Jesus bound and sent him to Caiaphas, his son-in-law, who was the high priest (18:24). Annas's actions illustrate his helplessness in the face of Jesus's words.

In India, Christian missionaries often suffer due to cases filed against them wrongfully. Once a person is falsely charged – for example, with proselytizing – they face trials by police and judicial authorities. A tragic example is the case of Father Stan Swamy, an eighty-four-year-old Jesuit priest – a Dalit and tribal rights activist – who died in 2021. Despite his deteriorating health because of Parkinson's disease, Swamy's repeated requests for bail were denied. The prison authorities treated him rudely and reportedly denied him basic medical care. He suffered unjustly – like Jesus. Although Article 25(1) of the Indian Constitution "guarantees equality of religious freedom to all," Christians are often denied this right. Nevertheless, they are called to speak up for justice and keep trusting God.

The narrator then turns the focus back to Simon Peter. While Jesus was slapped, bound, and sent to Caiaphas, Peter remained among the servants and officials, warming himself by the fire (18:25a). While Jesus was on trial inside the high priest's house, Peter was on trial outside. Once again – perhaps prompted by the servant girl's earlier remark – they asked him, "You aren't one of his disciples too, are you?" (18:25b). While the darkness and their unfamiliarity with Jesus's disciples caused them to be cautious in their questioning, the same courtesy was not extended to Jesus, who was slapped on the face at the trial before Annas. Peter responded as before, "I am not" (18:25c). This was Peter's second denial.

So far, Peter had only faced questioning by people who were unfamiliar with him. But at this point, someone who seemed certain of Peter's identity spoke up. He was a servant of the high priest and a relative of Malchus, whose ear Peter had cut off (18:10). Having been present at Gethsemane, this man challenged Peter: "Didn't I see you with him in the garden?" (18:26). Yet again, Peter denied it. This was Peter's third denial. At that very moment, "a rooster began to crow" (18:27). Jesus had predicted this earlier. When Peter had declared that he would lay down his life for him, Jesus had responded, "Will you really lay down your life for me? Very truly I tell you, before the rooster crows, you will disown me three times!" (13:38), demonstrating that he was truly a prophet by predicting Peter's denial.

In ancient times, the royal court of Koryo in Korea kept roosters as natural clocks to show time. Travelers would even carry roosters with them on long trips to ensure that they were awakened on time. In ancient Israel, similar practices probably existed to alert people to the coming of dawn – although roosters were not always accurate!

Peter's three denials took place around a fire in the courtyard outside the house. Jesus's trial happened inside. This contrast parallels the "from above" and "from below" theme that the narrator has been developing in this Gospel

18:28–40 JESUS BEFORE PILATE

The narrator omits what happened at the house of Caiaphas – to whom Annas had sent Jesus (18:24) – and goes straight to what happened in Pilate's courtyard: "The Jewish leaders took Jesus from Caiaphas to the palace of the Roman governor" (18:28a).[3] Pilate's official title was *Prefect of Judea*, which is loosely translated as "governor." Prefects were relatively low-ranking Roman officials who governed a region under the authority of a Legate. Pontius Pilate served under the Legate of Syria. But prefects had authority over centurions and other Roman officials. In the Indian context, they could be compared to the Chief Ministers of individual states.

By the time Jesus was brought before Pilate, it was early morning (18:28b), which meant that the trials before Annas and Caiaphas had taken place during the night. This violated Jewish law, which required that trials be held during the daylight hours. The Jews were in a hurry to bring Jesus to trial at the earliest possible time and used the cover of darkness to extinguish the light of the world. However, they did not want to enter Pilate's palace – the Praetorium – since this would have made them ceremonially unclean, preventing them from observing the Passover (18:28c). Despite ignoring the "holy one of God" (6:69), they took great pains to maintain ritual purity.[4] Therefore, they stood outside the Praetorium while Pilate "came out to them" (18:29). These details affirm that the narrator was an eyewitness, or someone acquainted with an eyewitness.

Pilate asked, "What charges are you bringing against this man?" (18:29). He wanted to make sure that this was a political charge against the Roman government. The Jewish leaders framed this as a criminal charge (18:30), reducing Jesus to the level of a common criminal. Since Pilate did not handle criminal cases, he responded, "Take him yourselves and judge him by your

---
3. The Greek text says that they took him to the praetorium (army headquarters) or "the hall of judgment" (KJV), but NIV explained it as "the palace of the Roman governor."
4. Similar hypocrisy exists in Hinduism: while they consider an animal (cow) holy, they consider fellow humans of a Dalit community unholy.

own law" (18:31a). Criminal cases were tried under local laws, not Roman laws. But the Jews categorically rejected Pilate's offer, saying, "But we have no right to execute anyone" (18:31b), which was not entirely true. Earlier, they had tried to stone a woman caught in adultery (7:53–8:11). What they wanted was not execution but crucifixion – a Roman form of torture and death. The narrator attests to this: "This took place to fulfill what Jesus had said about the kind of death he was going to die" (18:32). According to Deuteronomy 21:22–23, anyone put to death by being hung on a tree was considered "under God's curse." As Paul outlines in Galatians 3:10–14, Jesus – by his crucifixion – endured this curse to bear humanity's curse and then redeemed them from this curse by his resurrection. Thus, Jesus could not be stoned – as permitted by Jewish law – but had to be crucified according to Roman law, and the religious leaders unknowingly played a part in the fulfillment of this Scripture! The Jewish leaders and Pilate each tried to shift the responsibility for Jesus's case onto the other. In their tug-of-war, Jesus remained the innocent Lamb. Even today, political movements often try to use Christians as pawns in their conflicts.

Leaving the Jewish leaders outside, Pilate went inside the Praetorium and asked Jesus, "Are you the king of the Jews?" (18:33). This was probably the charge brought by the Jewish leaders – that Jesus was claiming kingship, setting himself in opposition to Caesar. Earlier, Nathanael had called Jesus the "king of Israel" (1:49), and perhaps that was what the Jews were referring to. Jesus, perhaps sensing that Pilate was sincere, asked, "Is that your own idea . . . or did others talk to you about me?" (18:34). Apart from Nathanael, the people themselves had tried to make Jesus king by force (6:15); during his triumphal entry to Jerusalem, they had even shouted, "Blessed is the king of Israel" (12:13). Had Pilate heard about these incidents and concluded that Jesus was Israel's Jewish king? It was not a crime to be a king of Israel under Rome rule. Herod the Great ruled as king of Judea during the reigns of Julius Caesar and Caesar Augustus. However, the title "king" had to be granted by Caesar – and none of Herod the Great's sons or grandsons received that title except Agrippa II. Therefore, while it was not an offense under Roman law to be a king of Israel, it was an offense to claim that title for oneself.

In response to Jesus's question, Pilate replied, "Am I a Jew? . . . Your own people and chief priests handed you over to me. What is it you have done?" (18:35). This implies that it was not just the chief priest but also the crowds who were against Jesus. Pilate's displeasure at being drawn into this matter is underscored by his question, "Am I a Jew?" His response makes it clear that he had been forced to take up this case because of pressure from the Jews (18:35b). Pilate's ignorance concerning this matter is made plain by his question, "What is it you have done?" (18:35c). Unlike Herod, who was curious about John the Baptist and Jesus (Mark 6:20; Luke 23:8), Pilate appears to have been indifferent to Jewish civil and religious matters and unfamiliar with the ministries of Jesus and John. This suggests that Jesus had not taught or acted in ways that posed a threat to Rome.

Jesus responded by explaining that his teachings focused on a non-earthly kingdom: "My kingdom is not of this world. If it were, my servants would fight to prevent my arrest by the Jewish leaders. But now my kingdom is from another place" (18:36). This statement must have puzzled Pilate. Could there be another kingdom apart from Rome? Was Jesus confused or insane? Pilate then said, "You are a king, then!" (18:37a). Again, Pilate might not have been greatly alarmed by the idea of Jesus being a king of the Jews since Rome worked with local rulers – for example, Herod the Great and Agrippa II. But he was unclear about when Jesus's kingdom was established and who had appointed Jesus as its king.

Jesus's reply was cryptic: "You say that I am a king. In fact, the reason I was born and came into the world is to testify to the truth. Everyone on the side of truth listens to me" (18:37b). He affirmed that he was indeed the king, although not of this world but of the world from above. His identity as king and the nature of his kingdom led to several misunderstandings among both the Jews and the Romans. Since Jesus intended to establish a spiritual kingdom – in contrast to the Roman Empire – his hearers struggled to grasp his message. Jesus's kingship and kingdom were not based on material power but grounded in truth and justice.

Misunderstanding Jesus's words, Pilate asked, "What is truth?" (18:38a). Perhaps he was wondering whether it was the people or Jesus who were telling the truth. Or perhaps he was asking an existential question. Regardless, Jesus had claimed, "I am the way and the truth and the life" (14:6). That very "truth" now stood before Pilate, yet he failed to recognize him. His question should not have been "What is truth?" but, rather, "*Who* is truth?" – to which the answer would have been, "I am."

Without waiting for a response, Pilate made up his mind. Going out to the Praetorium, he said to the Jews there, "I find no basis for a charge against him" (18:38b). The trial before Pilate revealed Jesus's innocence. Justice B. Pugalendhi of the Madras High Court once stated, "An impartial investigation is the basic requirement for any investigation. A fair investigation is also a part of constitutional right guaranteed under Articles 20 and 21 of the Constitution of India."[5] He also said, "Thousand culprits can escape, but one innocent person should not be punished."[6] This basic human rights principle was violated in the case of Jesus. It is also violated in the case of many Indian Christians who suffer unjustly due to false religious charges against them. Since Pilate knew that he had neither moral nor legal grounds to crucify Jesus, he looked for a way to release him.

Following the custom of releasing a prisoner during the Passover season as a gesture of goodwill between Rome and the Jews (18:39a), Pilate asked the crowd, "Do you want me to release 'the king of the Jews'" (18:39b). Having examined Jesus, Pilate was willing to accept Jesus as "the king of the Jews" (18:33b, 37, 39). Ironically, while the Jewish nation refused to accept Jesus as their king, a pagan Roman ruler affirmed him as the Jewish king.

The Jews were enraged. They shouted back, "No, not him!" They did not want Jesus – the miracle worker, worker of signs, healer, provider, restorer, Son of God, and God incarnate – to be released. Instead, they shouted, "Give us Barabbas!" (18:40b). From Mark 15:7, we know that Barabbas was an insurrectionist and a murderer. The narrator describes him as one who had "taken part in an uprising" (18:40b) – perhaps a revolution aimed at overthrowing Roman rule. Their preference for Barabbas over Jesus – a gentle healer, a kind provider, and God's own Son – reveals the depth of their hatred for Jesus.

Jesus was surrounded by people who were unable to recognize him, accept him as the truth of God, or perceive him for he truly was. In Asia today, many struggle with this same reality. They may accept Jesus as a great teacher but not as the Son of God, the truth, and the King! Despite having several opportunities to intervene to prevent Jesus's execution, the Jewish and Roman authorities failed to show care and compassion toward Jesus. As a minority community in many parts of Asia, Christians often face injustice. When they struggle and suffer, they are called to endure like Jesus.

---

5. Bhumika Indulia, "Madras HC | 1000 culprits can escape, but, one innocent person should not be punished: HC states in perfunctory investigation of a brutal murder," dated 9 September 2020. https://www.scconline.com/blog/post/2020/09/09/madras-hc-1000-culprits-can-escape-but-one-innocent-person-should-not-be-punished-hc-states-in-perfunctory-investigation-of-a-brutal-murder/.

6. Bhumika Indulia, "Madras HC | 1000 culprits can escape, but, one innocent person should not be punished: HC states in perfunctory investigation of a brutal murder."

19:1–15 PILATE'S FINAL ATTEMPT TO RELEASE JESUS

John 19 continues the narrative of the previous chapter, describing Jesus's trial before Pilate (19:1–15), his crucifixion and death (19:16–30), and his burial (19:31–42). Up to this point, Jesus faced three trials: before Annas, the previous high priest; Caiaphas, the high priest for that year; and Pilate, the Roman governor of Judea. John 19 resumes the narrative of the trial before Pilate.

Pilate was unsure what to do with Jesus. He probably thought flogging him would appease the Jewish leaders. So, he had Jesus flogged by the soldiers (19:1), who also mocked him as a king, twisting together a crown of thorns and placing it on his head (19:2a). This public disgrace was intentional within the honor-shame culture of the time. Since royalty usually wore purple robes,[7] the soldiers also clothed him in a purple robe (19:2b) and mocked him by chanting, "Hail, king of the Jews!" (19:3). Christians in Asia are often subjected to hate speech, sarcasm, mob violence, lynching, brutal attacks, and public humiliation that may even include being forcibly stripped and paraded in public. Jesus was indeed the king, but not in the way they mocked him. While a king is typically seen as an authoritative figure who executes justice and upholds righteousness for the people, Jesus was a suffering king, who was mocked by Roman soldiers. Just as a religious official had slapped Jesus for the way he addressed the high priest (18:22), the soldiers now slapped him in the face without cause (19:3b). In the same way, Christians in Asia – despite being God's chosen people, a royal priesthood, a holy nation, and God's special possession (1 Pet 2:9) – are often ridiculed, punished, and persecuted without cause. The mockery that Jesus endured can encourage and comfort them in such situations.

Pilate came out yet again and spoke to the Jews: "Look, I am bringing him out to you to let you know that I find no basis for a charge against him" (19:4). Ironically, Pilate said this after unlawfully flogging Jesus. When Jesus came out wearing the crown of thorns and purple robe, Pilate said to the Jews, "Here is the man!" (19:5).[8] His words, which emphasize Jesus's humanity, might have been intended as an insult – he was not a king but just a man.

However, the chief priests and the officials stood firm in their decision to crucify Jesus and shouted, "Crucify! Crucify!" (19:6a). Pilate responded, "You take him and crucify him. As for me, I find no basis for a charge against him" (19:6b). This was the third time Pilate declared that he found no basis

---

7. Blomberg, *Historical Reliability of John's Gospel*, 243.
8. Beasley-Murray, *John*, 337.

on which to charge Jesus with a crime (18:38; 19:4, 6). Therefore, since Pilate did not want to take responsibility for crucifying Jesus, he challenged the Jews to do so according to their own laws.

In 1999, the Australian Christian missionary Graham Staines and his two sons, Philips and Timothy, were burned alive in the village of Manoharpur, Odisha. A Hindutva mob, led by Dara Singh, falsely accused them of forcefully converting people to Christianity. Just as Jesus was falsely accused, so were the Staines. Similarly, many Christians in Asia are falsely accused and killed without receiving justice.

The Jewish leaders defended their stance, saying that Jesus had violated their law by claiming to be the Son of God and that he must die for it (19:7). Earlier, Nathanael had declared, "Rabbi, you are the Son of God; you are the king of Israel" (1:49). Martha had said, "Yes, Lord . . . I believe that you are the Messiah, the Son of God, who is to come into the world" (11:27). Jesus himself did not refer to himself as the Son of God, although he repeatedly said that he was the Son of the Father, that the Father and he were one, and that the Father had sent him. Jesus had also violated their interpretation of the Sabbath law. Earlier, the narrator had noted, "For this reason they tried all the more to kill him; not only was he breaking the Sabbath, but he was even calling God his own Father, making himself equal with God" (5:18). It was on this basis that the Jewish leader accused Jesus of blasphemy and wanted him killed.

Pilate must have realized the political implications of the issue because he became "more afraid" (19:8) and went back inside the palace to talk with Jesus again. He asked him, "Where do you come from?" (19:9a). In ancient cultures, kings and queens were often considered sons and daughters of gods. Pharaoh, for example, was seen as the son of the god Re. Pilate might have feared that Jesus was a king from another region – and he wanted to know what this region was. Jesus had already told him, "My kingdom is not of this world. If it were, my servants would fight to prevent my arrest by the Jewish leaders. But now my kingdom is from another place" (18:36). To Pilate's question about whether he was a king, Jesus had implied that he was (18:37). But Jesus remained silent (19:9b). His silence frustrated Pilate, who then said, "Do you refuse to speak to me? . . . Don't you realize I have power either to free you or to crucify you?" (19:10). Jesus replied, "You would have no power over me if it were not given to you from above" (19:11a). His response indicates that his trial before Pilate and the Jewish leaders was part of God's divine plan and purpose. Nevertheless, Jesus held the Jewish leaders accountable, saying, "The one who handed me over to you is guilty of a greater sin" (19:11b) – that is killing the Son of God.

Jesus's ultimate intention was to inaugurate God's kingdom among suffering humanity. This kingdom is based on righteousness, justice, truth, and peace on earth. Mahatma Gandhi, a seeker of truth, was influenced by Jesus's teachings and drew on them for his vision of a peaceful India – even though his dream was not realized.

Convinced of Jesus's innocence, Pilate tried to set him free (19:12a). But the Jewish leaders accused Pilate, saying, "If you let this man go, you are no friend of Caesar. Anyone who claims to be a king opposes Caesar" (19:12b). Although Rome sometimes appointed local kings – for example, Julius Caesar's appointment of Herod the Great as the Judean king – this new accusation was that Jesus's claim to kingship posed a threat to Caesar, and Pilate did not want to be an enemy of Caesar.

At the same time, Pilate knew that being king of a people group was not a crime against Caesar or Rome. So, he sat on his judge's seat – a symbol of legal authority – and decreed, "Here is your king" (19:13–14). Earlier, he had said, "Here is the man!" (19:5), but now he declared Jesus as their king. The narrator provides an explanatory note: The judgment seat was called "the Stone Pavement (which in Aramaic is Gabbatha)," it was "the day of Preparation of the Passover," and the time was "about noon" (19:13–14). Since Pilate was publicly recognizing or declaring Jesus as the Jewish king, the narrator records the place, date, and time, as would usually be done when a decree was established.

The Jewish leaders were not happy. They shouted, "Take him away! Take him away! Crucify him!" (19:15a). They did not want Jesus stoned, as was the Jewish custom – they wanted him crucified, as was the Roman custom. Pilate continued to resist, asking, "Shall I crucify your king?" (19:15b). Displeased that Pilate had referred Jesus as a king, the chief priests responded, "We have no king but Caesar" (19:15c). Pilate found no fault in Jesus, but the religious leaders were relentless. Eventually, Pilate gave in (19:16) because they kept evoking the name of Caesar. Despite knowing the truth, Pilate did not want to make Caesar his enemy and so, he caved under pressure. Even today, many who recognize the truth still cave under social, cultural, or political pressure, just like Pilate. But Christians are called to stand firm, following the example of Jesus, who boldly acknowledged his kingship and sonship even amid persecution.

19:16–30 THE CRUCIFIXION OF JESUS

Despite proclaiming Jesus's innocence three times (18:38; 19:4, 6) and even referring to him as the king of the Jews (19:14), Pilate succumbed to the threat that he would not be a friend of Caesar if he released Jesus (19:12) and handed Jesus over to be crucified (19:16). This, too, was part of the divine plan (19:11). Jesus's life and mission were guided by God's sovereign will, and it was part of God's purpose that his Son should suffer. Even today, religious authorities and political powers often come together to suppress the voices of the marginalized and minorities in Asia.

The narrator now shifts the focus back to Jesus. The king of the Jews carried his own cross and went to the place of the Skull (*kranion*) to be crucified (19:17a). Earlier, the soldiers had placed a crown of thorns on Jesus's head (*kefalē*) (19:2); soon he would bow his head (*kefalē*) and die, after which, Joseph of Arimathea and Nicodemus would bury him (19:38–40), with his head (*kefalē*) covered by a burial cloth (20:7). Thus, the narrator's reference to "the Skull" in connection with "the head" is intentional, and he provides its Aramaic name: Golgotha (19:17b). This is the third of four instances where the narrator provides the Aramaic translation of a place or a phrase, indicating his audience's familiarity with Aramaic. The four instances are: a pool near the Sheep Gate, called "Bethesda" in Aramaic (5:2), the judgment seat of Pilate, called "Gabbatha" in Aramaic (19:13), the place where Jesus would be crucified, which is "Golgotha" in Aramaic (19:17), and Mary's address to Jesus as "Rabboni," meaning "Teacher" (20:16).[9] At Golgotha, they crucified Jesus along with two others – "one on each side and Jesus in the middle" (19:18). Unlike the Synoptic Gospels, the Johannine narrator does not give details about the agony of the crucifixion – possibly because the early Christians would have been familiar with these.

Pilate's involvement in Jesus's death was not yet over. Having already declared Jesus as the Jewish king (19:14), he now wanted everyone else to know this as well: "Pilate had a notice prepared and fastened to the cross. It read: JESUS OF NAZARETH: THE KING OF THE JEWS" (19:19).[10] Many Jews read that notice because the place of crucifixion was near the city, which was a busy metropolis, and the notice was written in three common languages: Aramaic,

---

9. The narrator has one more reference to the Aramaic: the inscription on the cross above Jesus was written in Aramaic, Latin, and Greek (19:20). But he doesn't give the Aramaic or Latin phrase.
10. Okure, "John," 1570.

Latin, and Greek (19:20). The wording of the notice was Pilate's assertion of his power and a mockery of the Jewish leaders who had said, "We have no king but Caesar" (19:15). In effect, Pilate was saying, "Yes, you have a king, and here he is on a cross."

The chief priests, understanding his mockery, protested, "Do not write 'The King of the Jews,' but that this man claimed to be king of the Jews" (19:21). Other people had already acknowledged Jesus as king: Nathanael called him "the king of Israel" (1:49), the people tried to make him king by force (6:15), those welcoming Jesus as he rode to Jerusalem on a donkey proclaimed, "Blessed in the king of Israel" and said "Daughter Zion . . . see, your king is coming" (12:13, 15). But only to Pilate did Jesus make the acknowledgment, "You say that I am a king" (18:37) – and, based on those words of Jesus, Pilate refused to oblige the Jewish leaders. He replied, "What I have written, I have written" (19:22). In Greek, this is just three words – *ho gegrapha, gegrapha* – which have a grunting sound, conveying Pilate's impatience.

Just as Jesus was denied a fair and righteous trial by both the Jewish and Roman leaders, his followers also frequently suffer injustice. In 2023, several Kuki Christian women were paraded naked through the streets of Manipur, India, by Hindu fundamentalists. In such instances, it is God alone who will ultimately bring comfort and justice.

Although Pilate was willing to accept Jesus as the king of the Jews, the Jewish leaders were not. Although Pilate believed that Jesus should be freed, the Jewish leaders wanted him crucified. Ultimately, God's plan prevailed: Jesus was crucified and, through his death (and resurrection), truly became king – not just of Israel but of all people.

The soldiers then crucified Jesus (19:23a). Afterward, they took Jesus's clothes (plural) and divided them into four shares, one for each of them (19:23b), suggesting that four soldiers participated in Jesus's crucifixion. But when they examined the tunic (*chitōn*), they realized it was seamless, "woven in one piece from top to bottom" (19:23c).[11] Not wanting to tear it, they cast lots for it (19:24). With his clothing gone, Jesus would have been naked on

---

11. The NIV's translation "undergarment" might be an error. In other uses of *chitōn*, Jesus instructed the disciples if anyone wanted to take their *chitōn* to give them other clothing as well (Matt 5:40; compare Luke 3:11; 6:29; 9:3); when they went on their mission, not to take extra *chitōn*, sandals, or staff (Matt 10:10); and at Jesus's testimony, the high priest tore his *chitōn* (Mark 14:63). It's difficult to think that in these cases, *chitōn* referred to someone's undergarment.

the cross. This was the Roman way of humiliating a person even in death.[12] On the cross, Jesus became the "naked truth," while the world around him disguised or denied the truth about him.

Mary or Joseph might had given Jesus that seamless tunic (19:23b) as a gift.[13] Regardless of how it was obtained, the tunic must have been attractive enough that the soldiers did not want to divide it into four pieces but, instead, cast lots for it (19:24a). The narrator explains that this, too, was a fulfillment of prophecy: "They divided my clothes among them and cast lots for my garment" (19:24b). This prophecy came from one of David's psalms. David felt abandoned by God: "My God, my God, why have you forsaken me?" (Ps 22:1). He described his dire situation: "I am a worm and not a man, scorned by everyone, despised by the people. All who see me mock me; they hurl insults, shaking their heads" (22:6–7), "Many bulls surround me; strong bulls of Bashan encircle me. Roaring lions that tear their prey open their mouths wide against me" (22:12–13), and "All my bones are on display; people stare and gloat over me. They divide my clothes among them and cast lots for my garment" (22:17–18). Without a doubt, this is a messianic psalm, and the narrator sees it as being fulfilled in Jesus.

In India, in recent years, several missionaries were paraded naked through the streets because of their faith in Jesus and their efforts to spread the gospel. Jesus's nakedness on the cross is a paradigm for those who undergo suffering and humiliation. The crucified Jesus identifies himself with the poor, the naked, the marginalized, and the ostracized of society.

The narrator then turns his attention to Jesus and people whom he loved (19:25–27). Although most of the disciples had abandoned Jesus (Matt 26:56), four women stood at the foot of the cross, three of whom were named "Mary": Jesus's mother, the wife of Clopas, and Mary Magdalene (19:25). Mary the mother of Jesus, who appeared at the beginning of the Gospel (2:1–11), now reappears at the foot of his cross (19:25). In many Asian contexts, female followers of Jesus outnumber the men. Mary's sister and Mary, the wife of Clopas, appear only here. But Mary Magdalene plays a significant role in the following narrative (20:1–18).

Near these women stood one male – "the disciple whom [Jesus] loved" (19:26a), often known as the Beloved Disciple. Jesus said to his mother, "Woman, here is your son" (19:26b). As he had done before, Jesus addressed

---

12. Beasley-Murray, *John*, 347.
13. Okure, "John," 1570.

his mother as "woman" (2:4) – a culturally appropriate and respectful form of address. Jesus demonstrated his concern for his earthly mother by making provision for her even from the cross. He told the Beloved Disciple, "Here is your mother" (19:27a). Jesus was terminating his earthly relationship with Mary, but he was also ensuring that she would be cared for by entrusting her to someone he loved and trusted. At the foot of the cross, the Beloved Disciple was entrusted with a sacred responsibility. From that time on, he took Mary into his home (19:27b), and a new mother-and-son relationship was established – one that was both relational and spiritual.

Jesus's example challenges Christians in Asia – they are not to abandon their parents but to care for them. Despite emphasizing the priority of spiritual relationships over physical relationships (compare 1:13), children are to honor their parents (Exod 20:12). This passage focuses on the Christian bond of love that transcends flesh-and-blood relationships.

Jesus then went on to fulfill yet another prophecy of Scripture by saying, "I am thirsty" (19:28). Jesus might have been echoing Psalm 22:15: "My mouth is dried up like a potsherd, and my tongue sticks to the roof of my mouth." This was a messianic psalm that had already been quoted in the context of the soldiers casting lots for Jesus's tunic (19:24). Jesus might also have had in mind another messianic psalm, in which David says, "They put gall in my food and gave me vinegar for my thirst" (Ps 69:21; compare John 19:29). Whichever passage Jesus had in mind, he knew he had to feel the thirst and express it and fulfill the Scriptures before he died.

Ironically, the giver of living water (John 4:10, 13–14; 7:37–38) was now thirsty (19:28b). As prophesied in Psalm 69:21, Jesus was given vinegar from a jar of wine vinegar (19:29a). Jesus, who had turned water into wine (2:1–11) and described himself as the true vine (15:1–5), now received wine vinegar. The narrator emphasizes the details: "They soaked a sponge in [the jar of wine vinegar], put the sponge on a stalk of the hyssop plant, and lifted it to Jesus's lips" (19:29b). This evokes yet another Scripture. During the first Passover, the Israelites were commanded to "take a bunch of hyssop, dip it into the blood [of the lamb] in the basin and put some of the blood on the top and on both sides of the doorframe" (Exod 12:22). Now, the true Lamb of God (John 1:29, 36), while shedding his own blood for the sins of the world, received sour wine vinegar on a stalk of the hyssop plant (19:29).

Having received the drink, thereby fulfilling the prophecy about him, Jesus declared, "It is finished" (19:30a). Blum explains that this was a joyful cry that proclaimed his accomplishment of the salvation of the world.[14] It was also a statement that he had finished every task the Father had assigned to him. By fulfilling the will of the Father, completing the law of Moses, destroying the power of sin and Satan, offering his sacrificial blood on the cross, and fulling the mission of the Father, Jesus ushered in the hour of glorification of the Son and the Father.

Jesus then bowed his head and gave up his spirit. Bowing his head was a mark of his surrender before God, and giving up his spirit symbolized his return to the Father's house (19:30).[15] Just as Jesus had promised to give living water to anyone who was thirsty (7:37) and explained that the living water was the Spirit (7:39), he now gave up his spirit, making way for his followers to receive the Spirit of truth (15:26).

Just as Jesus accomplished the mission entrusted to him by the Father, Asian Christians, too, must fulfill the mission of God through their proclamation, acts of liberation, and lives of transformation. Like Jesus, we must be deeply committed to fulfilling God's will in our lives.

19:31–42 THE BURIAL OF JESUS

Jesus's trials before Annas, Caiaphas, and Pilate, his crucifixion, and his death took place on the day of Preparation, the day before the special Sabbath (19:31a). The Jewish leaders did not want the bodies left hanging on the crosses during the Sabbath (19:31b), perhaps because bodies hanging on a tree were seen as a curse upon the land (Deut 21:23; Gal 3:13). So, they asked Pilate to have the victims' legs broken so that they would die quickly and their bodies could be taken down (19:31c). Beasley-Murray comments, "Romans left crucified men to linger till their death, sometimes for several days, and then the vultures finished them off. If there was any reason for hastening the death of crucified men, their legs were smashed with an iron mallet, so causing great loss of blood and asphyxia."[16] Pilate agreed, and the soldiers broke the legs of the two men crucified alongside Jesus (19:32). When they came to Jesus, since they found that he was already dead, they did not break his legs (19:33). Although all three had been crucified at the same time, Jesus died earlier than the other two. Nevertheless, one of the soldiers pierced Jesus's side with a spear (19:34a). Immediately, blood and water flowed out of his side. This is a

---

14. Blum, "John," 340.
15. Moloney, *Gospel of John*, 508.
16. Beasley-Murray, *John*, 353.

symbolic portrayal of yet another prophecy: "Rivers of living water will flow from within them" (7:38; compare Isa 44:3; 55:1; 58:11; Zech 14:8). The flow of the last few drops of blood symbolizes Jesus's total sacrifice. He gave all his blood to the people. Similarly, as the giver of living water, he gave even the last drop of water in his body. In that sense, his mission was completed through his glorification on the cross (19:34).

The narrator speaks of an eyewitness to these events: "The man who saw it has given testimony, and his testimony is true. He knows that he tells the truth, and he testifies so that you also may believe" (19:35). John's Gospel speaks of many witnesses to Jesus: John the Baptizer (1:6–7), the disciples who beheld Jesus's incarnation (1:14), the Father (5:37; 8:18), the Scriptures (5:39), Jesus's works (10:25), the Holy Spirit (15:26), and now the unnamed eyewitness at the cross (19:34). All these testimonies serve one purpose: that people may believe in Jesus and, through believing, have life.

The narrator then explains why the soldiers did not break Jesus's feet. That, too, was in fulfillment of Scripture: "Not one of his bones will be broken" (19:36b). When the Exodus generation ate the Passover lamb, God had commanded, "[The lamb] must be eaten inside the house; take none of the meat outside the house. *Do not break any of the bones*" (Exod 12:46, emphasis added). This was probably the passage the narrator was referring to, although other texts also speak of the Messiah's bones not being broken (Num 9:12; Ps 34:20).

The narrator sees yet another fulfillment of prophecy in the soldier's action of piercing Jesus's side (19:34): "They will look on the one they have pierced" (19:37). This quotation is from Zechariah: "I will pour out on the house of David and the inhabitants of Jerusalem a spirit of grace and supplication. They will look on me, *the one they have pierced*, and they will mourn for him as one mourns for an only child and grieve bitterly for him as one grieves for a firstborn son" (Zech 12:10, emphasis added).

The entire context is associated with the events surrounding the crucifixion. The "Spirit of grace and of supplication" is poured out on the house of David and the inhabitants of Jerusalem in the first part of 19:10. A few verses later in 13:1 Yahweh (typically rendered as "Lord" in the OT) says, "In that day a fountain will be opened for the house of David and for the inhabitants of Jerusalem, for sin and for impurity" (Zech 13:1). The blood which flowed from Jesus's pierced side may well be what the author saw as the connection here, since as the shedding of the blood of the sacrificial victim it represents cleansing from sin. Although the Jewish authorities and Roman soldiers certainly *"looked on the one whom they have pierced"* as he hung on the cross, the author may also have in mind the *parousia* (second coming) here.[17] The context in Zechariah 12–14 is certainly the second coming, so that these who crucified Jesus will look upon him in another sense when he returns in judgment. Thus, the narrator emphasizes that all the events in Jesus's life were messianic, fulfilling what had been foretold in the Scriptures. Jesus fulfilled every prophecy concerning him.

In the final section of this chapter (19:38–42), the narrator explains what happened to Jesus's dead body. Finding Jesus already dead, the soldiers refrained from breaking his legs but, instead, confirmed his death by piercing his side with a spear (19:31–37). Thereafter, Joseph of Arimathea, a secret disciple of Jesus – secret because he feared the Jewish leaders – sought and obtained Pilate's permission to take Jesus's body for burial (19:38). Just as one Joseph was present at Jesus's birth, another Joseph was present at his burial. Nicodemus, who had earlier visited Jesus at night (3:1–10), "brought a mixture of myrrh and aloes, about seventy-five pounds" to embalm Jesus's body (19:39). At that time, many were not able to openly express their faith in Jesus due to their fear of the Jewish authorities and the threat of expulsion from the synagogue. Today, too, there are secret believers in Jesus – for example, within the *Khrist Bhakta Movement* and the *Yeshu ka Darbar* movement in Uttar Pradesh, India. Both myrrh and aloes would have been costly and were probably imported from Asia. Beasley-Murray comments, "Myrrh is a fragrant resin, often used by Egyptians in embalming, but by the Jews rendered aromatic sandalwood."[18] The actions of Nicodemus and Joseph of Arimathea reveal that both were followers of the teachings of Jesus and had placed their faith in him (19:39). Together, they took Jesus's body and wrapped it with spices in strips of linen (19:40a). The narrator says that this was done "in accordance with Jewish burial customs" (19:40b).

While Jesus's own disciples hid in fear of their lives, Joseph of Arimathea and Nicodemus worked quietly in the background. Earlier, Nicodemus had come to Jesus under cover of night to discuss theology (3:2); now, he had come to bury this famous teacher (19:39). Although Joseph and Nicodemus embalmed Jesus's body with spices, days earlier, Mary of Bethany had washed his body days in preparation for his death and burial (12:1–8).

---

17. NET footnote. Italics in original.
18. Old Testament references in Psalms 45:8 and Proverb 7:17. Beasley-Murray, *John*, 359.

Near the place of the Skull (19:17) – where Jesus was crucified – was a garden, and in that garden was a new tomb where no one had ever been laid (19:41). Since it was the Jewish day of Preparation and Sabbath observances would soon begin – which included not working – and since the tomb was nearby, Joseph of Arimathea and Nicodemus hastily placed Jesus's body in that tomb (19:42). The Passion Narrative begins in the garden of Gethsemane and ends in a garden near the place of the Skull. Soon, Jesus's resurrection would also take place in that same garden. Just as the first creation took place in the garden of Eden (Gen 2:8), the new creation would also begin in a garden.

The arrest, trial, passion, crucifixion, and death of Jesus mark the climax of Jesus's mission. He had come to lay down his life for the sheep (10:15, 17; 15:13) – and he did so. His martyrdom serves as an example for Asian Christians. Jesus was tried before several judicial authorities and found not guilty, and yet they crucified him. Similarly, Christians in hostile countries and cultures are often falsely accused of wrongdoing, misjudged, and ostracized. But, like Jesus, they must remain faithful and finish the work the Father has entrusted to them.

JOHANNINE CULTURAL DYNAMICS

Richard Niebuhr (1894–1962) outlines five paradigms to describe how Christ intersects with culture: Christ against Culture, Christ of Culture, Christ above Culture, Christ and Culture in Paradox, and Christ Transforming Culture.[1] We see these paradigms at work in John's Gospel.

Christ against Culture. This phenomenon is powerfully expressed in the "from above" and "from below" imagery found throughout John's Gospel. Jesus said to the religious leaders: "You are from below; I am from above. You are of this world; I am not of this world" (8:23). To Pilate, who claimed that he had power over Jesus's life, Jesus responded, "You would have no power over me if it were not given to you from above" (19:11a). The *Prologue* declares, "The Word became flesh and made his dwelling among us. We have seen his glory, the glory of the one and only Son, who *came from* the Father" (1:14, emphasis added). Jesus also said, "No one has ever gone into heaven except the one who *came from* heaven – the Son of Man" (3:13, emphasis added). He repeatedly told his disciples that he was going away where they could not yet follow (8:21) but promised that he would return to them (14:28) and also give them "another advocate" (14:16). Jesus functions *above* worldly culture, confronting the sinful nature of the world, aligning earthly realities with heavenly truths, and serving as ideal for the world to follow. John's Gospel presents a clear "Christ *against* Culture" scenario.

Christ of Culture. The mere fact that the Word became flesh and lived among ordinary people emphasizes the "Christ of Culture" dimension of the Gospel. In addition, Jesus participated in celebrations such as weddings (2:1–11) and sorrowful events like funerals (John 11). He ate bread and fish (21:1–13), provided food for multitudes (6:1–13), and turned water into wine to bring joy at a marriage celebration (2:1–11). These events affirm that Jesus came to be part *of* the culture.

Christ above Culture. When the religious leaders brought a woman caught in adultery to Jesus, they expected him to behave like a Jewish rabbi and punish her for her crime (7:53–8:11). But Jesus stood *above* the culture. He did not follow the cultural norm of punishing her without the testimony of multiple witnesses, including the man who had committed adultery with her. He was countercultural. He said, "Let any one of you who is without sin be the first to throw a stone at her" (8:7). This poignant statement pierced their consciences; and instead of stoning her, they walked away one by one, beginning with the oldest.

Christ and Culture in Paradox. One night, Jesus engaged in a theological discussion with a Pharisee – a member of the Jewish ruling council – about what it means to be born from above (3:1–11). On another occasion, he had a theological conversation with a Samaritan woman about drinking living water and worshiping God in the Spirit and in truth (4:4–26). The source of living water cried, "I am thirsty" (19:28), and the one who promised to send the Spirit of truth bowed his head and gave up his spirit (19:30). These are examples of the paradoxical nature of Jesus's life and teaching.

Christ Transforming Culture. Nicodemus came to Jesus at night with a paradox of his own: "We know that you are a teacher who has come from God. For no one could perform the signs you are doing if God were not with him" (3:2). Yet Jesus's life did not resemble that of a prophet, priest, or king. Over time, through Jesus's teachings and signs, Nicodemus experienced a transformation. On one occasion, he defended Jesus: "Does our law condemn a man without first hearing him to find out what he has been doing?" (7:51). Finally, Nicodemus came to Jesus – not at night but in the light of day – along with Joseph of Arimathea, bringing seventy-five pounds of myrrh and aloes to embalm the body of Jesus and place it in a tomb (19:39). A similar transformation took place in the life of the Samaritan woman. She had come to the well to draw water, but after her encounter with Jesus, she left her bucket behind, ran to her village, and brought many of the villagers to him. The man born blind, after receiving healing, boldly rebuked the religious leaders (John 9). These are just a few examples of how Christ transforms not just individuals but cultures.

Like Christ, Christians in Asia can engage culture in ways that are *against* it, *of* it, *above* it, *paradoxical* to it, or *transformative* of it. They can stand *against* the injustices of culture, be part *of* the culture by accommodating its moral and positive values, be *above* culture by foregrounding Christian ethics and morality that go beyond cultural norms, expose *paradoxical* aspects of the world in relation to divine values and virtues, and *transform* socioreligious and political-cultural taboos and structures to liberate the marginalized and ostracized. As persecution and suffering intensify across Asia, Christians are called to be *against*, *of*, and *above* culture to liberate people regardless of their caste, color, creed, gender, region, or ethnic identity. A faithful reinterpretation of Johannine cultural dynamics can foster the virtue of solidarity amid the turbulent realities of Asia.[2]

---

1. Richard Niebuhr, *Christ and Culture* (San Francisco: Harper & Row, 1951).
2. Johnson Thomaskutty, "Culture Dynamics in the Johannine Community Context," *One Gospel, Many Religions: Doing Theology in Context*, ed. Arren Bennet Lawrence (Minneapolis: Fortress Press, 2022), 135–60.

JOHN 20:1–31

THE RESURRECTION OF JESUS

The *Book of Glory* (13:1–20:31) has three major sections: the Farewell Discourse (13:1–17:26), the passion of Jesus (18:1–19:42), and the resurrection of Jesus (20:1–31).

The resurrection narrative of John 20 can be divided into four subsections: resurrection and the first witnesses (20:1–10); Jesus's appearance to Mary Magdalene (20:11–18); two appearances of Jesus to the disciples (20:19–29); and the Gospel's purpose statement (20:30–31). The resurrection narrative offers people hope by assuring them that their sufferings will one day come to an end and that a new beginning will emerge. The Johannine community would have found hope amid their hardships as they read this resurrection narrative. Asian Christians, too, can draw hope for their future from the resurrection story.

20:1–10 RESURRECTION AND THE FIRST WITNESSES

In John's Gospel, Mary Magdalene first appears at the foot of the cross with three other women: Jesus's mother, her sister, and Mary of Clopas (19:25). Now, she appears at the tomb: "Early on the first day of the week, while it was still dark, Mary Magdalene went to the tomb" (20:1a).[1] Graveyards and tombs are often the setting for tales of ghosts and spirits. Mary Magdalene, however, was a brave follower of Jesus, who wanted to see Jesus as soon as the Sabbath ended and a new day dawned. As she reached the tomb, she "saw that the stone [that had covered the entrance] had been removed from the entrance" (20:1b). Brant says, "A woman who comes alone in darkness to such a place abandons propriety and safety to commemorate Jesus with her grief. John represents her anxiety by focalizing the setting through her eyes: she sees the stone has been removed from the tomb (20:1)."[2] Mary's courage offers a model for Asian women to live boldly and bravely amid trials and sufferings.[3]

---

1. While other gospels present her in the company of other women at the tomb (Matt 28:1; Mark 16:1; Luke 24:10), in John she appears all alone (20:1). Thomaskutty, "Johannine Women as Paradigms in the Indian Context," 91–93.
2. Brant, *John*, 266.
3. Thomaskutty, "Johannine Women as Paradigms in the Indian Context," 94–95.

Without looking inside the tomb, Mary ran to Peter and the other disciple – "the one Jesus loved" – and said, "They have taken the Lord out of the tomb, and we don't know where they have put him!" (20:2). She must have thought that Jesus's body had been removed from the tomb by the Jewish leaders or Roman soldiers. Even at this stage, she acknowledged Jesus as her "Lord" (20:2). Mary's commitment to the Lord is demonstrated by her search for Jesus's body in the early hours of the morning, her concern for his body, and her urgency to inform the disciples.

Upon hearing Mary's report, Peter and the other disciple raced to the tomb (20:3). Both were running, but the unnamed disciple – the Beloved Disciple – outran Peter and reached the tomb first (20:4). Scholars have suggested that the Beloved Disciple may have outrun Peter either because of his youthfulness or because Peter hesitated to face the Lord whom he had betrayed.

The Beloved Disciple "bent over and looked in at the strips of linen lying there but did not go in" (20:5). Perhaps out of fear, or because he wanted to wait for Peter, the Beloved Disciple did not enter the tomb but only peered into it. The strips of linen lying there would have stirred his curiosity: What had happened to Jesus who had been wrapped in those strips? Perhaps he recalled the earlier scene at Lazarus's tomb, where the Lord had commanded people to unbind Lazarus from his funeral garments – "his hands and feet wrapped with strips of linen, and a cloth around his face" (11:44).

While the Beloved Disciple waited at the entrance, peering hesitantly into the empty tomb, Peter caught up with him and "went straight into the tomb" (20:6a). Like the Beloved Disciple, he also saw "the strips of linen lying there, as well as the cloth that had been wrapped around Jesus's head" (20:6b–7a). The burial cloth was folded and lay separated from the linen strips (20:7b)[4] as if the body had passed through leaving the cloths behind. If this had been a robbery,[5] why would the robbers have taken the trouble to remove the grave clothes? Later, the disciples would understand that the body had not been stolen but that Jesus had risen from the dead.

Once Peter went inside, the other disciple also entered the tomb (20:8a) – unlike modern tombs, this would have been a large room. When he saw the empty tomb and the neatly folded grave clothes where the body and the head

---

4. Brown, *Gospel and Epistles of St. John*, 127.
5. Robbing graves was a common practice in the First Century Judea. The *Nazareth Inscription* or *Nazareth Decree* is a marble tablet inscribed in Greek with an edict from an unnamed Caesar ordering capital punishment for anyone who involves in such crimes.

would have been, he believed (20:8b). But this belief was probably a reference to his recognition that Jesus's body was gone rather than belief in resurrection because, as the narrator says, "they still did not understand from Scripture that Jesus had to rise from the dead" (20:9). Mary Magdalene, Peter, and the Beloved Disciple had not yet grasped the idea of resurrection, but they were all convinced that Jesus's body had been taken (20:2).

In Asian cultures, there are various beliefs about death. For example, Chinese people spent a great deal on funerals and coffins, believing that this is a way of showing filial piety toward their ancestors. Hindus believe that unnatural deaths are dangerous because the souls of such people wander around harming others. Similarly, Jesus's death by crucifixion, the open tomb, and the missing body would have raised various concerns among the early witnesses. So, these disciples returned to where they were staying, most likely curious about what they had seen and trying to make sense of it all (20:10).

Mary's role was significant. She went to the tomb first – while it was still dark – saw that the stone covering the entrance had been removed and ran to report this to the other disciples. She remained silent while the male disciples examined the tomb. In the next section, however, Mary would encounter the risen Jesus and play an active role as a witness to his resurrection.

20:11–18 JESUS'S APPEARANCE TO MARY MAGDALENE

While Peter and the other disciple hurried back to where they were staying (20:10), Mary "stood outside the tomb crying" (20:11a). She missed her Lord and feared that someone had taken his body (20:1–2). Seeing the dead body of Jesus would probably have brought her greater comfort than not seeing him at all. She had not yet heard Jesus's words, "Blessed are those who have not seen and yet have believed" (20:29). At this moment, she just wanted to see her Lord. She wept outside his tomb, just as Jesus had wept outside Lazarus's tomb (11:35).

Still crying, Mary "bent over to look into the tomb" – perhaps hoping that the disciples had been wrong and Jesus might still be there (20:11b). Instead of Jesus, she "saw two angels in white, seated where Jesus's body had been, one at the head and the other at the foot" (20:12). These were the same places where the disciples had earlier seen his head cloth and linen wrappings (20:7). Now, the angels had replaced the burial clothes.

The angels asked Mary, "Woman, why are you crying?" (20:13a). Just as Jesus had addressed Mary as "woman" (2:4; 19:26), the angels used the same respectful form of address. She replied, "They have taken my Lord away . . .

and I don't know where they have put him" (20:13b), repeating the statement she had made to the disciples earlier (20:2). Mary was convinced that someone had taken Jesus's body, and she was greatly distressed that she could not see him and did not know where his body was. Mary's presence at the tomb, her distress about the body of Jesus, and her boldness in speaking to strangers about Jesus's body demonstrate her deep devotion to Jesus and serves as an example for Asian Christian women in particular.

As Mary spoke, she turned around and "saw Jesus standing there, but she did not realize that it was Jesus" (20:14). Perhaps the reason she failed to recognize him was her lack of faith in his resurrection, the tears clouding her eyes, the darkness of the early morning, or a divine "blinding" until the appropriate time. Regardless of the reason, Mary did not realize that this was Jesus. This was Jesus's first resurrection appearance, and Mary was his first witness – an unlikely candidate since she was not one of the Twelve and because she was a woman. Perhaps the Lord granted her the privilege of seeing him first because of her great devotion to him.

Jesus asked her, "Woman, why are you crying? Who is it you are looking for?" (20:15a). Jesus knew the reason – but he wanted her to answer that she was looking for Jesus. But Mary, assuming that he was the gardener, replied, "Sir, if you have carried him away, tell me where you have put him, and I will get him" (20:15b). This was the third time she expressed this same concern that someone had taken the body of Jesus and that she did not know where they had put him (20:2, 13). She wanted to ensure that Jesus's body remained in that tomb where Joseph and Nicodemus laid him. Her faith had not grown sufficiently to grasp the reality of Jesus's resurrection.

Jesus did not leave her in suspense any longer. He called her by name: "Mary" (20:16a). Earlier, Mary had failed to recognize his voice, but she did so now. Her eyes were open. "She turned toward him and cried out in Aramaic, 'Rabboni!'" (20:16b). That was an affectionate way of addressing her teacher in her native language. In Asian contexts, this would be like calling one's teacher *guru, lama, tulku, tinpoche, geshe,* or *khenpo*. Earlier, Jesus had said that the good shepherd calls his own sheep by name and that the sheep recognize the shepherd's voice (10:3). Here, Jesus called Mary by her name, and she recognized his voice – and the good shepherd and his sheep were reunited after a brief separation.

In her great joy, Mary clung – NIV translates this "hold on" – to Jesus (20:17a). Some translations, like the KJV, translate Jesus's response as "Don't touch me," which has given rise to various interpretations. The Greek verb *aptō* implies clinging or holding on to someone. Three times Mary had said that someone had taken her Lord away (20:2, 13, 15) and even said that if she knew where he was, she would carry him back to his tomb. Now, she was attempting to do just that – to hold on to him and not let him out of her sight so that no one would take him away again. Jesus comforted her, saying, "I have not yet ascended to the Father. Go instead to my brothers and tell them 'I am ascending to my Father and your Father, to my God and your God'" (20:17b). In other words, there would still be time – forty days – before Jesus ascended to heaven. In the meantime, Mary was commissioned to go and tell the disciples – "my brothers" – about Jesus's resurrection and ascension. By referring to God as "my Father and your Father" and "my God and your God," Jesus affirmed the new relationship that believers enjoyed with the Father God. His earlier prayer that "all of them may be one, Father, just as you are in me and I am in you" (17:21a) was being fulfilled.

Mary became the first witness to Jesus's resurrection and the first to receive his call to proclaim the resurrection message to others. She became an apostle to the apostles! What a privilege! Paul said that God wanted people everywhere to "seek him and perhaps reach out for him and find him, though he is not far from any one of us" (Acts 17:27). That invitation remains open – anyone who sincerely seeks the true God will find him for he is near to every one of us.

True to her commission, Mary Magdalene went to the disciples and declared, "I have seen the Lord!" and told them what Jesus had said (20:18). Mary demonstrated her devotion and faithfulness. She did not worry about whether the disciples would believe her or not. Her concern was to remain faithful to the Lord's commission and bear witness to what she had seen and heard. In doing so, she serves as an example for all Christians of what it means to trust and obey.

20:19–29 TWO APPEARANCES OF JESUS TO THE DISCIPLES

After appearing to Mary, the Lord Jesus appeared to his disciples. First, he appeared to ten of the Twelve – Judas had died, and Thomas was absent (20:19–23). Second, he appeared to the eleven, with Thomas present (20:26–29). In between these appearances, the narrator describes how Thomas – because he missed Jesus's first appearance – doubted Jesus's resurrection (20:24–25).

"On the evening of that first day of the week" – the same day that Mary Magdalene saw the resurrected Jesus – Jesus appeared to the disciples while they were gathered behind locked doors because they feared that the Jewish leaders might harm them (20:19a). Despite the locked doors, Jesus came and stood among them, proclaiming the traditional Hebrew greeting, *Shalom lech* or "Peace be with you!" (20:19b). Earlier, he had promised, "Peace I leave with you; my peace I give you" (14:27). Now, he offered them that same peace (20:19b).

Jesus then showed them his hands and side as evidence that he was the one the religious leaders had crucified just three days earlier (20:20a). His wounds now served yet another witness testifying to his identity. Seeing him, the disciples were overjoyed (20:20b). Their sorrow had turned into joy, just as the Lord had promised: "Now is your time of grief, but I will see you again and you will rejoice, and no one will take away your joy" (16:22).

Once again, Jesus said, "Peace be with you!" (20:21a) and then gave them a commission: "As the Father has sent me, I am sending you" (20:21b). This commission included both a vertical ("as the Father has sent me") and a horizontal ("I am sending you") dimension. They were to go into the world and be his witnesses.

In the first creation, "The LORD God formed a man from the dust of the ground and breathed into his nostrils the breath of life, and the man became a living being" (Gen 2:7). Similarly, Jesus breathed on the disciples and said, "Receive the Holy Spirit" (20:22).[6] Just as God created the first Adam – humanity – Jesus formed the new humanity with the power and authority of the Holy Spirit. All those who believe in Jesus can be part of this new humanity (20:22).[7] The Holy Spirit whom Jesus had promised to give them (14:26) was now being given (20:22).

Because they had received the Holy Spirit, the disciples were now entrusted with great authority: "If you forgive anyone's sins, their sins are forgiven; if you do not forgive them, they are not forgiven" (20:23). The disciples' mission included proclamation of the forgiveness of sins in the Lord's name. We, too, have the same privilege of bringing people to Christ so that their sins will be forgiven. The narrator does not elaborate on what else Jesus told them, whether he ate with them, or how he left them. Instead, the focus now shifts to Thomas.

Thomas, one of the Twelve, had exercised great faith earlier on.[8] When the other disciples – fearing death – were reluctant to go to Jerusalem, Thomas

---

[6]. In both accounts, the same word for breathing, *emfusaō*, is used. For further study, see Thomaskutty, *Gospel of John: A Universalistic Reading*, 108.

[7]. Blomberg, *Historical Reliability of John's Gospel*, 266.

[8]. Thomas had the nickname "Didymus" meaning a twin. Perhaps he had a physical twin brother or sister or he was so identical to someone else among the disciples in his appearance or behavior.

declared, "Let us also go, that we may die with him" (11:16). He was eager to follow Jesus, even when he did not really understand where Jesus was going (14:5). However, Thomas was not present when Jesus first appeared to the disciples on the evening of his resurrection (20:24). So, when the other disciples told him, "We have seen the Lord!" (20:25a), he remained doubtful. Earlier, Mary Magdalene had made the same declaration: "I have seen the Lord!" (20:18). Despite these testimonies, Thomas remained skeptical. He told his fellow disciples, "Unless I see the nail marks in his hands and put my finger where the nails were, and put my hand into his side, I will not believe" (20:25b). Thomas wanted evidence to believe. He wanted to verify Jesus's identity by feeling his wounds with his own hands.

The Lord Jesus was not offended by this request. He appeared to the disciples a second time, a week later, when Thomas was also present (20:26). Once again, the doors were locked, but that did not stop Jesus. He came and stood among them, repeating the same greeting, "Peace be with you!" (*Shalom lech*) – in Hindi, *shanti aapke sath raho*.

Then he told Thomas, "Put your finger here; see my hands. Reach out your hand and put it into my side" (20:27a). Although Jesus had not been physically present when Thomas had said, "Unless I see the nail marks in his hands and put my finger where the nails were, and put my hand into his side, I will not believe" (20:25b), he offered Thomas the evidence he had asked for, proving both his omniscience and the reality of his bodily resurrection. Thomas had said he would not believe without evidence. Now that the evidence was before him, Jesus told him, "Stop doubting and believe" (20:27b). Immediately, Thomas responded, "My Lord and my God!" (20:28).

Thomas's confession is probably the strongest statement of faith in John's Gospel. It also echoes and forms a bookend with the opening line of the *Prologue* – "In the beginning was the Word, and the Word was with God, and the Word was God" (1:1). Jesus was not only Lord but also God. Thomas's faith grew instantaneously as he recognized Jesus not only as Lord but also as God. Many people are willing to accept Jesus as a great teacher or an exemplary human being. But the Johannine narrator challenges the reader to believe, like Thomas, that Jesus is both Lord and God.

Jesus replied, "Because you have seen me, you have believed" (20:29a). Thomas's faith was experiential. Jesus continued, "Blessed are those who have not seen and yet have believed" (20:29b). In this way, Jesus proclaimed a blessing on future believers who would believe without seeing him. Earlier, he had prayed for future believers (17:20–23); now, he blessed them. This includes all of us in Asia who believe in Jesus. We have not seen him, yet we believe in him. As Peter writes, "Though you have not seen him, you love him; and even though you do not see him now, you believe in him and are filled with an inexpressible and glorious joy" (1 Pet 1:8). May it always be true of us – that we believe without demanding evidence!

20:30–31 THE GOSPEL'S PURPOSE STATEMENT

The Johannine narrator brings his narrative to a close in John 20:30–31. He says, "Jesus performed many other signs in the presence of his disciples, which are not recorded in this book" (20:30). This implies that the narrator of John wrote the entire Gospel as a "sign document," focusing on just a few signs rather than on all Jesus's miracles and wonders. From a broader pool of available materials, he carefully selected representative stories and events to include in order to persuade the community to believe and keep believing. The expression "which are not recorded in this book" makes it clear that in the process of crafting this narrative, the author selected some stories and rejected others (20:30b).

The narrator's goal was that people should have faith in the Messiah: "But these are written that you may believe that Jesus is the Messiah, the Son of God, and that by believing you may have life in his name" (20:31). His primary purpose was to lead people to believe in Jesus as the Messiah so that they would have life – eternal life – in his name. This theme of eternal life runs all through the Gospel: "Everyone who believes may have eternal life" (3:15), "God so loved the world that he gave his one and only Son, that whoever believe in him shall not perish but have eternal life" (3:16), and "Whoever believes in the Son has eternal life, but whoever rejects the Son will not see life" (3:36). The narrator invites people to have eternal life by believing in Jesus, the Messiah.

This is our call, too – to show the world that Jesus is the Son of the Father and that believing in him brings eternal life with the Father. The primary purpose of John's Gospel can be understood as a call to believe: Believing in Jesus and the Father is the hallmark of a true follower of Jesus; followers of Jesus acknowledge and believe that Jesus is the Messiah – about whom the Scriptures prophesied – and the Son of God; and by believing in Jesus, his followers have life in his name.

JOHN 21:1–25

THE EPILOGUE OF THE GOSPEL

The Gospel of John has four major sections: the *Prologue* (1:1–18), the *Book of Signs* (1:19–12:50), the *Book of Glory* (13:1–20:31), and the *Epilogue* (21:1–25).

The *Epilogue* (21:1–25) can be divided into three subsections: Jesus's appearance to seven disciples (21:1–14); dialogue between Jesus and Peter (21:15–19); and Jesus and the Beloved Disciple (21:20–25).

21:1–14 JESUS'S APPEARANCE TO SEVEN DISCIPLES

Thus far, the narrator has recorded three post-resurrection appearances of Jesus: Jesus's appearance to Mary Magdalene (20:11–18), Jesus's appearance to the disciples in Thomas's absence (20:19–23), and Jesus's appearance to the disciples with Thomas present (20:26–29). This chapter records another appearance of Jesus to the disciples by the Sea of Galilee (21:1). Seven of the eleven disciples were present on this occasion: Simon Peter, Thomas (called Didymus), Nathanael from Cana in Galilee (where Jesus turned water into wine, 2:1–11, and healed the official's son, 4:46–54), the sons of Zebedee, and two unnamed disciples (21:2). Among these disciples, Peter is mentioned most frequently in John's Gospel (1:42; 6:66–69; 18:10–11, 15–18, 25–27; 20:3–9; 21:2–19); Thomas appears in several places (11:16; 14:5; 20:24–29; 21:2); and Nathanael is mentioned just once (1:44–51) prior to this incident. The title "sons of Zebedee" does not appear in the main body of John, and the other two disciples remain unidentified.

The number seven may be symbolic, similar to the narrator's presentation of the seven signs and seven "I am" statements of Jesus. The seven signs are: a) turning water into wine (2:1–11); b) healing the royal official's son (4:46–54); c) healing the paralytic by the pool of Bethesda (5:1–15); d) feeding the five thousand (6:1–14); e) walking on water (6:16–21); f) healing the man born blind (9:1–41); and g) raising Lazarus from the dead (11:1–44). The seven "I am" statements are: a) "I am the bread of life" (6:35); b) "I am the light of the world" (8:12); c) "I am the gate" (10:7–9); d) "I am the good shepherd" (10:11, 14); e) "I am the resurrection and the life" (11:25); f) "I am the way and the truth and the life" (14:6); and g) "I am the true vine" (15:1). In Indian numerology, the number seven is regarded as mysterious and spiritual, ruled by the planet Neptune (*Ketu*), and associated with creativity and intuition.[1] Jesus met with these seven disciples to prepare them for their participation in the mission of God.

Simon Peter led the group, saying, "I'm going out to fish" (21:3a), and the other disciples immediately responded, "We'll go with you" (21:3b). They got into a boat and went out to sea but were unable to catch any fish that night (21:3c). The fishermen of Kerala, India, often return empty-handed from their fishing trips because of depleting marine resources caused by overfishing – and this failure worsens their already difficult circumstances, leaving them in greater poverty. The disciples' fruitless efforts throughout the night may have left them feeling hopeless and frustrated.

But their luck would soon change. Early in the morning, Jesus stood on the shore, waiting for them, but the disciples did not recognize him (21:4) – perhaps it was still too dark, or they were exhausted, or they were not expecting to see him. Just as Mary Magdalene had failed to recognize Jesus in the garden (20:15), the disciples did not realize that it was Jesus standing there (21:4).[2] And just as Mary had recognized Jesus after hearing his voice (20:16), the Beloved Disciple recognized Jesus after hearing his voice and seeing the miracle that unfolded before his eyes (21:5–7). The sheep recognized the good shepherd's voice (10:27). Jesus called out to them: "Friends [Children], haven't you any fish?" (21:5a).[3] Earlier, when Jesus explained to the disciples that they would grieve when he was gone but would rejoice again when he returned, he used this illustration: "A woman giving birth to a child has pain because her time has come; but when her baby [*paidion*] is born she forget the anguish because of her joy that a child is born into the world" (16:21). Now, he addressed them as children [*paidion*] because he had returned after a brief absence – during which they had grieved – bringing them joy. To his question, "Haven't you any fish?" they replied, "No" (21:5).

Jesus then gave a command: "Throw your net on the right side of the boat and you will find some" (21:6a). The disciples obeyed immediately. To their surprise, they caught so many fish that they were unable to haul the net in (21:6b). The narrator notes that they caught 153 fish and that, despite this

---

1. Mahima Sharma, "Number 7 in Numerology: Personality, Career, and Lucky Colour," The Times of India, 21 July 2023, https://timesofindia.indiatimes.com/astrology/numerology-tarot/number-7-in-numerology-personality-career-and-lucky-colour/articleshow/102013280.cms.
2. Blomberg, *Historical Reliability of John's Gospel*, 275.
3. The Greek text says *paidia* "children."

large catch of fish, the net did not break (21:11) – which may be understood as two more signs, even though they are not called "signs." Obedience to the Lord results in good outcomes – an important principle for Asian Christians to remember.

Jesus's voice and the miracle he performed opened the eyes of the disciple whom Jesus loved, and he said to Peter, "It is the Lord!" (21:7). Hearing this, Peter wrapped his outer garment around him – because he had taken it off and was standing in his undergarments – and jumped into the water (21:7).[4] Even today, fisher folk in India wear very little clothing when they go fishing. Peter's actions probably stemmed from reverence for Jesus and the desire to present himself properly before the Lord.

While Peter swam toward the shore, the other disciples followed in the boat, "towing the net full of fish, for they were not far from shore, about a hundred yards" (21:8). The narrator's mention of the distance effectively addresses skeptics' doubts about whether the disciples could have heard Jesus's voice from the shore while they were in the boat. It seems clear that a shout can be heard within a hundred yards.

When the disciples reached the shore, they saw "a fire of burning coals there with fish on it, and some bread" (21:9). Just as Jesus had provided bread and fish for five thousand hungry people (6:1–15), he provided food for his disciples. He knew they would be tired after fishing all night and disappointed that they had caught nothing. Just as Jesus met them in their weariness and discouragement, he does the same for us today – granting unexpected and miraculous provision when we least expect it.

As the disciples drew near, Jesus said, "Bring some of the fish you have just caught" (21:10). Just as he once asked the disciples to distribute the bread and fish he multiplied (6:10), he now invited them to contribute to the breakfast. The Lord wanted their participation in his provision – a principle that still holds true today. Simon Peter climbed aboard and dragged the net ashore. Although it held 153 large fish, the net was not torn (21:11). Two miracles!

This incident teaches several lessons: the disciples cannot do anything apart from Jesus; Since Jesus's presence is always with them, they must be mindful of their actions; they can witness God's miraculous working in their lives; and their calling is not just to fish but also to enjoy God's provision for them. Just as the disciples had gathered twelve baskets of leftovers after everyone had eaten their fill (6:12–13), seven people now had more than 153 fish to enjoy. Just as

---

4. Beasley-Murray, *John*, 400.

Jesus provided six large barrels of wine to the wedding couple when they ran out of wine (2:6, 9–10), he provided an abundance of fish for the disciples. Jesus always provides abundantly.

Jesus then said, "Come and have breakfast" (21:12a).[5] In Asia, breakfast symbolizes hospitality, nurturing relationships, and fostering a sense of identity. Those who host the meal and those who enjoy it develop a sense of mutuality and friendship in the process of serving and eating it. Indian mothers, for example, show their love, care, and hope by preparing breakfast for the whole family. As the most important meal of the day, breakfast holds a special significance that goes beyond mere nourishment. Jesus's act of preparing breakfast was symbolic and sacramental, preparing the disciples for a new movement and a new missional paradigm under the guidance of the Holy Spirit.

None of the disciples dared to ask Jesus who he was because they now knew it was the Lord (21:12b). Who else would perform such a miracle and provide for them in this way? They had now come to a full understanding of Jesus's identity. Just as the disciples moved from unrecognition to recognition, the Johannine narrator invites all his readers to move from unrecognition to recognition through the process of reading the Gospel narrative.

Jesus then "came, took the bread and gave it to them, and did the same with the fish" (21:13). These words would have reminded the disciples of Jesus's words and actions on the night before his death: "He took bread, gave thanks and broke it, and gave it to them, saying, 'This is my body given for you; do this in remembrance of me'" (Luke 22:19). In this sense, Jesus was symbolically reenacting that earlier scene. Then, he had served them bread and wine; now, he served them bread and fish.

The narrator says, "This was now the third time Jesus appeared to his disciples after he was raised from the dead" (21:14). The previous two appearances had taken place when the disciples were behind locked doors – first without Thomas (20:19–23) and later with Thomas also present (20:26–29). This third appearance occurred by the Sea of Galilee, where Jesus had begun his earthly ministry and was now bringing it to a close. Jesus initiated a new culture and a new movement on the shores of the Sea of Galilee. This new culture formed around Jesus is liberative and transformative – centered on faith and witness, and universal in its scope and mission.

---

5. The Greek verb *aristaō* can mean breakfast or lunch (Liddel & Scott). But because it was early morning when Jesus and the disciples ate, "breakfast" is an appropriate translation.

21:15–19 DIALOGUE BETWEEN JESUS AND PETER

John 21 has three main sections: Jesus with the seven disciples (21:1–14), Jesus with Peter (21:15–19), and Jesus with the Beloved Disciple (21:20–25). In John 21:15–19, Jesus has an extended dialogue with Peter.

There were many ups and downs in Peter's journey. When he first came to Jesus, Jesus had said, "'You are Simon son of John. You will be called Cephas' (which, when translated, is Peter)" (1:42). This declaration anticipated that Peter would be like an immovable rock in his faith. At times, Peter demonstrated that kind of faith. When many of Jesus's disciples left because they thought his teachings were too difficult and Jesus asked the Twelve if they also wanted to leave, Peter said, "Lord, to whom shall we go? You have the words of eternal life" (6:68). Yet when Jesus washed the disciples' feet, Peter did not understand and objected, "You shall never wash my feet" (13:8). However, when Jesus explained that unless Peter allowed Jesus to wash his feet, he could not have any part with Jesus. Peter said, "Then, Lord . . . not just my feet but my hands and my head as well!" (13:9). When Jesus spoke of his departure, Peter boldly said, "Lord, why can't I follow you now? I will lay down my life for you" (13:37). Not long after, however, he denied Jesus three times (18:15–27). When Jesus was being arrested, Peter bravely drew his sword to defend him – although his aim was poor (18:10). When the Beloved Disciples said that it was the Lord standing on the shore, Peter jumped into the water and swam toward Jesus (21:7). When Jesus wanted more fish for their breakfast, Peter climbed back into the boat and dragged the net ashore with the 153 fish in it (21:11).

His three denials of Jesus must have made Peter fearful and anxious. He may have wondered: Will Jesus still love me? Will he still trust me to lead? Knowing Peter's thoughts and feelings, Jesus took the first step in the process of healing and restoration. After breakfast, he asked Peter, "Simon son of John, do you love me more than these?" (21:15a). Jesus's question might have referred to whether Peter loved him more than fishing (if "these" is a neuter pronoun) or more than the other disciples (if "these" is a masculine pronoun). The text is unclear. Perhaps Jesus meant both. If the former, Jesus's might have intended to redirect Peter's attention from the fish in the sea to the "fish" that Jesus wanted him to catch – people (Matt 4:19).

The Johannine narrator establishes the priorities for Jesus's followers: They must invest in the "world above" rather than in the "world below." Although the world runs after material things, followers of Jesus must "set their minds" on the things of the "world above" (Col 3:2).

Peter responded, "Yes, Lord . . . you know that I love you" (21:15b). Much has been said about the two Greek verbs for love that are used in this section: *agapaō* and *philō*. In his first two questions, Jesus used *agapaō* (21:15a, 16a), and Peter replied using *philō* (21:15b, 16b,). The third time Jesus used *philō*, and Peter was hurt that Jesus asked him this question a third time (21:17a). Based on this use of two different Greek words, some scholars argue that *agapaō* refers to pure divine love – which Peter could not give Jesus – and that *philō* is brotherly love – which Peter was willing to give, and Jesus accepted the third time the question was asked and answered. However, the Gospel of John uses the terms *agapaō* and *philō* interchangeably. The Father's love for the Son is described using *agapaō* (3:35), as well as *philō* (5:20). Similarly, both *agapaō* and *philō* are used of the Father's love for the disciples (14:23; 16:27). Therefore, Peter's response to Jesus communicated his heartfelt love and commitment to the Lord (21:15b).

To Peter's confession of love, the Lord responded, "Feed my lambs" (21:15c). This command directed Peter to care for even the "little ones" of this world. In the same way, Asian churches today are called to focus on all generations, paying special attention to the younger generation, in their mission and ministry.

A second time, Jesus asked, "Simon son of John, do you love me?" (21:16a), this time without the additional phrase "more than these" (21:15a). Peter responded, "Yes, Lord, you know that I love you" (21:16b), and Jesus replied, "Take care of my sheep" (21:16c). This time, the Lord instructed Peter to care for the adult sheep. Churches in Asia must minister to both new and mature believers.

A third time, Jesus asked Peter, "Simon son of John, do you love me?" (21:17a). Peter was hurt when Jesus asked this question a third time. This time, Peter responded, "Lord, you know all things; you know that I love you" (21:17b). Repetition is a style used in pedagogy, legal inquiry, and courtroom discourse to emphasize a point, teach a lesson, or convey urgency. Since Peter's was a somewhat wavering personality, Jesus was determined to teach him an important life lesson. Earlier, Peter had denied Jesus three times; now, he confessed his love for Jesus three times. Jesus wanted to reaffirm his love for Peter and restore him to ministry before ascending to his Father. Jesus then said to Peter again, "Feed my sheep" (21:17c).

Jesus's commands – "feed my lambs" (21:15c), "take care of my sheep" (21:16c), and "feed my sheep" (21:17c) – emphasize that these were not Peter's lambs and sheep but Jesus's and that Peter's job was to feed and take care of them. When declaring that he was the good shepherd, Jesus said, "The one who enters by the gate is the *shepherd* of the sheep. The *gatekeeper* opens the gate for him" (10:2–3, emphasis added). The shepherd and the gatekeeper worked together. Similarly, Jesus is the owner of the lamb and sheep – they belong to him. Peter was not the owner but only the caretaker of the flock. Pastors and leaders in Asia must remember that the flock belongs to the good shepherd. Their job is to serve under the shepherd, feeding and taking care of the lambs and the sheep.

After reinstating Peter and commissioning him to care for God's flock, Jesus explained what would happen to Peter using a metaphor: "Very truly I tell you, when you were younger you dressed yourself and went where you wanted; but when you are old you will stretch out your hands, and someone else will dress you and lead you where you do not want to go" (21:18). The narrator immediately explains this metaphor: "Jesus said this to indicate the kind of death by which Peter would glorify God" (21:19a). Jesus prophesied Peter's martyrdom. In a sense, Peter's "old age" had already begun – he was already in danger of death (compare Acts 12:1–3). Tradition says that Peter was crucified upside down. Peter's martyrdom, like Jesus's crucifixion, glorified God (21:19b). For Asian Christians facing persecution, these words offer strength to persevere even in the face of death because they know that their death will glorify God and they will enjoy eternal life with the Father and the Son. "Precious in the sight of the Lord is the death of his faithful servants" (Ps 116:15).

Regardless of what lay ahead, Jesus had one call for Peter: "Follow me!" (21:19c), which echoes his call to Peter at the beginning of his ministry (Matt 4:19). Whatever happened, he wanted Peter to continue following Jesus. That same call comes to every Christian: Follow Jesus all your life!

21:20–25 JESUS AND THE BELOVED DISCIPLE

The disciple whom Jesus loved – often called the Beloved Disciple – is a somewhat mysterious figure who is mentioned at several crucial moments in John's Gospel. He reclined next to Jesus at the Passover meal (13:23). Jesus entrusted his mother to him (19:26). When Jesus stood on the shore and instructed the disciples to cast their nets on the other side, this disciple recognized Jesus and cried, "It is the Lord!" (21:7). Now, at the end of this Gospel, the Beloved Disciple appears once again. Peter, with whom Jesus had been conversing, "turned and saw that the disciple whom Jesus loved was following them" (21:20a). Just in case the audience have forgotten, the narrator explains that "this was the one who had leaned back against Jesus at the supper and had said, 'Lord, who is going to betray you?'" (21:20b).

Jesus had just prophesied about Peter's martyrdom (21:18). Curious about what would happen to the Beloved Disciple, Peter now asked, "Lord, what about him?" (21:21). Jesus said, "If I want him to remain alive until I return, what is that to you?" (21:22a). In other words, Jesus refused to answer him. It was not Peter's business to know what would happen to the Beloved Disciple or any other disciple. Instead, Peter was to focus on following Jesus (21:22b). For the second time that day, Jesus told Peter to follow him (21:19b, 22b). Just as Peter needed that repeated call, so did we.

The narrator says that because of Jesus's words about the Beloved Disciple, "the rumor spread among the believers that this disciple would not die" (21:23a). But the narrator clarifies that Jesus had only said, "If I want him to remain alive until I return, what is that to you?" (21:23c). Clearly, Jesus was not making a pronouncement about what would happen to the Beloved Disciple; instead, he was rebuking Peter for his curiosity.

The last two verses refer to the testimony of the disciple who wrote this Gospel (21:24) and acknowledge that Jesus did many more signs and wonders than were recorded in it (21:25).

The Lord Jesus has several witnesses in this Gospel: John the Baptizer, the Father, and Jesus's own works. Now, the author of this Gospel adds his own testimony: "This is the disciple who testifies to these things and who wrote them down. We know that his testimony is true" (21:24). From the beginning of the Gospel, the narrator identifies the author as an eyewitness – someone who witnessed the events in the life of Jesus. This claim is repeated here, providing a persuasive climax to the extended narrative. The phrases "the disciple" and "we know" suggest that one among the group – "the disciple" – wrote the Gospel, while others – "we" – testified to the truth of his account. The OT law decreed that "a matter must be established by the testimony of two or three witnesses" (Deut 19:15b). Both Jesus and the disciples had multiple witnesses who confirmed what Jesus did and what the disciples wrote about him. When doubts arise about the authenticity of Jesus or the reliability of God's word, we must remember these many witnesses.

The narrator concludes the Gospel by saying, "Jesus did many other things as well. If every one of them were written down, I suppose that even the whole world would not have room for the books that would be written" (21:25). If every detail about Jesus's life had been included, it would have been impossible to finish this Gospel. What the narrator has recorded is so deep and challenging that we could spend a lifetime studying it and still not fully comprehend it or be able to apply its meaning. But we have this assurance: "The Advocate, the Holy Spirit, whom the Father will send in my name, will teach you all things and will remind you of everything I have said to you" (14:26).

SELECTED BIBLIOGRAPHY

Abhishiktananda, Swami. *Hindu-Christian Meeting Point*. Übersetzt von Sara Grant. New Delhi: ISPCK, 1976.

———. *Saccidananda: A Christian Approach to Advaidic Experience*. New Delhi: ISPCK, 1974.

Achtemeier, Paul J., Joel B. Green, and Marianne M. Thompson. *Introducing the New Testament: Its Literature and Theology*. Grand Rapids: Eerdmans, 2001.

Allison, D. C. "Eschatology." *DJG*. Edited by Joel B. Green, Scot McKnight, and I. Howard Marshall. Downers Grove: InterVarsity Press, 1992.

Anderson, Paul N. *From Crisis to Christ: A Contextual Introduction to the New Testament*. Nashville: Abingdon, 2014.

Anderson, Robert T., and Terry Giles. *The Samaritan Pentateuch: An Introduction to its Origin, History and Significance for Biblical Studies*. Atlanta: Society for Biblical Studies, 2012.

Appasamy, A. J. *Christianity as Bhakti Marga: A Study of the Johannine Doctrine of Love*. Madras: Christian Literature Society, 1930.

Asiedu-Peprah, Martin. *Johannine Sabbath Conflicts as Juridical Controversy*. WUNT 132. Tübingen: Mohr Siebeck, 2001.

Ball, David Mark. *'I AM' in John's Gospel: Literary Function, Background, and Theological Implications*. Sheffield: Sheffield Academic Press, 1996.

Baltusen, Han. *The Peripatetics: Aristotle's Heirs (332 BCE-200 CE)*. New York: Routledge, 2016.

Bane, Theresa. *Encyclopedia of Spirits and Ghosts in World Mythology*. Jefferson: McFarland & Company, 2016.

Barrett, C. K. *The Gospel according to St. John: An Introduction with Commentary and Notes on the Greek Text*. London: SPCK, 1978.

Bartholomä, Philip F. "The Johannine Discourses and the Teaching of Jesus in the Synoptics: A Comparative Approach to the Authenticity of Jesus's Words in the Fourth Gospel." PhD dissertation, Leuven, Evangelical Theological Faculty, 2010.

Barus, A. "John 2:12–25: A Narrative Reading." *New Currents through John: A Global Perspective*. Edited by F. Lozada, and T. Thatcher. Leiden/Boston: Brill, 2006.

Basker, G. T. *Interpreting Biblical Texts: John and his Tamil Readers*. New Delhi: ISPCK. 2016.

Bauckham, Richard. *Jesus and the Eyewitnesses: The Gospels as Eyewitness Testimony*. Grand Rapids: Eerdmans, 2006.

John

———. *The Testimony of the Beloved Disciple: Narrative, History, and Theology in the Gospel of John*. Grand Rapids: Baker Academic, 2007.

Beasley-Murray, George R. *John*. WBC 36. Nashville: Thomas Nelson Publishers. 1999.

Bennema, Cornelis. *Encountering Jesus: Character Studies in the Gospel of John*. Bangalore: Primalogue, 2009.

———. *Excavating John's Gospel: A Commentary for Today*. Delhi: ISPCK, 2007.

Blomberg, Craig L. *The Historical Reliability of John's Gospel: Issues and Commentary*. Leicester: Apollos, 2001.

Blum, E. A. "John." *The Bible Knowledge Commentary: New Testament*. Hyderabad: Authentic, 1983.

Borchert, G. F. *John 12–21*. The New American Commentary. Vol. 25B. Nashville: Broadman & Holman Publishers, 2002.

Boyd, Robin M. *An Introduction to Indian Christian Theology*. Delhi: ISPCK, 1969.

Brant, Jo-Ann. *John*. Paideia Commentaries on the New Testament. Grand Rapids: Baker Academic, 2011.

Breneman, Mervin. *Ezra, Nehemiah, Esther*. The New American Commentary: An Exegetical and Theological Exposition of Holy Scripture NIV Text, Vol. 10. Nashville: B&H Publishers, 1993.

Brown, Raymond E. *Community of the Beloved Disciple*. New York: Paulist, 1979.

———. *The Gospel according to John*. Vols. 1–2. Garden City: Doubleday, 1966.

———. *An Introduction to the New Testament*. Bangalore: Theological Publications in India, 2009.

Bruce, F. F. *The Gospel of John: Introduction, Exposition, and Notes*. Grand Rapids: Eerdmans, 1983.

Bultmann, Rudolf. *The Gospel of John: A Commentary*. Philadelphia: Westminster, 1970.

Burge, Gary M. "'I AM' Sayings." *DJG*. Downers Grove: InterVarsity Press, 1992.

Carson, Donald Arthur. *The Gospel according to John*. Leicester: IVP; Grand Rapids: Eerdmans, 1991.

Casey, Maurice. *From Jewish Prophet to Gentile God: The Origin and Development of New Testament Christology*. Louisville: Westminster John Knox Press, 1992.

Charlesworth, James H. *The Beloved Disciple: Whose Witness Validates the Gospel of John?* Philadelphia: Trinity Press International, 1995.

Cho, Jae Hyung. *This is My Flesh: John's Eucharist and the Dionysus Cult*. Eugene: Pickwick Publications, 2022.

Clark-Soles, Jaime. "John, First-Third John, and Revelation." *The Bible and Disability: A Commentary*, edited by Sarah Melcher, Mikeal C. Parsons, and Amos Yong. London: SCM Press, 2018.

Coggins, R. J. *Samaritans and Jews*. Atlanta: John Knox Press, 1975.

Selected Bibliography

Collins, R. F. *The Things Have been Written: Studies on the Fourth Gospel*. Louvain: Peeters Press, 1990.

Coloe, Mary L. *Dwelling in the Household of God: Johannine Ecclesiology and Spirituality*. Collegeville: Liturgical Press, 2007.

Cullmann, Oscar. *The Johannine Circle*. London: SCM Press, 1976.

Culpepper, R. Alan. *Anatomy of the Fourth Gospel: A Study in Literary Design*. Philadelphia: Fortress Press, 1983.

———. *Design for the Church in the Gospel of John: Collected Essays 1980–2020*. WUNT 465. Tübingen: Mohr Siebeck, 2021.

———. "The Johannine *hypodeigma*: A Reading of John 13:1–38," *Semeia* 53 (1991): 133–52.

———. *The Johannine School: An Evaluation of the Johannine School Hypothesis based on the Investigation of the Nature of Ancient Schools*. Durham: Duke University, 1982.

De Boer, Esther A. *The Gospel of Mary: Listening to the Beloved Disciple*. London: T & T Clark, 2004.

Devin, Christine. *Hanuman or the Way of the Wind*. New York: Discovery Publisher, 2020.

Dodd, Charles Harold. *The Interpretation of the Fourth Gospel*. Cambridge: University Press, 1960.

Duke, Paul. *Irony in the Fourth Gospel*. Atlanta: John Knox Press, 1985.

Engberg-Pedersen, Troels. "A Question of Genre: John 13–17 as *Paraklēsis*." In *The Gospel of John as Genre Mosaic*, edited by Kasper Bro Larsen. Göttingen: Vandenhoeck & Ruprecht, 2015.

Frykenberg, Robert E., and Alaine Low, eds. *Christians and Missionaries in India: Cross-Cultural Communication since 1500: With Special Reference to Caste, Conversion, and Colonialism*. Studies in the History of Christian Missions. Grand Rapids: Eerdmans, 2003.

Gench, Frances Taylor. *Back to the Well: Women's Encounters with Jesus in the Gospels*. Louisville: Westminster John Knox Press, 2004.

———. *Encounters with Jesus: Studies in the Gospel of John*. Louisville: Westminster John Knox, 2007.

George, Sam. "*Motus Dei* (The Move of God): A Theology and Missiology for a Moving World." *Pharos Journal of Theology* 102 (2021): 1–12.

Ghai, Anita. *Rethinking Disability in India*. London: Routledge, 2015.

Green, Joel B. "Burial of Jesus." *DJG*. Edited by Joel B. Green, Scot McKnight, and I. Howard Marshall. Downers Grove: InterVarsity Press, 1992.

———. "Death of Jesus." *DJG*. Edited by Joel B. Green, Scott McKnight, and I. Howard Marshall. Downers Grove: InterVarsity Press, 1992.

John

———. "Passion Narrative." *DJG*. Edited by Joel B. Green, Scot McKnight, and I. Howard Marshall. Downers Grove: InterVarsity Press, 1992.

Griffiths, Bede. *A New Vision of Reality: Western Science, Eastern Mysticism and Christian Faith*. Edited by Felicity Edwards. New Delhi: Harper Collins, 1989.

———. *The Marriage of the East and West: A Sequel to the Golden String*. London: Collins, 1982.

———. *Return to the Centre*. London: Collins, 1976.

Gungwu, Wang. *Chinese Overseas: History, Literature, and Society* 12. Leiden: Brill. 2018.

Guthrie, Donald. *New Testament Introduction*. Revised Edition. Leicester: Apollos, 1990.

Haenchen, Ernst. *John 2: A Commentary on the Gospel of John Chapters 7–21*. Philadelphia: Fortress Press, 1984.

Hellholm, David. "The Problem of Apocalyptic Genre and the Apocalypse of John." *Semeia 36: Early Christian Apocalypticism, Genre and Social Setting*. Decatur: SBL/Scholars Press, 1986.

Hengel, Martin. *The Johannine Question*. London: SCM Press, 1989.

Hezser, Catherine. *Jewish Slavery in Antiquity*. Oxford: Oxford University Press, 2005.

Hoeck, Andreas. "The Johannine Paraclete: Herald of the Eschaton." *J. Biblic. Pneumatological Res.* 4 (2012): 23–37.

Hylen, Susan. *Allusion and Meaning in John 6*, BZNW 1377. Berlin: Walter de Gruyter, 2005.

Immanuel, Babu. *Acts of the Apostles: An Exegetical and Contextual Commentary*. India Commentary on the New Testament. Edited by Brian C. Wintle. Bangalore: Primalogue, 2016.

Irudaya, Raj. *The Gospel according to John*. Dalit Bible Commentary: New Testament. Vol. 4. New Delhi: Centre for Dalit/Subaltern Studies, 2009.

Jahan, Rounaq. "Women in Bangladesh." *Women for Women: Bangladesh 1975*. Dhaka: Women for Women Research and Study Group, 1975.

James, Manohar. *Religious Conversion in India*. Eugene: Wipf & Stock, 2022.

Jebaraj, Edwin, and Johnson Thomaskutty. "The Gospel of Mark." *An Asian Introduction to the New Testament*. Minneapolis: Fortress Press, 2022.

Kanagaraj, J. J. *The Gospel of John: A Commentary*. Secunderabad: OM Books, 2005.

———. *John*. New Covenant Commentary Series. Eugene: Cascade Books, 2013.

Kärkkäinen, Veli-Matti, ed. *Holy Spirit and Salvation: The Sources of Christian Theology*. Louisville: Westminster John Knox Press, 2010.

Kartveit, Magnar. *The Origin of the Samaritans*. Leiden/Boston: Brill, 2009.

Kaunda, Chammah J. "Mission as Witness." *The Expository Times* 134, no. 7 (October 2022): 299–308.

Selected Bibliography

Keener, Craig S. *The Gospel of John: A Commentary*. Vol. 1. Peabody: Hendrickson, 2003.

———. *The IVP Bible Background Commentary: New Testament*. Downers Grove: InterVarsity Press, 1993.

Keith, Chris. *The Pericope Adulterae, the Gospel of John, and the Literacy of Jesus*. Leiden/Boston: Brill, 2009.

Knoppers, Gary N. *Jews and Samaritans: The Origins and History of their Early Relations*. Oxford/New York: Oxford University Press, 2013.

Kohli, Surindar Singh. *The Sikh and Sikhism*. New Delhi: Atlantic Publishers, 1993.

Köstenberger, Andreas J. *John*. BECNT. Grand Rapids: Baker Academic, 2004.

Lalfakmawia, Joseph H. *Re-reading the Gospel of John from Indian Perspective*. Kolkata: SCEPTRE, 2013.

Lightfoot, R. H. *St. John's Gospel: A Commentary*. Oxford: Clarendon Press, 1956.

Lipton, Edward P. *Religious Freedom in Asia*. New York: Nova Science Publishers, 2002.

Löwner, Gudrun. *Intercultural Dialogue in Art and Religion*. New Delhi: Manohar Publishers. 2018.

Lozada, Francisco. "Contesting an Interpretation of John 5: Moving Beyond Colonial Evangelism." In *John and Postcolonialism: Travel, Space and Power*, edited by Musa W. Dube and Jeffrey L. Staley. London: Sheffield Academic Press, 2002.

Lukose, Wessly. "An Indian Pentecostal Reading on Conversion." *Religious Freedom and Conversion in India*. Bengaluru: SAIACS Press, 2017.

MacGregor, G. H. C. *The Gospel of John*. Moffat New Testament Commentary. London: Hodder & Stoughton, 1928.

Malina, Bruce J., and Richard L. Rohrbaugh. *Social-Science Commentary on the Gospel of John*. Minneapolis: Fortress Press, 1998.

Maniparampil, J. *Reading the Fourth Gospel: A Textbook for Students of Gospel according to John*. Bangalore: Claretian Publications, 2004.

Martyn, Louis J. *History and Theology in the Fourth Gospel*. Nashville: Abingdon, 1983.

Moloney, Francis J. *The Gospel of John*. Sacra Pagina Series 4. Collegeville: The Liturgical Press, 1998.

Montgomery, James A. *The Samaritans, the Earliest Jewish Sect, Their History, Theology and Literature*. Philadelphia: University of Pennsylvania, 1907.

Montijo, Ivonne. *Mary Magdalene: Beloved Wife, Beloved Disciple*. CreateSpace Independent Publishing Platform, 2017.

Morris, Leon. *The Gospel according to John*. NICNT. Revised edition. Grand Rapids: Eerdmans, 1995.

Myers, Jacob M. *Ezra, Nehemiah: Introduction, Translation and Notes*. The Anchor Bible 14. New York: Doubleday, 1965.

John

Narasu, Lakshmi, P. *The Essence of Buddhism*. New Delhi: Gautam, 2009.
Neyrey, J. H. "The 'Noble Shepherd' in John 10: Cultural and Rhetorical Background." *JBL* 120, no. 2, (2001): 267–91.
Nirmal, Arvind P. *Heuristic Explorations*. Chennai: Gurukul/Christian Literature Society, 1990.
Niebuhr, Richard H. *Christ and Culture*. San Francisco: Harper & Row, 1951.
Nworie, Ben, ed. *Integrating Faith and Special Education: A Christian Faith Approach to Special Education Practice*. Eugene: Wipf & Stock, 2016.
O'Day, Gail. "John 7:53–8:11: A Study in Misreading." *JBL* 111, no.4 (1992): 631–40.
Okure, Teresa. "John." *The International Bible Commentary*. Edited by William R. Farmer. Bangalore: Theological Publications in India, 1998.
Painter, John. *The Quest for the Messiah: The History, Literature and Theology of the Johannine Community*. Second edition. Nashville: Abingdon, 1993.
Parananda, Sri. *An Eastern Exposition of the Gospel of Jesus according to St. John being an interpretation thereof*. Edited by R. L. Harrison. London: William Hutchinson and Co., 1902.
Perkins, Pheme. "The Gospel according to John." *The New Jerome Biblical Commentary*. Edited by Raymond E. Brown, Joseph A. Fitzmyer, and Roland E. Murphy. Bangalore: Theological Publications in India, 2001.
Popley, H. A. *Paricutta Yōvān eḻutiṉa cuvicēṣam, mūlamum uraiyum, (The Gospel of John: Text and Commentary) ceṉṉai kirictava kalvi apivirutti caṅkam*. Chennai: SPCK, 1913.
Pummer, Reinhard. *The Samaritans: A Profile*. Grand Rapids: Eerdmans, 2016.
Rector, Rebecca Craft. *The Early River Valley Civilizations: The First Humans and Early Civilizations*. New York: Rosen Publishing, 2017.
Renner, George, and Mark Shaw. *Ten Great Ideas from First Corinthians*. Eugene: Wipf & Stock, 2021.
Resseguie, James L. *Narrative Criticism of the New Testament: An Introduction*. Grand Rapids: Baker Academic, 2005.
———. *The Strange Gospel: Narrative Design and Point of View in John*. BINS 56. Leiden: Brill, 2001.
Ridderbos, Herman. *The Gospel of John: A Theological Commentary*. Grand Rapids: Eerdmans. 1997.
Robertson, Archibald T. *The Fourth Gospel/The Epistle to the Hebrews*. Word Pictures in the New Testament 5. New York: Ray Long & Richard R. Smith, Inc., 1932
Robinson, John A. T. *The Priority of John*. London: SCM, 1985.
Sahi, Jyoti "An Artist Looks at the Fourth Gospel." In *India's Search for Reality and the Relevance of the Gospel of John*, edited by Christopher Duraisingh and Cecil Hargreaves. Delhi: ISPCK, 1974.

Selected Bibliography

Schnackenburg, Rudolf. *The Gospel according to St. John*. Vol. 2. London: Burns & Oates, 1980.

———. *The Gospel according to St. John*. Vol. 3. London: Burns & Oates, 1982.

Seng Ja, L. "The Letters of Peter." *An Asian Introduction to the New Testament*. Edited by Johnson Thomaskutty. Minneapolis: Fortress Press, 2022.

Singh, R. B. P. "Water Symbolism and Sacred Landscape in Hinduism: A Study of Benares (Vārāṇasi)." *Erdkunde*, Band 48, no. 3 (1994): 210–27.

Skinner, Tobias. *The Gospel according to Lazarus*. UK: Watersgreen House, 2022.

Smith, Dwight Moody. *John*. Abingdon New Testament Commentaries. Nashville: Abingdon, 1999.

Soares-Prabhu, George M. *The Dharma of Jesus*. Edited by Francis X. D'Sa. Maryknoll: Orbis, 2003.

———. "The Man Born Blind: Understanding a Johannine Sign in India Today." *India's Search for Reality and the Relevance of the Gospel of John*. Edited by Christopher Duraisingh and Cecil Hargreaves. Delhi: ISPCK, 1975.

Spiro, Abram. "Samaritans, Tobiads, and Judahites in Pseudo Philo." *PAAJR* 20 (1951): 279–335.

Stibbe, Mark W. G. *John's Gospel: New Testament Readings*. London and New York: Routledge, 1994.

———. *John*. Readings: A New Biblical Commentary. Sheffield: Sheffield Academic Press, 1993.

Subramaniam, Kamala. *Ramayana*. Mumbai: Bharatiya Vidya Bhavan, 2019.

Swartley, Williard M. *John: Believers Church Bible Commentary*. Harrisonburg: Herald Press, 2013.

Swinton, John. "Foreword: The Strange New World within the Bible: Some Reflections on the hermeneutics on Disability." In *The Bible and Disability: A Commentary*, edited by Sarah Melcher, Mikeal C. Parsons, and Amos Yong. London: SCM Press, 2018.

Thomas, V. V. *Dalit and Tribal Christians of India: Issues and Challenges*. Nilambur: Focus India Trust, 2014.

Thomaskutty, J. "Biblical Interpretation in the Global-Indian Context." *Fuller Magazine: Reading Scripture Globally* 8 (2017).

———. "Culture Dynamics in the Johannine Community Context." In *One Gospel, Many Religions: Doing Theology in Context*, edited by Arren Bennet Lawrence. Minneapolis: Fortress Press, 2022.

———. *Dialogue in the Book of Signs: A Polyvalent Analysis of John 1:19–12:50*. BINS 136. Leiden/Boston: Brill, 2015.

———. *The Gospel of John: A Universalistic Reading*. Biblical Hermeneutics Rediscovered 25. New Delhi: Christian World Imprints, 2020.

———. "Johannine Women as Paradigms in the Indian Context." *Acta Theologica Supplementum* 27. Bloemfontein: University of the Free State, 2019.

———. "Metaphors of Salvation in the New Testament and Their Implications in Asia." In *Exploring the New Testament in Asia: Evangelical Perspectives*, edited by Samson L. Uytanlet and Bennet Lawrence. Carlisle: Langham Global Library, 2024.

———. *Saint Thomas the Apostle: New Testament, Apocrypha, and Historical Traditions*. T & T Clark Jewish and Christian Texts Series 25. London/New York: Bloomsbury T & T Clark, 2018.

Thompson, Marianne M. "John, Gospel of." *DJG*. Edited by Joel B. Green, Scot McKnight, and I. Howard Marshall. Downers Grove: InterVarsity Press, 1992.

Tiénou, T. "The Samaritans: A Biblical-Theological Mirror for Understanding Racial, Ethnic and Religious Identity?" In *This Side of Heaven: Race, Ethnicity and Christian Faith*, edited by Robert J. Priest and Alvaro L. Nieves. Oxford: University Press, 2007.

Tupamahu, Ekaputra. "The Gospel of Luke." In *An Asian Introduction to the New Testament*, edited by Johnson Thomaskutty. Minneapolis: Fortress Press, 2022.

Vallianippuram, T. *New Society in John's Gospel*. Aloor: Biblia Publications, 2008.

Vandana, S. "From Death to Life." *India's Search for Reality and the Relevance of the Gospel of John*. Edited by Christopher Duraisingh and Cecil Hargreaves. Delhi: ISPCK, 1974.

Vashum, Y., ed. *Tribal Theology and the Bible: A Search for Contextual Relevance*. Tribal Study Series 19. Jorhat: Tribal Study Center, 2011.

Vivekananda, Swami. *Swami Vivekananda's Chicago Speech*. Kolkata: EditionNext, 2015.

Walzer, M., M. Lorberbaum, and N. J. Zohar, eds. *The Jewish Political Tradition*. Vol. 2. New Haven: Yale University Press, 2003.

Wead, D. W. *The Literary Devices in John's Gospel*. The Johannine Monograph Series. Revised and expanded edition. Eugene: Wipf & Stock, 2018.

Williamson, H. G. M. "Samaritans." *DJG*. Edited by Joel B. Green, Scot McKnight, and I. Howard Marshall. Downers Grove: InterVarsity Press, 1992.

Wise, M. O. "Feasts." *DJG*. Edited by Joel B. Green, Scot McKnight, and I. Howard Marshall. Downers Grove: InterVarsity Press, 1992.

Witherington, Ben. *John's Wisdom: A Commentary on the Fourth Gospel*. Louisville: Westminster John Knox, 1995.

Wright, Tom. *John for Everyone: Part I, Chapters 1–10*. Delhi: ISPCK, 2002.

Yong, Amos. *The Bible, Disability, and the Church: A New Vision of the People of God*. Grand Rapids: Eerdmans, 2011.

Zanchettin, Leo, ed. *John a Devotional Commentary: Meditations on the Gospel according to St. John*. Ijamsville: The Word Among Us Press, 2000.

Asia Theological Association
54 Scout Madriñan St. Quezon City 1103, Philippines
Email: ataasia@gmail.com Telefax: (632) 410 0312

OUR MISSION

The Asia Theological Association (ATA) is a body of theological institutions, committed to evangelical faith and scholarship, networking together to serve the Church in equipping the people of God for the mission of the Lord Jesus Christ.

OUR COMMITMENT

The ATA is committed to serving its members in the development of evangelical, biblical theology by strengthening interaction, enhancing scholarship, promoting academic excellence, fostering spiritual and ministerial formation and mobilizing resources to fulfill God's global mission within diverse Asian cultures.

OUR TASK

Affirming our mission and commitment, ATA seeks to:

- **Strengthen** interaction through inter-institutional fellowship and programs, regional and continental activities, faculty and student exchange programs.
- **Enhance** scholarship through consultations, workshops, seminars, publications, and research fellowships.
- **Promote** academic excellence through accreditation standards, faculty and curriculum development.
- **Foster** spiritual and ministerial formation by providing mentor models, encouraging the development of ministerial skills and a Christian ethos.
- **Mobilize** resources through library development, information technology and infra-structural development.

To learn more about ATA, visit www.ataasia.com or facebook.com/AsiaTheologicalAssociation

Langham Literature, along with its publishing work, is a ministry of Langham Partnership.

Langham Partnership is a global fellowship working in pursuit of the vision God entrusted to its founder John Stott –

> *to facilitate the growth of the church in maturity and Christ-likeness through raising the standards of biblical preaching and teaching.*

Our vision is to see churches in the Majority World equipped for mission and growing to maturity in Christ through the ministry of pastors and leaders who believe, teach and live by the word of God.

Our mission is to strengthen the ministry of the word of God through:
- nurturing national movements for biblical preaching
- fostering the creation and distribution of evangelical literature
- enhancing evangelical theological education

especially in countries where churches are under-resourced.

Our ministry

Langham Preaching partners with national leaders to nurture indigenous biblical preaching movements for pastors and lay preachers all around the world. With the support of a team of trainers from many countries, a multi-level programme of seminars provides practical training, and is followed by a programme for training local facilitators. Local preachers' groups and national and regional networks ensure continuity and ongoing development, seeking to build vigorous movements committed to Bible exposition.

Langham Literature provides Majority World preachers, scholars and seminary libraries with evangelical books and electronic resources through publishing and distribution, grants and discounts. The programme also fosters the creation of indigenous evangelical books in many languages, through writer's grants, strengthening local evangelical publishing houses, and investment in major regional literature projects, such as one volume Bible commentaries like the *Africa Bible Commentary* and the *South Asia Bible Commentary*.

Langham Scholars provides financial support for evangelical doctoral students from the Majority World so that, when they return home, they may train pastors and other Christian leaders with sound, biblical and theological teaching. This programme equips those who equip others. Langham Scholars also works in partnership with Majority World seminaries in strengthening evangelical theological education. A growing number of Langham Scholars study in high quality doctoral programmes in the Majority World itself. As well as teaching the next generation of pastors, graduated Langham Scholars exercise significant influence through their writing and leadership.

To learn more about Langham Partnership and the work we do visit **langham.org**

www.ingramcontent.com/pod-product-compliance
Lightning Source LLC
Chambersburg PA
CBHW062002220426
43662CB00010B/1202